Operations of Regulators of Healthcare Professionals

Principles and Processes for Regulating Healthcare Professionals

FIRST EDITION

Volume 4

Operations of Regulators of Healthcare Professionals

Marc Seale

WILEY

This edition first published 2026

Registered Office(s)
John Wiley & Sons, Inc., 111 River Street, Hoboken, NJ 07030, USA
John Wiley & Sons Ltd, New Era House, 8 Oldlands Way, Bognor Regis, West Sussex, PO22 9NQ, UK

For details of our global editorial offices, customer services, and more information about Wiley products visit us at www.wiley.com.

The manufacturer's authorized representative according to the EU General Product Safety Regulation is Wiley-VCH GmbH, Boschstr. 12, 69469 Weinheim, Germany, e-mail: Product_Safety@wiley.com.

Wiley also publishes its books in a variety of electronic formats and by print-on-demand. Some content that appears in standard print versions of this book may not be available in other formats.

Library of Congress Cataloging-in-Publication Data
Names: Seale, Marc, author.
Title: Operations of regulators of healthcare professionals / Marc Seale.
Description: Hoboken, NJ : Wiley, 2026. | Includes index.
Identifiers: LCCN 2025011952 (print) | LCCN 2025011953 (ebook) | ISBN 9781394333639 (paperback) | ISBN 9781394333653 (adobe pdf) | ISBN 9781394333646 (epub)
Subjects: LCSH: Medical care–Law and legislation. | Medical laws and legislation. | Medical policy. | Medical ethics.
Classification: LCC K3601 .S423 2026 (print) | LCC K3601 (ebook) | DDC 344.04/1–dc23/eng/20250501
LC record available at https://lccn.loc.gov/2025011952
LC ebook record available at https://lccn.loc.gov/2025011953

Cover Design: Wiley
Cover Image: © yewkeo/Getty Images

Set in 9.5/12pt STIXTwoText by Straive, Pondicherry, India

This book is dedicated to my wife Carole and my children Alexander and Jessica.

Contents

Author Biography

Marc Seale has a wealth of knowledge and practical experience in the regulation of healthcare professionals. From 2001 to 2020, Marc was the first Chief Executive and Registrar of the UK's Health and Care Professions Council, the multi-professional regulator of 350,000 healthcare professionals from 15 professions. He has held a number of ministerial appointments including membership of the 2005 Foster review of non-medical regulation and the working group on herbal medicines and traditional herbal medicines. Marc was also a member of over three dozen government working groups related to the Department of Health and has appeared as a witness to numerous Parliamentary committees. He was a Professor of Practice at the University of Cumbria and an Honorary Visiting Fellow at the Anglia Ruskin University. He is a graduate of the University of St Andrews and the London Business School and was awarded an Honorary Doctor of Science by the University of Hertfordshire in recognition of his service to health. His international regulatory experience has included participation in numerous European regulatory projects relating to the Recognition of Professional Qualifications Directive and was rapporteur for the focus group on Physiotherapy. In 2009, he was elected to the US-based Council on Licensure, Enforcement and Regulation, becoming its president in 2014. Before regulation, Marc worked for a number of major commercial companies including Metal Box plc and British Gas plc. He also worked for INMARSAT, the Intergovernmental Organisation satellite operator. His responsibilities have included general management, finance, marketing, and strategy. Marc has over 25 years of experience as a non-executive director including West London Mental Health NHS Trust, the Centre for Rail Skills, and the Passenger Council. He is married to Carole, lives in London, and has two grown-up children Alexander and Jessica.

Preface

Many professions throughout the world are regulated. Most readers will be familiar with the grandees of regulated professions, such as doctors and lawyers, whose practice is regulated in virtually every country. However, what will probably be less well known to some is that hundreds of other occupations such as farriers, medical secretaries, and barbers are regulated in various countries.

In the United Kingdom, the regulation of a profession usually involves the publication and maintenance of a list, or register, of individuals, or registrants, who have achieved specific standards of education and training; maintain their knowledge skills, values, and behaviours; and have the exclusive right to use a particular job title or to undertake a distinct function. The register is a public document, which is available for inspection by all. The keeper of the register is the regulator, whose function is to ensure that standards to join and remain on the register are maintained.

A brief review of the regulation of professionals will quickly identify a range of interrelated topics, such as standards of education and training, fitness to practice, public involvement, grandparenting, etc. The number of topics is extensive, indeed there are over three thousand entries in the index of the book. The reader may start to speculate on which topics are important or controversial, how they work, how they are evolving, and how they relate to one another.

To explore these issues, the inquisitive reader will readily find a plethora of academic research papers, doctoral thesis, technical journals, and specialist books, but no single comprehensive reference guide. Grey literature such as legislation, consultation documents, and reports of government inquiries also provides further information as do the numerous publications of the regulators of healthcare professionals, consisting for example of standards, guidance, policy documents, and annual reports. Unfortunately, they are often written without any explanation of how they fit into the wider regulatory arena. Also, the authors of these publications frequently support a particular stance on how regulation should, or could, work. In addition, many of the authors often have no practical experience or knowledge of the actual challenges faced in the day-to-day operations by a regulator. Further barriers also arise from the use of impenetrable jargon, that is made worse by a lack of clear definitions. For example, what exactly is a professional, and why are some professions regulated whilst others are not? What is the rationale for this?

The inquisitive reader may rapidly become perplexed and frustrated, as there is no obvious, single comprehensive source that rigorously analyses all the components and their relationships of the principles and processes for regulating healthcare professionals.

The book has therefore been written to correct this deficiency and provide a single thorough reference guide to the principles and processes used to regulate healthcare professionals in the United Kingdom at the start of the twenty-first century. It may also assist those who extemporise on the regulation of healthcare professionals.

The book does not support or reject a particular set of permutations of the many variables that form the regulatory environment of healthcare professionals. Rather, it aims to identify the principles and processes of a particular regulatory topic and then to assess the pros and cons of each variable and position each on a spectrum of choice. It is for others to decide on the merits or otherwise of a particular set of options. It also aims to assist the reader to clearly identify how a particular issue fits into the overall regulatory landscape.

The readership of this book, in terms of the their detailed understanding and familiarisation of the regulation of healthcare professionals, is potentially broad, ranging from newly appointed employees working in junior administrative roles of a regulator to knowledgeable board members of regulators with long careers and varied experiences. This raises the challenge of where to pitch the level of observation, examination, analysis, and explanation of each individual topic addressed in the book. The approach I have adopted is to assume the reader is not familiar with the topic and to start with basic principles. Readers with greater knowledge or experience in a particular area may therefore choose to skip certain sections where they have a firm grasp of the issues of the particular topic.

The potential audience of this book is as broad and varied as the issues addressed in it. Readers may work in institutions and organisations directly concerned with the regulation of healthcare professionals, or they may be on the periphery of the sector. However, the book has been written primarily for a number of specific audiences, including:

- Consumer organisations
- Educators and trainers of healthcare professionals
- Employees of regulators
- Employers of professionals
- Government officials

- Healthcare professionals
- Members of the governing bodies of regulators of professionals
- Professional associations
- Researchers
- Student healthcare professionals

I have sought to make the book as accessible to as wide an audience as possible. To accommodate the range of potential readers, the book is deliberately not written in the style of an academic journal or book. For clarity, wherever possible each section of the book addresses a discrete topic, and a limited number of publications have been referenced. I have also sought to avoid duplication. However, readers may on occasions need to refer to a number of sections to gain a broad understanding of a particular regulatory process or principle. For example, there is a single section on supervision, which covers its use in the initial education and training of healthcare professionals, the return to practice process and periods of adaptation used by professionals applying to join a register from a different jurisdiction.

The principles and process of regulating healthcare professionals relate to a range of academic fields and disciplines. They include:

- Economics
- Ethical and moral philosophy
- Healthcare sciences
- History of healthcare and science
- Jurisprudence
- Pedagogy
- Political science
- Public administration
- Psychometrics
- Sociology

I do not expect the readers of this book to be polyglots. However, although it is tempting to explore equally all of these neighbouring disciplines, I have sought to closely align the scope of the book to reflect its title. As a result, there are a number of disciplines that are not examined in the same level of detail as those that directly relate to the principles and processes of the regulation of healthcare professionals.

I have therefore only provided relatively cursory introductions to a number of significant areas of human knowledge and endeavour such as jurisprudence and pedagogy. For those individuals, such as members of the legal professions and educationalists, who require further information on these topics, there are numerous papers and reference books that they will no doubt find more appropriate.

Likewise, fields such as accountancy, communication, quality assurance, and statistics are beyond the scope of the book and are therefore not explored in depth. However, where appropriate, clear signposts are provided for those interested in venturing further afield.

I have also attempted to minimise the use of jargon and buzzwords. Where their use is unavoidable, I have aimed to provide clarity through a thorough explanation of their meaning supported by a glossary.

The book deliberately focuses on the principles and processes that are used in the United Kingdom. Thus, a majority of examples are drawn from this jurisdiction, and they specifically refer to why and how healthcare professionals are regulated in the United Kingdom. However, the principles and processes of the regulation of healthcare professionals vary from country to country. What might be appropriate for an economically developed country may be wholly inappropriate for a country ravaged by war, natural disasters, or economic deprivation. The use has therefore been made of examples from other countries to enable the reader to compare and contrast the different methods adopted to contend with the challenges of a particular geographical area or jurisdiction.

Besides healthcare professionals, many other professions are regulated including, to name but a few, actuaries, architects, teachers, and veterinary surgeons. The book may therefore be of interest to those working outside the healthcare delivery system. Also, although the book focuses on the principles and processes used to regulate healthcare professionals, many of the issues discussed may be of interest to those concerned with the regulation of occupations ranging from nursing assistants to taxi drivers, who have a markedly different set of knowledge and skills compared to the competence level of professionals.

Finally, all regulated sectors, such as communications or financial services, evolve in parallel with developments in economic activity, government, industry, and society in general. The regulation of healthcare professionals is no exception to this rule, and it is currently undergoing rapid development driven by changes in the attitude of society, technology, the healthcare delivery system, and demographics.

This is therefore a snapshot of the world of the regulation of healthcare professionals at the start of the second decade of the twenty first century and will need to be periodically updated.

Lastly, it is not my intention to instruct you what to do in any particular situation. Rather, I have sought to enable you to analyse the what, and why, the situation is as it is. It is then up to you and your organisation to use a range of tools and frameworks to select and make the right decision and to successfully implement a workable solution.

Operations of Regulators of Healthcare Professionals

The fourth volume has 10 chapters.

CHAPTER 1 – ADMINISTRATION AND MANAGEMENT OF REGULATORS

Government can use a range of different structures to regulate professionals. Regulators in turn must align their operating models to deliver their objectives, whilst remaining operationally effective and efficient. Despite regulators not being subjected to the rapidly changing financial and economic constraints found in commercial markets, the healthcare delivery system continuously evolves and government may conclude that the regulators are either no longer required or new ones should be established. These issues are explored in the chapter.

CHAPTER 2 – COMMUNICATION

Regulators rely on effective and efficient processes to receive and transmit communications to and from their stakeholders. In turn stakeholders must be aware of the regulators' roles and responsibilities and know how to communicate with them. To do this, regulators use a range of processes including publishing, consultations and face-to-face meetings, which, if well managed, can maintain and enhance their reputation.

CHAPTER 3 – GOVERNANCE

Regulators must be well governed. Making use of the considerable amount of published research that supports best practice, the chapter explores the principles and processes of governance that are used by the board of regulators to control, direct and manage the organisation.

CHAPTER 4 – SERVICE STANDARDS AND OPERATIONAL PERFORMANCE OF REGULATORS

Every one of us has numerous daily experiences of the standards of service provided by organisations and individuals. Whether it is the time waiting in a queue at the supermarket checkout, the accuracy of a utility companies' bill, or the quality of a lawyer drafting a will, we all have expectations and experiences of good, bad and indifferent services.

The regulators of healthcare professionals are service organisations and the standards of service that they provide to their users are as important as any other service provider. It is therefore entirely reasonable that standards for the services that regulators provide should be set and used to measure, evaluate and improve their performance.

In addition to the service standards used and created by a regulator, they can also adopt standards set by other organisations such as standards organisations. Lastly, other public authorities set standards that regulators must abide by, for example standards relating to data protection and freedom of information.

CHAPTER 5 – REGULATORY FAILURE

A cursory trawl of the internet will rapidly identify a litany of individual healthcare professionals, organisations operating in the healthcare delivery system and regulators of healthcare professionals, where the expectations of stakeholders have been woefully let down by regulatory failure. These types of incidents, besides harming patients, are the primary trigger for the public and governments to lose their trust and confidence in regulators. As a result, these high-profile events often trigger government intervention and in many cases in due course have dire organisational consequences for regulators. This section examines historic examples from various jurisdictions of regulatory failures when the regulatory processes have gone seriously awry. By understanding the causes of regulatory failure, counter measures can be adopted to change regulatory principles and process that should lead to an increase to the chances of detecting and preventing similar events occurring in the future.

CHAPTER 6 – STANDARDS FOR REGULATORS

Government has a responsibility to be informed about whether or not regulatory interventions and individual regulators are delivering their objectives. To achieve this they must firstly set the standards they expect regulators to achieve. Government can then assess its regulators using qualitative and quantitative assessment tools either directly or indirectly by commissioning auditors and/or oversight organisations to ensure that regulators comply with their objectives and standards. In effect, regulators are subjected to a regulatory process. In turn, these processes have resulted in regulators evolving characteristics and attributes that enable them to meet the required standards.

CHAPTER 7 – ROUNDUP

The chapter addresses a range of eclectic topics ranging from national emergencies, to professional indemnity insurance, to the regulation of service delivery facilities and workforce planning. However, whilst each is distinct and important in the context of the principles and processes of regulating healthcare professionals, they don't merit separate chapters of their own.

CHAPTER 8 – HISTORY AND REFORM OF REGULATING HEALTHCARE PROFESSIONALS

The history of the development of the regulation of healthcare professionals is inextricably linked to the histories of the healthcare delivery system, the healthcare professionals and their education and training. Whilst these fields are somewhat on the periphery of the subject of the book, each has had an influence on the principles and processes of the regulation of healthcare professionals. A brief detour into each is therefore in order. The chapter then concludes by exploring what triggers governments to reform the regulation of healthcare professionals and the processes that they employ to achieve this.

CHAPTER 9 – PLANNING AND RESEARCH

All organisations must allocate their limited resources so that they can plan and execute their strategy to deliver their objective of protecting the public and run their day-to-day operations. This chapter looks at a range of tools and techniques that can be used to plan for the future. It also explores the role of research in this endeavour.

CHAPTER 10 – FUTURE OF THE REGULATION OF HEALTHCARE PROFESSIONALS

I have consciously attempted not to bowdlerize the book by suggesting that all issues relating to the statutory regulation of professionals are agreed and uncontroversial.

However, before concluding, I would like to briefly explore my predications for what I believe will be the "Big issues" relating to the regulation of healthcare professionals that in the future will be controversial and will need to be resolved.

Acknowledgements

The book would not have been completed without the encouragement and mentoring of a number of friends and colleagues. They include Adam, Anna, Claire, Di, Ewan, Giba, Greg, Guy, Jacqueline, Jane, John, Jonathan, Kelly, Louise, Martin, Michael, Neil, Norma, Richard, Rick, Robert, Roy, Ros, Steve, Sylvia, and Tony.

About the Companion Website

This book is accompanied by a companion website:

www.wiley.com/go/seale/regulatinghealthcare

The website includes:

- Abbreviations
- Bibliography
- Charts List
- Consultations
- Glossary
- Guidance
- Index
    - Legislation
    - Organisation
    - People
    - Subject
- Journals and research papers
- Policy Topics
- Practice Notes
- Principles for regulating healthcare professional
- Reports
- Standards
- Summary Chapters & Sections
- Tables List

Introduction

When I set out to pen this book, my intention was to establish a single-source reference and guide on the subject of regulating healthcare professionals and that it would be structured around two broad themes:

Firstly, to identify and observe, and then record the principles that are used to regulate healthcare professionals and to provide an explanation why it is so.

Secondly, to identify and observe, and then record the processes that are, or in the past, have been, used to regulate healthcare professionals.

Hence, the title:

Principles & processes for regulating healthcare professionals
A reference guide in four volumes

INTENDED USE

The volumes are arranged on the assumption that they will be primarily used as a reference guide to individual topics relating to the regulation of healthcare professionals. Therefore, each section is intentionally designed to be more akin to a briefing note, rather than a text-heavy discourse. Although, on occasions, a few brave souls may read the whole of the reference guide from cover-to-cover.

STYLE, LAYOUT, AND DESIGN

The style, layout, and design make considerable use of bullet points, charts, labelled paragraphs, and tables. Lists of charts and tables are also provided on the companion website. The charts include timelines for a selection of the UK regulators of healthcare professionals that provide the key dates in their historic development.

FRAMEWORKS

Over twenty frameworks are used. Each provides a diagram of the basic structure of a subject or topic. They are intended to facilitate the exploration of the structural relationship of the components used in the principles and processes of regulating healthcare professionals.

ARRANGEMENTS OF CONTENTS

The reference guide is arranged into a total of forty-two chapters, each of which focuses on a specific subject, for example continuing competence, standards, and tribunals. The chapters are then subdivided into individual sections, each covering a specific topic. There are approximately two hundred sections.

ORDERING OF SUBJECTS AND TOPICS

It is intended that each subject and topic is only explored in detail once in the four books. Therefore, wherever possible, I have addressed the subjects in a logical sequence. My intention is that when a topic is addressed for the first time, if it is dependent on an understanding of other related topics, then wherever possible, these have been addressed in the preceding sections.

For example, if the reader where to be confronted by the sentence:

> *A* **regulator** *will seek to minimise* **risk of harm** *by establishing* **standards** *for* **professionals** *who seek to return to the* **register** *using a* **return to practice process**.

Thus, in this hypothetical example, each of the six subjects are addressed in a sequential order, 'regulator' first and 'return to practice' last.

CROSS REFERENCING

Limited cross-referencing is provided, which primarily directs readers to proceeding sections.

GLOSSARY

To the uninitiated, the regulation of healthcare professionals is often made impenetrable by a reliance on the use of jargon, lack of clarity, and ambiguous and confusing definitions.

Therefore, a glossary is provided on the companion website that defines words and phrases that are commonly used in the world of regulating healthcare professionals.

When used for the first time, a definition is provided in the body of the text, as follows:

Definition: Glossary
Alphabetical list of words and definitions relating to a specific subject with an explanation of the meaning of the word.

PRINCIPLES FOR REGULATING HEALTHCARE PROFESSIONALS

Some 65 principles are identified that are used in the regulation of healthcare professionals.

In a similar way that the glossary is constructed, at the point in the book when a new regulatory principle is referred to for the first time, it is highlighted by way of the stylized approach. As follows:

Principle: High Standards of Conduct
The standards of conduct of healthcare professionals are expected to be higher than the typical members of the public at all times.

INDEXES

There are four separate indexes. They are:

- Legislation
- Organisation
- People
- Subject

The subject index has over 3,250 entries. In addition, the relevant legislation relating to each section is provided at the end of each section.

PUBLICATIONS

For the intrepid reader seeking to explore any of the subjects discussed in the book in greater detail, there are numerous sources to consult. They include:

- Books
- Conference papers and proceedings
- Reports
- Theses and dissertations

The secondary sources, sometimes referred to as 'Grey Literature', make the task of exploration more complex as the number of publications is continually increasing. This is particularly true of the publications produced by the vast majority of the key stakeholders in the regulation of healthcare professionals who are all avid publishers. It is therefore beyond the scope of the book to include every relevant publication. In essence, those that are included are intended to be a 'taster menu' rather than a definitive source of all these types of published material. Notwithstanding this, eight types of publications are provided in the companion website. They are as follows:

1. Books
2. Consultations
3. Guidance
4. Journals and Research papers
5. Policy Topics
6. Practice Notes
7. Reports
8. Standards

Wherever possible an International Standard Book Number (ISBN), or an International Standard Serial Number (ISSN), is provided. In addition, at the end of each section, the relevant publications are also listed. Where cross-reference locations are provided, consultations are marked with a C, guidance with a G, standards and codes with S&C, and reports with an R.

JOURNALS AND RESEARCH PAPERS

It should be noted that only a small number of primary source publications from journals have been provided. Again, this decision is driven by the need for brevity. For those seeking further sources of these types of publications, the numerous academic search engines such as Academia.edu, Google Scholar, and RefSeek, as well as other publications, are all rich sources.

EXERCISE AND QUESTIONS

Lastly, at the end of each section a number of exercises and questions are provided. It is hoped that some readers may find it interesting to explore these further issues, particularly, if they are involved in one of the numerous organisations connected to the issues raised.

Administration and Management of Regulators

CHAPTER 1

INTRODUCTION

Government can use a range of different structures to regulate professionals. Regulators in turn must align their operating models to deliver their objectives, whilst remaining operational effective and efficient. Despite regulators not being subjected to the rapidly changing financial and economic constraints found in commercial markets, the healthcare delivery system continuously evolves and government may conclude that the regulators are either no longer required or new ones should be established. These issues are explored in the chapter.

The chapter has eight sections:

1.1 Structures for regulating healthcare professionals

1.2 Operating models of regulators of healthcare professionals

1.3 Policy and strategy development

1.4 Financial characteristics of regulators of HCPs

1.5 Economics of regulating professionals

1.6 Monopolies, professionals, and their regulation

1.7 Establishing new statutory regulators

1.8 Abolishing regulators and transferring registers

1.1 STRUCTURES FOR REGULATING HEALTHCARE PROFESSIONALS

INTRODUCTION

Throughout the world there are many different ways to structure the regulation of healthcare professionals. These differences can be identified by reference to twelve variables. A framework can then be constructed to compare and contrast the structure of a regulator either within or across jurisdictions. This is of particular use when considering amending the legislation of a regulator.

VARIABLES OF THE STRUCTURE FOR REGULATING HEALTHCARE PROFESSIONALS

Twelve variables can be used to analyse the structure for regulating healthcare professionals. They are as follows:

1. State compulsion to register
2. Autonomy and independence of regulator from the state
3. Alignment with systems and structures of government
4. Board composition
5. Degree of integration of regulators' eight processes and nine standards
6. Collaboration, joint working and delegation between regulators
7. Number of professions regulated by regulator
8. Harmonisation and sharing of standards, rules, and processes by regulators
9. Source of funding
10. Legislative harmonisation
11. Board structure
12. Board member inclusion in judgment decisions

However, it should be noted that the identification and selection of the 12 variables is my subjective opinion, and it is entirely reasonable for others to have different views on what should or should not be included. In addition, each of the variables can be implemented using markedly different approaches. To illuminate this, a framework can be used. The framework allows the different approaches to each variable to be positioned along a spectrum between two extremities, as illustrated in Chart 1.1 – I, on the next page:

Operations of Regulators of Healthcare Professionals, Volume 4, First Edition. Marc Seale.

Companion website: www.wiley.com/go/seale/regulatinghealthcare

Chart 1.1 – I **Structures for regulating healthcare professionals – framework**

State compulsion to register 1	Autonomy & indepedence of regulator from the State 2	Aligment with systems & structures of Government 3	Board composition 4	Degree of integration regulators' processes & standards 5	Colaberation joint working between regulators 6	Number of professions regulated by regulator 7	Harmonisation & sharing of standard & rules processes by regulators 8	Source of funding 9	Legislative harmonisation 10	Board structure 11	Board inclusion in judgment decisions 12
1 State compulsion to register	2 Autonomy & indepedence of regulator from the State	3 Aligment with systems & structures of Government	4 Board composition	5 Degree of integration regulators' processes & standards	6 Colaberation joint working between regulators	7 Number of professions regulated by regulator	8 Harmonisation & sharing of standard & rules processes by regulators	9 Source of funding	10 Legislative harmonisation	11 Board structure	12 Board inclusion in judgment decisions

Each of the twelve variables will now be elaborated upon and in turn the above chart can be populated with examples of each variable:

1. **State compulsion to register**

   The requirement by the state for professionals to be regulated varies considerably across different jurisdictions. There are five approaches. At one end of the spectrum there is compulsory statutory regulation, whilst at the other end, there may be no requirement whatsoever.

   Compulsory statutory regulation

   In this approach to regulation, the state grants statutory powers to regulators that requires professionals to register. This is the most frequently used approach for this variable to regulate healthcare professionals.

   Virtually every country in the world requires at least one healthcare professionto be regulated, for example, medical practitioners are regulated in 123 of the 145 countries recognised by the United Nations. However, some professions are only regulated in a minority of countries, for example, dieticians. The reasons for this are predominantly historical or economic, and the issues surrounding the history of the regulation of healthcare professionals are discussed further in Section 8.3, volume 4.

   Proxy regulation

   In a small number of jurisdictions the state does not establish its own regulator. Instead it requires healthcare professionals to be registered with a regulator based outside its own jurisdiction. If a professional is not on the register of the proxy regulator they do not have the right to practise in the state.

   An example of this type of structure is found in the Isle of Man and the Channel Islands. This is because they are both small independent countries and some of the UK regulators of healthcare professions, such as the HCPC, have no jurisdiction in them. In these types of arrangements the government and regulator will have a formal agreements, often a memorandum of understanding (MoU), see Section 1.4, volume 1, that stipulate how the two parties will cooperate with one another, for example, by agreeing to cooperate with the provision of information relating to complaints about professionals.

   Encouraging voluntary regulation

   The next approach to this variable is used in relation to the regulation of healthcare professionals, is where employers or a non-governmental organisation requires individual professionals to be members of a voluntary register. An example of this is where a health insurance company will only reimburse a patient for the cost of their health treatment if it has been provided by a healthcare professional who is a member of a professional association. In other situations an employment agency or an employer will only employ professionals if they are members of a voluntary register.

   An example of this type of situation is that in the UK until July 2009 forensic psychologists were not statutorily regulated by the Health Professions Council; the Prison Service required all forensic psychologists that it employed to be members of the professional association, the British Psychology Society (BPS), which incidentally has chartered status.

   However, some professionals may choose not to be members of a professional association and accept the consequences of possibly being unable to supply services to specific organisations.

   Voluntary regulation

   In this approach professional associations may operate a system of non-statutory regulation where they have no powers to comply or force professionals to become members of the organisation. However, there is a degree of protection of title, since only members can use a title that indicates their membership of the professional association.

   An example of this in the UK are nutritionists who are not statutorily regulated, but a membership organisation, the Nutrition Society, manages a voluntary register for individuals who reach certain education standards. There is no compulsion by the state to join the register and they can't prevent anyone using the title nutritionist as the title is not protected. However, it should be noted that to complicate matters in the UK there are a number of different professional associations for nutritionists.

   No regulation

   If there is neither regulator nor professional association in a particular jurisdiction, then there is in effect no regulation whatsoever. However, others will choose to join or remain on a register based and operating in another jurisdiction which they have previously belonged to before taking up practice in the new jurisdiction

   In addition, many healthcare professionals when they are working in an environment where there is no statutory or voluntary regulation will abide by their own perception of how a professional should behave. This can sometime be referred to as self-regulation; see Section 1.1, volume 1.

   More than one system in a single jurisdiction

   To add to the complexity, it should be noted that, many jurisdictions require some professions to be statutorily regulated, whilst at the same time they encourage other professions to use a voluntary system.

2. **Autonomy and independence of regulator from the state**

   The second variable that can be used to structure the regulation of healthcare professionals is the degree of autonomy and independence of the regulator from government. This issue is explored in detail in Section 1.1, volume 1, in particular the advantages and disadvantages of autonomous and independent regulators.

There are three broad options:

i. Direct government control of regulator
ii. Semi-autonomous and semi-independent from government
iii. Self-governing autonomous and independent from government

i. Direct government control of regulator

An example of the use of this type of arrangement is in Saudi Arabia where doctors are regulated by the Ministry of Health. The regulatory organisation is based in the ministry, and the employees are civil servants and they run the day-to-day operations. Similar arrangements are found in Japan. In a few USA, some states such as Colorado regulate some professions where the regulator is managed by a state official without recourse to a board.

An example in the UK of this type of arrangement is the regulation of teachers by the Teaching Regulation Agency, which is an executive agency and is sponsored by the Department of Education in England. The relevant legislation is the Teachers' Disciplinary (England) Regulations 2012.

When the structure of regulation is such that government has direct control of the day-to-day running of the regulator, it can exert a strong influence by the use of a number of levers, including:

- **Appointment of the chair, board members, and senior executives**
  The government has the ability to directly appoint the board members and/or key members of the senior executive of the regulator. Alternatively, the government has a right to be consulted over appointments to the board or senior positions of the regulator. It may also have a veto over appointments.
  In some jurisdiction, there is a degree of separation between the ministry and the organisation that appoints the board members of the regulator. An example of this type of arrangement is to be found in Philippines where the Professional Regulation Commission confers the responsibility to license healthcare professionals to profession-specific regulatory boards
  In some instances government may not make the direct appointments but can heavily influence the appointment process.
- **Employee contracts**
  Employees of the regulator may be engaged using civil servant employment contracts with standard terms and conditions.
- **Ownership**
  Government in effect has ownership of the regulator in a similar way that a commercial enterprise is controlled by the major shareholder. Special powers for government in the body's constitution may also indicate control.
- **Regulatory outcomes**
  The government, when it has day-to-day control of the regulator rather than just setting the objectives and policy of the regulator, may seek to set or constrain the outcomes of the regulator; see Section 1.1, volume 1.
- **Reporting**
  The government may demand certain reports or information from the regulator.
- **Financial surplus**
  The government can determine the way in which the regulators' financial surpluses should be utilised. This included using financial surpluses for non-regulatory purposes.

ii. Semi-independent and semi-autonomous from government

This is the most frequently occurring arrangement, whereby government, rather than having day-to-day control of the regulator, may step back and rely on indirectly control of the regulator who is constituted as a public authority.

It can be argued that all statutory regulators are given specific powers by the state and are therefore never truly independent of the state however weak the link is.

However, as a quid pro quo, the amount of formal reporting by the regulator to government may be considerable. This type of reporting may include an annual report and annual performance reports. In addition, committees of the legislature may scrutinise the workings of the regulator.

An example of this arrangement is in the Netherlands where the Centraal Informatiepunt Beroepen Gezondheidszorg (BIG) works as an implementation, or executive organisation, for the Ministry of Health, Welfare and Sport.

iii. Self-governing autonomous and independent from government

In the third option there is no direct control by government and no delegated legislative powers. In effect the profession manages its own affairs using a system of certification – voluntary.

Gauging independence from government

When examining the issue of the independence of regulators from government, the degree of independence can be gauged by reference to the regulators' standards and rules. One way to do this is to examine the ability of regulators to establish and amend their standards and make rules and/or byelaws (rule-making powers), without the approval, or interference from, government; see Chapter 4, volume 1, and Sections 8.3 and 8.4, volume 1. This means that at one end of the spectrum a certification – voluntary system may be non-prescriptive and allow inconsistent standards to be set and different rules to be established for different healthcare professions. At the other end of the spectrum, which uses a prescriptive system with detailed primary or secondary legislation that requires specific rules and is inflexible; it forces consistency between different regulators. In effect the standards of the regulator are tightly controlled by government.

3. **Alignment with systems and structures of government**
In Section 8.6, volume 1, the different ways that the system and structures of government can be organised are explored. The way that regulation is then aligned with these systems and structures of government is then of great importance. For example, there may be a single national/unitary/central government that has complete control of the regulation of healthcare professionals. Alternatively, in some countries, the federal government has no power relating to the regulation of healthcare professional and the power to regulate is embedded in the devolved or regional government. Whatever the arrangements, wherever it be centralised, federal, devolved, or a regional system, it has a significant impact on the organisation of the regulation of healthcare professionals.

4. **Board composition**
The board of a regulator can comprise two distinct types of members, namely, those who are professionals or those who are lay; see Section 3.2, volume 4, Structure, composition, and size of boards.

However, it is not just a matter of the ratio of lay members to professions members of the board that is important but also the relationship of the professional members to their professional association.

The relationship between the professional association and regulator is important and as discussed in Section 10.6, volume 2, Relationship between regulators and professional associations, a business-like relationship is desirable. Unfortunately, conflicts can, and often do, arise between the two organisations because many areas of their respective responsibilities and interests overlap. In terms of the relationship, as with all key stakeholders, the professional associations must be in a position to be able to influence the regulator. But at the same time they must not be in a position to marshal undue influence.

The desired outcome of the relationship is that the regulatory contract should be balanced, so that the advantages of professional regulation outweigh the disadvantages; see Section 7.1, volume 1.

The central challenge relating to board composition is that of the possibility that the board of the regulator comes under the control of the professional association of the profession that it regulates. This should be avoided at all costs since in the eventuality that it happens, then the regulator may suffer regulatory capture and may operate to the benefit of the profession and to the detriment to other stakeholders, in particular members of the public.

It should however be emphasised that control by the professional association will not automatically be detrimental but in today's world of consumerism, there could very well be a perception that there is.

Therefore, when considering the variables of the structure for regulating healthcare professionals the desired level of influence on the board of the regulator by the professional association of the profession(s) regulated should be taken into account.

Bearing this in mind, there are two alternative ways that board composition can be structured in relationship to:

i. Percentage of the regulators' board members who are members of the profession

ii. Degree of integration of regulators' board and the professional association's board

The actual percentage of the regulators' board members who are members of the profession can vary significantly. Thus, when the board is controlled by a significant majority of members who are professionals, it is referred to as professional statutory self-regulation:

Definition: Professional Statutory Self-regulation
Statutory regulator of a profession where a significant majority of the board of the regulator are members of the profession it regulates.

Where the board of the regulator is still controlled by members of the profession but their majority is small, the arrangement can be referred to as profession-led al-statutory regulation.

Definition: Profession-Led-Statutory Regulation
Statutory regulator of a profession where a small majority of the board of the regulator are members of the profession it regulates.

At the other end of the spectrum is consumer-oriented regulation, where the members of the profession are not in a majority. Thus:

Definition: Consumer-Oriented Regulation
Statutory regulator of a profession where the majority of the board of the regulator are not members of the profession it regulates.

Degree of joint board membership of the regulator and the professional association

The alternative way to examine the issue of board composition is to consider the degree of joint membership that individual board members have of the board of the regulator and the board of the professional association. There are five options. They are as follows:

- **i.** Identical membership of the board of regulator and professional association
- **ii.** Majority of the regulator's board members are also board members of the professional association
- **iii.** Half of the board members of regulator also on board of professional association
- **iv.** Minority of the regulators board members are also board members of the professional association
- **v.** No joint membership of the boards of the regulator and professional association

It should be pointed out that it should not be assumed that all professionals will be members, or active members of their professional association, or that they will diligently support the position of their professional association. Notwithstanding this, there may however be a perception that they are and will.

In the UK it is now considered that there is a fundamental conflict of interest if the regulator's governance structures and arrangements are not clearly separate from the professional association.

For example, in the UK the Royal College of Veterinary Surgeons who is the regulator of veterinary surgeons and the British Veterinary Association who is the professional association are totally separate organisations. Again in the UK, the regulation of medical practitioners, the General Medical Council (GMC) is partly separated from the Royal Colleges, for example, the Royal College of Surgeons, who act as a professional association and in particular set post-registration qualifications.

In conclusion, this can be expressed as a principle:

Principle: Autonomy of Regulator
Regulators, by adhering to their legislation, should be able to act independently, govern themselves, and control their own affairs without interference from government, professional associations, and employers.

5. **Degree of integration of regulators' eight processes, and nine standards**

   Section 3.1, volume 1, Framework for the regulation of healthcare professions, proposed a framework consisting of a register, eight regulatory processes, and nine standards.

One of the main benefits of an integrated approach to regulation is that lessons and experience gained from one part of the regulator can relatively seamlessly be transferred to another part of the organisation. So, for example, a greater understanding of the causes of fitness to practise (FTP) complaints can be transferred to the standards for education and training of new professionals. In a sense integration leads to a beneficial positive feedback loop.

However, not all regulators of healthcare professionals slavishly undertake all eight processes and use all nine standards. This is because some of the regulatory process under the legislation of a jurisdiction will be the responsibility of a separate and independent organisation. Or, the regulator has the power to contract out one or more of the eight processes to another organisation.

Therefore when examining the alternative structures that can be used to regulate healthcare professionals the extent that all eight processes and nine standards are under the direct organisation and management a single regulator should be considered. There are a range of options and practical examples:

Fully integrated processes within regulator

In this structure a single regulator is responsible for all eight processes and use all nine standards. This is the structure used in the UK by the General Dental Council (GDC) and the Health and Care Professions Council (HCPC).

However, in relation to education and training and FTP to a greater or lesser extent the service may be organised and managed by external organisations.

Degree of integration of the education and training processes

Different regulators may have markedly different processes to:

- Directly quality assure education and training programmes against the standards for approving education and training programmes that lead to initial registration
- Manage exams to assess the performance of prospective professionals who have the required qualifications and are seeking to enter the profession

Some regulators will be directly involved in both processes. Alternatively, both processes may be provided by others. For example, professional associations may set the exams or the regulator may contact out the process to QA E&T programmes, as the NMC does in the UK.

Another example from the UK was the Postgraduate Medical Education and Training Board (PMETB), which was responsible for the structure and quality of the postgraduate education and training of medical specialists and GPs in England from 2005 to 2010 when it was abolished and its responsibilities transferred to the GMC.

Degree of integration of ftp process
Section 3.1, volume 3, explores how the FTP process can be organised and structured using five different options. They include: full integration, legally required internal separation, voluntary separation, separate public authority independent from regulator, and lastly the use of government's legal service.

Additional integration of other non-regulatory processes
A small number of regulators of healthcare professional may have additional responsibilities outside regulation. For example, workforce planning.

6. **Collaboration, joint working and delegation between regulators**
Regulators should be effective and efficient. This can be partly achieved both by cooperating, see Section 1.5, volume 1, and collaboration with one another, which can be defined as:

Definition: Collaborate
Working together to create a shared goal.

Encouraging collaboration between regulators
Politicians and their civil servants, who are seeking greater collaboration or joint working of regulators, may make statements to encourage and cajole them to take action. These encouragements may focus on either minimising duplication of regulatory effort or reducing the impact on those enterprises or individuals they regulate. Areas of potential collaboration include, for example:

- Common ICT systems
- Gathering existing data from existing sources rather than collecting again
- Harmonisation or common standards
- Information sharing of data amongst different regulators
- Regulators inspect the same service delivery facilities concurrently
- Shared general functions such as finance and HR
- Shared or collocated office accommodation
- Sharing best practices
- Training and career development of employees

Regulators often respond by the issuing of joint statements articulating the many benefits of collaboration and joint working, but examination will usually fail to identify any hard evidence of significant change. The apparent lack of demonstrable appetite for these types of projects is possibly because of the perceived threat to board independence or indeed their existence if the collaboration is successful.

An exemplar of a more forceful approach has taken place in Nova Scotia, Canada, where the Regulated Health Professions Network Act, Chapter 48 of the Acts 2012, as amended by 2015, c. 52, s. 33, facilitated the establishment of the Nova Scotia Regulated Health Professions Network. Notwithstanding this, in a number of jurisdictions, words of encouragement from politicians and oversight organisations may in the long term be replaced by threats of the introduction of legislation.

Finally, it should be noted that since regulation has cross border implications, their collaboration and cooperation can be both within jurisdictions and between jurisdictions.

Contracting out or delegation
In the UK since 2022, the regulators of healthcare professionals have been given legal powers to either contract out or delegate their regulatory processes to other regulators of healthcare professionals or third parties. And at the same time they have been given powers to undertake processes delegated to them by other regulators of healthcare professionals.

However, responsibility for processes delegated to third parties remains with the delegating regulator.

7. **Number of professions regulated by regulator**
If only one healthcare profession is regulated in a particular jurisdiction then, obviously, there will only be a need for one regulator. However, if the number of regulated healthcare professions in a jurisdiction is greater than one, different approaches must be utilised.

There are three options:

i. **Single regulator for each profession**
As each new profession is brought into the system of regulation a new independent regulator is created to regulate the additional profession. This, for example, is the approach used in the Canadian Province of Ontario, where there are over 20 independent regulators or colleges.

ii. **Multi-professional regulator – related family of professions**
As new professions are brought into regulation, closely related professions are regulated by the same regulator rather than creating additional separate regulators. This approach is sometimes used with dentists and pharmacists and their related professions or 'team'.

In terms of corporate governance there is a single board, and the processes used by the regulator are identical wherever possible or at least very similar for each of the professions. In the UK two examples of this structure are firstly the GDC who regulate the 'dental team' consisting of dentists, dental nurses, and dental technicians and secondly the General Pharmaceutical Council (GPhC).

iii. Multi-professional regulators – unrelated professions
Regulators using single acts and common processes operate in a number of jurisdictions. For example, AHPRA in 2010, HCPC in 2001, and CORU in 2007

These types of regulators are referred to as multi-professional regulator, which can be defined as:

Definition: Multi-professional Regulator
Regulator established by single piece of legislation to regulate more than one profession using uniform principles, processes, and standards.

It should be noted that the term multidisciplinary regulator may also be used.

Of interest is that in June 2024 British Columbia established two multi-professional regulators, the College of Health Care Professionals of BC and the College of Complementary Health Professionals of BC. In a sense both the BC regulators sit somewhere betwixt and between the second and third options described above.

Increasing emergence of multi-professional regulators
It can be argued that there is an increasing emergence of multi-professional regulators. The cause of the phenomenon can be linked to advantages and disadvantages of multi-professional regulation, which are now explored.

Advantages and disadvantages of multi-professional regulators
There are a range of both advantages and disadvantages to multi-professional regulation. They include:

Advantages

- Board membership quality will increase since the best candidates will only be recruited by one organisation
- Fewer civil servants and less government resources required to administer a multi-professional regulator
- Single communications channel for employers of the professionals, patients, and service users reduces task of communication by the regulator
- Consumer advocacy organisations become more familiar with a single FTP process increasing their ability to support consumers/patients and service users
- Consistency of approach increases the quality of processes
- Court rulings and decisions apply to numerous healthcare professions rather than each regulator having to test its own legislation
- Economic benefits; see Section 1.5
- Employers of professionals
  - One set of FTP standards and processes to follow when engaging with regulator, particularly relating to decisions about whether to refer a professional to the regulator
  - One set of continuing competence standards and processes to support for numerous professions
- Education and training providers of programmes for different healthcare profession on the same campuses can be subjected to the same standards and quality assurance making it straightforward to meet the standards
  - Share knowledge of regulator's standards and processes
  - Practise placements requirements
- FTP sanctions should be consistent across numerous professions
- Governance is improved as the regulator's governing body is more inclined to focus on regulatory issues rather than on single-profession non-regulatory issues
- Joint working between regulators, including both collaboration and cooperation, is simplified if the number of regulators is reduced
- Legislative body will have fewer pieces of legislation to keep up to date
- Immigrating professionals will have a common application process which will increase the understanding of the process by interested parties
- Multi-disciplinary team working should be enhanced since healthcare professionals will share many of the same standards and with their greater understand and expectations of their co-workers should be more willing to hold their fellow professionals to account if they display standards below what is expected of them
- Parity of professions means that all the regulated professions are treated equally in relation to each another
- Professional associations' and trade unions' greater knowledge of how to support their members involved in the regulator's processes such as continuing competence, FTP, return to practise, and initial registration
- Regulatory capture less likely since stakeholders such as professional associations and trade unions will have less influence on a single multi-professional regulator compared to a number of smaller separate regulators

- Stakeholders find it easier to understand the single identical processes for all healthcare professions
- Standards, see multi-professional standards in Section 4.5, volume 1, sharing standards, where common standards can be shared across many professionals; this will lead to a better understanding across the professionals of what is expected of them and their co-professionals
- Workforce planning will be enhanced by common data sets amongst numerous professions
- Workplace multi-professional regulation better reflects changing work place practices and environment.

Disadvantages

- Professional associations influence on the regulatory contract will be reduced and may lead to their disenchantment and support of regulation
- Regulatory failure of the single regulator would mean that the consequences would be greater compared to a number of smaller separate regulators. This may generate a 'too big to fail' mentality
- The detachment of the board from the individual professions may result in a reduction of the enthusiasm and passion for the healthcare professions they regulate
- Level of understanding of the healthcare professions they regulate may result in the board focusing on the internal day-to-day operations of the regulator rather than the professions
- Limited resources will be spread too thinly across the responsibilities of a multi-professional regulator and will be unable to maintain appropriate relationships with key stakeholders.

Governance arrangements for multi-professional regulators

Notwithstanding the advantages vs. the disadvantages of multi-professional regulators, there are different ways that their governance can be structured. These include:

Multi-professional regulator – unrelated professions – single board

At one end of the spectrum a single regulator regulates numerous professions. The governance arrangement consists of a single board or central agency. Wherever possible, there is a propensity to have common regulatory standards and processes.

Examples of this type of arrangements include:

- HCPC in the UK
- The Department of Regulatory Agency (DORA), Colorado, USA
- The Regulated Industries Complaints Office, Hawaii

Multi-professional regulators – unrelated professions – multiple boards

At the other end of the spectrum a federated governance organisation is used. This consists of a central board that governs with the assistance of other autonomous boards, each of which is associated with a particular profession. There is a considerable variation in the powers of the autonomous boards. For example:

- The central board facilitates joint discussions with the autonomous boards who have no other roles
- The central board controls all budgets and operations and the autonomous boards set some standards
- There are no requirements to have similar processes or standards. The central board provides some regulatory processes such as the register to the autonomous boards who may be responsible for the FTP process

Examples of this type of arrangements include:

- Health Professions Council, South Africa
- Health Professions Council, Texas, USA
- Professional Regulation Commission, Republic of the Philippines

However, when reviewing the governance arrangements of multi-professional regulators with multiple boards, careful examination of their legislation is required, since it is often challenging to understand who exactly is responsible for which regulatory process and standard.

This challenge can be ascertained by reviewing two regulators: APHRA in Australia and CORU, the Health and Social regulator in the Republic of Ireland.

In summary it can be concluded that the selected regulatory structures used within a multi-professional regulators can bring benefits. After all, even a Martian arriving to investigate the regulation of healthcare professionals in the UK would surely question the need for so many regulatory organisations delivering identical objectives using similar operating models and processes. However, if the legislation incorporates weak regulatory principles and processes, the fact that it is a multi-professional regulator in comparison to a single professional regulator, its structure will not magic away any inbuilt defects.

8. **Harmonisation and sharing of standards, rules, and processes by regulators**

   Regulators, although they regulate different sectors, should logically work in similar ways. For example, if a particular process or standard works in one sector then it is reasonable to assume that it may be applicable in another regulated sector and it should be adopted wherever possible by other regulators in other sectors.

And even though duplication of effort can also be decreased by reducing the number of regulators, the structure of regulation in a jurisdiction can also be arranged so that there is harmonisation of standards and processes without reducing the number of regulators.

This approach, which can be seen as an alternative to establishing multi-professional regulators, occurs when two or more independent regulators agree to harmonise and share their standards and at the same time they may also share their processes. The objective of both organisations is to make them more effective and efficient.

For example, sharing and harmonisation can include:

- Common guidance, for example, on confidentiality
- Commonality between the standards of proficiency
- Harmonised rules
- Identical process for renewing registration
- Identical standards of conduct for all professions
- Similarities for continuing competence audits and/or assessments

In addition, harmonisation is not just limited to regulators working in one jurisdiction since the approach can apply just as well to regulators in different jurisdictions. However, where different regulators have different legalisation, harmonisation of the standards of regulation is challenging.

At the current moment in time, there appears little interest and support to establish these types of relationships. The reason for this may be that the boards of regulators see it as a first step to full integration and the possibility of the demise of their board. Also, professional associations may perceive the process as one that will reduce their direct influence on their regulator. Lastly, the public has little interest and impact on the adoption of the process.

Despite this challenge, noteworthy are processes to harmonise standards across jurisdictions; for example, in the USA and Canada nurses use the same standards of entry to practise.

9. Source of funding

The subject of how regulators are funded is introduced in Section 1.1, volume 1, Introduction to regulation and regulators, and is explored further in Section 1.4, financial characteristics of regulators of healthcare professionals.

In essence, without the appropriate funding a regulator can't deliver its regulatory objectives. There are two options for providing the financial resources required by a regulator of healthcare professionals, namely:

i. The State

ii. The Professionals

The issue of funding is an important variable when considering the structure of regulation because stakeholders who fund the regulator may seek to influence the regulator. This can lead to a reduction to the autonomy and independence of the regulator. See Section 1.4, volume 1, Autonomy, independence, accountability, and scrutiny of regulators.

For example, if the regulator is funded solely by the professionals that it regulates, the professionals may seek to gain influence over the regulator to deny it funds to undertake its functions or to curtail its process such as continuing competence audits.

On the other hand, a government that provides funds to the regulator may seek to gain control over how that funds are used. Also, the government may be reluctant to allow the regulator to raise its fees on the ground that it is in effect a tax on employment.

The issues is slightly muddied because in many jurisdictions the cost of the annual registration fees paid by professions to the regulator can be partly, or fully, offset against personal taxation. Thus the tax rebate transfers some of the cost of regulating healthcare professionals to the tax payer.

In addition, in some instance, particularly in the USA, not all funds raised by the regulators are retained for their own exclusive use because a percentage may be retained by the government and is deposited in the state's General Fund for its own purposes. In other words, not all the funds raised by the regulator are used by the regulator.

10. Legislative harmonisation

When there is more than one statutory regulator in a single jurisdiction there is a choice between either each regulator having broadly similar legislation, referred to as omnibus, or alternatively, different legislation in the form of multiple acts. The advantages and disadvantages of single or multiple acts of legislation are explored in Section 8.3, volume 1, Legislation.

11. Board structure

An important variable in the structure of regulators is the exclusion or inclusion of the executives as executive directors on the board, serving as equal with the non-executive board members. At one end of the spectrum there are no employees on the board. At the other end of spectrum the executive can compose of up to 49% of the composition of what is referred to as a unitary board.

These alternative board structures are examined in further detail in Section 3.2, volume 4, Structure, composition, and size of boards.

12. Board member inclusion in judgment decisions

The pros and cons of members of the board of the regulator acting as assessors, are explored in detail in Section 1.2. Different jurisdictions have markedly different approaches, from allowing members of the board to act as assessors, to their complete exclusion.

Returning to Chart 1.1 – I it can now be populated with examples of each variable, as depicted in Chart 1.1 – II, on the next page:

Chart 1.1 – II **Structures for regulating healthcare professionals – framework, populated**

State compulsion to register 1	Autonomy & indepedence of regulator from the State 2	Aligment with systems & structures of Government 3	Board composition 4	Degree of integration regulators' processes & standards 5	Colaberation joint working between regulators 6	Number of professions regulated by regulator 7	Harmonisation & sharing of standard & rules processes by regulators 8	Source of funding 9	Legislative harmonisation 10	Board structure 11	Board inclusion in judgment decisions 12
Compuary statutory Regulation	Self Governing	Unitary State	Majority board members lay	Fully Integrated	Legislative requiment to collaberate	Numerious	Maximum Harmonisation of Processes & Standards	100% funding by Professionals	Single Act	Unitary Board	Board members Excluded
Proxy Regulation											
Encouraged Voluntary regulation	Limited State Control	Federal	Equal lay professional board members	Education or FTP separate	Collaboration			% of Registration Fees Tax Deductible		Board involved in day-to-day operations	
Voluntary regulation											
No Regulation	State Control	Regional	Majority board members professionals	FTP & Education separate	Minimal Cooperation	One	Minimum Harmonisation of Processes & Standards	100% State Funded	Multiple Acts	Two Tier Strategic Advisory Board	Board members participate

1 State compulsion to register | 2 Autonomy & indepedence of regulator from the State | 3 Aligment with systems & structures of Government | 4 Board composition | 5 Degree of integration regulators' processes & standards | 6 Colaberation joint working between regulators | 7 Number of professions regulated by regulator | 8 Harmonisation & sharing of standard & rules processes by regulators | 9 Source of funding | 10 Legislative harmonisation | 11 Board structure | 12 Board inclusion in judgment decisions

Role of government in defining structures

It has been proposed in Section 1.2, volume 1, that government is responsible for setting the policy objective of its regulators. They also have an important role of selecting which permutation of the twelve variables described in the proceeding paragraphs to adopt and then to impose the structure by way of legislation, see Section 8.3, volume 1. However, rather than stepping back and leaving the regulator to its own devices to deliver the policy objective, government should from time to time reconsider what is the most appropriate structure and thus avoid ossifying the regulators and hindering their evolution and adaptation.

Selecting or changing structurers for regulating healthcare professionals

For those who are contemplating the selection or changing the structure for regulating healthcare professionals it is worthwhile to take the following four points into your consideration:

Firstly, the social, economic, and political structures that influence the healthcare delivery system that are identified in Section 11.2, volume 3, introduction to country profiles, should be taken into account.

Secondly, more often than not, the particular set of structural variables adopted in a jurisdiction is the result of its socio-political history, culture and economic development, rather than a conscious, logical, objective, and rational choice by government.

Thirdly, the existing arrangements in any one jurisdiction are usually an accident of history, albeit strongly influenced by the rise of consumerism. The issue is explored in greater detail in Section 8.4, volume 4, history of the regulation of the healthcare professions. And in particular the metamorphosis from profession statutory self-regulation to profession-led statutory-regulation and in turn the emergence of the consumer oriented regulation are examined.

Fourthly, there is no 'correct way' to structure the regulation of healthcare professionals.

This leads to a regulatory principle:

Principle: Structure for Regulating Healthcare Professionals
There is no intrinsic ideal permutation.

CONCLUSIONS

The taxonomy of the structure of regulators of health professionals is not particularly complicated. The different permutations of the variables have evolved over time driven by the increasing number of regulated healthcare professions and the strength of lobbying of particular stakeholders to ensure that their views are adopted in the legislation of the jurisdiction. However, there are dynamic and evolving tensions in the system, namely:

1. The strength of the monopoly granted to the profession by government
2. The level of public protection versus the economic advantages to the professions
3. The degree of influence on the regulatory process from key stakeholders

Lastly, for statutory regulators, pressures for desirable changes to their structures pose challenges, since if the structures are set down in their legislation, further legislation is required to make amendments and the timetable for any change process is measured in years.

EXERCISES AND QUESTIONS

Exercises

- Using your knowledge of a regulator that you are familiar with, using Chart 1.1 – I, plot the twelve variables that comprise the structure or regulators.
- For a regulator that you are familiar with, how and why would you change its structure to improve the delivery of its regulatory objectives?
- How do the structures of regulators operating in different sectors vary? And are they markedly different or fairly similar?

Questions

- In addition to the twelve variables discussed in this section, what alternative variables can be used to examine the structures for regulation healthcare professionals?
- What are the three most important variables that can be used to examine the structure for regulation healthcare professionals and why?
- Within a single jurisdiction should all healthcare professionals be regulated using identical principles and processes or is it acceptable to have a variety?

LEGISLATION

Examples of UK Legislation

The Teachers' Disciplinary (England) Regulations 2012 L

Example of International Legislation

Canada

Nova Scotia

Regulated Health Professions Network Act, Chapter 48 of the Acts 2012, as amended by 2015, c. 52, s. 33 L

FURTHER READING

Enabling Excellence: R
Autonomy and Accountability for Healthcare Workers, Social Workers and Social Care Workers
Department of Health (UK)
Stationery Office
ISBN: 9780101800822
Cm 8008
16 February 2011
31 pages

Fundamentals of Regulatory Design B
Sparrow, M K
ISBN-13: 979-8670959285
Independent publication
30 July 2020
145 pages

Health Workforce Regulation in the Western Pacific Region R
World Health Organization – Western Pacific region
ISBN: 9789290617235
January 2016
48 pages

International Council of Nurses on Regulation R
Towards a Twenty First Century Models
M Styles and F Affara
OCLC Number 48764597
1998
49 pages

Models of Self-regulation; B
An overview of Models in Business and the Professions
National Consumer Council
ISBN-13: 9781899581863
1 October 1999
66 pages

Nursing Regulation: From Principle to Power: R
A Guidebook on Mastering Nursing Regulation
International Council of Nurses, (ICN), with the support of the W.K. Kellogg Foundation
NLM Unique ID: 9417880
1992
184 pages

Paradoxes of Professional Regulation: In Search of Regulatory Principles B
Michael J. Trebilcock
University of Toronto Press
ISBN: 9781487543051, 1487543050
March 2022
168 pages

Review of the Regulatory Framework for Legal Services in England and Wales R
Sir David Clementi
December 2004
139 pages

Self-Regulation for Nurses: Issues and Opportunities R
Percival, E
International Council of Nurses
ISBN: 9295005279
2001
43 pages

Washington State Medical QA Commission R
Efficient, Transparent, Responsive: a Safer Patient, a Respected Profession a Modern Medical Board
Fourth Substitute House Bill 1103 Pilot Project Report
Ref: DOH 658-019
3 December 2012
106 pages

1.2 OPERATING MODELS OF REGULATORS OF HEALTHCARE PROFESSIONALS

INTRODUCTION

The functions of a regulator can be divided into either general functions used by many types of organisations or specialists functions that together are primarily found in regulators. They then use a variety of organisational designs to deliver their numerous functions effectively and efficiently.

OPERATING MODELS

This description of the way an organisation functions and works is called its operating model, which can be defined as:

Definition: Operating Model
Description of how an organisation functions and works.

The use of the term operational model is a relatively new addition to the lexicon of organisational jargon, and it should be noted that there are a number of alternative analytical techniques that can be used to examine an organisation, for example, economic, financial, functional, and information flows.

FUNCTIONS

The functions referred to in the definition of an operating model are discrete activities that organisations, including regulators, can use to organise themselves.

FUNCTIONS OF REGULATORS

In relation to the regulators of healthcare professionals, the functions fall into two broad categories.

Firstly, general functions. These are activities that are found not only in regulators but also in many other organisations such as commercial businesses. Typically, they will also be found in medium-sized enterprises (MSE) in a developed economy.

The second category of activities are specialist regulatory functions that together are primarily found in regulators. And whilst each function is not unique to regulators, they tend to be less commonly found in non-regulatory organisations.

It should be noted that, this section does not go into the minutia of each function. For example, how a communications or a human resources (HR) department is organised and managed, as there are many other better reference sources. What is however highlighted, are the particularly important or unusual responsibilities of each function within a regulator of healthcare professionals.

The types of general and specialist functions of regulators of healthcare professionals are listed in Table 1.2 – I , below:

Table 1.2 – I Functions of regulators

General functions
1. Business continuity
2. Contact centre
3. Chief executive officer, registrar, and chair
4. Communications and public affairs
5. Complaints service function and enterprise complaints
6. Compliance, internal audit, service standards, SOPs, and quality assurance
7. Executive management team (EMT)
8. Facilities and office services
9. Finance and accounting
10. Human resources (HR)
11. Governance
12. Information, technology, and communications (ITC)
13. Learning and development
14. Miscellaneous
15. Planning and forecasting
16. Policy and strategy
17. Project management
18. Procurement and purchasing
19. Research and data analysis
20. Risk management
21. Secretariat
Specialist regulatory functions
1. Assessors
2. Continuing competence
3. Education and training
4. Examinations
5. Fitness to practise (FTP)
6. Inspection of service delivery facilities
7. Legal service
8. Professional advisory service
9. Registration
10. Regulation of businesses and partnerships
11. Standards and guidance
12. Workforce planning

GENERAL FUNCTIONS

The general functions are now explored in greater detail.

1. **Business continuity**
   The function of business continuity, which is also sometimes referred to as crisis management or disaster recovery, is to ensure that the organisation will be resilient and can continue to operate following an event such as a natural disaster. These include events such as a flood that causes significant damage or other manmade events such as a long period of disruption to the electricity

supply. The frequency that rehearsals of simulated business continuity scenarios are organised, will be important in maintaining appropriate preparedness.

In addition to preparing a business continuity action plan, the regulator may seek and gain ISO 22301 Business Continuity; see Section 4.3, volume 4, Standards organisations for more details. In addition, they may use ISO 31000: Risk Management.

2. **Contact centre**
Regulators must be able to manage a high volume of voice and electronic communications and, to a markedly decreasing extent, letters. These are predominantly received from the professionals they regulate and members of the public. The function is normally managed in a contact centre, although it is usually embedded in the registration department due to the prevalence of operations related to communications from the professionals on the register.

The contact centre function will probably be responsible for:

- Responding to all types of communications from most stakeholders
- Act as the first port of call and then transfer queries to other functions including communications, education, and FTP
- Systems for receiving and banking financial transactions
- Credentialing of documents
- The contact centre may also provide a walk-in customer service for functions such as applications for registration

Fluctuating Demand for Services
One of the challenges of managing a contact centre can be the wide fluctuations in demand for its services. For example, the number of newly qualified professionals who apply to join the register following graduation in the summer. Or, the renewal of a professional's registration, occurring by a specific date, will all lead to a high demand on only a small percentage of the days in the year.

The patterns of rapid rises and falls in demand may result in a reduced service standard during periods of peak demand compared to other less busy times of the year. Processes may be adopted to 'shave the peak in demand', for example, by the use of self-service systems such as using the web to renew registration online.

Compared to commercial organisations, regulators will often, because of the small scale of their operations, run suboptimal operations and are unable to offer 24/7 services; see Section 1.5, Economic aspects of regulating professionals.

Commercial organisation often contract this type of customer service function to specialist commercial providers. This is advantageous where the complexity of the issues raised by customers is relatively limited, for example, banking. However, given the small scale of the operations of regulators and the complexity of the queries they receive, this option is rarely used by regulators of healthcare professionals.

3. **Chief executive officer, registrars, and chair**
The role of the chief executive, nowadays often referred to as the chief executive officer (CEO), will probably include the following responsibilities:

- Day-to-day management of the operations of the regulator
- Board/executive relationship
- Communication
- Culture of the organisation
- Leadership
- Operational performance
- Stakeholder management

It is of note that the CEO's responsibilities overlap all the factors that are identified as influencing the reputation of a regulator; see Chart 2.5 – I, volume 4.

In the UK there is a legal requirement to appoint a registrar, who has the responsibility to maintain the register along with other governance responsibilities. Thus:

Definition: Registrar
Individual responsible for keeping and maintaining a register.

Although the position of registrar does not have to be the CEO, they usually are. In addition, a deputy and or assistant registrars can be appointed. In addition, in the UK the CEO will be the accounting officer; see Section 1.4.

The roles and responsibilities of the chair and the board are addressed in Chapter 3, volume 4, Governance.

4. **Communications and public affairs**
The responsibilities of the communications and public affairs function embraces the typical portfolio of communications processes found in a commercial organisation. These may include:

i. Advertising
ii. Corporate identity
iii. Digital communication
iv. Events management
v. Internal communications
vi. Market research
vii. Media relations
viii. Monitoring media

ix. Newsletters

x. Print / publications

xi. Public affairs

xii. Reputation management

xiii. Social media

xiv. Stakeholder engagement

xv. Web site design and content management

The regulator will probably have a documented subsidiary communications strategy. This may also include a digital communication strategy. The processes of market research, public affairs, and reputation management are explored in greater detail in Chapter 2, volume 4, Communication.

5. **Complaints service function and enterprise complaints**
An enterprise complaint can be defined as:

Definition: Enterprise Complaint
Complaint about an organisation.

Regulators will inevitably receive enterprise complaints, and to a lesser extent positive feedback, from the users of its services including both members of the public and the professionals it regulates.

It should be noted that these enterprise complaints are not the same as the concerns and complaints received by the regulator concerning the professionals that it regulates; see Chapter 2, volume 2, Concerns about professionals.

The complaints service function, see Section 4.4, volume 4, Complaints about services of regulators, will focus on the handling of enterprise complaints concerning the quality and timeliness of the services that the regulator provides. The role of the complaints service function is to receive, investigate, and respond to these types of complaints. However, analysing the cause of complaints and triggering the development of long-term solutions to eliminate the cause of enterprise complaints in the first place, is also an important responsibility of this function. It is likely to work closely with the quality assurance function if one exists.

The regulator may seek and gain ISO 10002 Customer Service Complaints Management; see Section 4.3, volume 4, standards organisations, for more details.

Enterprise complaints concerning commercial transactions of professionals
Some healthcare professionals provide services and products to their patients on a commercial basis, for example, via a high-street shop selling hearing aids. Complaints received from patients by regulators of healthcare professions concerning commercial transactions between themselves and professionals may be dealt with by the regulator establishing a dedicated internal function. Alternatively, the function may be contracted to an external service supplier. In the UK, an example of this type of service relationship is provided by the Dental Complaints Service which has been established and is funded by the General Dental Council (GDC).

6. **Compliance, internal audit, service standards, SOPs, and quality assurance**
The processes and procedures that a regulator uses to ensure that it delivers its statutory objectives in an efficient and effective manner are mission critical. There are a number of functions that a regulator can undertake to reassure itself that it is undertaking regulation as intended. These functions include:

i. Compliance

ii. Internal audit

iii. Service standards

iv. Standard operating procedures (SOPs)

v. Quality assurance

i. **Compliance**
This is the function of monitoring the implementation of legislation, rules, and regulations to ensure that they are being followed correctly by the regulator. Compliance looks at the present and towards the future, thus providing assurance that the regulators' policies and procedures are in place and are being adhered to.

The compliance function should have a degree of independence from the management of the regulators' other functions but with a strong element of cooperation, so that it can educate and advise the organisation effectively. The independence may be reinforced by having the management of the function reporting directly to the chief executive of the regulator.

In effect, compliances ensures that a regulator does what it is required to do and, if not, it informs those who need to know. Lastly compliance can be audited.

ii. **Internal audit**
Internal audit is concerned with risk management, internal controls, and governance. It provides assurance that all the organisations' activities and internal controls are undertaken in accordance with its policies and procedures. It looks at the past and present. Internal audit should preferably, but not necessarily, be fully independent of the day-to-day management of the organisation. To this end the internal audit function and the head of internal audit usually report to the audit committee.

Chart 1.2 – I **Internal audit vs. compliance**

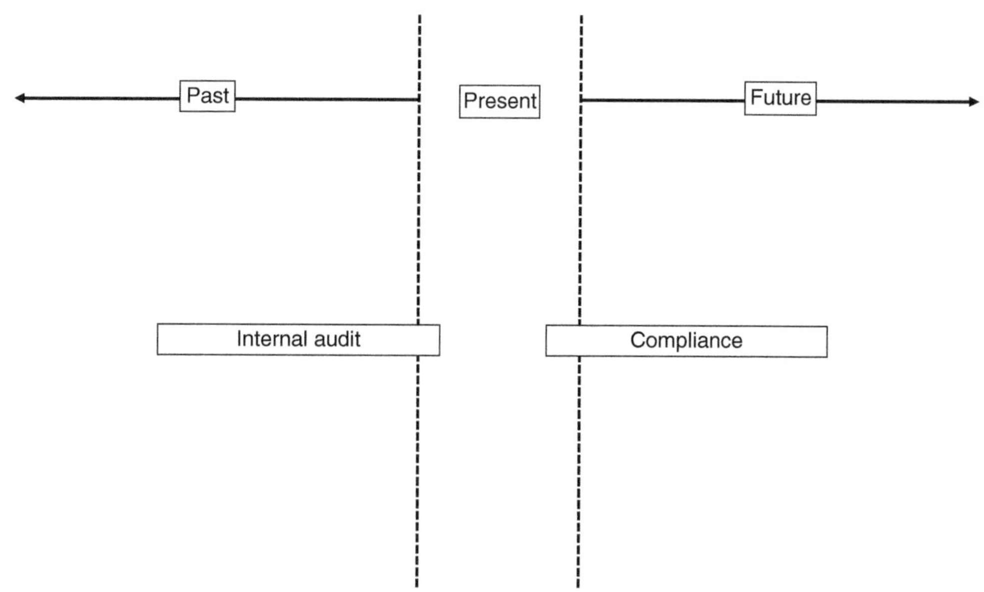

In effect, internal audit provides assurance that the regulator is doing what it said it would do.

The difference between internal audit vs. compliance is illustrated in Chart 1.2 – I. The chart depicts how internal audit looks at the past and present. Whereas, compliance is concerned with the present and the future.

Both compliance and internal audit functions can either be managed internally by in-house teams, or alternatively, they can be provided by external or independent organisations.

External delivered solutions by third parties auditors are overseen as part of the governance arrangements of the regulator such as the regulator's audit committee. Also, oversight organisations, for example, in the UK the Professionals Standards Authority (PSA), in effect make use of compliance and internal audit processes.

iii. Service standards

A regulator, once it has devised and implemented its standard operating procedures (SOPs), should monitor and evaluate its performance against both internal service standards and external service standards; see Section 4.2, volume 4, Evaluating operational performance of regulators. The internal service standards are those set by the regulator itself; see Section 4.1, volume 4, Service standards and operational performance of regulators. Whereas external service standards are set by various standards organisations, see Section 4.3, volume 4, Standards organisations for more details.

iv. Standard operating procedures

Given the repetitive nature of many of the processes of regulators of healthcare professionals they can and do make use of SOPs. Regulators can:

- Derive and publicise their SOPs
- Ensure their employees adhere to them
- Measure their performance against the SOPs

In the context of the functions of a regulator, SOPs provide employees with a reference on how to undertake common business practices, specific business rules activities, or tasks. New employees can use SOPs to answer questions on their jobs without having to interrupt supervisors to ask how an operation is performed. Documented SOPs can also be useful for regulators to communicate with those that they regulate to explain both how monitoring and compliance is undertaken.

SOPs are usually supported by guidance and process flow charts; see Section 1.1, volume 1. As a result they are a key component of the business practice of continuous quality improvement and compliance with quality management system such as ISO 9001 90002 (2015); see Section 4.3, volume 4, Standards organisations, for more details.

However, as a word of warning, regulators must not become over-wedded to their policies and procedures and slavishly apply them in all situations. A 'Tick Box' mentality must be avoided.

v. Quality assurance

In terms of regulators, quality assurance is slightly different from internal audit and compliance.

A number of key processes of a regulator require assessors to use judgment. For example, to assess the competences of a professional involved in an FTP tribunal or the process to approve a programme of education and training. In this context, the purpose of quality assurance is to ensure that, based on the evidence available, the judgment made is satisfactory and that the process is formally recorded. At the same time it facilitates an internal review of compliance with policies and procedures and that service standards are being met or surpassed. The issue is explored further in Section 4.2, volume 4, Evaluating operational performance of regulators.

7. **Executive management team (EMT)**
Typically, there will be an EMT that is responsible for the operational day-to-day management of the regulator. It may also be referred to as the executive committee. The executive team is usually led by a CEO or registrar and comprises the senior members of key functions of the regulator such as the communications, FTP, ITC, and registrations. The EMT may have joint responsibilities that include:

- Allocation of resources
- Budget monitoring and delivery
- Culture of the organisation
- Project prioritisation and delivery
- Recruitment and retention
- Service quality

The relationship between the executive and the board is reviewed in Section 3.5, volume 4. It can be formally defined by a scheme of delegation; see Section 3.1, volume 4.

8. **Facilities and office services**
The facilities and office services function is unlikely to have any unusual responsibilities, and many of the services it provides are contracted out to third-party suppliers either in part or fully.

The responsibilities of the function will embrace all, or some of:

- Catering
- Cleaning
- Environmental services
- Maintenance of accommodation and equipment
- Postal and courier services
- Reception
- Security

The decision to rent, lease, or purchase accommodation will have significant impact on the size of the function because some services may be provided by the landlord or owner of the accommodation.

The department may also be responsible for health and safety issues such as fire evacuation and first aid training. Security includes not only the physical security of the building and its contents but also the security of employees and visitors. This may be particularly important in relation to FTP tribunals.

Usually regulators locate all their functions on a single site. However, they sometimes have physically separate accommodation for their FTP tribunal services. This facilitates the separation of what can be a challenging and stressful process from the more routine day-to-day functions of the regulator.

Other regulators have additional small offices often located in the capital city of their jurisdiction or in the provincial capitals in a federated jurisdiction. The smaller peripheral offices provide functions such as communications, public affairs, and stakeholder engagement.

In UK the GMC's small head office is located in central London with a large secondary office in Manchester, where registration and FTP function are provided. It also has peripheral offices in the capital cities of Northern Ireland, Scotland, and Wales. The Australian regulator APHRA has a main office in Melbourne with a network of regional offices.

In a number of jurisdictions regulators, to reduce costs, share office space with each other. Examples of co-location include New Zealand (Wellington) and in British Columbia (Vancouver), Canada, and the UK HCPC and GCC (London).

9. **Finance and accounting**
The financial characteristics of regulators of healthcare professionals are explored in detailed in Section 1.4. They are relatively straightforward because:

- Capital requirements are low
- Income is predictable
- Reserves are limited and usually invested in low-risk assets
- Single-site operations
- Service organisations
- Taxation is not complicated

Also, the ability of the regulator to manage its affairs without the recourse to raising capital, the relatively low level of capital investment, or the need to financially reward shareholders strongly influence the functions of the finance departments of regulators.

The one area of relative operational complexity is that the professionals it regulates pay their fees to the regulator frequently and in small amounts; see fee collection, Section 4.6, volume 2.

The accounting function of a regulator, in a similar vein to its finances, is relatively straightforward. Its responsibilities may include:

i. Accounts payable and receivable
ii. Annual budgeting preparation and monitoring
iii. Annual report and accounts
iv. Asset management
v. Costing model for services
vi. Financial and accounting policy, including a financial reserves policy
vii. Financial accounts
viii. Financial controls
ix. Financial planning
x. Financial statement
xi. Insurance
xii. Investment portfolio management
xiii. Management accounts
xiv. Project accounting
xv. Pay role
xvi. Tax planning and compliance
xvii. Treasury

10. **Governance**
The governance arrangements of regulators and the structure and function of the board are addressed in Chapter 3, volume 4, Governance.

11. **Human resources (HR)**
Sometimes referred to as human capital management, the HR function will probably include the following responsibilities:

i. Employee assistance and support
ii. Employee forum
iii. Employee grievance procedure
iv. Employee relations
v. Employee surveys
vi. Equity, diversity, and inclusion (EDI) initiatives and policy
vii. HR policies, guidance, plans, and strategy
viii. Publication of HR information (internal and external)
ix. Recruitment – internal and external – and retention policy and processes including annual performance appraisals
x. Remuneration and terms and conditions
xi. Supporting the remuneration committee
xii. Retirement processes
xiii. Succession planning
xiv. Training
xv. Whistleblowing

Unusually, the HR function may be responsible for three specific areas relating to the regulation of healthcare professionals. They are:

i. Criminal record checks for prospective employees
ii. Recruitment, remuneration, learning and development, and appraisal of assessors
iii. Provision of health support to FTP case managers involved in the management of emotionally challenging cases, so that their mental health wellbeing is not adversely affected. The service may be provided by an employee assistance programme or specialist professionals such as councillors or psychotherapists

Some of the functions will be contracted out to specialist service providers such as training organisations.

The regulator will probably have a documented subsidiary HR strategy.

12. **Information, technology, and communications (ITC)**
The ITC function is likely to use processes found in commercial or large public organisations. Resources are directed towards enterprise software systems that are either user-facing services or alternatively internal ITC services.

User-facing services
These will include developing and maintaining ITC systems for the various functions, both external and internal facing, of the regulator. They include:

- The register
- Continuing competence
- FTP case management system (CMS)
- Education and training
- Finance and accounting, HR, and office services
- Management information system (MIS)
- Web site

Internal itc services
These will include the functions that ITC has to undertake to manage its own systems and processes. They include:

- Back-up systems
- Connectivity including mobile telephones and mobile PCs
- Databases
- Employee support
- Remote working
- Security and resilience
- Telephones
- Web services

When selecting and acquiring new ITC technology the decision about the need to either configure as opposed to customising the solutions will be important.

The regulator will probably have a documented subsidiary ITC strategy. The regulator may also seek and gain ISO 27001 Information Security; see Section 4.3, volume 4, standards organisations, for more details.

Lastly, it should be noted that it is a key role of the department to facilitate the substitution of physical transactions by the use of ITC.

13. Learning and development
Learning and development of employees and board members may be a separate function or embedded in the HR function. It can't be underemphasised that adequate resources must be allocated, not only to new employees but also existing employees. A 'sheep dip' approach should be avoided on issues such as the ethics and culture of the organisation

The regulator may have a documented subsidiary learning and development strategy.

14. Miscellaneous
A range of miscellaneous responsibilities may be embedded within the other general functions of the regulator, including:

- Archiving historical documents
- Business analysis
- Change and operations management
- New service development
- Retention, storage and retrieval of data, documents, and other records
- Service providers relationship management

In some of these functions the process to improve the effectiveness and efficiency of the regulator may be driven with the use of various business techniques including innovation, reengineering, continuous quality improvement, and six sigma process improvement.

15. Planning and forecasting
The planning and forecasting function will incorporate both financial and operational processes. Of particular interest will be forecasting the number of regulated professionals and the FTP process. The responsibility for the task, whilst not necessarily embedded in a single function, may be shared across the organisation and co-ordinated by the finance department.

This function may also take the lead in examining and proposing solutions to the intractable requirement of a regulator of professionals to forecast and implement plans to balance factors including:

- Capacity of its functions
- Capabilities
- Costs
- Efficiency
- Types and level of fees
- Funding requirements
- Quality of its services
- Productivity
- Resource requirements, both financial and human
- Timeliness of its services
- Impact of new technology

16. Policy and strategy
Different solutions are found across regulators in terms of how they organise their policy and strategy functions. In this respect regulators differ little from commercial or other types of organisations. The responsibility can be either concentrated in a single function or it can be distributed across many functions each with their own dedicated policy and strategy team.

However organised, the policy and strategy function is likely to responsible for two different types of tasks:

i. Those similar to other public sector and commercial policy and strategy functions

ii. Those unique to the regulation of healthcare professionals

The functions not unique to the regulators of healthcare professionals include:

- Coordination and publication of the regulators' planning process; see Section 9.1, volume 4
- Policy development; see Section 1.3
- Undertaking or commissioning research into the basis for regulating healthcare professionals; see Section 9.3, volume 4
- Undertaking and responding to other organisations' consultations. Whether or not required by legislation a considerable effort may be directed to undertaking public consultations; see Section 2.3, volume 4

- Regulatory impact assessments; see Section 6.1, volume 4
- Responding to Parliament and government departments request for information and providing advice on regulatory matters.
- Managing task and finish groups
- Strategy development process in terms of the regulator as a whole
- Assisting other parts of the organisation such as IT and HR to develop their subsidiary strategies
- Horizon scanning
- Facilitating the use of scenarios
- Influencing the drafting of primary, secondary, and tertiary legislation; see Section 8.3, volume 1, Legislation

The function may also be responsible for forecasting registrant numbers. This may be linked to a workforce planning responsibility if required by the regulator's legislation.

The functions unique to the regulators of healthcare professionals that may be undertaken by a policy and strategy department include:

- Drafting and revising standards and guidance; see Sections 4.4 and 5.1, volume 1
- Assessing the suitability of professions for statutory regulation; see Section 11.2, volume 3

In terms of policy the regulator is likely to have a range of published policies relating to various regulatory issues that may, for example, include:

- Continuing competence; see Section 7.7, volume 2
- Memorandums of understanding; see Section 1.5, volume 1
- Return to practise; see Section 8.2, volume 1

Further examples are included in the index and on the Companion Website.

17. Project management

The ability to deliver projects in scope, on time, within budget, and to the anticipated quality is a key and critical organisational skill for virtually all organisations including regulators. In the UK the Prince II methodology for project planning is often used by regulators.

The responsibilities of the project teams will include:

- Proposing project priority
- Project management
- Progress monitoring
- Risk register of projects
- Post completion review

The projects of the regulator will often be cross functional with a resulting increase in complexity. For example, the process to regulate a new profession.

18. Procurement and purchasing

A procurement and purchasing function may be established, although this may be placed in the portfolio of the finance and accounting function. For European regulators, this function will be responsible for compliance with EU public bodies purchasing requirements; see Section 10.3, volume 3, European internal market, for further details. They may also be responsible on behalf of other functions for the commercial contract negotiations and, in particular, the terms and conditions of the regulators' relationship with external suppliers.

19. Research and data analysis

Some regulators may have the resources and inclination to undertake research into regulation. This will probably include evidence informed research into the principles and processes of regulation of healthcare professionals; see Section 9.3, volume 4, Research into the evidence base for regulating of healthcare professionals. The reasonability is often allocated to the policy and strategy function. Many regulators will however commission the work from external specialists' organisations such as management consultants or universities rather than undertaking the research themselves.

The capability to analyse data is also particularly important to try and understand the causes of FTP. It is also important in relation to workforce planning; see Section 7.5, volume 4.

20. Risk management

The function of risk management needs to be embedded into the functioning of the regulator. However, given the size of regulators they are unlikely to establish a specific department. Notwithstanding this, whoever is responsible, it must devise and maintain the regulators' risk register; see Section 2.3, volume 1, Enterprise risk management, for further details.

21. Secretariat

The secretariat function within a regulator of professionals is likely to share many similarities to a commercial organisation and in particular a publicly owned company. This means that the board secretary of a regulator will have many similar responsibilities as the company secretary of a commercial organisation.

Within a regulator of healthcare professionals the secretariat function will have a wide range of responsibilities, many of which operationalise the governance arrangements. They may include:

- Administering council and committee meetings including arranging the meetings, and the distribution of agendas and papers
- Provide guidance to the board on procedural matters relating to the running of the board meetings
- Scheduling dates for board meetings
- Ensuring that board meetings are quorate
- Record, draft, circulate, and publish the formal minutes of meetings
- Monitor the implementation of all board decisions on an annual or more frequent basis
- Archive of data, both physical and electronic and both current and historical archives
- Organise offsite board meetings
- Quality control board and committee papers
- Process to recruit and appoint board and committee members which may include directly managing elections or contracting the service to specialist service suppliers or coordinating a public appointment process
- Board and committee member induction
- Board and committee ongoing training
- Administer the system to appraise board and committee members
- Supported by policies and procedures, maintain and publish the register of board members interests and senior executives

The committee structure of the regulatory is likely to have a large impact on the size of the function. The roles and responsibilities of committees are covered in Section 3.6, volume 4.

The secretariat function may also be responsible for the processes associated with data protection, record retention and disposal, and freedom of information; see Section 4.5, volume 4, Data protection; and Section 4.6, volume 4, Freedom of Information. In addition, operational responsibility for environmental, social, and governance (ESG) and corporate social responsibility (CSR) may be led or coordinated by the secretariat function.

And in some regulators, a degree of executive day-to-day support may be provided by the secretariat to the chair of the board.

SPECIALIST REGULATORY FUNCTIONS

The general functions described above are unremarkable in that they will probably be found in any typical medium-sized commercial enterprise. The specialist regulatory functions of a regulator of healthcare professionals are quite the opposite in that they are mostly not found together in other organisations.

As a reminder the specialist regulatory functions may include:

1. Assessors
2. Continuing competence
3. Education and training
4. Examinations
5. Fitness to practice (FTP)
6. Inspection of service delivery facilities
7. Legal service
8. Professional advisory service
9. Registration
10. Regulation of businesses and partnerships
11. Standards and guidance

Workforce planning

The specialist regulatory functions will now explored in greater detail.

1. **Assessors**
   The processes used by regulators of healthcare professionals frequently require judgments to be made; see Section 6.4, volume 1, and all are high-stake decisions. The process can include the assessment of data and information, conducting face-to-face interviews with the professional, or observation of their work. However, rather than being based within a single function of the regulator assessment processes using judgment take place within the following six processes:

   i. **Continuing competence assessments**
   Undertaking the assessment of the data and information submitted by a professional and /or conducting interviews with the professionals, to confirm that they have met the standards of continuing competence.

   ii. **Fitness to practise tribunals**
   Assessors are involved in assessing complaints against professionals. Assessors can either have a collective responsibility as a FTP panel or committee members. Alternatively, they are solely responsible for the task and are referred to as case examiners.

   Other assessors will be engaged in the FTP process to undertake performance assessments of professionals, either based on written documentation or via face-to-face interviews.

   iii. **Grandparenting applications**
   Reviewing grandparenting applications to join the register when a profession is regulated for the first time.

   iv. **International applications**
   Considering if an application by a professional from another jurisdiction possesses the competences to

be eligible to join the register. This may include establishing the equivalence of the applicants' qualification. The individuals making the assessment may be referred to as registration assessors.

v. **Education and training programme approval**
Deciding if a new or established domestic programme of education and training meets the regulators' standards. The individuals making the assessments are in the UK called visitors. A similar process may be used if programmes of education and training that are physically based in other jurisdictions can be approved.

vi. **Registration appeals**
Reviewing decision to reject an applicant to be admitted to the register.

Interestingly, if you refer back to the framework for the regulation of healthcare professionals in Section 3.1, volume 1, it can be seen that all these types of judgments are made at the interface between the processes of a regulator of professionals as illustrated in Chart 3.1 – IV, volume 1.

The individuals, who are engaged by the regulator to make these judgments, are called assessors. They can be defined as:

Definition: Assessor
Person who is knowledgeable in a particular field and who can evaluate the quality of a person or thing.

It should be noted that they may also be referred to as visitors and partners.

Types of assessors
There are two types of assessors. Firstly, some, but not all, assessors will be drawn from the professions that the regulator regulates. This is because the assessors must have the knowledge and skills in fields such as the body of knowledge or the education and training of a particular professions. The second type of assessors will be non-professional or lay. However, the key characteristic of an assessor, whether professional or lay, is to be able to make decisions based on judgment.

It should be noted that in some jurisdictions the role of assessors will be specified in legislation. For example, in the UK the Health Professions Council (Functions of Assessors) Rules Order of Council 2002, SI 2203 NO 1577.

Assessors can potentially be engaged from three different sources:

i. **Board members**
The first traditional approach that is used in many jurisdictions is to exclusively use members of the board of the regulator to be directly involved in making judgments relating to its regulatory process.

This may not be practical if the regulated profession is large in terms of the number of individual professionals, or the regulator is a multi-professional, since the task is greater than the capacity of the board members

Notwithstanding this, in the UK, board members used to be directly involved in establishing the policy and strategy of the regulator and, in turn, setting and monitoring its performance. It was therefore argued that the board members of regulators who are public authorities should not themselves be directly involved in the processes requiring assessors. For example, admitting international applicants to the register or directly involved in FTP tribunals The reason for this is that the board member concerned, may be tempted to manipulate the process to justify the policy and performance of the regulator. In addition, there may be a public perception that board members who are professionals may make decisions that are more advantageous to the profession rather than the public.

As a result the legislation of the regulators of healthcare professionals prohibits board members from being appointed as assessors; see Section 8.2, volume 1, legal principles and processes. This is also supported by the principle of the separation of powers and the avoidance of conflicts of interests.

The solution is to engage non-board members as assessors.

ii. **Non-board members**
The second option for the regulator to engage individuals who are not board members to be assessors. They are in effect individual service providers hired to undertake specific tasks on an ad hoc basis. The contractual arrangements should specify the tenure of the appointment and the expected quality standards. The regulator makes no specific commitment to the number of hours to be worked in a given period of time, and the assessors are only called upon when there is a demand. However, they are not obliged to accept the work if they have other pre-commitments.

This approach is used by the multi-professional statutory UK regulator, the Health and Care Professions Council (HCPC). The assessors, referred to as partners, are recruited, trained, and regularly assessed. In 2015 when the HCPC regulated 16 professions; it had over 800 Partners, split 60:40 between professionals and lay. The partners were remunerated usually on a daily or a per task basis.
Advantages of this approach include:

- The capacity of the various processes is not restricted by the availability of members of the board

- Assessors may be used more frequently than board members and therefore become more component
- Dedicated use of assessors leads to greater consistency of decision making
- The use of numerous individual professionals as assessors helps forge the relationship between the regulator and profession it regulates

Arguments against this approach include:

- Board members may become less familiar with the process of the regulator

iii. Commission another organisation to undertake assessment tasks
The third option is for the regulator to purchase the services of independent organisation to undertake the work, for example, a professional association whose members can undertake the task on behalf of the regulator. The drawback of this approach is that there may be inherent conflicts of interests between the two organisations. For example, a professional association may be tempted to reject international applications to reduce future competition to its members. Or, it may set education standards that are too high to limit access to the profession. Likewise, if an employer is involved in assessing continuing FTP, they may be reluctant to fail assessments as they may reduce the size of their own workforce.

Employing assessors
Lastly, in line with the principle of separation of power, in the UK the legislation of regulators of healthcare professionals prevents employees from being assessors.

Competences, recruitment, and training
Whatever recruitment process is used, assessors are typically selected against competences. Once selected they should be given contracts specifying its limited duration, the need for annual appraisal, and any reappointment process.

Successful applicants must undergo education and training before they start participating in the regulators' processes. Continuing education and training is also important to ensure that they are kept abreast of any developments. It is likely that additional and specialist education and training will be required for tribunal chairs.

To ensure that there is no possibility of inappropriate interference by members of the regulators' board in the process to select and reappoint assessors, using the principle of separation of power, some regulators may establish a tribunal advisory committee with the specific task of recruiting and appraising assessors.

In terms of remuneration, assessors are normally remunerated but not as employees but rather as contractors or a periderm basis or for each completed task. This can include payments for not only for attending meetings but also for time spent preparing for meetings.

2. Continuing competence
The next specialist regulator function of the regulator of healthcare professionals is continuing competence that is explored in detail in Chapter 7, volume 2. The delivery of this important regulatory process may be managed across different departments of the regulator.

For example, the policy and strategy department may set the principles and standards used. Assessors and subject matter experts may be hired by the HR department. The FTP department may organise the hearing of appeals against a decision to remove a professional from the register for failing to meet the standards of continuing competence. The registration department will have a pivotal role in communicating with the professions undergoing continuing competence audits and or assessments. They may also be involved in the selection of professionals for assessment of compliance with the standards of continuing competence.

3. Education and training
Chapter 10 examined how UK regulators of healthcare professionals' quality assures education and training programmes of the next generation of professionals using approval and monitoring processes. On the assumption that this is the case, the regulator will need to have a specialist function within their operating model that will need to deliver the operational aspects of the quality assurance processes.

4. Examinations
As discussed in Section 1.6, volume 2, many regulators have the responsibility to organise examinations for those seeking to be admitted to their registers. If this is the case and the service is not contracted out, then their operating model will need to deliver the operational aspects of the examination process.

5. Fitness to practise (FTP)
Stating it bluntly, the organisation and management of the FTP process is the most complex and resource-intensive process managed and operated by regulators of healthcare professionals. To address the challenge the FTP process can be organised in a number of different ways; see Sections 3.1, volume 3, and 1.1, volume 1. On the assumption that the process used is fully integrated within the regulator, the FTP function, in terms of employee numbers and operating costs, will probably be the largest.

As discussed in Section 4.7, volume 3, regulators employ case managers to manage their FTP process using case management systems (CMSs) supported by guidance provided by practice notes. As the size of regulators increases specialisation within the FTP department will become more easily achievable and it is probable that it will be organised around specialist teams relating to the various processes depicted in Chart 3.1 – I, volume 3, Fitness to practise framework – concern to restoration.

For example, large regulators may sub-divide their FTP departments into five teams, namely:

i. Case reception
ii. Investigation
iii. Adjudication
   - Case presentation
   - Management of tribunals
iv. Appeals
v. Post tribunal compliance with sanctions

The FTP department will also need to provide a range of support functions. They will include:

Advisory service for ftp
Regulators will often provide a separate and dedicated service to provide advice to raisers of concerns, the healthcare professionals involved in the FTP process, and other stakeholders such as employers of healthcare professionals.

Forecasting, planning, and scheduling
The FTP function will need to be able to forecast the number of concerns and complaints received. It will then need to plan for the forecasted investigations, tribunals, appeals, and review hearings in terms of operational numbers and financial costs. In turn, scheduling officers will also need to ensure that all documents and participants are available to attend the tribunals and other meetings that are planned to be held at a given time and place.

Quality assurance
The FTP department will probably have a specialist quality assurance team dedicated to review the FTP departments' processes and in particular the case files for each complaint concerning a registrant. Other issues of concern will be the number of cases per case manager; see Section 4.7, volume 3.

6. **Inspection of service delivery facilities**
The legislation of some regulators of healthcare professionals requires them to undertake the inspection of the facilities that various professionals use to deliver their services. An example of this type of specialist regulatory function is where the regulator of pharmacists also has a responsibility to inspect their pharmacies. To deliver this function the regulator will have to employ subject matter experts who may be professionals and ancillary support staff. For further details see Section 7.3, volume 4, Regulation of service delivery facilities.

7. **Legal services**
In the UK statutory regulators of healthcare professions will inevitably require the advice and practical expertise of members of the legal professions in the form of both solicitors and barristers, across many aspects of their day-to-day functions and in particular the FTP process.

The types of legal services required by a regulator of healthcare professionals fall into four areas. They are as follows:

i. **General legal advice**
A range of general legal services will be required. The services may relate to:
   - Contracts
   - Data protection
   - Employment
   - Freedom of Information
   - Governance
   - Litigation
   - Memorandum of Understanding (MoU)
   - Property
   - Procurement and purchasing

ii. **Public law**
A range of general public law services will be required. The services may include:
   - Drafting of legislation
   - Drafting of rules
   - Judicial reviews

iii. **Fitness to practise**
Legal advice is required in relation to two stages of the FTP process, driven in part by the nature of their high-stake decision and the confrontational tribunal process of testing in public both the evidence and witnesses.

Firstly, in the preliminary investigating and evaluation of the allegation stages information and documentation are gathered to reach a decision or whether or not to pursue a potential FTP case.

Secondly, before and during the case preparation and the adjudication by tribunal stages, legal professionals may be engaged to take witness statements and other evidential documents required during the presentation of the regulators' case and the cross examination of witnesses.

And as a reminder, regulators may employ their own presenting officers to undertake all or some of the work. The presenting officers may be either qualified lawyers or hold no legal qualifications; see Section 4.3, volume 3, Participants in tribunals.

iv. **Appeals**
Section 8.5, volume 1, appeals and judicial reviews, explores the principles and processes to facilitate appeals against the decision of the various processes of a regulator. Appeals may either be direct to the courts or, alternatively, may

commence as internal appeals within the regulator, before potentially transferring to the courts. It is best practice that lawyers undertaking work associated with the tribunal should not be involved in the appeal process, so different lawyers will be required for the two processes.

The regulator will therefore need systems to hire, brief, and work with solicitors and barristers to work on their behalf in any appeal process.

In house vs. External legal services
In terms of the annual financial budget of a regulator of healthcare professionals the provision of legal services is likely to be one of the largest cost items purchased from external suppliers. The decision to either provide the service in-house by hiring lawyers as employees, or to purchase the service from external legal organisations, or to use both internal and external resources will be a significant strategic decision for the regulator. The issue is explored further in Section, volume 4 Financial characteristics of regulators of healthcare professionals. In terms of organisation, internal legal services can be deployed in one department or distributed across the regulator.

8. **Professional advisory service**
Regulators usually provide various types of advisory services, including their contact centre and specific advisory services for those involved in raising or the receipt of concerns relating to professionals.

On the other hand professional advisory services are typically provided by professional associations; see Section 10.4, volume 2, and not regulators of healthcare professionals. However, there is a degree of controversy on whether or not regulators should also provide a professional advisory service to those they regulate. This is because it can be argued that advice relating to the practice of the profession is an area perhaps best served by professional associations who are the keepers of the body of knowledge of the profession. It is also argue that the provision of such a service by a regulator is tantamount to straying into the legitimate territory of the professional associations, learned societies, and trade unions.

However, it should be noted that in Canada such professional advisory services are provided by some professional colleges, and historically in the UK this type of service has been provided by some regulators in the past and then withdrawn, for example, the UKCC.

Notwithstanding this, regulators of healthcare professionals do provide guidance to all their professions on numerous issues; see guidance in Section 5.1, volume 1.

9. **Registration**
For a typical regulator of healthcare professionals the process to manage and maintain an accurate and up-to-date register is likely to be its second largest function in terms of number of employees. This is because maintaining the accuracy and integrity of the data on the register is uppermost in importance in terms of the responsibility of the organisation.

The processes that registration department are responsible for are described in detail in Chapter 4, volume 2, Registers and registration. They cover a range of functions including the handling initial registration, the international applications for registration, and renewal of registration. Generically three processes are used:

i. Processing registration applications
   - Domestic
   - Grandparenting
   - International
   - Return to practise

ii. Maintaining the accuracy of data held on the register

iii. Responding to information request about the register

Registration is characterised as being a high-volume transaction function. For this reason the regulators' contact centre rather than being organised as a separate operating unit may be embedded in the registration department. The process has traditionally been very labour intense focusing on the processing of paper applications. This has now been largely replaced by the use of ITC and the internet.

In parallel with the registration function, the process to manage fee payments from registrants and others may be the responsibility of the registration department. Alternatively, it may be shared with the finance department or managed exclusively by them. Its components are as follows:

- Processing payments
- Refunding overpayments
- Calculating account balances
- Processing information requests

Some regulators in terms of the handling of applications will divide the registration department into a domestic and an international team. If the number of employees allows, the separation of duties within the international registration team may assist with the detection of fraudulent applications; see Sections 4.5, volume 2, 8.1, volume 3, and 9.3, volume 3. If one is maintained, a credential database can be managed by the international team.

10. **Regulation of business and partnerships**
Some regulators may be responsible for regulating business and partnerships. This issue is explored in detail in Section 7.3, volume 4.

11. **Standards and guidance**
The drafting and revision of the regulators' standards and guidance can be viewed as a specialist function. The function may be undertaken by a dedicated group or the policy and strategy function.

12. **Workforce planning**
Some regulators have a specific responsibility in their legislation to undertake workforce planning; see Section 7.5, volume 4, Workforce planning.

ORGANISATION AND MANAGEMENT STRUCTURE OF REGULATORS OF HEALTHCARE PROFESSIONALS

Having reviewed both the general functions and the specialist regulatory functions of regulators, the issues of how they design their organisation and what management structures they can adopt can be addressed. However, before considering these two issues, it is worth briefly exploring how public authorities such as statutory regulators differ from commercial organisations.

CHARACTERISTICS OF THE OPERATING ENVIRONMENT OF PUBLIC AUTHORITIES

UK statutory regulators of healthcare professionals are characterised by their responsibility to administer process enshrined in legislation. The environment that public administration operate within is markedly different from the environments that organisations such as commercial enterprises, charities, religious institutions, or universities, to name but a few, operate in.

In the UK the environment that public authorities such as the regulators of healthcare professionals operate within has a number of distinct characteristics. They include:

- There are no, or very limited, alternative services to those provided by public authorities
- There is usually a financial requirement for the public authority to break even or make a modest surplus, and they must avoid financial distress. However, there is no requirement to make a significant profit or to pay a dividend
- Access to capital is limited and subject to governmental financial constraints
- Public authorities operate in a relatively stable operating environment in terms of sudden unpredictable or unforeseen market changes but are subject to political decision making
- The rate of change of the operating environment of regulators is relatively stable and predictable
- Public authorities are subject to considerable public scrutiny of their operations and the standards and costs of their services
- There is a requirement for public authorities to be open and transparent.
- Governmental and political oversight and inspection operate; see Section 6.4, volume 4, Auditing and overseeing regulators
- In a jurisdiction with devolved administration public authorities may have to operate within more than one legal system
- Employee's remuneration packages are related to public sector terms and conditions and often made public
- Public authorities decisions can be readily scrutinised by the courts
- The governing boards of public authorities and regulators usually include part-time non-executives appointed by a public appointment process and their remuneration is relatively modest
- There are usually few or no executives who are members of the board of the public authority

These characteristics of the operating environment have a significant influence on how the regulators organise their affairs and in turn the organisations of their functions.

ORGANISATIONAL DESIGN AND MANAGEMENT STRUCTURES

Organisational design is the process of mapping, arranging, and coordinating an organisation into a systematic whole. Once complete, the functions of an organisation are arranged into a management structure and potentially a departmental structure.

ORGANISATIONAL DESIGN OF REGULATORS

To quote the maxim of the architect Louis Sullivan:

Form (ever) follows function.

And this is true for the organisational design of regulators, where the organisation should facilitate the effective and efficient delivery of its objectives and policies.

However, before settling on a particular organisational design regulators should take into consideration six factors:

1. Legislative requirement to undertake specific functions
2. Provision of functions by external suppliers
3. Sharing general functions with other regulators
4. Sharing specialist regulatory functions with other regulators
5. Provision of consultancy services
6. Relationship between of size of regulator and its organisational design

These six factors will now be expanded:

1. **Legislative requirement to undertake specific functions**
The legislation governing regulator dictates which function they will have to have. However, not all regulators undertake all the 8 processes or use the 9 standards, that are depicted in Chart 3.1 – III, volume 1, Regulatory framework – 8 processes and 9 standards, since they can be undertaken by other organisations. For example, in some jurisdictions regulators will not be responsible for approving education and training programmes or managing FTP tribunals.

2. **Provision of functions by external suppliers**
Not all the functions required by a regulator are, or need to be, provided internally by the organisation, since they can be 'contracted out' to external suppliers. These include both general functions and also specialist regulatory functions.

General functions

- Contact centre
- Office cleaning
- Payroll
- PC help desk

Specialist regulatory functions

- Approval and monitoring of E&T programmes
- Assessments of international applications for registration
- Examinations and test centres
- Legal services

Specialist non-regulatory functions

- Election to the board
- Research

Subject matter experts and consultants

- These will be sought if and when required.

In general the decision to acquire services from external suppliers should be driven by the appropriate trade-off between cost and quality of service requirements. Interestingly, the UK regulators of healthcare professionals have markedly different approaches particularly in relation to the provision of legal services. Some contract in external suppliers to provide legal services, whilst others do exactly the opposite.

3. **Sharing general functions with other regulators**
In theory general functions can be shared with other regulators. For example, some regulators may contemplate providing general functions such as HR or financial functions to other regulators on a commercial basis. However, achieving this is often more challenging when attempting to put into practise. The challenge is that there are many commercial organisations that have successful businesses providing these types of services. Regulators, with little or no previous experience or knowledge of this type of business, are unlikely to be able to provide these types of service on a commercial basis to other organisations.

4. **Sharing specialist regulatory functions with other regulators**
When considering the provision of specialist regulatory functions to other regulators the central challenge is different legislation for different regulators. For example, if two regulators require their professionals to undertake continuing competence using different standards and processes, it will be challenging for one regulator to manage and operate both processes simultaneously.

However, if the regulator is a multi-professional regulator and it has the same legislation for all the different professions it regulates, this problem does not occur; see Section 1.1, for further details.

In the UK the issue has been partly resolved by amending the regulators' legislation to allow regulatory processes of one regulator to be undertaken by or delegated to another. However, responsibility remains for the quality and cost of the service with the delegating regulator.

5. **Provision of consultancy services**
A regulator may seek to establish a commercial business to provide advice to other regulators and stakeholders, such as government, by creating a consultancy service.

Whilst an initial proposal to provide consultancy services on a commercial basis may appear to be an attractive proposition, reassurance should be forthcoming about its financial viability, and in particular:

- What happens if the consultancy service makes a financial loss?
- Will separate accounts be published?
- Will and how enough work be generated to justify fixed HR resources?
- How will central costs be allocated across the organisation?
- How is the cost of capital calculated?

6. **Relationship between size of regulator and its organisational design**
The comparative size of a regulator in terms of the number of professions and individual professionals it regulates, or the number of employees or its annual income, can vary enormously. This has a significant impact on what type of organisational design they adopt.

In terms of organisation, small regulators, with say 10–50 employees, may organise themselves around individuals with a portfolio of linked responsibilities. Thus smaller regulators often consolidate the delivery of related functions into single departments. For example, an operations department may be responsible for business continuity, internal audit, project management, and quality assurance. Or the finance department may also be responsible for ITC. And, for example, as the size of a regulator increases in terms of the number of employees, informal and undocumented process will need to be replaced by structured and codified systems.

Whereas larger regulators with more than say 100 employees will, more often than not, have more clearly delineated functions and departments. And, as the size of regulators increases beyond one hundred employees, the organisation around distinct departments will tend to become almost universal.

COMMONALITY OF ORGANISATIONAL DESIGN OF REGULATORS

Taking all these factors into account, it is somewhat unsurprising that regulators of healthcare professionals, in whatever jurisdiction they are based in, have a tendency to adopt similar organisational designs. This may be partially due to the fact that regulators' operating environment is relatively stable and predictable and that many regulators have been in existence for decades. An example of a typical regulator's organisation structure is that of the HCPC in 2019, see Chart 1.2 – II below.

COMPOSITION OF EXECUTIVE MANAGEMENT TEAM

The composition of the EMT of regulators of healthcare professionals typically consists of a team of five to six individuals. In addition, some regulators have a larger operational management team of up to a dozen individuals reporting to it. In general there is little significant variation between different regulators of a similar size. However, the choice of the EMT composition to some extent is usually dependent on the propensity of the organisation to have a flat or hierarchal management culture.

CULTURE OF REGULATORS

In Section 1.3, volume 1, it is proposed that society expects regulators to be effective, efficient, and ethical and that its board members, employees, and contractors should always behave ethically and maintain appropriate ethical standards. Also in Section 1.3, volume 1, it is argued that the importance of the right type of culture of all organisations, including regulators, is intrinsically linked to their performance and success. In other words, regulators with poor cultures are unlikely to be effective, efficient, or ethical.

It is therefore important that before drawing this section to a conclusion that when examining the operating model of a regulator in terms of functions, organisation, and management, the issue of culture should not be forgotten. Culture embraces not only all the employees but also members of the board,

Chart 1.2 – II **Organisational structure HCPC 2019**

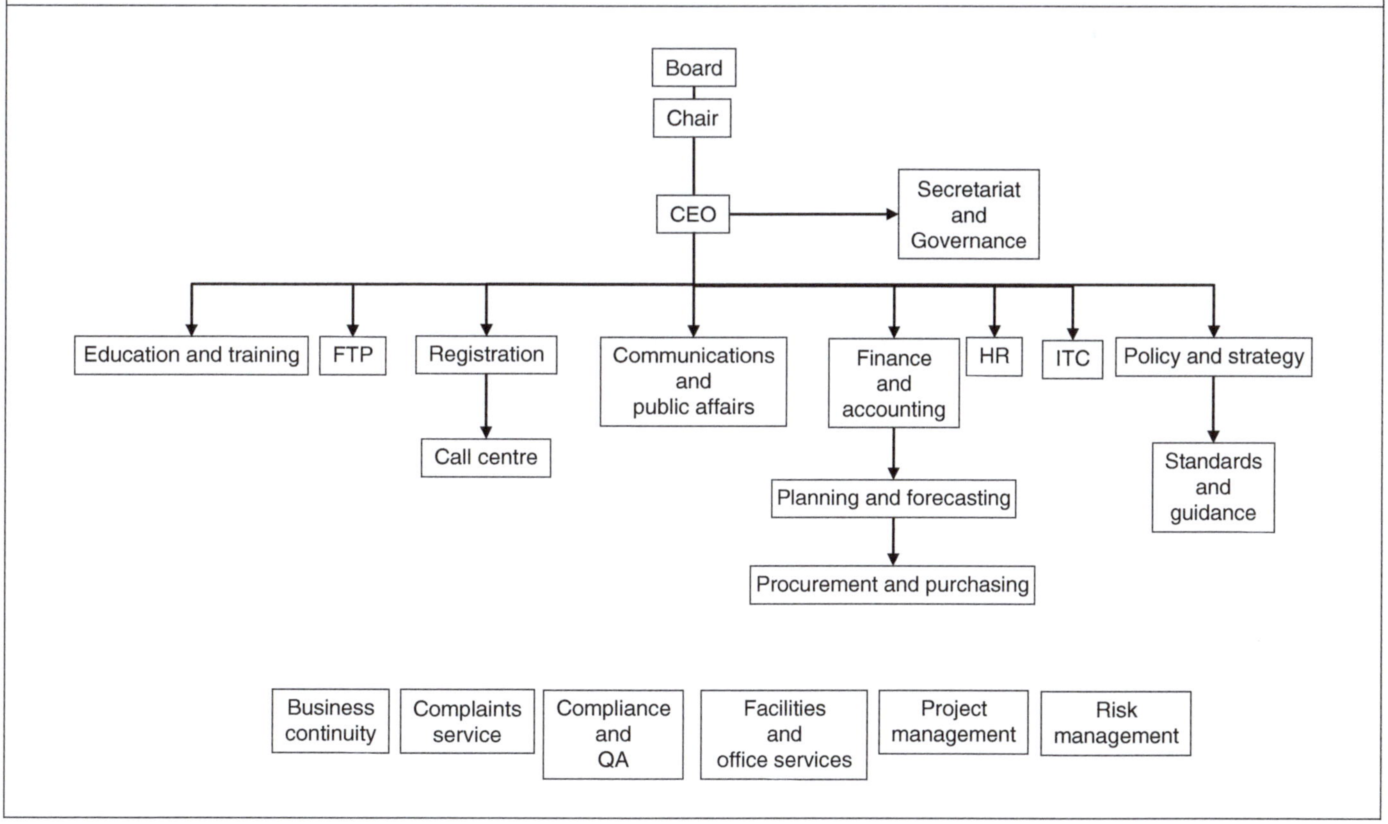

secondees, consultants and, contractors. The culture of a regulator is not imposed by management but created by those working in and for it. So if employees wish to have a programme of corporate social responsibility, should this be opposed by the board?

And, since the culture of a regulator is the responsibility of everyone in the organisation, the regulator should have a code of conduct to support its culture. In turn, its adoption and implementation should be reinforced in the processes to recruit, train, and appraise everyone who works for the organisation.

CONCLUSION

What this section has hopefully demonstrated is that regulators of healthcare professionals do not have particularly complex operational models compared to, for example, a nuclear power station, an acute care tertiary hospital, Big Science projects like the European Organization for Nuclear Research (CERN), or a multinational investment bank. Also, it is clear that both the regulators' general and specialist regulatory functions can be found in other organisations. What is unique is that they can be found together in regulators. What is distinct is that regulators also have to make high-stake decisions. For example, the implications of the decision on the behaviour or a registrant at the end of a FTP tribunal or the consideration on a decision to withdraw approval from a programme of education and training. Lastly, it should be emphasised that all organisations should strive to be more effective and efficient; thus, the functions and their organisations are a snapshot in time and should be continuingly evolving.

EXERCISES AND QUESTIONS

Exercises

- What functions of your regulator should and should not contract out to third-party supplies?
- Does the business model of your organisation make the best use of new technologies?
- Does the size of your regulator maximise the most economic structure?

Questions

- What types of legal services should a regulator of healthcare professionals provide in-house?
- Should a regulator of healthcare professionals employ healthcare professionals on a full-time basis or should they be commissioned on a case-by-case basis?
- How can regulators use ICT to enable the professionals they regulate to access services directly without recourse to direct interaction with the regulator's employees?

LEGISLATION

Example of UK Legislation

Rules

The Health Professions Council (Functions of Assessors) L
Rules Order of Council 2002
SI 2203 NO 1577

FURTHER READING

Collisions and Collaboration: The Organization of Learning in the ATLAS Experiment at the LHC B
Max Boisot, Markus Nordberg, Saïd Yami, Bertrand Nicquevert
Oxford University Press
ISBN-13: 978-0199567928
28 July 2011
336 pages

The Medical Council of New Zealand B
A personal and informal perspective of events during my time as Chief Executive/Secretary/Registrar from 1986 to 2000
Georgina Jones
Medical Council of New Zealand
191 pages

STANDARDS, CODES, GUIDANCE, CONSULTATIONS, POLICIES, AND PRACTICE NOTES

Standards and Codes

Standards for Performance Assessors S&C
GMC
8 pages

1.3 POLICY AND STRATEGY DEVELOPMENT

INTRODUCTION

The utterances and publications of government and regulators are peppered with references to policy and strategy. This section focuses firstly on defining what policy and strategy are. And, secondly, in the context of regulation, it examines how they are both created and developed by government and regulators.

POLICY AND STRATEGY

The challenge to understand policy and strategy is that the two terms sit adjacent to one another and have a high degree of overlap. In seeking to tease the two apart, policy is often used in the bailiwick of government and has a tendency to use a principles-based approach. Whereas strategy tends towards the world of commerce and practical plans of action.

On the presumption that policy and strategy are not one and the same thing, two working definitions are in order:

Definition: Policy
Principle or course of action adopted or proposed by an organisation or individual.

Definition: Strategy
Making important irreversible choices under conditions of uncertainty.

This section of the book will now firstly examine how government, public authorities, and other types of organisations approaches policy. And, secondly, how organisations approach strategy.

GOVERNMENT AND POLICY

A government can be defined by its policies. If one unpicks the various policies of a government they cover virtually all aspects of the running of a country. To grasp the sheer scale of government's policies a web search will identify hundreds of UK government policies, with subjects ranging from taxing sugar in food to asylum.

EXAMPLES OF POLICY REVIEWS

In relation to healthcare the UK and other jurisdictions are awash with examples of reports and publications that either define government policy or are instrumental in setting a new or revised policy. As ever, in this arena there are is rich seam of published documents that can be used to identify the processes used by government to set and revise policy. In the UK examples of these type of documents include:

- Acts of Parliament
- Command papers
- Consultations
- Green papers
- Hansard
- Houses of Parliament select committees reports
- Law Commission reports
- Public enquiries reports
- Researcher briefings published by the House of Commons library
- Responses to consultations by government
- Royal Commissions
- Statutory instruments
- White papers

TRIGGERS FOR CHANGES TO GOVERNMENT POLICY

There are a number of triggers that may cause government to introduce or change its existing policies including those policies relating to the regulation of healthcare professionals. These triggers for policy change may include:

1. Changes to adjacent or overlapping government policy
2. Election of a new government
3. Government policy reviews
4. Lobbying by stakeholder
5. Ministerial appointments
6. Regulatory failure

These six triggers will now be explored in greater detail:

1. **Changes to adjacent or overlapping government policy**
   In relation to the regulation of healthcare professionals, adjacent or overlapping policy areas may include:
   - Education and training
   - Employment
   - Fiscal policy
   - Immigration controls
   - Regulation in general
   - Universal health coverage and equality of access

   As a result, changes to the regulation of healthcare professionals may occur as a consequence of a change in policy in a related area. This is particularly important where the state is responsible for either the funding of the healthcare delivery system and is also responsible for the management of parts of the systems, for example, hospitals. This multifaceted responsibility may lead to tensions, for example, the desirability of keeping wages low versus the need to satisfy the supply of healthcare professionals by increasing their wages.

2. **Election of a new government**
To state the obvious, different political parties usually have markedly different agendas on the key areas of government such as, the economy, education, health, and taxation. Before an election, the competing political parties will set out what their intentions are if they win the election in the form of party manifestoes.
Thus the election of a new government may trigger significant changes in broad policy areas such as the desire to reduce the cost of government or increase government spending. In turn other policies will emerge in related areas. For example, if the intention is to reduce regulation across all areas of government, a consequence may be to decrease the number of professions regulated or a decrease in the funding of regulators.

3. **Government policy review**
In addition to the election of a new government, an existing government may shift its policies for various reasons that are triggered by unforeseen events. Examples of changes to the policy of government are provided in Section 8.5, volume 4, Reforming the regulating healthcare professionals.

4. **Lobbying by stakeholder**
Government policy may change in response to lobbying by stakeholders, including regulators; see communication channels and techniques in Section 2.2, volume 4.

5. **Ministerial appointments**
In a similar vein to policy changes triggered by the election of a new government, the appointment of a new government minster may mean that the new incumbent introduces a new set of policy initiatives.

6. **Regulatory failure**
The principles and processes of regulation can fail. Unfortunately, in recent times there have been numerous examples of notorious and catastrophic failures both in the UK and other jurisdictions, including Bristol Royal Infirmary, Shipman and Winterbourne View Hospital as discussed in Chapter 5, volume 4. And to quote a saying attributed to Winston S. Churchill:

"Never let a good crisis go to waste"

As a result when the regulation of healthcare professionals fails government usually instigates a public inquiry and the subsequent publication of the inquires' report and recommendations, often act as a catalysts for policy change.

HOW DOES GOVERNMENT UNDERTAKE POLICY DEVELOPMENT OR REVIEWS?

Once a government has decided to embark on the task of considering introducing or changing its policy on a particular issue, it has a range of options for who will be commissioned to undertake the work.

In the UK historically a Royal Commission would be established by Parliament. Nowadays, government policy reviews may be produced by a considerable range of 'suppliers', ranging from parts of government itself to commercial organisations. They include:

- Academics
- Civil servants
- Committees of Parliament
- Experts and expert groups
- Management consultants
- Policy institutes and think tanks

Policy reviews by government are characterised by the length of time they take with timetables often running into years. The process can involve consultations, summoning witnesses and substantive analysis and research. The reports are often voluminous, some running into hundreds of pages. However, the inevitably slow process can be justified, if consensus can be established on how to proceed, since policies that have a high degree of broad support are more likely to achieve their goals.

Lastly, it should be noted that in recent times the approach to some policy formation has shifted and can be noteworthy for its speed and brevity.

PUBLIC AUTHORITIES AND POLICY

In addition to government, virtually all public authorities also develop policies, in the form of policy papers, on a wide range of issues.

In relation to regulators, they should have policies on two different types of topics. Firstly wide-reaching policies relating to regulation in general. For example, the advantages and disadvantages of regulating healthcare professionals or if healthcare occupations should be regulated.

Secondly, they should also produce policies on numerous other topics that can be considered to be inward facing, such as postponed initial registration or vexatious complaints and assisted dying and many others that are listed in the index.

In an ideal world a regulator should publish a position paper before establishing their policy on a given topic. These can be substantive aids for stakeholders to better understand and/or generate public discourse on the specific issues. The production of position papers also provides opportunity for the board and the executive to work together in partnership to create policy.

NON-GOVERNMENTAL ORGANISATIONS AND POLICY

On occasions many non-governmental organisations seek to persuade government that there is a need for a change in policy and will create their own new policies or seek to amend existing ones. These organisations include many stakeholders associated with the regulation of healthcare professionals, including charities consumer advocacy organisations, employers, and professional associations and think tanks. Stakeholders may achieve their ends by a number of routes including the publication and dissemination of independently produced policy reviews. Often their work is underpinned by evidence informed research. Recent UK examples of this type of trigger include *Rethinking Regulation*, the PSA 2015 and *Fit for Purpose*, The Health Foundation 2016.

And as a reminder in the process to develop policy in the regulatory arena:

- There is a clear need for the inclusion of the consumers' voice
- Participation of the consumer must be on equal terms with all other stakeholders

LINK BETWEEN POLICY AND LEGISLATION

Lastly, it should be borne in mind that if a change in policy requires new or legalisation, any changes may take many years to come to fruition.

STRATEGY

It is said that if you ask one hundred strategists for their definition of strategy you will receive one hundred and one answers. In other words, there is little or no agreement on what strategy is. To avoid an intractable metaphysical debate on the correct or best definition of strategy, I would support the argument that strategy has four characteristics, namely:

1. Strategy is about **making irreversible choices** under conditions of **uncertainty**
2. Strategy is concerned with **long-term implications** of choices made in the short term
3. Strategic choices are made when there are **resource constraints** that impose the requirement to make difficult trade-offs. In an unreal world, if an organisation could pursue any course of action and fund and resource all projects, then no strategic decisions would be required
4. A strategy is not just the process of making choices. The organisation must agree to a particular strategy and it must then be **implemented** or **executed**. Hence the saying

"Strategy is action".

So an organisation considering its strategy will be facing an uncertain future and making short-term choices about the deployment of limited resources.

UNDERTAKING STRATEGIC DEVELOPMENT

So if strategy exhibits the four characteristics identified in the preceding paragraphs, what is involved in establishing or reviewing a strategy? Unfortunately, again there is absolutely no consensus on how this can or should be achieved. And again, to short circuit the debate, I will explain a process that requires five steps, namely:

1. Strategic analysis
2. Decision matrix – options and criteria
3. Layers of choice
4. Action
5. Horizon scanning

1. **Strategic analysis**
   There are dozens and dozens of competing methods that can be employed to analyse a business, market, or organisation. Six popular methodologies include:

   i. **SWOT**
   A SWOT analysis is the most basic form of strategic analysis. It is a framework that identifies an organisation's **strengths**, **weaknesses**, **opportunities**, and **threats**.

   ii. **Porter's 5 forces**
   Michael Porter's 5 Forces model is a framework for identifying **threats** and **opportunities** within the environment of an organisation. It analyses the relative strengths of suppliers and customers including distributors, the threat of new entrants and substitutes, as well as degree of competition within an industry.

   iii. **Boston Consulting Group**
   The BCG Matrix analyses market share against the market growth rate for an organisation's products, services, or customer segments. These are then plotted on a metric as either stars, cash cows, questions, or dogs

   iv. **The McKinsey 7S**
   The McKinsey 7S analyses an organisation in terms of the strengths and weaknesses. Of its 'Hard' elements: **strategy**, **structure, and systems** and four 'soft' elements **staff**, **skills**, **strategy**, and **shared values.**

   v. **PESTLE**
   The PESTLE framework considers opportunities and threats in terms of political, economic, social (or socio-economic), technological, legal, and environmental opportunities and threats in an organisation's environment.

vi. **Diamond model**
The diamond model is an economic model developed by Michael Porter in his book The *Competitive Advantage of Nations.*

2. **Decision matrix – options and criteria**
Let's take a relatively straightforward question. What is the best way of travelling from London to New York? There are a range of transportation options, some realistic for the average member of the public, others less so. The list of **options** could include:

- Airship
- Commercial airline
- Commercial ship
- Cruise line
- Military fighter aeroplane
- Private executive jet
- Rowing boat
- Sailing yacht
- Submarine
- Rocket

In terms of comparing the options listed above, a range of **criteria** could be used. For example:

- Age group suitability
- Availability
- Comfort
- Cost
- Duration of journey
- Food quality
- Risk
- Weather – impact of inclement conditions

Each **option** is then assessed against each **criterion** and used to populate a weighted decision matrix (Chart 1.3 – I):

3. **Layers of choice**
Choice is not a unidimensional analysis. There will be multiple layers of choices.

4. **Action**
The fourth step assumes that a strategy analysis is of no use unless it leads to action. Resources, both human and financial capital, and systems must be obtained deployed and controlled. This is not just a process of stating the obvious, but there are many examples of organisations that have undertaken strategic analysis, options assessment, and then taken no action.

5. **Horizon scanning**
The fifth and last step is the need for regulators to be constantly alert for what might be coming over the horizon. Resources can be deployed to detect early signs of important impending changes using a methodology called horizon scanning. An example of this type of approach is to review how government is adapting regulation in other sectors and other jurisdictions, since new ideas cross borders with impunity.

Chart 1.3 – I **Weighted decision matrix**

		Options					
Criteria	Weight	Option I		Option II		Option III	
		Score	Total	Score	Total	Score	Total
A							
B							
C							
D							
E							
	Total						

LEVELS OF STRATEGY – SUB-STRATEGIES

It should also be noted that as with commercial and other organisations, strategies of public authorities can be for both the totality of the organisation and for some of the different functions of an organisation. This means, for example, that a regulator will have an overarching strategy for the whole organisation that may be supported by a number of separate strategies, for example, communication, ITC, and HR. These are sometimes referred to as sub-strategies.

REQUIREMENT FOR A STRATEGY

Do regulators of healthcare professionals actually require a strategy?

To conclude this section by posing such a question may be seen by some readers to be provocative. So why pose the question? Consider the following situation:

- The legislation of the regulator is up to date and requires minimal amendments
- The regulator's degrees of choice are heavily constrained by their legislation
- The regulator has agreed and implanted its numerous polices
- The regulator has subsidiary strategies for its communications, HR, and ICT functions
- It has achievable annual and medium-term operating plans
- It makes use of scenarios

Since strategy has been defined above as '*making important irreversible choices under conditions of uncertainty*', is it unclear what the purpose of regulators' strategy would be, other than to consolidate and summarise what is already in existence but under different names? However, how can any organisation not have a strategy? One solution is therefore indeed to consolidate and summarise the processes and documents listed above in terms of a strategic intent. This should square the circle to the satisfaction of most stakeholders.

CONCLUSION

The process to introduce new or change government's policy relating to the statutory regulation of healthcare professionals is mission critical for all concerned. In the process of establishing government's policy impacting the regulation of healthcare professionals, the regulator can either take an assertive proactive stance that seeks to strongly influence the process. Alternatively, they can be a passive player, relying on the quality of their requested formal input into the process. Whilst it is clearly desirable that the policy of government is supported by the regulator and vice versa, since deliverables can then be synchronised. Notwithstanding this, agreement is not always forthcoming and tensions may arise between government and regulator if their respective policy objectives diverge.

Finally, it should be noted that this is a cursory review of a complex area and as in other areas related to the principles and process of regulating professions there are numerous other detailed sources of information on the topic of policy and strategy development that those readers interested in this topic may find useful to refer to.

EXERCISES AND QUESTIONS

Exercises

- What is the government's strategy for the regulation of healthcare professionals in your jurisdiction?
- Locate the strategy of a regulator of healthcare professions. How can it be improved?

Questions

- Find alternative definitions of strategy. Which one is the best and why?
- Why does a regulator of healthcare professionals need a strategy since it can be argued that all it needs to do is implement its legislation?
- How is innovation implemented in your organisation?

FURTHER READING

Artificial Intelligence: Opportunities and Implications for the Future of Decision Making R
Government Office for Science
GS16/19
9 November 2016
21 pages

Competitive Advantages of Nations B
Porter, Michael E
Palgrave Macmillan
ISBN-13: 978-0333736425
26 April 1998
886 pages

Ensuring Effective Public Protection R
UK Central Council for Nursing, Midwifery and Health Visiting, (UKCC)
London
2000

Ensuring Public Safety, Enabling Professionalism R
New strategic direction
NMC
(Undated)
20 pages

Futures Toolkit R
Tools for Futures Thinking and Foresight across UK Government
Government Office for Science
November 2017
113 pages

Involving Consumers in the Development of Regulatory Policy R
Working Group discussion paper by Martin Coppack, Francis Jackson and James Tallack
UK Regulators Network
July 2014
20 pages

Quality of Public Administration – A Toolbox for Practitioner R
Publications Office of the European Union Luxembourg
DOI: 10.2767/879305 KE-04-17-933-EN-N
August 2017
119 pages

Shifting the Balance; R
A better, fairer system of dental regulation
General Dental Council
13 December 2017
64 pages

Strategizing National Health in the Twenty First Century: A Handbook R
World Health Organisation
Editors Gerard Schmets, Dheepa Rajan and Sowmya Kadandal
ISBN: 9789241549745
2016
712 pages

1.4 FINANCIAL CHARACTERISTICS OF REGULATORS OF HCPs

INTRODUCTION

The financial characteristics of different organisations vary considerably, and regulators of healthcare professionals are no exception to this observation. This section reviews how regulators generate income and in turn what use is made of their financial resources.

STRUCTURES OF REGULATORS AND THEIR FINANCIAL CHARACTERISTICS

As previously discussed in Section 1.1, volume 4, regulators of healthcare professionals are structured in numerous different ways. The way that the structures of regulators vary by, for example:

- The regulator is embedded in a government ministry and civil servants manage its day-to-day operations
- The regulator is independent of government and is responsible for most regulatory processes except FTP
- The regulator is responsible for one small profession but is not responsible for approving education and training programmes

In turn, the type of structure used has a direct and significant impact on the financial characteristics of the regulator concerned.

However, before delving into the details of their financial characteristics, it is useful to remind ourselves of their operating environment.

PUBLIC AUTHORITIES

Regulators of healthcare professionals are public authorities and as part of the system of government share common characteristic with other public authorities.

NON-COMPETITIVE

Regulators have no competitors for the services that they provide to their 'customers'. The professionals have to pay the regulators' fees if they want to work as professionals, and they can't move their allegiances to another regulator if they are dissatisfied with the service they receive. As such regulators can be described as monopolists. Notwithstanding this, government can, and does occasionally, abolish and merge regulators when they fail to deliver their primary objectives; see Section 1.8, volume 4.

SERVICES BUSINESS

Regulators do not produce tangible goods or wares. They provide intangible services. They therefore have the operational and financial characteristics of a service business.

CAPITAL REQUIREMENTS

Their capital requirements of regulators are relatively small, and the majority of their expenditure is for operating expenses.

LARGE NUMBERS OF FEE PAYERS

The vast majority of the income of regulators of professionals is generated from thousands, and in some cases hundreds of thousands, of annual renewal of registration fees paid by individual professionals. The annual renewal of registration fee paid by each professional therefore represents a microscopic proportion of the regulators total annual income.

CHARACTERISTICS OF THE BUSINESS OF REGULATORS OF HEALTHCARE PROFESSIONALS

To simplify the examination of the financial characteristics of regulators, this section focuses on UK regulators of healthcare professionals who are independent of government, are self-funding, and are responsible for all eight regulatory processes.

FINANCIAL CHARACTERISTICS OF REGULATORS OF HEALTHCARE PROFESSIONALS

The financial characteristics of regulators are explored under 15 topics. They are as follows:

1. Requirements for financial resources
2. Surplus, reserves, and losses
3. Funding
4. Types and level of fees charged by regulators
5. Attitude of professionals to regulators' fees
6. Requirement for government approval
7. Legal powers to impose fees
8. Setting and revising the level of fees
9. Timing and frequency of changes to fees
10. Income from sources other than professionals
11. Fees and multi-professional regulators
12. Reduced fees for dual registered professions
13. Transfer pricing and fee sharing
14. Taxation liabilities of regulators
15. Charitable status of regulators

These 15 topics will now be expanded:

1. **Requirements for financial resources**
   The regulators require financial resources for three items, namely: operating expenditure, capital expenditure, and working capital:

Chart 1.4 – I **Operating Expenditure Regulators of healthcare professionals**

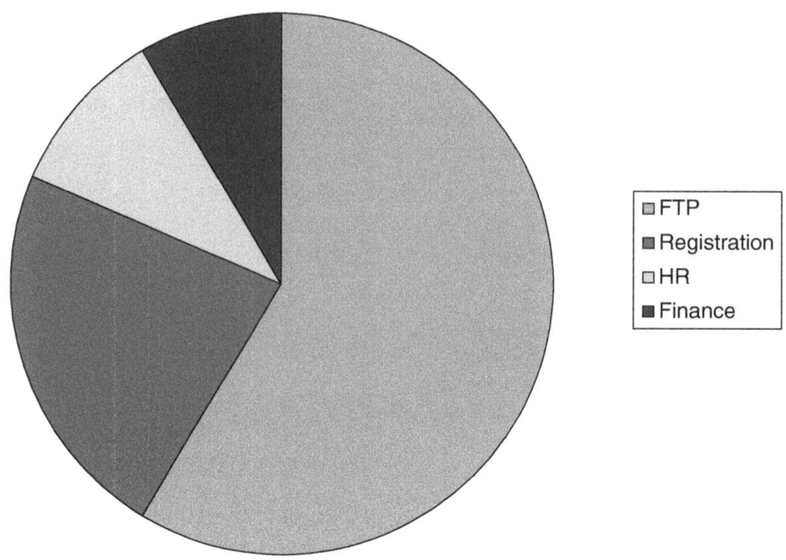

i. **Operating expenses (OpEx)**
The allocation of operating expenses across the functions of a regulator is illustrated in Chart 1.4 – I, above: HCPC broken down by function for the FY 2010–2011. Excludes deprecation.

The chart illustrated that operating expenses are predominantly related to FTP, employee salaries, and legal services.

Fitness to practise costs
It is worth considering at this junction, why does FTP absorb such a high proportion of the costs of regulators of healthcare professionals? There are a range of reasons. They are as follows:

Complexity hinders automation
- Each case is normally unique and requires a bespoke solution

Costs of legal services
- It is structurally difficult to negotiate low prices for the provision of externally provided legal services

Employee salaries
- FTP is a labour-intensive process
- A large variety of different occupations most of which require specialist knowledge and skills are involved in the process including employees of the regulator and external service providers

Planning and execution is slow
- FTP cases can take a long time from start to finish, 18 months being a typical average
- One party may not want the process to conclude and procrastination is used as a legal delaying tactic
- Gathering all participants together for a tribunal is challenging

Thoroughness trumps speed
- Although *'justice delayed is justice denied'*, the thoroughness that a FTP case is dealt with by a regulator trumps the time taken

ii. **Capital expenditure (CapEx)**
Regulators are not capital-intense operations. However, capital is required for ITC and working capital and, if not leased or rented, office accommodation.

iii. **Working capital**
Once established, regulators can finance their working capital requirements by charging their fees in advance.

2. **Surplus, reserves, and losses**
Unlike commercial organisations regulators are not organised to seek to maximise their profits. However, they will need to make surpluses to enable them to purchase capital assets which will be used and depreciated over a number of years.

Regulators also need to have reserves for unexpected costs, for example, unusually high litigation costs arising from FTP cases. As a result, over time the annual fees will need to be slightly higher than just the annual operating expenses, so that resources can go towards capital expenditure and the building of reserves.

The surplus will be held in reserves and the regulator should establish as part of its overall financial and accounting policy a financial reserves policy for its level of reserves. There are no hard and fast rules on the appropriate level of reserves, but the equivalent of three months operating expenses is usually considered to be adequate. If as a result of continuing positive cash flows, reserves grow to a high level throughout the financial year, it is legitimate for registrants to enquire if the fees that they are required to pay have been set too high and should be reduced. If on the other hand losses become the norm, action must be taken by the board of the regulator and government, since the registrants are not responsible for the financial wellbeing and management of the regulator. The reserves are usually held as a portfolio of short-term cash deposits in banks, or government debt, and in some cases portfolios of low-risk equity investments.

Other uses of surplus funds
In the USA, some states deliberately set the annual fee charged by regulators to be higher than their expenditure. The annual surplus is then transferred to the states' general fund. The funds can then be used for purposes other than the regulation of professionals.

3. **Funding**
Regulators require financial funds and throughout the world the most frequently used method to finance the majority of the costs of regulating healthcare professionals is to charge the professionals to join and then to remain on the regulators' register.

In the UK the historical justification to support this position was that since the healthcare professionals were the prime benefactors from regulation, there was no justification for the tax payer to fund the cost of regulation, although of course they do gain the benefit of enhanced public protection.

However, besides the fees paid by the professionals to the regulator there are two other sources of funding that can be considered, namely, the government and/or employers.

Should government directly fund the regulator?
In some jurisdictions fees are not levied on the regulator professionals to pay for the cost of the regulator. Under this type of arrangement the regulator is structured so that it is embedded in a government ministry, and most of the funding requirements are met from the general resources of government via taxation. Advocates of this type of funding arrangement argue that this is fair, since the tax payer should fund the cost since they also gain advantages from regulation and not just the regulated professionals

However, this type of system where government directly funds the costs of regulation is subject to criticism for four reasons:

i. The income of the regulators will be wholly or partially dependent on the state of government finances and budgets may be cut arbitrarily during times when their finances are constrained

ii. The normal independence of regulators from government may be compromised as:

"he who calls the piper pays the tune."

iii. Unless every regulator in the jurisdiction is funded by this type of the policy, it will be seen as unfair to those who are not

iv. The cost of regulation will be less noticeable and therefore interest to the profession and professionals, and they will be less concerned in the affairs of the regulator

An example of this type of funding occurred when the Department of Health (England) subsidises the General Social Care Council (GSCC) who was the regulator of social workers in England from its foundation in 2000 until it was abolished in 2009. However, after a review by the PSA, the regulator to demonstrate its independence from government was required to become self-funding. Unfortunately, its proposed level of fees was assessed to be problematic in relation to the financial wellbeing of the individual social workers that it regulated. This was one of the reasons the GSCC was abolished and its register transferred to the HPC.

Should employers pay regulators' fees?
Although not very common, in a few instances the employer of the professionals will reimburse the professionals for all or part of the cost of their regulation.

For example, in the 2000s the UK's Department of Health in England awarded certain professionals including nurses an extra pay rise to pay a small proportion of the regulators' fees. This was a temporary measure and was discontinued after three years. The justification for the policy was the then low wage increases being awarded to certain professions such as nurses.

The counter arguments against employers paying all or part of the regulator's fees is that it is unfair to the self-employed and it breaks a link between the regulator and those it regulates.

It therefore follows that if government is unable or unwilling to directly finance its regulators and employers of the professions will not fund the regulator, then regulators have three alternative sources that they can use to obtain financial resources to maintain their operations, namely:

i. Government grants

ii. Borrowings

iii. Fee income from users of their services

i. Government grants
Firstly, on occasions single one-off non-returnable grants may be made by government to regulators. The grants are usually made because it is considered unreasonable for the existing professionals to pay for a government initiative relating to the regulating of healthcare professionals.

Recent examples in the UK of such an approach include the Department of Health making grants to regulators to cover the costs to:

- Establish a new regulator
- Expedite the immigration of international professionals
- Regulate a new profession

The grant payments from government will often be reported in the annual report and accounts as a separate type of income to differentiate it from other sources of fee income.

However, it should be noted that very occasionally the UK Government has made grants to regulators to cover operating expenses so that an increase in registrant fees can be avoided. Government is usually reluctant to take this cause of action since it may cause disquiet with other professionals who do not benefit from the subsidy to the regulator.

ii. **Borrowings**
Secondly, in the UK the regulators of healthcare professionals have the powers in their legislation to borrow. If borrowings are used they are predominantly for capital expenditure such as ITC, land, and buildings. If and when regulators need to and are allowed to borrow capital they are considered low risk by lenders and thus are charged relatively low rates of interest.

iii. **Fee income from users of their services**
Lastly, in addition to fees changed to professionals for joining and remaining on the register, fees can be charged to the users of the services provided by regulators. For example, approving programmes of education and training. Typically this represents only a small minority of the source of the income for regulators of healthcare professionals, particularly if cross subsidisation is not permitted.

4. **Types and level of fees charged by regulators**
On examination it will be seen that there are a complex range of many different fees that can be charged by regulators. The fees fall into two broad types: subscription and transactions.

Subscription fees
These are fees for a service provided by the regulator for a fixed period of time that are paid in advance. Examples of subscription include:

- Renewal of registration
- Specialist registers

Transaction fees
All other fees are charged as a result of a single transaction. Examples of transaction fees may include:

- Examinations to gain entry to the register
- Grandparenting applications
- Initial registration
- International applications
- Readmissions to the register
- Return to practise
- Statement of professional standing

Level of fees
For comparative purposes the annual retention fees charged by the UK regulators of healthcare professionals are detailed in Table 12.2 – II, volume 3. It can be seen that there is a considerable variation in the fees charged by the regulators. The reasons for the differences are discussed in Section 1.5, volume 4 Economics of regulating professionals. And it should be remembered that the fees charged by regulators to the professionals they regulate are relatively small as a percentage of their annual incomes, and they represent only a few hours pay per year and are partially tax deductible.

Again, it should also be borne in mind that cross subsidisation of different services within a single public authority is generally not permitted and should be avoided; see Section 1.5, volume 4. To this end, regulators will probably have a detailed cost model for the services they provide.

5. **Attitude of professionals to regulators' fees**
The fees imposed by regulators on professionals, even though they only represent a small percentage of their annual wages, are often seen by those who have to pay them as unwelcome and burdensome. Some professionals argue that it is the equivalent to an unfair taxation and brings about as much pleasure to them, as purchasing fuel for a car.

It is therefore important that the regulators' fees in totality really do reflect the amount of resources they require to be an effective and efficient regulator and at the same time only cause a minimal burden on those they regulate. Thus, the regulators' fees must not reduce the ability of the professionals to maintain a sound financial position, which is an important component of the regulatory contract; see Section 7.2, volume 1, and in particular:

> *"The regulated profession is able to maintain a sound financial footing to delivery economic, cost effective services of an appropriate quality."*

In addition, because regulators in effect impose the equivalent of a tax on professionals, government takes a range of measures to ensure that the resources of the regulator are managed appropriately. These measures can include:

- The legislation of the regulator makes specific reference to its powers to raise its finances by the use of fees
- The regulator is required to keep and publish a financial statement or the annual report and accounts
- The government's auditor, in the UK, the National Audit Office (NAO) are required to audit the regulators accounts
- The regulator has to follow the governments' requirements for how it manages its financial resources and financial probity
- The CEO is appointed as the regulators' Accounting Officer and can be held accountable by Parliamentary committees

6. **Requirement for government approval**
In an attempt to square the circle, government often insists that they scrutinise and approve the setting and revision of the regulator's fees and before approval is sought, requiring them to undertake a consultation. Nowadays, regulators who attempt to raise their fees unreasonably should consider the possibility of the likelihood of a judicial review by those stakeholders who have a legitimate expectation that one will be undertaken. It is worth noting that a minority of stakeholders will support fee increases where they are seen as justifiable and reasonable.

These measures mean that regulators are not wholly financially independent from government control when managing their finances, in that they must to a certain degree take account of government's policies and procedures.

7. **Legal powers to impose fees**
In the UK the ability of regulators to impose fees on registrants is established in their legislation which may be an act or statutory instrument and the details that may be provided by rules. In some instances the ability to impose a particular fee is set down in the regulators' legislation. Alternatively, the legislation may be more flexible and the regulator has powers to impose fees where they see fit.

8. **Setting and revising the level of fees**
To state the obvious a regulator must be in a sound financial position if it is to deliver effective, efficient, and ethical regulation. Thus, to discharge their objectives, regulators must be properly funded.

In a commercial business operating in rivalrous competition for their goods or services, the market will set, or at the very least strongly influence, prices. As public authorities and monopolists, regulators obviously can't use this process.

The pragmatic solution is for regulators to set their fees to reflect their costs which in return should reflect the quality and level of services they provide. This should result in all the operating expenses of the regulator being recovered from fees charged to the professionals and other individuals and organisations.

But returning to the non-competitive market, the major challenge with this method for setting the level of fees is that the regulator is a monopoly. So, for example, what level of quality of service should they provide to the users of its service or should they pay above market rates for key employees?

Or, is it unreasonable to assume that they set their fees as set as high as the regulator believes that they can get away with, in an environment where the individual 'customer' has little impact on the process?

Compared to commercial organisations operating in competitive markets, the operating environment of regulators is relatively stable and predictable. For example, because it takes three years and more to educate and train the next generation of healthcare professionals, regulators should be very confident in the medium term about the number of new individuals joining the register who have been educated and trained in their jurisdiction. Compare this to a commercial business operating in the international ICT market.

Notwithstanding this, from time to time the fees charged by regulators will need to be revised as their costs will inevitably increase caused by inflation or a government requirement to provide new services, of their own desire to provide improved or more efficient services.

To some extent regulators should also be continually seeking to reduce their costs by, for example, utilising the web and the internet, or to facilitate professions to update their data held on the register or renew their registration on-line.

Occasionally, more fundamental changes do occur when new legislation requires them to deliver new responsibilities such as continuing competence. However, such changes are usually preceded by government policy development and legislation, both of which proceed at a slow pace.

The first stage in the process to set or revise fees is the construction of a medium-term operational plan and financial budget as part of the planning process that is explored in Section 9.1, volume 4, planning processes.

Once the plans that demonstrate the need to revise the regulators' fees are completed they should be approved by the board, followed by four other steps, namely:

i. Consultation
ii. Governance approval
iii. Changes to legalisation to permit fee increase
iv. Communication

Despite the best efforts of regulators to only impose reasonable and justifiable increases to their fees, a proposal to increase them can instigate a strong hostile reaction from the professions. For example, in March 1970 the proposed introduction by the GMC of a £2 annual retention fee led to a sizeable minority of the UK medical professional boycotting fee payments. To resolve matter a working party chaired by Sir Brynmor Jones was established. In more recent times the reaction of a proposed fee increase by the GDC led to a very public dispute with the British Dental Association (BDA); see BDA v General Dental Council [2014] EWHC 4311 (Admin), [2014].

9. **Timing and frequency of changes to fees**
In the UK the arrangements whereby fees are charged by regulators to professionals can be considered to be a contract. This means that the renewal of registration or retention fee purchases the right of the professional to be on the register for a given period for a given fee. Fee changes can only be imposed at the point of renewal and a fee increase can't be retrospectively applied. Therefore fees can't be increased during the period of registration. The implication of this is that if renewal of registration occurs once every three years, then any changes to the renewal fee of an individual registrant can only occur once every three years.

If a regulator decides to use a period of registration longer than one year, it will take a corresponding length of time for all the professionals on the register(s) to be pay the increased fee. As a result the total financial impact of an increase in fees may not be fully felt for a number of years.

Further complications can arise if the need to link fee changes to the renewal cycles is combined with the need to gain approval from the legislature, is imposed on the regulator by its legislation. This is because frequent and small increases will be seen as desirable by the regulator and preferably by registrants but not the legislature. Whereas large and infrequent changes may be objected to by the profession and the legislature.

A pragmatic solution is for the regulators' legislation to permit future fees to be set for longer periods than their renewal cycle. For example, a regulator that requires the professions to renew their registration every two years may decide to set fees for a longer period, for example, £100 pa for the next two years, then £120 for the third year, and £125 for the fourth year.

10. **Income from other sources other than professionals**
Regulators of healthcare professional do have a number of potential sources of income beside monies raised directly from the fees from the professionals they regulate. They are as follows:

Education and training programme providers
Regulators may have the powers to charge fees to the providers of programmes of education and training. The fees can be derived from approving new programmes, periodically monitoring them, and occasionally reapproving existing programmes. The fees can apply to providers both within and outside the regulators' jurisdictions.

Consultancy services
Some regulators have established consultancy services, which are managed on a fee-generating commercial basis, for example, GMC Services International. Again, regulators may seek business within and outside their jurisdiction. However, there is little evidence of significant fee generation from the provision of these types of consultancy services.

If should also be noted that if regulators seek to establish commercial business, care should be given on how they are funded and the treatment and responsibility for any financial losses if they occur and the ability to demonstrate that all costs are ring-fenced and recovered.

Service delivery facilitates inspection
Some regulators charge a fee for the inspection and accreditation of service delivery facilities; see Section 7.3, volume 4.

Selling contents of register
Historically, regulators would sometimes sell the contact details of their registrants to other organisations for commercial marketing purposes. This is no longer the case.

Fines and financial penalties
Although not strictly a fee, some jurisdictions may permit regulators to impose fines or other financial penalties on a professional as a sanction of an FTP proceeding; see Section 4.6, volume 3.

Tribunal costs recovery
Regulators may seek to recover their legal costs in relation to appeals of decisions of FTP tribunals; see cost awards, Section 4.6, volume 3.

11. **Fees and multi-professional regulators**
When a regulator is responsible for regulating more than one profession it is possible that the costs of regulating the different professions may vary. The cost variations may be due to a range of factors including:

- The number of concerns received per 1,000 professionals
- The number of HEI programmes
- The complexity and length of FTP investigations and tribunals

On the assumptions that the costs are significantly different, should a multi-professional regulator therefore charge the same fee for all professionals, whatever their profession? Or, alternatively, should the professionals pay different fees depending on the costs associated with their particular profession?

There are advantages and disadvantages for charging fees directly relating to the different costs of each profession. They are as follows:

Different fees for different professions

- It seems fair to the professionals from a low-cost profession that they do not have partially fund another profession whose costs are higher
- Resolves the issue of cross subsidisation
- The regulation of a small profession will not capture the economies of scale of a large profession and their fees will be disproportionally higher
- Small professions may have widely varying annual fees due, for example, to one-off costly FTP tribunals
- Year-on-year variations in cost differentials between professions would require adjustments to annual fees to some of the professions
- Requirement to maintain separate set of accounts for each profession.
- May be complex to administer and communicate
- Requires complex and costly management accounting processes

Uniform fees for all professions

- Year-on-year variations in cost differentials between professions would not require adjustments to annual fees
- Straightforward to administer and communicate
- Less complex and costly management accounting systems required

On a practical level referring to three multi-professional regulators, ARPHA in Australia does set different fees for different profession, whereas the UK's HCPC and CORU in the Republic of Ireland have uniform fees.

12. **Reduced fees for dual registered professions**
In a single jurisdiction, a very small number of practitioners may be qualified and registered as more than one profession, for example, a paramedic who may also be a nurse, a physiotherapist who may also be an occupations therapist, or a dentist who is also a medical practitioner. Reduced fees for dual registration are usually not forthcoming, since regulators have costs associated with both professionals such as continuing competence audits and assessments and cross subsidisation should be avoided.

13. **Transfer pricing and fee sharing**
When regulators provide services to other organisation or services are purchased from external providers the price set for the service must represent the true cost. Similarly, when income is shared between regulators, an audit trail must be forthcoming to demonstrate the correctness of the division.

14. **Taxation liabilities of regulators**
The financial implications of taxation need to be taken into consideration by regulators. In the UK regulators may be subject of taxation if they make an operating surplus, or they earn income from interest or dividends from reserves. Also, in the UK regulators must pay VAT but can't reclaim it.
And as a reminder, many jurisdictions allow the registration fees paid by professionals to their regulator may be offset, or partially offset, against personal tax; see Section 4.6, volume 2. This in effect transfers a proportion of the cost of regulation to the taxpayer.

15. **Charitable status of regulators**
In the UK charities have a favourable tax status and some regulators gain advantages as registering as charities; see Section 3.1, volume 4.

CONCLUSION

The financial characteristics of the UK regulators of healthcare professions are not particularly complex. However, because the fees of regulators are in many ways similar to taxation government may impose various restraints. Regulators must therefore take these into account when considering how and when to raise their fees.

EXERCISES AND QUESTIONS

Exercises

- Should regulation be funded by the state rather than those who are regulated?
- What percentage of a regulator's annual budget should be allocated to communication, continuing competence, and governance? Justify your decision.

Questions

- The wages of nurses have not increased for three years. How should government react to a regulator who seeks to increase their fees due to rising costs?
- Should government allow different professions to have to pay the different fees to be regulated?

FURTHER READING

Cost of Capital Annual Update Report R
UK Regulator Network (UKRN)
December 2020
31 pages

Following the Pound R
The Accounting Officer in Central Government
Institute for Government
Josh Harris
3 September 2013
41 pages

Managing Public Money R
HM Treasury
ISBN: 978-1-910835-51-7 & PU1805
July 2013, revised September 2019
217 pages

Regularity, Propriety and Value for Money R
Treasury officer of accounts
HM Treasury
52 pages
November 2004

LEGISLATION

Example of UK Legislation

Legal Cases

British Dental Association v General Dental Council [2014] EWHC 4311 (Admin), [2014] L

STANDARDS, CODES, GUIDANCE, CONSULTATIONS, POLICIES, AND PRACTICE NOTES

Guidance

Accounting Officers' Survival Guide G
Treasury officer of Accounts
HM Treasury
December 2015
14 pages

Consultations

Clear and Certain: A New Framework for Fee-setting C
Consultation outcome report
General Dental Council
November 2018
24 pages

Our Fees Consultation Document C
Health Professions Council
20061019cPOLUB
November 2006
17 pages

1.5 ECONOMICS OF REGULATING PROFESSIONALS

INTRODUCTION

A number of economic terms are referred to in the book. To assist readers the various terms are mustered together and examined in the section.

The economic terms are listed in alphabetic order:

1. Barrier to entry
2. Cost, fixed, semi-variable, and variable
3. Credence
4. Cross subsidisation
5. Distortionary price
6. Division of labour
7. Economies of scale
8. Intangible asset
9. Labour demand/supply curve
10. Learning curve
11. Long-run cost curve
12. Market
13. Minimum efficient scale
14. Moral hazard
15. National competitiveness and foreign direct investment
16. Positive consumption externality
17. Productivity
18. Public choice theory
19. Rent seeking
20. Rivalrous competition
21. Scarcity of resource
22. Wage premium

The 22 terms will now be expanded and explored:

1. **Barrier to entry**
   In relation to the regulation of professionals a barrier to entry can be defined as:

Definition: Barrier to Entry
Obstacle or difficulty that prevents or restricts individuals or organisation entering a market.

Because barriers to entry protect the incumbent professionals by restricting competition in the market for their services, it can lead to distortionary prices. However, it should be noted that both government regulation and regulation of professionals do not necessarily fit the various classic economic definitions of a barrier to entry.

2. **Cost**
   From the perspectives of accounts and economists there are three types of costs that can be identified in relation to how they change as the production of goods or services change. They are fixed, variable, and semi-variable:

   Fixed cost
   Fixed costs do not change as production of goods or services increases or decreases. Examples include tax on property and property insurance.

   Variable cost
   The costs change as production of goods or services increases or decreases. Examples include overtime pay.

   Semi-variable cost
   Costs comprising both fixed and variable components. Examples include the costs of operating a delivery lorry.

3. **Credence**
   Many services provided in the healthcare delivery system by healthcare professionals can't be judged by patients in terms of quality or benefit. Healthcare services are therefore a classical example of a credence service; hence, the definition:

Definition: Credence
Good or service where the consumer finds it difficult or impossible to ascertain their utility.

This is often the situation in healthcare. For example, consider the same patient visiting two dentists. If dentist A recommends to the patient a treatment for £250 and dentist B suggests a treatment to the same patient which will cost £500 for exactly the same dental problem, how does the patient rationally decide which is the best course of action?

A similar problem arises for the purchase if both suppliers charge the same amount but one provides a good service the other does not and the patient is unable to judge the quality of the services of one compared to the other. In the UK as the NHS provides a universal healthcare service that is free at the point of service, in theory patients as consumers are not required to make these types of decisions.

4. **Cross subsidisation**
   Cross subsidisation can be defined as:

Definition: Cross Subsidisation
Lower prices paid by one group of consumers are subsidised by higher prices charged to another group of consumers.

Cross subsidisation could occur in relation to a regulator of healthcare professionals if the cost of the infrequently international application process is relatively high in comparison to the frequently used initial registration process. The regulator could in theory decide to use cross subsidisation to lower the fee charged for international applicants by transferring income generated from the initial applicants to lower the costs charged to the international applicants.

However, in the context of the statutory regulation of healthcare professionals the practice of cross subsidisation is normally discouraged. The rationale for this is that the legislature requires the professionals to complete the initial registration process and the professionals have no choice in the matter. So, for example, it is therefore considered unreasonable for domestic registrants to be compulsorily required to fund part of the costs of the process for international applicants.

5. **Distortionary price**
These can be defined as:

Definition: Distortionary Price
Price that should occur with restrictions on supply and demand.

6. **Division of labour**
The microeconomic theory of the division of labour proposes that workers who cooperate together by dividing and sharing parts of a single process between themselves can reduce the requirement for labour compared to the same process where there is no specialisation of labour. The division of labour can be defined as:

Definition: Division of Labour
Organisation of a process into separate tasks each performed by different individuals who specialise in the task, to gain efficiency provided that sufficient volumes of goods or services are produced.

In the healthcare delivery system scientific discoveries have enabled the division of the healthcare professions into groups of workers who undertake similar tasks. As a consequence society has gained from the resulting economic benefits of specialisation.

7. **Economies of scale**
Economies of scale is a macroeconomic term that can be defined as:

Definition: Economies of Scale
Cost advantages that enterprises obtain due to their size, output, or scale of operation, such that the cost per unit of output generally decreases with increasing scale as fixed costs are spread out over more units of output.

Economic benefits arise from scale because organisations can spread their fix and semi-variable cost over more widgets or customers. Compared to smaller operations, they can obtain lower supply prices due to volume discounts. They may be able to pay higher wages and attract higher quality employees. As large organisations they are likely to gain from experience at a faster rate compared to smaller organisations, as they in effect move down the learning curve faster.

Economies of scale of regulators of professionals
It can be assumed that there are no fundamental difference in the processes used by the nine UK regulators of healthcare professionals, since they have the same primary and secondary objectives. Regulators of professionals demonstrate economies of scale in relation to some of their processes. The scale, or size, of a regulator, can be measured by using a number of parameters. For example, income, number of professionals on the register, or the number of FTP cases. These economies of scale should result in regulators with large registers having lower annual registration fees. This can be demonstrated by showing the comparative relationships between the numbers of professionals regulated by a regulator and the annual renewal fee in a given jurisdiction and is illustrated in Chart 1.5 – I, on the next page.

From the graph it can be deduced that:

- Regulators undertaking identical or similar process are able to impose widely different fees on different healthcare professions
- Government permits, or at the very least, do not intervene to reduce significant fee outliers
- Small regulators with, say, less than 50 employees or 50,000 regulators are of a sub-optimal scale.

What are the consequences of regulators who are running sub-optimal scale organisations? One important issue is that they will not have the resources to deliver services to match the public expectations who they interact with. And the public's high expectations of quality is based on their interaction with modern service organisations that provide self-service via the internet, fast communication response times, and so on and so forth. It may also mean that regulators' ability to adapt rapidly to changing circumstances is also comparatively slow due to their cumulative position of the learning curve.

Reason for lack of government intervention
Government does have the tools to intervene, particularly if they adopt multi-professional regulators who clearly have the ability to extract economies of scale for the benefit of all stakeholders. This then raises the question of why government is either apparently indifferent to the fees charged by regulators or is not supportive of the position of professional associations of their desire to see limitations on fees and their possible increase. One suspects that it all comes down to the

Chart 1.5 – I **Economies of scale of regulators of professionals**

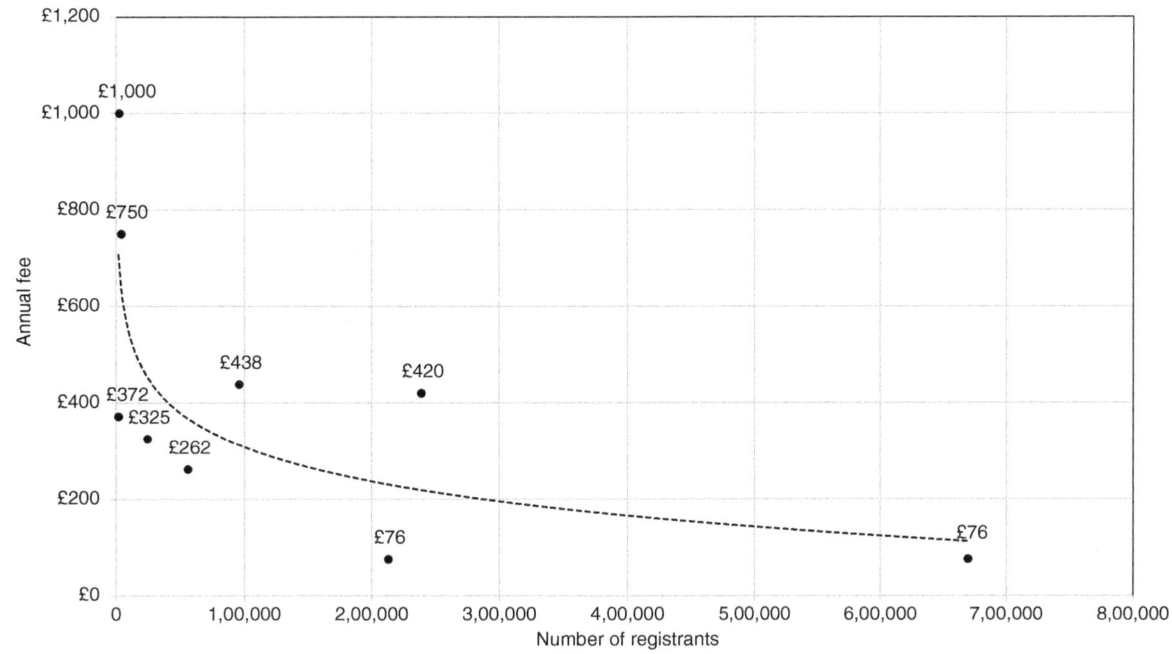

difference in stakeholders' ability to influence government action, or in this case inaction.

8. **Intangible asset**

Tangible assets include things like buildings, machinery, and vehicles. Intangible assets are things that *'you cannot see or drop on your foot'* and include software and brands. These different types of assets are of interest to those studying regulators because organisations and businesses that make little use of tangible assets can grow their business more rapidly than those that are dependent on tangible assets.

Scalability of the operating model of a regulator of healthcare professionals is therefore easily achieved.

In contrast, organisations utilising intangible assets are less able to restrict their use by other organisations. For example, a regulator that purchases software from a third party to develop a regulatory system will find it difficult to prevent the software developer supplying similar software to other regulators. This phenomenon is called 'spillover'.

9. **Labour demand/supply curve**

The supply and demand for labour are related. The macroeconomic proposition is that if the supply of labour is restricted and the demand for labour remains the same, then wages will increase.

To understand the argument a graph can be constructed showing the demand/supply curve for labour, where the horizontal axis or x-axis represents the quantity of labour. The vertical axis or Y-axis represents the wage rate for labour.

A demand curve is a graphical representation showing the different demand for labour provided at every possible wage rate.

The demand curve for labour is negatively sloped for two reasons. Firstly, a rise in the wage rate increases the costs of business providing the service, forcing them to raise their selling prices. As the price of the service rises, consumers will purchase less of it and less output will be provided. This will lead to a fall in demand for labour. Secondly, a rise in wages makes labour more expensive relative to capital. Businesses will substitute capital for labour. This results in less labour being used to provide services whatever output the businesses sell.

A supply curve is a graphical representation showing the different quantity of labour supplied at every possible wage rates.

The supply curve is positively curved and will rise from left to right, since as the price of a service increases, the quantity supplied increases.

If the wage rates are free to adjust in response to market forces, they will move to a point where the demand for labour equals the supply. This is sometimes referred to as equilibrium.

This is illustrated in Chart 1.5 – II. The chart represents the relationship between the quantity of labour and wage rates in terms of demand and supply. The point Q1 W1 represents equilibrium in a flexible labour market.

Chart 1.5 – II Labour demand/supply curves in flexible labour markets

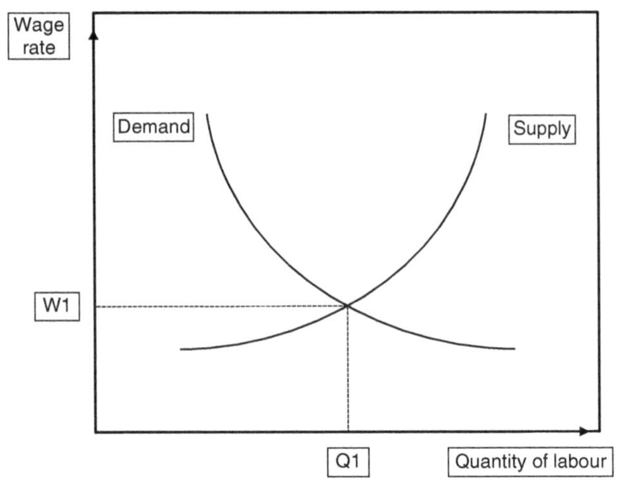

Chart 1.5 – III Labour demand/supply curves in inflexible labour markets

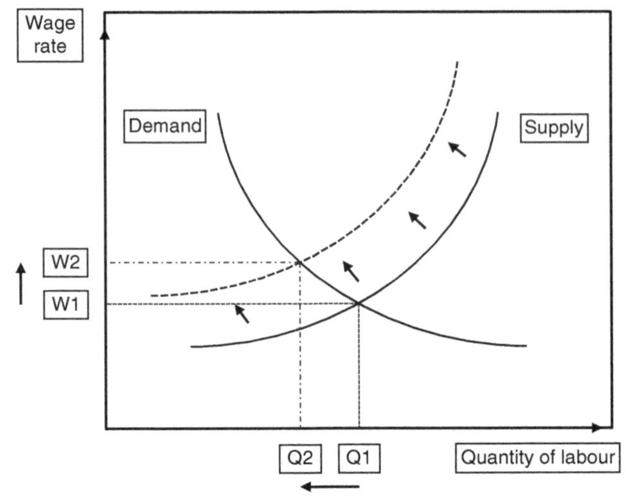

In Section 7.1, volume 1, the advantages and disadvantages of regulating professionals are explored in detail. It is argued that there is a strong case against the public utility of professional regulation. This is because regulated professionals gain a disproportionate economic influence compared to other non-regulated workers, due to their ability to limit or reduce the supply of the use of their knowledge in a particular market. When considering whether or not to regulate a new group, the regulatory impact assessment should consider the effects on the earnings, or wages, of professionals caused by regulation and also those individuals who will no longer be able to work in the particular market.

The effect of regulating professionals on the labour market is to make it more inflexible. If supply is reduced by the imposition of barriers such as long periods of training then for a given demand for labour, the quantity wages at equilibrium increase as the supply curve rises.

This is illustrated in Chart 1.5 – III. The chart represents the relationship between the quantity of labour and wage rates in terms of demand and supply. The point Q2 W2 represents equilibrium in an inflexible labour market.

10. Learning curve

A learning curve can be defined as:

Definition: Learning Curve
Over time the cumulative experience of making goods or providing services increases efficiency in the use of labour and materials resulting in lower costs per unit of output

The term experience curve can also be used.

11. Long-run cost curve

This is another economic term that demonstrates that an organisation will benefit from economies of scale, since costs should fall the longer in time that it produces goods or provides services.

12. Market

There is a degree of inconsistency on what economist mean by '*a market*'. Three examples include:

Definition: Market
The term has three different meanings: System of coordinating using prices to convey information between economic entities to control production and distribution. and Arrangement between buyers and sellers to exchange goods or services for money either directly or through mediating agents or institutions. and Groups of individuals or organisations delineated by geographic, demographic or socioeconomic, psychographic, behavioural, or sectoral that make up the pool of actual and potential customers for their goods and services

13. Minimum efficient scale

The minimum efficient scale can be defined as:

Definition: Minimum Efficient Scale
Scale of production reached when the average cost is at its minimum and therefore the same as the marginal cost.

The term minimum efficient plant size (MEPS) can also be used.

The minimum efficient scale can be calculated by considering the dynamic relationship production and marginal and average costs.

This is because when a small number of widgets are produced, the average cost per widget would be high because the bulk of the costs would come from fixed costs. For example, the cost of renting factory space and labour costs on the production line.

Contrast this to the same manufacture producing more widgets in the same factory using the same number of workers. Here the average costs incurred per widget will be lower as the fixed costs are spread over a larger number of widgets. Thus the marginal cost is below the average cost, pulling the latter down.

The efficient scale of production is then reached when the average cost is at its minimum and therefore the same as the marginal cost.

If the scale is below the MES it is said to be sub-optimal.

In terms of the regulation of healthcare professionals the impact of MEPS come into effect when the size of the register of a profession is small. Thus small regulators have relatively high fees.

14. Moral hazard

The term moral hazard is an economic term that occurs in relation to the regulation of healthcare professionals. It is defined as:

Definition: Moral Hazard
Transaction when one party with more information about its actions or intentions has a tendency or incentive to behave inappropriately from the perspective of the other due to party with less information resulting from an asymmetrical knowledge base.

It should be noted that the term moral hazard has two meanings; see Section 7.2, volume 4.

15. National competitiveness and foreign direct investment

It is argued that the excessive regulation of professionals harms a nation's competitiveness. In turn, lack of competitiveness will lead to slower economic growth. In this argument 'excess' refers to firstly, the amount of regulation used to regulate professionals and secondly, the number of professions that are regulated.

This economic argument is that too much regulation of professionals reduces inward and outward foreign direct investment (FDI) and may reduce trade in terms of exports in downstream industries. There are two effects. Firstly, if a particular country makes it difficult for a foreign national or corporation to establish themselves within the country, then the intensity of competition within the country for the service will be reduced. The flat-footed domestic incumbents will avoid competition from interlopers with their fleet of foot. This will drive up prices and reduce service levels. Secondly, it will reduce the competitiveness of in-country service providers, and they will be less able to compete in foreign markets.

FDI takes place when a foreign investor establishes a new operation in a country, or alternatively, purchases and then controls an established business in the country. Its supporters champion the potential to transfer technology and the increased investment in employees' knowledge and skills. Its distractors are more focused on the risks arising from the control of companies in the defence or ICT sectors by a foreign organisations.

The Organisation for Economic Co-operation and Development (OECD) measures the degree of competition in the service industries of each country by way of a services trade restrictive index (STRI). The STRI is an inventory of trade policy measures and domestic regulation for services. Examples of the components of the index include restrictions on the ownership of companies by foreigners and barriers to competition and the movement of people into and from a country.

The number of professions regulated in a country varies. According to the OECD, in 2013 Estonia regulated 47 professions, whereas the Czech Republic 404 were regulated. The OECD argues that the total number of professions and occupations in a country directly relates to a high STRI score. In essence, the greater the numbers of professions and occupations regulated, then the less efficient a country's service industry is

16. Positive consumption externality

Economists refer to the cost or benefit that affects a party who did not choose to incur that cost or benefit, as an externality. Externalities can relate to both production and consumption and can have both positive and negative effects. Hence, when a vaccination is given to a child the term positive consumption externality can be applied, since herd immunity is generated.

17. Productivity

Productivity can be defined as:

Definition: Productivity
Economic measure of output per unit of input.

In economic theory inputs include labour costs and can be measured as output per hour, output per job, and output per workers' capital. If productivity grows it reflects an economy that is producing output more efficiently. It also means that pay can be increased without triggering the risk that the rate of inflation will increase. It should also be noted that productivity can also change due to capital investment or the use of technology.

Should one therefore assume that in terms of the healthcare delivery system, increasing productivity means that more can be delivered for less? Since the healthcare system is labour intensive, small increases in productivity should have large impacts on costs.

Unfortunately, the labour costs of healthcare employees tend to rise without productivity gains. This is due to the cross elasticity of demand, or in other words, not only is the demand for a product or service set by its demand, but also the price of related services or products.

And, as described by the America economists William J Baumol and William G Bowen in the 1960s, wages in one sector can rise without productivity gains, at the same time as wages rise in another sector experiences productivity gains.

18. Public choice theory

The public choice economic theory assumes that individuals are motivated by their own self-interest. Thus in relation to the regulation of healthcare professionals, it can be defined as:

Definition: Public Choice Theory
Practitioners seek regulation to reduce competition and increase their market power.

19. Rent seeking

Rent-seeking can be defined as:

Definition: Rent-seeking
Economic process where organisations or individuals seek to gain increased wealth without creating new wealth.

One way to consider rent-seeking is that the owners of an input of production such as labour, machines, intellectual property, and capital are able to legally extract more profit than they would gain in a competitive market.

In relation to the regulation of healthcare professionals, rent-seeking manifests itself when professionals using their negotiating power derived from their monopoly, demand higher wages without an increase in productivity or an improvement to patient outcomes.

Monopolies also facilitate a form of rent-seeking:

20. Rivalrous competition

See Section 10.5, volume 2.

21. Scarcity of resource

Scarcity of resource is an economic theory based on the observation that many resources are limited. Thus:

Definition: Scarcity of Resource
When the demand for a resource is greater than its supply, it leads to a decline in the available resource.

This means that when resources are scarce both individuals and organisations must make trade-offs between competing alternative courses of action and in effect undertake one course of action as opposed to another alternative.

As a consequence ideally regulatory intervention should be proportionate and focused so that the maximum benefit at the lowest economic cost can be achieved.

22. Wage premium

Certain groups in the labour market such as trade union, public sector employees, and professionals are able to extract higher earning in comparison to workers in other sectors and occupations. This is referred to as a wage premium:

Definition: Wage Premium
Average wages of members of a group are greater than the population as a whole.

CONCLUSION

The discipline of economics provides both theoretical and practical methods to explain and justify how and why regulation works. A sound command of both, supported by the economic terms explored in this section, should therefore be of use to many of stakeholders concerned with the regulation of healthcare professionals.

EXERCISE AND QUESTION

Exercise

- What benefits arise to governments if it permits small regulators to operate?

Question

- Should high-earning professions be required to pay higher fees to their regulator?

FURTHER READING

Bottleneckers B
Gaming the Government for Power and Private Profit
Mellor, W Carpenter D
Encounter Books
ISBN: 978-1594039072
13 December 2016
446 pages

Capitalism Without Capital: The Rise of the Intangible Economy B
Jonathan Haskel and Stian Westlake
Princetown University Press
ISBN: 9781400888320
7 October 2017
287 pages

Competition in Professional Services 1999 R
OECD Policy Roundtable Competition Committee
DAFFE/CLP(2000)2
23 February 2000
214 pages

Cost-efficiency Review of the Health Professional Regulators R
Centre for Health Service Economics and Organisation
Jenny Ball|Alistair Rose Stuart Redding|Jonathan White
Report number 4, plus Annexes
November 2012
52 pages

Costs of Fitness to Practice: A Study of the Health and Care Professions Council R
HCPC
Publication code: REDDING–NICODEMO15
ISBN: 9781910938003
2005
60 pages

Encyclopaedia of Law and Economics, Volumes I – V B
Edited by Boudewijn Bouckaert Gerrit De Geest, Charles F
Edward Elgar Publishing
ISBN: 9781858985657
April 2000
4304 pages

Macroeconomics B
Hugh Granville and Ray Reese Prentice Hall
ISBN: 0-582-40487-8
1981
738 pages (3rd Edition)

Occupational Regulation in the EU and UK: Prevalence and Labour Market Impacts R
Queen Mary, University of London
Maria Koumenta, Amy Humphris, Morris Kleiner, Mario Pagliero
July 2014
116 pages

Regulation of Professions: B
A Law and Economics Approach to the Regulation of Attorneys and Physicians in the Us, Belgium, the Netherlands, Germany A (Law and Economics (Antwerp, Belgium).)
Finsinger, Jorg
Maklu Uitgevers N.V.
ISBN-13: 9789062153343
July 1993
430 pages

Review of the Economics of the Nine UK Regulators of Healthcare Professionals R
Evidence Report 40
UK Commission for Employment and Skills
ISBN: 978-1-906597-77-1
October 2011
202 pages

Valuing Professional Licensing in the US R
The Alliance for Responsible Professional Licensing and Oxford Economics
January 2021
39 pages

JOURNALS AND RESEARCH PAPERS

The Effects of Licensing on the Wages of Radiological Technologists JRP
Edward J Timmons, Robert J Thornton
Journal of Labour Research
Volume 29, No 84
2008

1.6 MONOPOLIES, PROFESSIONALS, AND THEIR REGULATION

INTRODUCTION

The process that requires healthcare professionals to demonstrate high attainment levels of education and training in combination with the regulatory protection of title and/or function restricts those seeking to join the professions. Although the process has been established and used with good intentions, in economic terms it creates barriers to enter the labour market.

As in most markets for goods or services, the higher the barriers to enter the market, the greater the likelihood that the successful entrants will be able to restrict competition and create a monopoly, thus reaping the resulting excessive financial rewards. However, the regulation of healthcare professions is contradictory. This is because it leads to increased safe and effective practice, clearly a public good, whilst at the same time it creates monopolies for the health professionals, which in general are against the public interest.

Since most, but not all, monopolies are seen to be against the public interest, stakeholders should be aware of the negative effects related to monopolies and particularly those of regulated healthcare professionals and if appropriate how they can be limited or curtailed.

COMPETITIVE MARKETS

When there is more than one organisation in a market it is reasonable to assume that they should and will compete with one another. The intensity of their competitive rivalry will depend on a number of factors. Michael Porter in his ground breaking book, *The Competitive Advantage: Techniques for Analyzing Industries and Competitors*, identifies four components of the rivalry, namely, the threat of new entrants or substitution and the bargaining power of supplies or buyers.

Ironically, unfettered rivalrous competition found in an efficient commercial market often leads to consolidation and a reduction of entities. The process is challenging since economists in the western liberal democracies are enthusiastic advocates and supporters of competitive market economies. Why so? In a competitive market producers compete with other producers and consumers compete with other consumers. The competitive process in a market economy directs the flow of resources to where they are most needed and to where they can be used most efficiently. In an effectively working comparative market prices accurately signal costs and benefits.

Indeed, Section 1.1, volume 1 identifies that one of the purposes of regulation is to ensure the efficient working of various markets by ensuring monopolistic powers are contained, reduced, or eliminated.

And to note, as discussed in Section 10.5, volume 2, the degree of intensity of rivalrous competition between professionals is influenced by their regulation.

ANTI-COMPETITIVE MARKETS

An anti-competitive market is one where the incumbents distort free and effective competition. This can be achieved by competitors colluding together to fix prices or to produce goods and services that are the same – a practice known as operating a cartel. Other ways to distort the market is for the incumbents to drop their prices to the point that the new entrant cannot sustain their continued participation, a process called predatory pricing. Participants may also abuse their dominant position for, by example, limiting production capacity, markets, or technical development to the prejudice of consumers.

COMPETITIVE VS. ANTI-COMPETITIVE MARKETS

In general competition in markets between suppliers of goods and services is seen by economists and politicians as a benefit to consumers. Although unfettered competition is to some degree discouraged by the western liberal democratic countries, it usually uses regulation to protect and to facilitate competitive markets. On the other hand, monopolies where competition is absent are seen as having negative consequences for consumers.

MONOPOLIES

A monopoly can be defined as:

Definition: Monopoly
Exclusive possession or control of the supply of a trade in a commodity or service.

The monopoly does not mean that the incumbent must have total control of the market. It is usually assumed that a 25% market share establishes a monopolist. It also leads to irreconcilable arguments about what constitutes the market.

The reason for the existence of a monopoly is that the incumbent can provide goods and or services at a lower marginal cost than its competitors. This is a good outcome for consumers. However, if contestants are forced to withdraw from the market, the resulting monopolist may be tempted to make supernormal profits by raising prices and restricting output to the detriment of consumers. Monopolists will be in a better position to try and dissuade potential competitors from entering the market with restraint of trade agreements.

In addition to economic factors, geography may also create monopolies, for example, the only supplier of a service on an isolated island.

In addition, the ownership of intellectual property rights may bestow monopolies on market participants.

EXAMPLES OF MONOPOLIES

Monopolies come in various guises that have evolved over the centuries. They include:

- In the US in the nineteenth century the Carnegie Steel Company and Standard Oil which dominated their respective steel and oil markets are both often colloquially cited as examples of monopolies created by predatory pricing
- In the UK in the latter part of the twentieth century, the flat glass manufacture Pilkington Glass had the intellectual property rights for the float glass manufacturing process. In the USA AT&T is a good example of a monopolist created by physical technological networks
- In the twenty-first century the basis for monopolist powers has shifted, and many global participants in the social media and information technology and communication (ITC) industry have been in conflict with governments for their alleged monopolistic behaviours

ADVANTAGES AND DISADVANTAGES OF MONOPOLIES

Monopolies have both advantages and disadvantages. Whilst the advantages of a monopoly fall almost exclusively on to the organisation or individuals who create or hold the monopoly, it is the consumer who loses out. Therefore, the assessment of the advantages and disadvantages varies enormously depending on the perspective of the controller of the monopoly compared to that of the user of the monopoly.

The criteria that can be used to assess the advantages and disadvantages of monopolies are detailed in Table 1.6 – I, see below:

Table 1.6 – I Criteria to assess advantages and disadvantages of monopolies

- Consumer choice
- Economies of scale
- Efficiency
- Income inequality
- Innovation in goods, production, and services
- Intellectual property rights
- Investment
- Political influence
- Prices
- Profits
- Resource allocation
- Tax losses
- Wealth creation

GOVERNMENT, REGULATION, AND MONOPOLIES

Governments have a mixed relationship with monopolies. In general they pursue four different policies, namely:

1. Government grants monopolies to individuals or commercial organisations. The monopoly is usually limited to a specified period of time. These types of monopolies are referred to as a government-granted monopoly. In undemocratic jurisdictions the government may seek to gain financially or politically from these types of arrangements
2. Government intervenes to protect consumers by eliminating or preventing the creation of the monopoly. This process is often undertaken by regulators. Examples in the UK include the Competition and Market Authority and in the USA the Federal Trade Commission
3. Government tolerates monopolies but using regulation, seeks to minimise their disadvantages
4. Government itself or via public authorities is the sole provider of a service to the market. Referred to as a state or government monopoly

TOLERATING MONOPOLIES

There are also two other monopolies which government will tolerate, namely, natural monopolies and duopolies:

NATURAL MONOPOLY

A natural monopoly can be defined as:

Definition: Natural Monopoly
Market where maximum economies of scale are achieved by single organisation.

An example of a natural monopoly is the distribution of electricity. In one jurisdiction a non-contestable market such as a single electricity distribution network may result in maximising lowest cost due to maximising the economy of scale. In these types of sectors such as the energy utilities and rail transportation, government allows the monopoly but regulates the sector to protect the consumer.

These markets are sometimes refer to as coercive monopolies.

DUOPOLIES

In some markets two suppliers dominate the market to such an extent that they are both monopolists. A duopoly can be defined as:

Definition: Duopoly
Market supply controlled by two organisations.

An example is the sector for the large-scale manufacturers of commercial airlines where Airbus and Boeing currently supply the vast majority of large commercial aeroplanes. Here governments tolerate or indeed are supportive of their national incumbent and the limited market competition due to the high cost of innovation, design, and manufacturing.

STATE MONOPOLIES

In some markets the government or a public authority is the sole supplier of goods or services. These can be defined as:

Definition: State Monopoly
Market where the government or a public authority is the only supplier of a service and competition is prevented by law.

These types of monopolies occur in two different categories.

Firstly, state monopolies where the state is the owner, manager, and operator of the organisation, for example in the USA the Postal Service and in Canada the retail selling of alcohol in British Columbia. In both these examples the criminal law is used to strictly exclude competitors from entering the market.

Secondly, public authorities are single suppliers of government services. For example, in the UK HM Revenue and Customs is the only organisation that collects tax. In addition, statutory regulators also fall into this category.

IMPLICATIONS OF SINGLE-SUPPLIER STATUS OF PUBLIC AUTHORITIES

Because public authorities are the only suppliers of services, government may establish process to monitor and scrutinise the services that they provide. This can be undertaken by the process described in Section 1.4, volume 1, Autonomy, independence, accountability, and scrutiny of regulators. In addition, government may establish auditors and/or oversight and organisations; see Section 6.4, volume 4.

IMPLICATIONS OF MONOPOLY IN THE REGULATION OF HEALTHCARE PROFESSIONALS

Having reviewed the difference between competitive and non-competitive markets, what are the implications of monopolies for regulators and healthcare professionals? There are six effects, namely:

1. Regulators are monopolist organisations
2. Lack of incentives for market consolidation
3. Regulators establish barriers to the labour market
4. Regulators establish professions as monopolists
5. Monopolies create social power
6. Earning powers of professionals

1. **Regulators are monopolist organisations**
Regulators are monopolist in that there is only one organisation providing the service.
If a consumer is not satisfied with the service they purchase from a commercial organisation they have a range of options. These include attempting to resolve the cause of the dissatisfaction with the supplier and more importantly, they can take their future purchasing decisions to an alternative supplier or competitor. For example, if you do not like supermarket A, provided an alternative is accessible, you can do your weekly shopping to supermarket B.
However, dissatisfied consumer of the services of a regulator can't take their business to an alternative supplier. A potential detrimental consequence of this situation may mean that the regulator is less concerned about the effectiveness or the efficiency of the services that it is meant to provide.
To balance this potential deficit, regulators are often required to provide service to a specified standard set by external organisations or within their legislation. Regulators should therefore set and publish their own service standards and report their performance they provide to their stakeholders and internal users. This issue is explored in Chapter 6, volume 4, Standards for regulators.

2. **Lack of incentives for market consolidation**
Because regulator are both public authorities and monopolies there is no ability or incentive to merge or acquire other regulators. So if they are not providing an adequate service to their stakeholders the management is not under threat that another organisation will take them over and they will lose their jobs. However, government may intervene; see Section 1.8, Abolishing regulators and transferring registers.

3. **Regulators establish barriers to the labour market**
Regulators enhance the barriers to enter the markets for healthcare service provided by healthcare professionals. This restricts the number of individuals competing to provide services resulting in higher prices and lower levels of service compared to a competitive market.
This can be summarised in the following principle:

Principle: Monopolies
Healthcare professionals' monopolies are enhanced by regulation.

In Section 3.5, volume 1, 11 processes are identified that can be used to restrict access to the labour market. The greater the restriction to enter the labour market, the greater the ability of those working in the occupation who are able to exploit any monopolistic benefits. In addition, as the strength of the barrier to enter the market increases, the greater the monopolistic benefits that arise to the incumbents.

This means that a system of licensing without examination has a minimal monopolistic effect, certification – voluntary has some monopolist effects, whereas occupational licensing has the greatest monopolistic effect. The following Chart 1.6 – I illustrates this effect, that as barriers to entry to the labour market increase, the strength of the monopoly of the incumbent also increases.

Another example of different regulatory processes having variable effects on the strength of the monopoly in the market for the services of healthcare professionals is the use of either protection of function or protection of title. This is illustrated in Chart 1.6 – II, opposite. The chart depicts how the strength of the monopoly increases as level of protection of function or titles increases barriers to entry the labour market.

If there is a message here, it is to make the legislative hurdles into the labour markets as low as possible whilst establishing the standards for safe and effective practice. It therefore follows that when considering if and how to regulate a profession consideration should be given to limiting barriers of entry to the labour market:

Principle: Barriers to Entry to the Labour Market
The regulation of professionals should be organised to minimise the barriers to entry to the labour market.

4. **Regulators establish professions as monopolist**
The regulation of healthcare professionals explicitly creates monopolies. The consequence of this is that whilst an individual nurse or dentist is obviously not a monopolist, the totality of the profession consisting of all its members if they act in coordination, can behave as a monopolist.

This type of anticompetitive behaviour is as old as the profession themselves. To quote Adam Smith from his book *The Wealth of Nations* published on 9 March 1776:

AND THE DISTORTION OF TRADE

> *"People of the same trade seldom meet together, even for merriment and diversion, but the conversation ends in a conspiracy against the public, or in some contrivance to raise prices.... But though the law cannot hinder people of the same trade from sometimes assembling together, it ought to do nothing to facilitate such assemblies, much less to render them necessary."*
> *The Wealth of Nations, Book IV Chapter VIII, p. 145, para. c27*
> *"A regulation which obliges all those of the same trade in a particular town to enter their names and places of abode in a public register, facilitates such assemblies.... A regulation which enables those of the same trade to tax themselves in order to provide for their poor, their sick, their widows and orphans...renders such assemblies necessary. An incorporation not only renders them necessary, but makes the act of the majority binding upon the whole. In a free trade, an effectual combination cannot be established*

Chart 1.6 – I **Restricting access to the labour market and strength of monopoly**

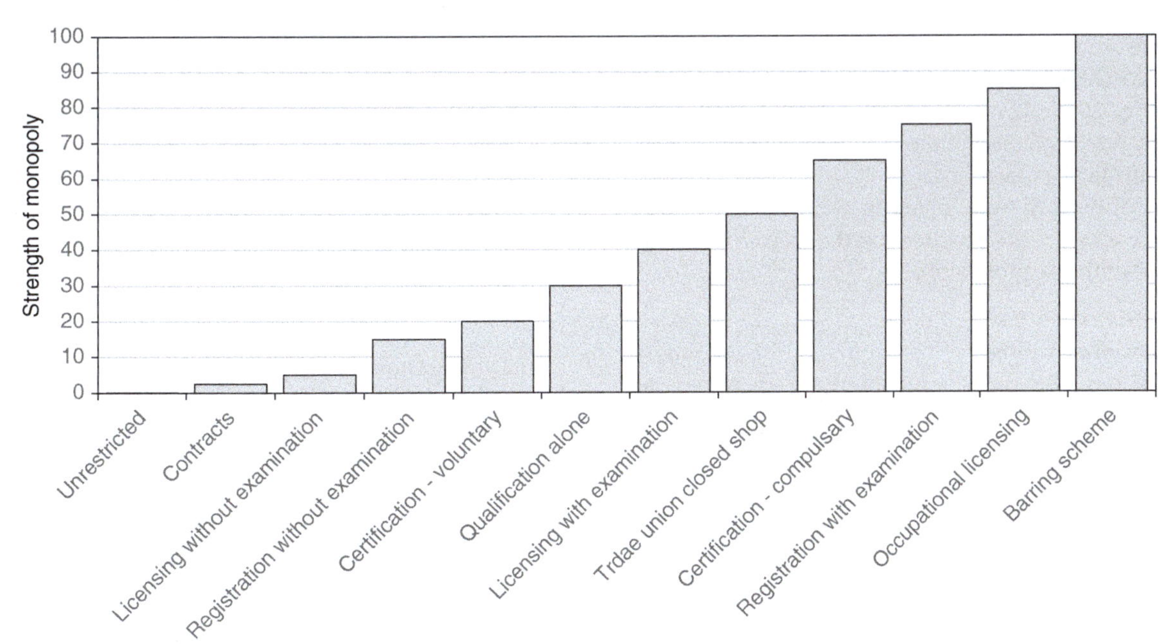

Chart 1.6 – II **Protection of title vs. protection of function**

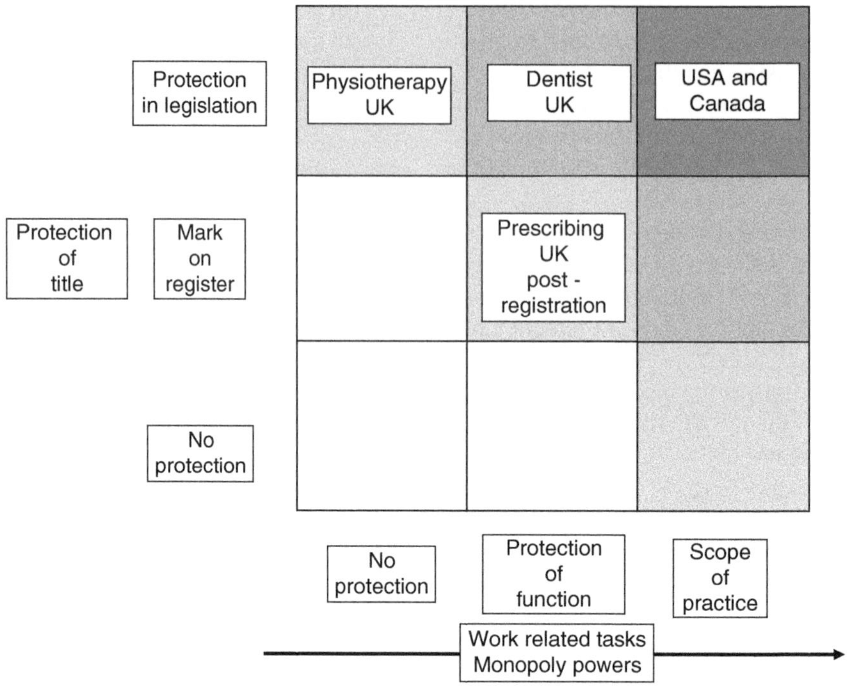

but by the unanimous consent of every single trader, and it cannot last longer than every single trader continues of the same mind. The majority of a corporation can enact a bye-law, with proper penalties, which will limit the competition more effectually and more durably than any voluntary combination whatever."

The Wealth of Nations, Book IV Chapter VIII, v. ii, p. 660, para. 49

A modern example of the impact of anticompetitive behaviour, research published by the *Economist* magazine on 31 January 2015, demonstrated that in the USA, states where scopes of practise limited the provision of services by non-medical professionals such as nurses, then the earnings of doctors were higher in comparison to states where there were less restrictions on the scopes of practise of other healthcare professionals.

5. **Monopolies create social power**
There are also a range of consequential or secondary effects of the creation of a monopoly in areas such as social power.

Definition: Social Power
Amount of influence that an individual or organisation has amongst their peers and society as a whole.

This results in professionals having comparatively stronger social power than others in society resulting in their ability to use their status to disproportionally influence politicians and in turn seek or gain political patronage.

For those readers interested in how to gauge the economic influence of the profession is to consider their position in class stratification schemes devised by John Goldthorpe and the UK's ONS National Statistics Socio-economic classification.

6. **Earnings of professionals**
The last effect of the monopolies of professions is that they can extract a 'wage premium' on their earnings. In addition, they may behave with rapacity.

An example of the consequence of a limited supply of healthcare professionals on their earnings was published by the *Economist* magazine on 31 January 2015.

They plotted the distribution of earnings of internal medicine doctors in the USA. The data provided by Doximity, the US online networking service for medical professionals, demonstrated that where there is a limited number of doctors earnings increase by up to 65% in comparison to areas where there are many doctors. Thus, the lowest rates of earnings were in Massachusetts and the highest in Alabama. In this example the healthcare professionals were not deliberately restricting the supply of practitioners in a particular area in an anticompetitive manor. Rather, doctors were assumed to prefer living in Boston or

New York, rather than in a rural and remote location such as Alabama.

Before concluding this section, it is interestingly to note that Beth Redbird, Assistant Professor, at North Western University published a paper in the American Sociological Review on 3 May 2017; pp. 600–624 entitled 'The New Closed Shop? The Economic and Structural Effects of Occupational Licensure' in which she argues that, contrary to established wisdom, licensure does not limit competition, nor does it increase wages, but instead creates a set of institutional mechanisms that enhance entry into the occupation, particularly for historically disadvantaged groups, while simultaneously stagnating quality.

CONCLUSION

In general monopolies are assessed as being detrimental to the public.

Because the regulation of professionals may lead to the establishment of monopolies, government must consider two processes. Firstly, to curb any excesses to limit harmful barriers for entry of the professionals and secondly the possibility of anticompetitive behaviour by the professionals.

To again quote Adam Smith:

> *"To widen the market and to narrow the competition, is always the interest of the dealers... The proposal of any new law or regulation of commerce which comes from this order, ought always to be listened to with great precaution, and ought never to be adopted till after having been long and carefully examined, not only with the most scrupulous, but with the most suspicious attention. It comes from an order of men, whose interest is never exactly the same with that of the public, who have generally an interest to deceive and even oppress the public, and who accordingly have, upon many occasions, both deceived and oppressed it."*
>
> The Wealth of Nations, Book IV Chapter VIII, p. 145, paras. c29–30

To counteract this, government often establishes regulators of monopolists. However, a central problem with the then regulation of professionals is that under certain circumstances it creates a strong monopoly by restricting access to the labour market.

EXERCISE AND QUESTION

Exercise

- What is the evidence that rent seeking by healthcare professions is a conspiracy theory?

Question

- Are the wages of nurses reasonable compared to other occupations? if they are not, what is the reason?

FURTHER READING

The Competitive Advantage: Techniques for Analyzing Industries and Competitors

Porter, Michael E B
New York Free Press
1 October 1980
ISBN: 100029253608 13 – 9780029253601
397 pages

First Thing We do, Let's Deregulate all the Lawyers B
Clifford Winston, Robert W Crandall and Vikram Maheshi
Broking Institution Press
ISBN: 978-0-8157-2190-1
2011
110 pages

Guild-ridden Labour Markets: The Curious Case of Occupational Licensing B
Kleiner, Morris M.
Published by W E Upjohn Institute for Employment Research
ISBN-13: 9780880995016
ISBN-10: 0880995017
2015
117 pages

Income from Independent Professional Practice B
Milton Friedman and Simon Kuznets
National Bureau of Economic Research, Inc New York
1954 / 1945
594 pages

Wealth of Nations
An Inquiry into the Nature and Causes of the Wealth of Nations B
Adam Smith
Everyman's Library – Publisher Alfred A Knopf, Random House, New York, 1991
IBSN 978 1 85715 011 7
9 March 1776
620 pages – in a five book series

1.7 ESTABLISHING NEW STATUTORY REGULATORS

INTRODUCTION

Following a decision by government to establish a new statutory regulator of healthcare professionals a well-trodden path can be used and the process is reviewed in the section.

TRIGGERS FOR ESTABLISHING NEW STATUTORY REGULATORS

There are two different starting points for establishing a new regulator. They are as follows:

1. **Profession has never been statutorily regulated**
   Historical UK examples of this position were:

Council for Professions Supplementary to Medicine (CPSM)	1961
General Chiropractic Council (GCC)	1994
General Osteopathic Council (GOsC)	1993

2. **Regulatory responsibility transferred from another organisation to new regulator**
   This can occur under two different eventualities, namely:
   - **i.** Transfer of regulatory functions from a professional association to a new statutory regulator
   - **ii.** Transfer of regulatory functions from an existing regulator to a new regulator

Historical UK examples of this process occurred in July 2008 when the then Health Professions Council (HPC) becoming responsible for the regulation practitioner psychologists when some responsibilities relating to their certification – voluntary process were transferred from the professional association the British Psychological Society (BPS). And in 2001 when the new HPC took over regulatory responsibilities from the CPSM.

PROCESS TO ESTABLISH A NEW REGULATOR

The process to establish a new regulator is similar to the process to regulate an aspirant group; see Section 11.2, volume 3, and in particular Chart 11.2 – I, volume 3. There are, however, a number of significant differences, which may or not be included depending on the nature of the project. They include:

- **Variables of the structure for regulating healthcare professionals**
  Government must decide on the combination of the twelve variables to structure the new regulator; see Section 1.1, volume 1
- **Enacting legislation**
  Government must enact new legislation to establish the regulator; see Section 8.4, volume 1
- **Standards used by new regulator**
  The standards used by the new regulator must be devised and published; see Section 3.1, volume 1, and in particular Table 3.1 – II, volume 1
- **Processes used by new regulator**
  The new regulator must establish, organise, and manage the processes used by regulators of professionals; see Section 3.1, volume 1, and in particular Table 3.1 – I, volume 1
- **Operating model**
  An operating model must be selected and established that can deliver the new regulators' general and specialist regulatory functions.

GOVERNANCE ARRANGEMENTS

To provide governance for the process and to establish a new regulator a shadow board of directors comprising both non-executives and possibly executive directors is typically appointed. Board members commence their terms of appointment before the legislation for the new regulator is enacted. During this initial phase the shadow board has the authority to make preliminary decisions relating to all aspects of the regulator. The shadow board formally becomes the board when the legalisation is enacted and before the register is opened. Once this is completed they can retrospectively and expeditiously formally approve any of their preliminary decisions that were made when they were operating as a shadow board.

FINANCIAL ASPECTS OF ESTABLISHING A NEW REGULATOR

The start-up costs of establishing a new regulator fall into two distinct categories. There are those that are incurred before the register is opened and those that are incurred after the register is opened.

COSTS ARISING BEFORE THE REGISTER IS OPENED

At this stage the regulator will require funding to pay for the following types of capital and operating costs:

- Communication
- Consultation
- Drafting and approval of legislation
- Establishing the operating model of the regulator
- Establishing processes
- Establishing stakeholder relationships
- Establishing standards
- Shadow governance arrangements

And, since the register is not opened, it will have no income from registrants.

COSTS OCCURRING AFTER REGISTER IS OPENED

Once the register is opened, income will start to flow into the organisation. However, it may take some time before there are enough registrants to cover fixed, semi-variable, and variable costs. This means that it may be many months or some years before a breakeven point is reached, and the costs of the regulator are completely funded by income.

FUNDING THE COST OF ESTABLISHMENT

The financial costs of establishing a new regulator of healthcare professionals are significant. Since the timetable to establish a regulator may take at least 18–24 months the financial resources required can run into the order of three to five millions pounds, in 2025 values.

Government needs to consider how it will fund the opening of the register and the period from then to the point that financial breakeven is reached and a stable self-funding organisation is established.

The only two sources of funding the cost of establishing a new regulator are either the registrants or, alternatively, the government via the taxpayer. In recent times the UK Government included in the legalisation for the establishment of the HPC and the NMC the provision to provide financial grants to pay for the initial capital and operating start-up costs of the two new regulators. However, government will also need to provide financial support to cover the operating expenses of the regulator from the point the register is opened until financial breakeven is achieved.

Lastly, it should be pointed out that in the UK regulators have the power to borrow money. In theory this means regulators could fund the costs of establishment up to a breakeven point. However, this type of funding arrangement has never been used.

CONCLUSION

The process to establish a regulator uses a number of well-defined processes. This means that the project should be relatively low risk, provided that government provides adequate financial resources to complete the process at the point the regulator generates enough income to cover its annual costs.

EXERCISE AND QUESTION

Exercise

- Estimate how much it would cost to establish a new regulator up to the point that it is covering all of its costs from fees from registrants.

Question

- Should government loan the capital cost of establishing a new regulator and expect it to be repaid in due course?

FURTHER READING

Making of a Multi-professional Regulator: The HCP Council 2001–2015 R
Research Report
Anna Van de gaag
2015
64 pages

Regulation of Health Professions: Report of a Review of the Professions Supplementary to Medicine Act (1960) with recommendations for new legislation R
J. M. Consulting Ltd, Bristol, England
Department of Health, England
April 1996
100 pages

STANDARDS, CODES, GUIDANCE, CONSULTATIONS, POLICIES, AND PRACTICE NOTES

Consultations

Establishing the New Health Professions Council C
Report on the statutory consultation
NHS Executive
Department of Health
Ref: TBC
February 2002
999 pages

Establishing the New Nursing and Midwifery Council C
Report on consultation
NHS Executive
Department of Health
Ref: 24717 1P
1 August 2000
21 pages

The Future; A Paper for Consultation C
Health Professions Council
July 2002
140 pages

Key Decisions: HPC Consultation 2002 C
Health Professions Council
November 2002
15 pages

Modernising Regulation: The New Health Professions Council C
A Consultation Document
NHS Executive
Department of Health
Ref: 24717 1P
1 August 2000
52 pages

Modernising Regulation in the Health Professions C
Consultation Document
Department of Health
Ref: 24717 1P
August 2001
15 pages

Modernising Regulation: The new Nursing and Midwifery Council C
A Consultation Document
NHS Executive
Department of Health
Ref: 24717 1P
1 August 2000
76 pages

Your Responses C
HPC consultation 2002
Health Professions Council
July 2002
40 pages

1.8 ABOLISHING REGULATORS AND TRANSFERRING REGISTERS

INTRODUCTION

On occasions statutory regulators of professionals are no longer required or fail to deliver their intended regulatory policy objectives and as a result are abolished. Their register is then either discontinued or transferred to another regulator. In addition, voluntary registers are transferred from professional associations to statutory regulators. What causes these types of regulatory reorganisations, how is the process managed, and what are the advantages and disadvantages of the alternative ways to continue to maintain the registers?

PROCESS TRIGGERING THE ABOLITION OF REGULATORS OF PROFESSIONALS

From time to time regulators of professionals are abolished. The process can be triggered by a number of different events, including:

1. The profession no longer exists
2. Regulation is no longer justified
3. Sunset review is implemented; see Section 8.4, volume 1
4. The incumbent regulator fails to deliver its intended policy objectives and it can't redress its problems and be turned around
5. Political policy to reduce regulation in general and the adoption of a 'one in, two out' policy in terms of the number of regulators

ABOLITION PROCESS

The abolition process then has four different routes:

1. The register is closed and the regulator is abolished unless it is a multi-professional regulator and remains in operation
2. The profession continues to exist, but their register is transferred to an existing statutory regulator. The incumbent regulator is then abolished
3. The profession continues to exist, but register is transferred from an independent regulator to a department of government. The incumbent regulator is then abolished
4. The profession continues to exist, but their register is transferred to a newly established regulator. If the incumbent regulator is a multi-professional regulator, it remains in operation

Examples of these four abolition processes are now explored. It should be noted that some of the following examples are drawn from non-healthcare professions.

1. **The profession no longer exists**
As the healthcare delivery system evolves a point can be reached where there is no longer any demand for a particular profession. An example in the UK concerned the remedial gymnasts.

Remedial gymnasts
In the UK the healthcare profession of remedial gymnasts had a scope of practice closely aligned to physiotherapists. Although they are still in existence in a few countries, such as Hungary, in the UK the profession's scope of practice gradually changed to the point that it was indistinguishable from physiotherapy. Regulated by the CPSM in 1967, in 1986 the register was closed and the 233 registrants were subsumed into the physiotherapy register as physiotherapists. In September 1989 the Society of Remedial Gymnastics and Recreational Therapy merged with the Chartered Society of Physiotherapists (CSP).

The relevant legislation was the Professions Supplementary to Medicine (Winding up of Remedial Gymnasts Board) Order of Council 1 April 1986 SI No 630.

2. **The profession continues to exist but their regulation is transferred to an existing regulator. The incumbent regulator is then abolished.**
Examples of this type of process include:

Hearing aid dispensers
In the UK hearing aid dispensers sell hearing aids directly to patients and were regulated under the Hearing Aid Council Act 1968. In contrast audiologists, who work in the NHS, also provide hearing aids but are not regulated since the hearing aids are not sold to the patient.

In March 2010 the UK statutory regulator for hearing aid dispensers, the Hearing Aid Council, was abolished under the Health and Social Care Act 2008, sections 123 (1) and (2). The register was then transferred to the then Health Professions Council (HPC) on 15 July 2008, when the Health Professions (Hearing Aid Dispensers) Order 2010 SI 233 came into effect.

The process was instigated by a shift in the UK Government's policy to reduce regulation and the Hampton Review that recommended a wholesale change to regulation and regulators.

Social workers in england
Following a review by the PSA in September 2009 which made recommendations including the need for self-financing, in August 2012 the General Social Care Council(GSCC) who was the statutory regulator for Social Workers in England was abolished. The register was transferred to the HCPC. The relevant legislation was the General Social Care Council (Transfer of Register and Abolition – Transitional and Saving Provision) Order of Council 2012 18 June 2012 Statutory Instrument 2012 No. 1480.

In both examples, the Hearing Aid Council and the GSCC, who were the original regulators, were abolished once the register had been transferred.

3. **The profession continues to exist but regulation is transferred from an independent regulator to a department of government. The incumbent regulator is then abolished.**
The cause of these rare occurrences is the failure of the regulatory contract; see Section 7.2, volume 1, and in particular those relating to the obligation of professionals to society. Often the situation is exaggerated because the structures for regulating the profession are inappropriate; see Section 1.1.

Teachers in british columbia
An example of the abolition of a regulator of a profession occurred in Canada when the British Columbia College of Teachers was closed on 9 January 2012 when chapter 449 Teaching Professions Act 1996 was introduced and its functions transferred to the Teacher Regulation Branch of the BC Ministry of Education. The decision was on the grounds that the college failed to work in the public interest and was dysfunctional.

Teachers in england
A similar process occurred in the UK with the General Teaching Council which was established by the Teaching and Higher Education Act 1998 to regulate teachers in England. In 2009 it was abolished by amending the Educating Act 1996 with Education Act 2011 which created the Teaching Regulation Agency, an organisation embedded in the Department of Education.

4. **The profession continues to exist but their regulation is transferred to a newly established regulator. The incumbent regulator is then either abolished or, alternatively, if it is a multi-professional regulator and remains in operation**
There are a number of examples of this type of process. They include:

Healthcare professionals in australia
On 1 July 2010 over 90 separate regulatory organisations were replaced by the Australian Health Practitioner Regulation Agency (AHPRA); see Section 12.3, volume 3, the eight States and Territories having adopted identical legalisation across the different jurisdictions. This meant that a single organisation could administer the regulation of healthcare professionals across numerous jurisdictions.

Social workers in england
The statutory regulator of social workers in England has passed through a number of phases. The idea of regulating the profession, then called Almoners, by the late 1950s was rejected and they were not regulated by the CPSM. In 2000 they were brought into regulation but not by an independent statutory regulator but by an arm's length body, the General Social Care Council GSCC. This was abolished in 2009 and the HCPC became responsible for their regulation. In 2018 a new statutory regulator, Social Work England, was established for the social workers in England and the register transferred from the HCPC. The HCPC continued as a multi-professional regulator of 15 professions.

The cause of this process is complex. The profession, their education and training, and their regulation have, in England, been challenging and complex. For those readers interested in the regulation of social workers in England a range of government reports are provided in Section 13.3, volume 3.

Pharmacists in Great Britain
A similar process occurred with the Royal Pharmaceutical Society of Great Britain. Founded in 1841, it is the professional association of pharmacists and pharmacy technicians. Until September 2010 it was also the statutory regulator when the regulatory role was transferred to the newly created General Pharmaceutical Council GPhC.

PROCESS TO TRANSFER REGULATORY RESPONSIBILITY BETWEEN REGULATORS

It is often thought that the process to transfer regulatory responsibility between regulators is the same as a merger of acquisition that takes place between two commercial organisations. However, in the UK, this is not the case.

The UK process, to transfer regulatory responsibility between regulators, is markedly different from either a merger or an acquisition undertaken by a commercial organisation. The process is initiated by government and is referred to as a reorganisation of a public authority. It has three central characteristics:

1. The cost is funded by government not the regulators
2. Employee protection rights are limited
3. No assets or liabilities are transferred between the regulators

1. **Costs of funding the process**
Abolishing regulators or transferring registers between regulators requires financial resources. They are required for:
   - Asset disposal
   - Financial liabilities
   - HR costs, including financial compensated for loss of employment
   - ITC
   - Legal advice
   - Underfunded pension liabilities

Since these one-time transaction costs are a result of changes to government policy, it is usually assumed that government and the tax payer are responsible for all the costs of the process and not the remaining regulator and their registrants. In support of this principle, in the eventuality that there is a financial surplus remaining at the end of the process, it goes to the government.

2. **Employees and employment protection**
If two organisations join together and they operate in similar sectors it is likely that after the process has been completed there will be excess employees. This will inevitably lead to the need to make employees redundant.

In the UK when organisations operating in the private sector merge or one is acquired by another, the legal rights of employee are protected by legislation commonly referred to as TUPE. TUPE refers to the Transfer of Undertakings (Protection of Employment) Regulations 2006 as amended by the Collective Redundancies and Transfer of Undertakings (Protection of Employment) (Amendment) Regulations 2014.

This means that when a commercial organisations takes over the operations of another the jobs of the employees in the acquired companies have limited protection. For example, if jobs are lost as a result of the transfer of operations, then employees from both organisations are allowed to compete for the remaining jobs.

However, in relation to mergers of government organisations such as public authorities, TUPE does not apply. Instead, in the UK a code and guidelines issued by government called Cabinet Office Statement of Practise (COSoP) are used to support employees when work is being transferred between departments within the civil service or across the wider public sector. In effect this limits employment protection to those individuals whose work is being transferred.

In relation to regulators of healthcare professionals, employment protection only covers those directly and exclusive involved in regulation and therefore only includes registration officers, FTP case managers, and junior policy officials. All other employees including the HR and finance functions and managers are considered to be out of scope and are not required to be transferred from one regulator to another.

This significantly reduces the challenges of integration to large groups of employees from two different organisations.

3. **Treatment of assets and liabilities**
In commercial transactions, if two organisations combine, then the ownership of assets and liabilities will normally transfer to the organisation making the acquisition. In the case of a merger, the new entity will own all the assets and liabilities. In both cases this will include assets such as employees, facilities, and software and liabilities such as borrowings and financial liabilities, including leases.

However, this does not apply to UK public authorities including regulators. This means that no financial or commercial assets or liabilities are transferred from the regulator that is being abolished to the remaining regulator. Once the keeper of the transferring register is abolished and closed, any remaining net assets or liabilities are transferred to the UK Government.

Transferring the register from professional association to regulator

The process to transfer a register from one statutory regulator to another compared to the process to transfer a voluntary register managed by a professional association to a statutory regulator, see Section 11.3, volume 3, is similar, but there is however one significant difference.

The difference is that when a register is transferred from a professional association to a regulator, the process of the professional association can be abandoned and the regulator then starts them afresh.

However, when the process that is used by the regulator with the register to be transferred is substituted by the process of the remaining regulator, the regulatory processes must continue seamlessly.

The relevant process includes:

- Incomplete applications to join the register
- Approval of education and training programmes
- Investigation of concerns raised about registrants

To achieve as seamless as possible a transfer of the regulatory functions, the principle used is to either keep the process of the regulator whose register will transfer operating as long as they can complete the process by the day of the register transfer. Alternatively, when this can't be achieved, the process is stopped some time before the day of the register transfer. The process is then reinstated on the day of the transfer but using the new regulator's process.

The process now passes through three stages:

i. Data transfer

ii. Adjustments to operational processes of the remaining regulator

iii. Wind down and abolition of the surplus regulator

During the process a principle is now applied. This is that once the new register is opened the new regulator uses the principles and processes of its legislation. It does not take account of the now-defunct legislation of the previous regulator.

i. Data transfer
During this stage highly confidential data will be transferred between the regulator whose register will transfer and the remaining or newly established regulator. The type of data may concern information about FTP process, the

registration process and the process to approve programmes of education and training. Working within the terms of the Data Protection Act 2018, see Section 4.5, volume 4, a Data Sharing Agreement (DSA) between the regulators and a Data Transfer Scheme between the government and regulator are therefore drafted and agreed.

Other processess include:

Fitness to practise
All unresolved concerns are handed over to the new regulator on the day the register is transferred in the form of 'open case files'.

The regulator transferring the open cases may choose to allocate additional resources, sometimes with grant monies from government, with the objective of expediting the conclusion as many cases as possible before the transfer date.

The receiving regulator may be given access to the case files before the transfer date under a strict confidentiality and data protection protocols. This usually only covers a short period of two to three months before the transfer and enables the FTP department of the receiving regulator to become familiar with cases.

Conditions of practice
A number of professionals who transfer to the new regulator will, as a result of an FTP process of the previous regulator, probably have had conditions of practice imposed on them. The receiving regulator will have to review any existing conditions of practice to ensure that they are recorded in the new register.

Protection of title and/or protection of function cases
Case files relating to protection of title and/or function will be transferred and continued by the receiving regulator.

Appeals
All ongoing appeals will become the responsibility of the receiving regulator.

Struck-off professionals
The receiving regulator will require the names and contact details of any individual who has been struck off the register of the old regulator so that if they apply to join the register their application will be properly scrutinised by the new regulator.

Initial registration applications
Initial registration applications are processed by the regulator whose register will transfer until two to three days before the register is transferred. The timetable should be linked to the average time it takes to process an application.

All applications are then processed by the receiving regulator.

International applications
The regulator whose register will transfer stops accepting new international applications that can't be accessed before the register is transferred. This occurs a few weeks before the register is transferred. The applications are returned to the applicant with an explanation of the situation. All open applications will be transferred to the new regulator the day the register is transferred and will be dealt with using the principles and processes of the new regulator.

Other processes
Other processes including continuing competence, education, and training programme approval renewal of registration, return to practise are stopped by the regulator whose register will transfer and will be replaced by the processes of the existing or newly established remaining regulator.

ii. **Adjustments to operational processes of the remaining regulator**
There is limited adjustment to operational process:

- Capacity of the receiving regulation will have to be adjusted to reflect increased demands for its services
- Transferring employees will be inducted into the regulator
- Communication resources will increase before and after the transfer
- Governance arrangements of the receiving regulator may need to adjusted to incorporate the transferring profession
- There is no grandparenting process since the professional title is already protected by the regulator whose register will transfer.

iii. **Wind down and abolition of surplus regulator**
The third and final stage occurs if there is a surplus regulator to be abolished. It commences once the register has been transferred. Although the to-be-abolished regulator no longer has a register it will need to remain in existence for a period of a few months while it winds itself down. This requires:

- Archiving of historical documents and records
- Disposal of assets
- Funding of outstanding liabilities such as pension funds and commercial leases
- Making employees redundant
- Publication of final set of accounts

The surplus regulator is then abolished and any remaining assets transferred to the government.

TRANSFER AGREEMENT

Lastly, a formal legally binding agreement that details the process is agreed between the regulators and sometimes the government department concerned.

AMALGAMATION OF REGULATORS

It should be noted that in addition to abolishing regulators and transferring register, the Canadian province of British Columbia has legislated for regulators to amalgamate. This in effect abolishes the former regulatory colleges, transferring all their assets, liabilities, and processes into a new organisation.

In 2024, in Nova Scotia, the currently separate colleges of nursing and midwifery colleges are considering amalgamation.

COMBINING VS. ESTABLISHING NEW REGULATORS

As previously stated, when an existing regulator fails to deliver its intended regulatory policy objectives it can't redress its problems and be turned around and government intends to continue the regulation of the profession as two distinct choices.

1. It can either transfer the regulatory responsibilities to a newly established regulator
2. Or alternatively, the regulatory responsibility is transferred to an existing regulator thus establishing, or increasing in size, a multi-professional regulator

PROPONENTS OF MULTI-PROFESSIONAL REGULATION

The proponents of separate regulators for each profession will focus their arguments by reference to the disadvantages of multi-professional regulators; see Section 1.1, volume 4.

Suffice to say that transferring a register to an established multi-professional regulator leads to immediate benefits. These include:

- Can charge the same registration fee whatever the size of the transferred register
- Experience of working with different professions with varying practitioner numbers
- Minimal changes to existing governance arrangements
- Minimal changes to existing shared regulatory standards and processes
- Possible experience of supporting professional association post-transfer of register

In addition, if the organisation, and particularly its senior and middle management, has undertaken similar projects in the recent past it will have gained and retained experience. The proven ability to deliver similar projects on time and within budget should correlate with a lower risk of failure.

DISTRACTORS OF MULTI-PROFESSIONAL REGULATION

The proponents of having a separate regulator for each healthcare profession in every single jurisdiction put forward a number of arguments to support their views. They include:

Pluralism

There is a strong argument that society benefits by having many institutions. For example:

- Civil society can defend itself from the tyranny of dominance of a single individual or political party
- A greater number of organisations with members of the public participating in the governance of those organisations will strengthen and embed the link between the process of government and those governed

This argument is called pluralism and can be defined as:

Definition: Pluralism
Theory that society benefits from having numerous public institutions.

Supporters of pluralism argue that reducing the number of public institutions, reduces democracy, since members of the public will have less influence on the few, large, and powerful organisations.

Too Big to Fail Risk

The consequence of a multi-professional regulator failing will be much greater compared to one of a number of regulators. Placing regulatory responsibilities in fewer organisations should therefore be rejected.

Institutional Self-interest

However, the argument put forward by distractors should be taken in the context of institutional self-interest. This is because if two regulators are combined, then the total number of board members and employees is likely to be considerably less after the project is completed. The individuals concerned, who are more likely to lose their jobs and positions, are rationally going to be against the processes. A proposal to reduce the number of regulators by combining them will often be resisted by the boards and employees of the institutions who will disappear.

Rewards and Risks of Combining Organisations

There are both risks and rewards associated with the combination of organisations. The potential rewards include operational benefits such as technology transfers, larger production facilities, and more customers. There are also potential financial benefits such as lower central costs and increased margins. In the commercial world the benefits should lead to, but often don't, enhanced financial returns for the owners or shareholders.

However, unlike the combination of commercial companies, the concept of shareholder benefit, both in terms of the selling shareholders and the acquiring shareholders, plays no part when considering the potential success of the reorganisation of government enteritis.

This makes the projects to combine regulators in comparison to commercial transactions inherently less risky. Despite this, the distractors of proposals to increase multi-professional regulation often focus on arguments more associated with the risks of commercial transactions. So what are the risks associated with combining organisations and regulator in particular?

Risks Arising from Combining Organisations

The risks that the successful combination of two organisations will fail are often associated with ten factors; they include:

1. Combinations of organisations from different sectors
2. Cross border transactions
3. Cultural Integration
4. Loss of customers
5. Post-merger operational integration
6. Correct assessment of the wellbeing of merging operations
7. Financial distress or turnaround situations
8. Preplanning period
9. Relative size differences
10. Valuation

1. **Combinations of organisations from different sectors**
   Combining organisations that operate in significantly different sectors increases the probability that the processes will fail, both in terms of anticipated operational and financial benefits. The history of failed industrial merges is well endowed with examples including British Aerospace and British Leyland Cars, Chrysler and Mercedes Benz, and media and ICT.
   However, in relation to the combination of two regulators of healthcare professionals this risk does not arise since they both operate on the same sector and will have probably have the same eight regulatory processes; see Section 3.1, volume 1.

2. **Cross border transactions**
   The merger of two commercial companies operating in different jurisdictions increases the risk of post-merger failure compared to one within the same country or jurisdiction. The causes of this risk are numerous but include legal, cultural, and language issues.
   Clearly, these issues do not arise when two regulators of healthcare professionals based in the same jurisdiction are combined.

3. **Cultural integration**
   Two organisations considering combining will often have markedly different and incompatible cultures. The process to integrate different cultures can be challenging and is often cited as a reason that mergers do not work or take considerably longer to successfully integrate than originally envisaged. Indeed, this can be exacerbated when organisations attempt to combine across countries and jurisdictions
   If the merger involves a limited transfer of employees then cultural clashes between different groups are less likely to arise in comparison with mergers when large numbers of employees from both organisations transfer into the combined operations.
   In the UK, because only employees relating to a small minority of functions transfer from the regulator transferring its register, the impact on the culture to the receiving regulator will be minimal.

4. **Loss of customers**
   When commercial operations are combined there is a possibility that some existing customers of either organisation will not be enamoured with the newly combined operations and will seek the provision of goods or services from other sources. This may result in a loss of customers who decide to take their business to rival companies.
   Regulators are monopolies and therefore registrants can't move to another regulator; thus, this type of risk does not arise.

5. **Post-merger operational integration**
   The history of integrating recently merged business is littered with numerous examples of failed projects. This is particularly true when the merging organisations have differing customers and suppliers and make use of different technology. This type of risk appears to be present when two regulators of healthcare professionals are merged. However, the process focuses on the transfer of databases and FTP cases. There is therefore no requirement to integrate IT systems and financial system, or operational processes such as registrations or FTP. In essence whole areas of post-merger operational integration complexity are avoided and the risks are relatively low.

6. **Correct assessment of the wellbeing of merging operations**
   When organisations merge there is a risk that the pre-merger assessment of the wellbeing of either party will

be incorrect and the true state of affairs will only come to light once the transaction has been completed. This risk applies to both commercial and government projects. To some extent this risk can be mitigated by due diligence and audit before the merger goes ahead.

However, in the case of regulators of healthcare professionals that are public authorities, it is more likely that the operational and financial states of both organisations is well understood by all relevant stakeholders.

7. **Financial distress or turnaround situations**
If one or both of the merging operations is in a poor financial state or is facing operational problems that are in need of a turnaround the chances of the failure of the merger are increased. This applies to commercial and non-commercial mergers.
However, in the case of two regulators of healthcare professionals only the databases and FTP cases are transferred and in effect all financial challenges remain with the regulator whose register is transferred. And if as a result they have no register they will be abolished in due course.

8. **Preplanning period**
When two organisations join together the more preparation that can be undertaken on issues such as post-merger integration before the merger takes effect, the greater the changes of its success whether the transaction is commercial or within a governmental organisation.
One advantage that arises in government-instigated reorganisations is that often legislation is required to facilitate the process, and the time taken for the legalisation to be approved by the legislature can be used to plan the merger.

9. **Relative size differences**
When organisations join together the relative size of the organisations to one another has an impact on the likelihood of the success of the project. Small organisations taking over larger organisation than themselves, or two organisations of equivalent size merging can sometimes throw up risks.
However, large organisations, including regulators, when they take over smaller regulators, are relatively less risky projects.

10. **Valuation**
In a commercial transaction, such as mergers and acquisitions, there is a risk that either the buyer will overvalue the price paid or the seller will sell the business too cheaply.
In combining two regulators of healthcare professionals the process is transacted between two government-controlled entities and there is no 'seller' and no 'buyer', and therefore the risks associated with an incorrect valuation do not arise.

THE REASON WHY REGULATORS ARE NOT COMBINED

In efficient commercial market rivalry and competition lead to consolidation and a reduction of competing entities. Although the market for regulators of healthcare professionals is clearly not a commercial one, given the numerous benefits that arise from the combination of regulators to members of the public, the taxpayer and individual professionals, given time, one would expect a reduction in the number of regulators

What are the reasons that multi-professional regulators are absent from many jurisdictions?

- Firstly, since regulators are not commercial companies with shareholders, the market alone is unable to achieve this end
- Secondly, those stakeholders who may directly benefit from the combination of regulatory institutions, struggle to get their voices heard
- Thirdly, the public or taxpayer is not in a position where they can see the cost benefit advantages or indeed measure the outcome of adopting multi-professional regulation
- Fourthly, there are strong interests that operate to prevent combinations and those who advocate for them tend to be a minority

Coercion is therefore required by external agencies and in particular government therefore must take the lead.

FUTURE PROOFING

Before concluding this section it is interesting to note that some jurisdictions are future proofing their existing legislation by making provisions to facilitate abolishing or merging regulators without recourse to seek further approval from the legislature.

CONCLUSION

The transfer of a register to a new or existing statutory regulator is a relatively straightforward and low-risk endeavour. However, the project requires careful planning and good communication with all stakeholders.

EXERCISE AND QUESTION

Exercise

- If two regulators want to combine, should the cost be funded by government?

Question

- Should the number of regulators in a jurisdiction that you are familiar with be reduced?

LEGISLATION

Example of UK Legislation

Collective Redundancies and Transfer of Undertakings (Protection of Employment) (Amendment) Regulations 2014 L

Data Protection Act 2018 L

Education Act 1996 and 2011 L

The General Social Care Council (Transfer of Register and Abolition – Transitional and Saving Provision) Order of Council 2012 18 June 2012 Statutory Instrument 2012 No. 1480 L

Hearing Aid Council Act 1968 (Repealed) L

Health and Social Care Act 2008 L

The Health Professions (Hearing Aid Dispensers) Order 2010 SI 233 L

Professions Supplementary to Medicine (Winding up of Remedial Gymnasts Board) L
Order of Council 1 April 1986 SI No 630
ISBN: 0110666305

Teaching and Higher Education Act 1998 L

Transfer of Undertakings (Protection of Employment) Regulations 2006 L

Example of International Legislation

Canada

British Columbia
Teaching Professions Act SO 1996, Chapter 449 L

FURTHER READING

Abolition of Hearing Aid Council and transfer of responsibilities to Health Professions Council R
Impact Assessment
Department of Health
9 pages
12 October 2009

Advice to the Department of Health and the Pharmacy Regulation and Leadership Oversight Group on Aspects of the Establishment of the General Pharmaceutical Council R
CHRE
November 2008
31 pages

The creation of Ofcom: Wider Lessons for Public Sector Mergers of Regulatory Agencies R
National Audit Office (NAO)
Report by the Comptroller and Auditor General
HC 1175 Session 2005–2006
5 July 2006
45 pages

A College Divided R
Report of the Fact Finder on the BC College of Teachers
Donald J Avison
October 2010
34 pages

Getting more for less from public bodies: 10 key lessons from the abolition of the Hearing Aid Council R
Annual Report 2009–2010
HC 322 2010-11
ISBN: 9780102962048
Published by The Stationery Office (TSO) www.tsoshop.co.uk
29 July 2010
76 pages

Liberating the NHS R
Report of the arm's-length bodies review
Department of Health
Gateway Reference 14482
26 July 2010
46 pages

Principles of Good Employment Practice R
Cabinet Office, (UK)
13 December 2010
4 pages

Report of the Independent Inquiry into a Professional Body for Pharmacy R
The Clarke Inquiry
Commissioned by the Royal Pharmaceutical Society of Great Britain
April 2008

Report of the Working Party on Professional Regulation and Leadership in Pharmacy R
Chair, Lord Patrick Carter of Coles
Department of Health
Stationary Office
May 2007

Supporting a strong and sustainable Ontario College of Trades R
Minister of Training, Colleges and Universities
Tony Dean
20 November 2015

STANDARDS, CODES, GUIDANCE, CONSULTATIONS, POLICIES, AND PRACTICE NOTES

Guidance

Short Guide to Reorganising Arm's Length Bodies G
National Audit Office
DP Ref: 009522-001
21 December 2010
12 pages

Staff Transfer in the Public Sector G
Cabinet Office Statement of Practice (COSoP)
Cabinet Office
January 2000, revised December 2013
10 pages

Consultation

The Regulation of Private Hearing aid Dispensers by the HPC C
A paper for consultation
Department of Health
Gateway Ref: 11553
April 2009
17 pages

The Health Professions (Hearing Aid Dispensers) Order 2009 C
Consultation Report: September 2009
Gateway Reference; 12495
22 October 2009
19 pages

Communication

CHAPTER 2

INTRODUCTION

Regulators rely on effective and efficient processes to receive and transmit communications to and from their stakeholders. In turn the stakeholders must be aware of the regulators' roles and responsibilities and know how to communicate with them. To do this, regulators use a range of processes including publishing, consultations, and face-to-face meetings, which, if well managed, can maintain and enhance their reputation.

The chapter has five sections:

2.1 Communication

2.2 Communication channels and techniques

2.3 Consultation

2.4 Promoting professions and professionals

2.5 Reputation management

2.1 COMMUNICATION

INTRODUCTION

Regulators to be effective and efficient must establish in the minds of their stakeholders, firstly, an awareness of their objectives, principles, and processes and, secondly, how to communicate with the regulator. However, stakeholders' awareness levels and understanding of regulation vary considerably. Therefore, regulators must be cognisant of these differences before developing and using processes to communicate bidirectionally with their stakeholders.

THE COMMUNICATION CHALLENGE

To work effectively and efficiently many of the principles and processes described in the preceding chapters are dependent on stakeholders' understanding and being aware of the role and responsibilities used to regulate professionals and, if the situation requires, how to communicate with the regulator. In an ideal world all stakeholders would be equally knowledgeable about the roles and responsibilities of regulators and how and when to communicate with them. However, a regulator should obviously not assume that this is the case. While it is reasonable to assume that some stakeholders will have an in-depth understanding and awareness of regulation and regulators, for example, the head of a UK university education and training programme for healthcare professionals, others such as members of the public will be at the other end of the understanding spectrum. They may not even be aware of the existence of a particular regulator of a healthcare profession in a specific jurisdiction and will not know when or how to make contact, let alone what its roles and responsibilities are.

How can regulators approach this challenge?

STAKEHOLDERS' PERSPECTIVE

It is imperative that regulators develop insight into the awareness, concerns, expectations, and understanding of regulation and regulators of their stakeholders from their perspective. This is because a competent regulator, rather than assuming that they are intuitively insightful about their stakeholders, should actively seek out their perspective. This can be achieved by using techniques such as stakeholder mapping; see Section 3.3, volume 1. Also, in analysing their stakeholders, their interests and concerns should be identified as illustrated in Table 3.2 – II, volume 1, Stakeholder subgroups in the regulation of healthcare professionals.

Once the analysis of shareholders' perspective has been completed it should identify that their relative level of awareness of the regulators' principles and process will fall into two broad groups. For the purposes of the following discussion the two broad groups of stakeholders will be referred to as 'knowledgeable' stakeholders and 'seeker' stakeholders.

'KNOWLEDGEABLE' STAKEHOLDERS

The first group of stakeholders can be assumed to have a well-developed understanding of the roles and responsibilities of the regulator. In general they will frequent engage with the regulator during their day-to-day work.

Operations of Regulators of Healthcare Professionals, Volume 4, First Edition. Marc Seale.

Companion website: www.wiley.com/go/seale/regulatinghealthcare

'SEEKER' STAKEHOLDERS

The second group of stakeholders can be assumed to have none or a very limited understanding of the roles and responsibilities of the regulator. In general, they have never needed to contact the regulator.

Examples of stakeholders from the two groups will now be explored in greater detail.

1. **Organisations**
   It can be assumed that most organisations and their employees that have to engage regularly with the regulator will have the resources and experience to do so with little difficulty. For example, civil servants working in a government department overseeing regulators can be assumed to be one of the most knowledgeable of the regulator's stakeholders. Others, such as the managers of HEI programme providers, will be in regular communication with the regulator, for example, confirming the awards of qualifications to their graduating students. However, some organisations, such as the HR departments of hospitals, will often be less informed.

   In general, most organisations like the ones described above can be considered to be knowledgeable stakeholders. They will understand the principles and processes of the regulator, will be aware of the regulator, and have well-established communications channels with them.

   In turn regulators should be able to develop insight into their awareness, concerns, expectations, and understanding of regulations and regulators.

2. **Members of the public**
   The members of the public present a unique set of communicating challenges to the regulator of healthcare professionals.

   In general from their awareness, concerns, expectations, and understanding of regulation and regulators they can be assumed to:

   - Expect all healthcare professionals and occupations to be regulated
   - Generally aware of some of the broad principles relating to ethical healthcare and the regulation of healthcare professionals, such as confidentially and treating patients with respect and dignity
   - Have a high level of expectation of the competences that professionals have and display
   - Hold healthcare professionals in high esteem
   - Possibly unclear on how and when to contact a regulator
   - Probably unaware of which regulator to contact

   However, since very few professionals transgress the standards of the regulator that can lead to concerns being raised about them, the vast majority of members of the public throughout their lives will never need to raise a concern about a healthcare professional with their regulator. And this is compounded by the number of concerns as a percentage of discrete treatment episodes, as discussed in Section 4.7, volume 3.

   Regulators should therefore assume that the public will have a low awareness level of their roles and responsibilities and will not necessarily know how to communicate with them.

   So what does a member of the public do if they perceive that the conduct or behaviour of a healthcare professional is inappropriate or that the treatment they received from a healthcare professional was significantly below the standard that they had expected? To take action they will need to know:

   - Wherever or not their concern is justified
   - Which organisation they should contact
   - How to bring their concerns to the attention of the regulator
   - What action may be taken as a result of their concern or complaint

   In effect, they are likely to be seeking access to information or to discuss their concerns with helpful and approachable advisers within the regulator, so that they can make an informed decision on how they wish to proceed.

'DRILLER' STAKEHOLDERS

There are however some stakeholders who fall between the two broad groups of 'knowledgeable' and 'seeker' stakeholders. These are predominantly individuals who have some knowledge about the roles and responsibilities of regulators but required very detailed information relating to the principles and processes of regulators and regulations.

For example, it should not be assumed that because professionalism and regulation are so intertwined with one another, that all individual healthcare professionals possess detailed knowledgeable about all aspects of the processes of the regulator.

As a consequence some stakeholders such as regulated professionals, prospective professionals, and emigrating and immigrating professionals will seek clarification on issues such as the renewal of registration or the continuing competence processes. These stakeholders who are in effect drilling down into the detailed operational matters of regulating will require the regulator to communicate with them in a different way.

Once a regulator has established an understanding of their stakeholder's perspective, they should be cognisant of three other issues. They are:

1. Resources required to achieve brand recognition
2. Legislative requirement to communicate
3. Resource allocation to regulators' communication budgets

1. **Resources required to achieve brand recognition**
Large multinational commercial organisations that produce products and services on a global scale such as Apple, BMW, Coca Cola, Google, and Rolex share one thing in common. That is throughout the world many members of the public are aware of their existence of their products, services, and brands. To achieve high levels of brand recognition organisations and commercial business in particular must firstly produce and distribute goods and services that are desirable by consumers. They then need to support this process by investing significant ongoing resources in communication over many decades to build and then maintain the level of recognition. However, other types of organisation such as belief systems, museums, nation healthcare delivery systems, and universities have also established high levels of brand recognition. This is not the place to discuss the merits of this type of investment which is more a phenomenon of financially affluent economies that consume vast quantities of goods or services. What however is important and gleanable from the examples is that significant amounts of time and resources are required to establish high levels of brand recognition.

2. **Legislative requirement to communicate**
As discussed in Section 3.1, volume 1, the process of communication is somewhat different than the eight processes used in the regulatory framework in that there are no standards directly associated with it. Despite this, communication remains critical to the regulation of professionals. To emphasise this, a number of regulators of healthcare professions have legislation that specifically require regulators to communicate.
For example, the Health Professions Order 2001 states:
(13) The Council shall inform and educate registrants, and shall inform the public, about its work.

3. **Resource allocation to regulators' communication budget**
Regulators when consideration the amount of resource to allocate towards their annual communications budgets should take into the following challenges:
   - Regulators' status as public authorities
   - High level of disquiet if public authorities spend monies on what can be considered to be overt advertising or marketing
   - Regulators' overall budgets mean that they have scare resources to allocate to communications
   - Communication budgets should target members of the public and the regulated professionals
   - Imperative that members of the public who need to contact a regulator can do so rapidly
   - Members of the public have a low level of understanding of regulation and recognition of regulators
   - Significant majority of members of the public will never in their lifetimes need to make contact with a regulator of healthcare professionals
   - Regulators' fees can be considered by some professionals to be a tax

UK regulators of healthcare professionals do address the challenges outlined above by allocating resources to communication. The following Table 2.1 – I, lists 2022/23 communication budgets of two UK regulators of healthcare professionals by annual income and the number of regulated professionals:

Table 2.1 – I Communication budgets of UK regulators of healthcare professionals

Regulator	Annual income	Communications budget	No. of professionals regulated
GMC	£150m	£1.7m	378k
NMC	£103m	£2.9m	789k

Source: Annual report & Accounts FY 2022/2023.

Given that in 2024 the population of the UK was approximately 69 million, it is therefore relatively straightforward to deduce that regulators have minuscule communication budgets in terms of annual financial resources per head of the adult population. The above example approximates to four pence per person, per regulator, per year.

CONCLUSION

Regulators of healthcare professions must ensure that all their stakeholders are aware of their roles and responsibilities and know how to communicate with them. In particular this applies to the small number of members of the public and organisations who have concerns about healthcare professionals and should be able to bring them to the attention of the regulator. Regulators should therefore assume that every single one of their stakeholders may at some point in the future seek to communicate with them to gain access to their knowledge library. To facilitate this process they should aim to ensure that their communication channels are easily accessible, straightforward to use, and freely available via spoken, physical, or electronic means. To achieve this aim regulators using their limited resources must overcome low levels of public recognition by implementing a subsidiary communications strategy; otherwise, they will not deliver public protection. How these communication challenges can be overcome is addressed in the next section.

EXERCISES AND QUESTIONS

Exercises

- How does/should a regulator decide what their annual communication budget should be?
- What is an acceptable public level of awareness of a regulator of healthcare professionals?

Questions

- Identify jurisdictions where barbers, cash delivery drivers, farriers, florists, and interior designers are regulated.
- Who regulates the workers in the care homes in the area where you live?

LEGISLATION

Example of UK legislation

Health Professions Order 2001 No 254 L

2.2 COMMUNICATION CHANNELS AND TECHNIQUES

INTRODUCTION

The section starts by considering the importance of regulators' knowledge libraries and the use that can be made of them in their communication strategy. Regulators are spoilt for choice in terms of different communication channels that they can use to engage with their stakeholders. However, communication with different types of stakeholders must be adapted to reflect their level of knowledge of regulation. Consideration of a range of communication techniques should therefore be made before selecting which communication channels to use.

REGULATORS' KNOWLEDGE LIBRARY

Regulators possess a wealth of knowledge that may be of use to their stakeholders. This knowledge library is extensive and includes numerous types of data and information as listed in Table 2.2 – I, below:

Table 2.2 – I Knowledge library of regulators

- Annual report and accounts
- Consultations
- Board and committee meetings papers and minutes
- Databases
  - Continuing competence
  - Education and training
  - FTP
  - Register
- Governance arrangements
- Guidance
- Historical records
- Market research
- Policy and position papers
- Process documentation
- QA site inspection and accreditation reports
- Research reports
- Risk register
- Standards
- Thematic reviews and annual reports

VALUE OF KNOWLEDGE LIBRARY

As public authorities, regulators should make their knowledge libraries' freely accessible to their stakeholders, with the caveat that there is a need to maintain confidentiality in limited and defined areas. This leads to a regulatory principle:

Principle: Knowledge Library
The knowledge library of regulators should be freely accessible to stakeholders.

The knowledge library of regulators is important because it is the foundation of why and how communication takes place with their stakeholders.

COMMUNICATION STRATEGY

If the central theme of the subsidiary communications strategy of a regulator is to communicate the content of their knowledge library to all of their stakeholder on the lines of:

Anything, anywhere, anytime.

And as discussed in Section 3.1, volume 1, stakeholders and the public in particular must be aware of the existence of the processes used to regulate healthcare professionals. Since if the regulator and its register were unknown the regulatory process would be ineffective and inefficient. The communication must therefore be bidirectional since stakeholders must receive information from the regulator, 'outward distribution' communication. And stakeholders must also in turn be able to communicate with the regulator via 'Inward reception' communication.

KNOWLEDGEABLE STAKEHOLDERS AND SEEKER STAKEHOLDERS

Having established, see previous section, the expectations of both their knowledgeable stakeholders and seeker stakeholders, regulators must select the most appropriate communicate channels and communication techniques to use in relation to the two broad groups.

COMMUNICATION CHANNELS

To deliver their communications strategy the regulator must select and use or more of the numerous communication channels, available, as detailed in (Table 2.2 – II).

The challenge is to select the most appropriate channel(s) at the most appropriate quality/cost combination point and then to decide the optimum time to deploy.

Table 2.2 – II Commutation channels

- Advertising
- Broadcasting (TV and radio)
- Conferences and seminars
- Consultations
- E-communication
- Marketing material for professionals
- The media – local and national and specialist
- News letters
- Press releases
- Public meetings 'Outreach programmes'
- Print/publications
- Social media, the internet, and the World Wide Web
- Stakeholder engagement

However, although it should be the responsibility of the communications and public affairs department to do this, an exploration of the process to select which communication channel(s) to use is beyond the scope of the book.

COMMUNICATION TECHNIQUES

However, in parallel with the process to select the most appropriate communication channel(s) to use, a range of communication techniques should also be examined and in turn consider for future deployment. These include:

1. Communication campaigns
2. Conference and seminars
3. Fitness to practise
4. Public affairs, public relations, and lobbying
5. Market research
6. Consumer panels
7. Signposting
8. Thematic reviews and annual reports
9. Social media, the internet, and the World Wide Web
10. Face-to-face meetings

The 10 techniques will now be explored in greater detail:

1. **Communication campaigns**
   Regulators can and should manage communication campaigns to raise awareness, educate, and inform their stakeholders. The topics of communication campaigns vary but can include:

   Knowledgeable – stakeholders
   - Changes to process used by prospective or existing registrants
   - Consultations particular relating to policy formation or adaption
   - Introduction of new or revised standards or guidance
   - Publication of research papers and findings
   - Recruitment of board members
   - Timetable for renewing registration

   Seeker – stakeholders
   - Arrangements for public meetings organised by the regulator
   - Benefits of regulating healthcare professionals
   - Benefits of using a regulated healthcare professional
   - Business continuity process during disaster recovery processes
   - Checking the status of healthcare professionals on the register
   - Educating and informing the public on the role of regulator
   - Grandparenting arrangements
   - International registration process
   - Students and the role of regulation and the regulator
2. **Conferences and seminars**
   Regulators are likely to have the option of frequently participating in both national and international conferences and seminars where professionals attend. Whether online or in person, regulators need to judge the relevance of these types of events and if attending as either as speakers or members of the audience, what message if any, they are seeking to convey to other attendees.
3. **Fitness to practise**
   Communications relating to the regulator's FTP process are complex and specialised. In general the FTP and communications and public affairs departments should work together on all communications relating to FTP. The issue is explored in detail in Section 7.1, volume 3, Publication of tribunal information.
4. **Public affairs, public relations, and lobbying**
   Public relations, lobbying, and public affairs occupy a crowded and overlapping space, and regulators must be cognisant of the need to embrace or avoid them.

   While not everyone will necessarily agree with the wording, the following three definitions will be used:

Definition: Public Relations
Process to influence the link an individual may have with a business and its goods or service.

Definition: Lobbying
Act of attempting to lawfully influence the opinions and the decisions made by politicians and government officials.

Definition: Public Affairs
Process to engage with government to influence public policy and law making.

Public relations

It can be seen from the definitions used above that public relations is generally the focus of organisations operating in the world of commerce. It is more akin to persuasion and while it can be argued that regulators provide services to its registrants, it is not an activity that is expected of public authorities.

It can be argued that public relations is not for regulators, and in particular lobbying is an area that regulators should defiantly be avoid. Despite this point of view, as experts in their field regulators have a legitimate and normally welcomed role in assisting government set their policy by the use of public affairs within their overall subsidiary communication strategy.

Lobbying

The policies of government are logically of great interest to many organisations including public authorities. In the commercial and third sector the process for individuals or organisations to try and directly influence the policy of government and future changes to legalisation would be classified under the general heading of lobbying. This can be done by either direct contact with or government officials – civil servants in the UK and politicians. Lobbying can also be undertaken in relation to individual members of Parliament but in this situation is more focused on changing the opinions of individual MPs.

Lobbying is undertaken by many types of people and organisations including:

- Commercial business
- Consumer advocacy organisations
- Individual members of the public
- Organised groups
- Professional associations
- Specially interest groups
- Third sector, voluntary and charity
- Trade unions

In terms of actual activities, lobbying may embrace:

- Face-to-face meetings with politicians and their officials
- Direct letters and e-communication to politicians and their officials
- Submitting written briefing material
- Making presentations
- Mass rallies in or near parliaments

In the UK the process of lobbying, and the lobbyists who undertake the work, is generally seen by many in a poor or negative light. Because of its negative reputation there is growing pressure to control lobbyists, and regulation (ironically) is periodically threatened. Lobbyists may be required to register to reduce possible corruption and increase transparency.

Lastly, it should be noted that the UK has specific legislation to control lobbying, the Transparency of Lobbying, Non-party Campaigning and Trade Union Administration Act 2014.

Shaping government policy

Effective and efficient statutory regulation is dependent on good legislation. Good in the sense that it is up-to-date and facilitates the standards and processes of the building blocks of regulation. In the UK since the government is the main route to either introducing new legislation or amending existing legislation, should a regulator have a role in shaping the outcome of the process?

However, it can be argued that it is not appropriate for a regulator to lobby because it is not undertaken in a transparent way, is usually conducted behind closed doors, and has a poor reputation.

Role of regulators to influence government policy and legislation

The role of regulators to influence government policy and developing, enacting, amending, revising, and repealing legislation has therefore the potential to be controversial. There are arguments that support the participation of regulators in the process and those against.

Supporting arguments

- Regulators are, or should be, subject matter experts
- They will understand the views of stakeholders
- Practical experience of how to operationalise proposed new policy or legislation

Distractors

- Since regulators are public authorities they should not interfere in the process used by government and legislature
- It is not a legitimate use of the regulators' resources

Public affairs

On the assumption that regulators do have a legitimate and welcomed role in shaping the policy of government and regulation in particular but at the same time avoid lobbying, how should they go about this? Or to put it another way, what communication resources should they deploy to encourage government to deliver legislation that is fit for purpose?

The legitimate agenda of a regulator's public affairs can focus on a limited range of activities, namely:

- Actively engaging with civil servants, government, and politicians to build a close working relationship based on mutual trust and openness
- Building the evidence for the need for change, including research, in-depth of developments in other jurisdictions and publishing position papers on policy reviews
- Building workable, low-risk, and pragmatic solutions preferably aligned with the views of others
- Engaging with stakeholders to build awareness and support for change
- Advocating for change

The public affairs effort may be directed at both regional and national governments. In Europe, it may also include the European Union (EU) in Brussels. In some instances the process may be undertaken by associations or groups of likeminded organisations including regulators and their domestic and international associations. In the UK, the Alliance of UK Health Regulators on Europe (AURE) acts as a lobbying umbrella organisation for the nine regulators of healthcare professionals in their engagement with the EU particularly when the Directive on the recognition of professional qualifications was being modernised.

5. **Market research**
In the context of the regulation of healthcare professions market research can be defined as:

Definition: Market Research
Process to gather and analyse information about consumers' needs and preferences.

Market research can therefore be seen as a different technique compared to researching the evidence base for regulating healthcare professionals; see Section 9.3, volume 4. Market research can incorporate many different types of techniques including focus groups. The topics addressed by market research can include, for example, the perception of the public about regulation. If this method is used there are advantages if the work can be repeated on a regular basis so that trends can be identified and acted upon. Typically, a two-year cycle is adopted.

And, as with other types of communication services such as advertising, market research will usually be purchased from specialist providers.

6. **Consumer panels**
Market research can be seen as a project-driven solution to increasing the regulators' understanding of the public's expectations and perception of regulation and regulators. An alternative approach to the ephemeral ad hoc engagement with members of the public is to establish a semi-permanent independent group of people.

The brief of these types of so-called consumer panels is to embed the views of the public into the day-to-day policy and processes, or the 'consciousness', of the regulator and to advise the board and executive of the regulator accordingly. For the panel to be successful the regulator must engage in a meaningful manner and avoid the creation of a talking shop with limited outputs and actions.

Examples of these types of panels include:

Citizens Advisory Group Health Regulatory Colleges, Ontario, Canada

Community Reference Group of the Australian regulator AHPRA

Consumer Panel of the UK's regulator, the Financial Conduct Authority (FCA).

Consumer Panel of the UK's regulator, the Legal Services Board

In terms of governance arrangements, the consumer panels are independent of the board of the regulator, but in general their arrangements are similar to those of the committees of the regulator. Membership should turnover with staggered terms of appointment along similar lines to a board. However, establishing these types of panels is not without challenges. For example:

- Overtime, will the consumer panel lose its original independence and inevitably become absorbed into the workings of the regulator?
- Can the members still be considered to be members of the public once they have become members of the panel?
- Should the role be undertaken by the board of the regulator rather than a consumer panel?

7. **Signposting**
It is important that members of the public are informed about the role of the regulator and if required, how to make contact with them if need be. As a result some regulators will occasionally run communication campaigns targeted at the public. However, given the limited resources that regulators can direct to these types of tasks, it is doubtful if they are effective in reaching the majority of the public.

As an alternative, a signposting process can be used. The process facilitates other organisations or individuals if asked, to point the person making the inquiry in the direction of the correct regulator. This is based on the supposition that if a member of the public does not know if, whom, or how to approach a regulator, their first port of call may be to contact an individual or organisation that they believe may be able to assist them. These potentially informed advisers may include:

- Citizen's advice centres
- Consumer advocacy organisations
- Healthcare professionals
- Law enforcement agencies
- Local councillors
- Ombudsman
- Media
- Members of Parliament/legislature
- Profession associations
- Solicitors
- Trading standards

It is therefore desirable that regulators increase the awareness in these stakeholders of their role. It also has the benefit of being a cost-effective communication approach.

8. **Thematic reviews and annual reports**
Thematic reviews and annual reports on the performance of the regulators of healthcare professionals are an important component of the process to inform and communicate with stakeholders. Regulators on their own volition may publish a range of these types of reviews and reports relating to their regulatory processes, including continuing competence, education and training, and FTP.

The reviews and reports serve a number of purposes, including:

- Part of the regulators' accountability process
- Education of stakeholders by providing exemplars and learning points
- Demonstrating the regulator's performance, in particular their effectiveness and efficiency
- Historical record of achievements
- Provides data for research

One-off reports and thematic reviews
In addition to their regular reviews and reports, regulators may also publish reports and thematic reviews on one-off processes such as regulating a new healthcare profession and the related grandparenting process or abolishing a regulator or transferring registers.

Legislative requirement to publish
In most jurisdictions as with all commercial organisations, there is a legal requirement for public authorities such as regulators to prepare and publish a financial statement, historically the annual report and accounts concerning their financial and operational performance. In the UK, as some regulatory powers are the responsibility of the devolved administrations, the reports are sent to, or in the vernacular 'laid', in the various parliaments and assemblies.

Operational plan
Setting aside the financial statement, there may be a legislative requirement to publish an operational plan and a strategy.

Examples of these types of publications include:

AHPRA
Annual Report 2019/20
SSN 1858-5060
158 pages

GDC
Annual Review of Education 2013/14
General Dental Council
67 pages

GMC
Annual Statistical Report – 2012
For Our Investigations into Doctors' Fitness to Practise
GMC/2012AS/0913
September 2013
23 pages

GMC
The State of Medical Education and Practice in the UK 2020
November 2020
1974 pages

HPC
Continuing professional development annual report
2008 09
Ref CPDreport10
March 2010
32 pages

HCPC
Fitness to Practise Annual Report 2018
Protecting the public Promoting professionalism
Publication code: 20171012F2PPUB
November 2018)
72 pages

Medical Practitioners Tribunal Service (MPTS)
Medical Practitioners Tribunal Service report to Parliament 2021
July 2022
46 pages

9. **Social media, the internet, and the World Wide Web**
It would be inappropriate not to make at least a passing reference to social media, the internet, and the World

Wide Web. They have all undoubtable made radical changes to the ease, range, and cost of communications. For example, printing registers and advertising in printed telephone directories such as yellow pages is now confined to the history books. The web now acts as a common portal to the processes of regulators.

Initially, there have been barriers to their adoption. For example, in some jurisdictions it may not be permissible to use email to send communications to certain stakeholders, such as witnesses involved in a FTP tribunal. Instead there is a specific requirement to only send paper communication by post. In other instances electronic communication can be substituted for paper communication. However, an organisation can't impose the use of electronic communication on the users of its services, and it is only possible if the service user takes a decision to opt into the process.

Other challenging areas that a regulator must confront is its sheer scale, ranging from the use of social media through to real-time customer reviews and feedback sites.

How to resolve this universe of challenges, like a number of other fields, is beyond the scope of the book. However, some regulators take the pragmatic decision to construct a specific digital communication subsidiary strategy to address and manage this area.

10. Face-to-face public meetings

The last technique within the portfolio of communication techniques are face-to-face meetings. It can be tempting to assume that communication can all be successfully undertaken via the internet. However, those readers who have attended meetings open to the public where participation is actively encouraged and facilitated will be aware of the advantages.

Regulators should therefore be encouraged to arrange public meetings with the professionals they regulate on a regular and frequent basis both in urban conurbations and rural and remote locations.

Accessibility

Before concluding this section it goes without saying that not all individuals and organisations will have the same ability to communicate with regulators of healthcare professionals. Regulators should adapt their communication techniques to ensure that those stakeholders who are considered to be part of the 'hard-to-reach communities' can easily access the regulator by removing or reducing any barriers.

This may include:

- Adapt use of language and images in all forms of publications
- Disclose employee names during communication
- Opening hours to mirror user expectations
- Provide call back options
- Telephone numbers with zero or low tariffs
- Translation services for multiple languages
- Use Plain English

In addition, it should be remembered that in jurisdictions with more than one language regulators may be require to, and should, meet specific communication requirements relating to both officially recognised and other languages.

CONCLUSION

Regulators need to make best use of their limited communications resources to create and maintain a good level of awareness in their stakeholders of the principles and processes used to regulate healthcare professionals.

But while consumer recognition levels achieved by international brands are beyond the wildest dreams of even the largest and longest established regulators of healthcare professionals, they can still make efficient and effective use of communication channels and techniques.

EXERCISES AND QUESTIONS

Exercises

- What communication channels does your organisation use? Are any not included or are actively excluded?
- What, if any, difference is there between public relations and public affairs?
- How do regulators who organise public face-to-face meetings with those regulated gain from the process?

Questions

- Do you agree that regulators of healthcare professionals should not undertake lobbing?
- Does a regulator that you know have a Consumer Representative Committee? If it does what is it tasked with?

LEGISLATION

Example of UK Legislation

Transparency of Lobbying, Non-party Campaigning and Trade Union Administration Act 2014 L

FURTHER READING

HCPC Stakeholders: Perceptions Audit R

ComRes & HCPC
March 2019
130 pages

A Social Strategy B

Mikolaj Jan Piskorski
Princetown University Press
ISBN: 978-0-691-15339-1
(2014)
275 pages

2.3 CONSULTATION

INTRODUCTION

In theory, regulators have two broad choices on how they can make decisions. Either, they can make decisions in complete isolation without any formal or informal input from their stakeholders. Alternatively, they can seek to involve their stakeholders in their decision-making process. For UK public authorities such as statutory regulators, the first option is no longer acceptable, and the process of seeking the views of stakeholders and interested parties about the future options on the function of regulators is now enshrined in the consultation process.

WHAT IS A CONSULTATION?

A consultation can be defined as:

Definition: Consultation
Process to seek opinions and discuss options on a proposal.

The terms public consultation and public comment may also be used.

From this definition it can be seen that consultation can and should be, an informal on-going process. For example, for a regulator this could include regular meetings with professional associations or civil servants. However, many readers will be more familiar with the more formal and regimented process of what is usually referred to as public consultations.

WHY CONSULT?

Given the expertise of the board of a regulator and the knowledge of the executive it could be argued that regulator should have all the answers to the numerous issues about its principles and processes that it has to resolve. This is of course nonsensical.

For example, in comparison to a regulator, other organisations and individuals may:

- Have more expertise in the area and have a better understanding of the issues
- Have alternative views to any potential regulatory challenges and may have different and more effective solutions
- Have a better understanding of how the proposals can be implemented
- Be better able to present the views of a particular stakeholder

Understanding the opinions, rationale, and desires of stakeholders is important. Consultation facilitates regulators to tap into this external knowledge and thus improve their thinking and decision making.

It therefore follows that the quality of decision making of the regulator concerning substantive issues is enhanced by welcoming input into the process by its stakeholders.

ISSUES TO CONSULT ON

A consultation should be undertaken before a significant decision has to be made. This may not sound specific enough to be helpful. But the reality is that what a public authority should consult on is a question of judgement and not a scientific processes. However, both under and over consultation should be avoided.

Regulators of healthcare professionals should however at a minimum consult on the following range of issues:

- Fees, including what to charge for, initial setting and changes
- Governance arrangements
- Guidance
- The eight processes used by regulators of healthcare professionals, but not minor adjustments
- Legislation
- Regulation of new professions
- Rules
- Standards

In the UK the legislation of public authorities may be prescriptive in defining what events should trigger a legal duty to consult and who should be consulted.

For example, the Health Professions Order 2001 states under Article 3 (14), states:

> (14) Before establishing any standards or giving any guidance under this Order the Council shall consult representatives of any group of persons it considers appropriate including, as it sees fit, representatives of –
>
> **a.** registrants or classes of registrant;
>
> **b.** employers of registrants;
>
> **c.** users of the services of registrants; and
>
> **d.** persons providing, assessing or funding education or training for registrants or prospective registrants.

A litmus test relating to the necessity to consult can be linked to regulatory impact assessments; see Section 6.1, volume 4. In essence it is probable that if a regulatory impact assessment will be generated when considering a significant decision then a consultation should be undertaken. In addition, the regulatory impact assessments should be included in the consultation document.

GOVERNANCE

Given the importance of consultations the boards of regulators should be involved in the process from inception to the conclusion of the process.

WHOM TO CONSULT?

The answer is straightforward, anyone, or any organisation, who has an interest in the issue – in other words stakeholders. For a regulator of hundreds of thousands of professionals treating millions of members of the public this can be a daunting task to select who to consult with. To make the process more manageable it is usual to proactively consult with a carefully drawn-up list of stakeholders. The original list will incorporate obvious organisations such as professional associations and consumer advocacy organisations but will grow over time as new organisations and individuals are added. Indeed, the regulator should proactively seek those who want to be consulted, by seeking new participants during each new consultation. Alternatively, to better improve participation other similar organisations will often share their list of stakeholders that they consult with. Websites can also be used to gather more consultees. Regulators can also publish their current consultation list. Where stakeholders can be considered *'hard to reach'* communities, organisations that represent their interests should be engaged both to respond on behalf of their members but also to facilitate communication directly with their members. Lastly, the list of those who should be consulted should be adapted to each consultation to ensure only those who have a reasonable view on the issues should be asked to spend time and resources responding to the consultation.

In addition, the individuals and organisation that must be consulted may be prescribed in the legalisation governing the regulator.

CONSULTATION PROCESS

In the UK the consultation process is well established and guidance is freely available from various organisations. Notwithstanding this, a number of topics should be adhered to, particularly as aggrieved stakeholders may seek legal redress by judicial review if the result of the consultation does not match their desired outcome.

CONFIDENTIALITY

Potential respondents should be made aware that their individual responses will be confidential unless they formally informed the regulator that they can be placed in the public domain.

PARTICIPATION

Regulators should actively encourage all their stakeholders to participate in and respond to their consultations. Larger organisations may well have the resources to respond to consultations. However, this may not be the case for some smaller organisations from the charity, voluntary, and the third sector and also members of the public. However, participation can be increased by holding public meetings.

PLAIN ENGLISH

The consultation should be written in plain English and employ open-ended questions.

TIMETABLE

A detailed timetable should be published before the consultation takes place. The working assumption is that consultations should run for three months, although this can be extended or reduced or a case-by-case basis. It should allow ample time for responses to be considered, drafted, and despatched. The timetable must include the date of the publication of the regulators' document analysing the response to the consultation, which should ideally not be more than three months after the deadline for receipt of responses. The timetable should also include an indicative timetable for the regulator to adopt and incorporate any resulting changes into its principles and processes.

ANALYSIS OF RESPONSES

Once the consultation process has finished an analysis of the responses should be undertaken. The analysis can commence as soon as the first response is received rather than waiting to the end of the consultation. Some regulators may commission third parties to undertake the analysis to reassure stakeholders of lack of any bias in the process.

PUBLICATION OF CONCLUSION AND DECISIONS

Subsequent to the publication of the analysis of the responses to the consultation, a final and second report is then published which should include the following topics:

- Process used
- Who and how many responded
- Detailed analysis of the responses
- Conclusions
- Decisions

RESPONDING TO OTHER ORGANISATIONS' CONSULTATIONS

It should be borne in mind that in addition to undertaking consultations themselves, regulators will also be invited to participate in consultations by other organisations. In the UK in the 2010s the number of consultations where the views of the regulator were sought could be in the order of 25 a year. For the regulator, some of the consultations will be pertinent and will require a response, others less so. This raises three issues:

1. Which consultations to respond to?
2. Who in the executive is responsible for analysing the responses and drafting the regulators' possible amended position?
3. Should board approval of the response be sought by the executive for some or all of the response to the consultation?

Some regulators will go as far as holding their own consultation on how to respond to a consultation of another organisation. This has the advantage of providing gravitas to the response.

In terms of drafting responsibility, larger regulators will probably allocate this task to the policy and strategy function, on the assumption that they have one; see Section 1.2, volume 4. The response may include attending and/ or giving evidence at public meetings of the organisation conducting the consultation.

REFERENDUM VS. INFORMATION GATHERING

Lastly, it is important for all involved in consultations to understand that the consultation is not a formal endorsement by stakeholders in the sense that they provide a binding vote on the proposal. Regulators as both instigators and recipients of consultations should always remember that they are information-gathering process and they are not referendums.

CONCLUSION

For UK public authorities the consultation process has become a way of life. It not only improves the quality of the decisions of the regulator, but it is one of the ways that they can be used to promulgate their principles and processes. It also helps to ensure stakeholders are engaged with the regulator, and they can influence its direction of travel.

EXERCISES AND QUESTIONS

Exercises

- Obtain the list of organisations and individuals that your regulator uses for its consultation. Is it up to date and does it exclude any stakeholder that you had expected to be included?
- What were the last three consultations that your organisation submitted a response for? Do you agree with the responses?

Questions

- Compose a regulator's response to a professional association explaining why although 95% of their members opposed an increase in the regulator's fees, the regulator is still going to increase their fees
- Why do members of the public tend not to respond to consultations by regulators of healthcare professionals?

LEGISLATION

Example of UK Legislation

Health Professions Order 2001 L

STANDARDS, CODES, GUIDANCE, CONSULTATIONS, POLICIES, AND PRACTICE NOTES

Standards and Codes

Code of Practise on Consultations S&C
Better Regulation Executive
URN 08/1097
July 2008
16 pages

Consultation Principles S&C
Cabinet Office
19 March 2018 (Updated)
2 pages

2.4 PROMOTING PROFESSIONS AND PROFESSIONALS

INTRODUCTION

Society benefits greatly from the services provide by the healthcare professions. Therefore, should the role of the professions and individual professionals be promoted? This can be achieved by, for example, increasing stakeholders' understanding of the role of professionals, encouraging recruitment to the profession, or providing information about the availability of the service that they provide.

If the answer to this question is yes, then who should be responsible for these tasks and in particular, what role, if any, should a regulator of healthcare professions have?

PROMOTION OF THE PROFESSIONS

Promoting the profession can be defined as:

Definition: Promoting the Profession
Increasing the understanding and knowledge about a profession.

However, it should be noted that the term is nuanced and in comparison with representing the profession or advocating for the profession; see Section 10.4, volume 2, promotion can be seen in comparison, to be more assertive and forceful.

To promote a profession a number of stakeholders may be targeted, including:

- Civil servants
- Employers of professionals
- Media
- Patients
- Politicians
- Prospective students
- Public

It should be noted that they are not the same group as the regulator's key stakeholders, in the regulation of healthcare professionals see Table 3.3 – II, volume 1.

TOPICS FOR PROMOTION

To promote a profession there are numerous topics that should be of interest to the various stakeholders. They include:

- Benefits of using a regulated professional
- Career prospects and progression in the profession
- Costs of the service provided by the profession
- Demographics of the profession
- Existing and future employment and earnings data
- Qualifications and experience required to enter the education and training programmes for the profession
- International perspectives about the profession
- Location and distribution of the professionals
- Provision of education and training programmes including capacity, costs, and quality
- Provision of new services
- Research undertaken by the profession
- Roles and services provided by the profession

RESPONSIBILITY FOR PROMOTING THE PROFESSION

In Section 2.1, volume 1 it is argued that regulators have a responsibility to communicate to their stakeholders to increase their awareness about its responsibilities and processes. This may include the benefits of using the services of a regulated professional in comparison to those who are not. And to assist this process, the regulators can provide access to their four main databases. An example of this is in the State of Colorado in the USA, where the Department of Regulatory Agencies manages the Healthcare Professions Profile Program (HPPP). This is an online database to help consumers find a healthcare provider that meets their needs and expectations.

However, although the profession as a whole is promoted by the benefits of regulation and professionalism, the regulators' legislation rarely requires it to proactively promote the profession, the assumption being that this responsibility lies with the profession's professional association.

METHODS TO PROMOTE THE INDIVIDUAL PROFESSIONAL

An exploration of the methods to promote an individual professional is beyond the scope of the book and is therefore not explored. It does however include some of the communication channels and techniques explored in Section 2.2, volume 1.

PROMOTING SERVICES PROVIDED BY INDIVIDUAL PROFESSIONALS

In the UK while the majority of healthcare professionals work in the NHS, only a minority of healthcare professionals work in the private sector and their earnings are on a fee for service basis.

One of the roles of a professional association is therefore to promote the services provided by their members to the fee-paying public. This can be achieved by, for example, facilitating members of the public to make contact with professionals in their locality, by recommending a number of relevant professionals to them. They also undertake similar services when a member of the public is seeking to contact a specialist.

They may also provide advice to other organisations such as the courts and insurance companies. This group of professionals is therefore more likely to be interested in the professional association promoting the services that their members provide to organisations rather than the fee-paying public.

This aside, some professionals working in the private sector will undertake their own advertising and marketing, remembering of course that the standards of conduct address the particular need to maintain truthfulness.

CERTIFICATION MARKS

Promoting the individual professionals is essentially outside the bailiwick of regulators. However, one area where regulators can provide assistants to the professionals that they regulate, is by managing a system of certification marks. Certification marks can be defined as:

Definition: Certification Mark
Symbol indicating that a product or service complies with the standards of a third party.

The term trademark of kitemark may also be used.

In the UK examples of organisation using certification marks include the British Standards Institute (BSI), the Professional Standards Authority (PSA); see Section 6.4, volume 4, and the College of Radiographers. The issuing of certification marks is usually run on a commercial basis to generate income for the organisations.

Notwithstanding this, some regulators of healthcare professionals do provide certification marks for individual professionals which can be both physical and electronic. Individual practitioners can then promote and market themselves by display the certification mark, in this case the name and logo or branding of the regulator, to demonstrate that they are a regulated professional. Certification marks can also be used in relation to premises or facilities.

CONCLUSION

Promoting the professions is usually an important role of its professional association and not the regulator. However, regulators can legitimately promote the benefits of regulation and professionalism. And, they can also provide certification marks to individual professionals.

EXERCISES AND QUESTIONS

Exercises

- Identify what type of support regulators provide to members of the healthcare profession who are working outside the NHS.
- Research the web sites of a professional association of physiotherapists and ascertain if you can recommend a professional in your locality.

Questions

- What is your view on the statement that 'regulators should not promote a profession'?
- When more than one profession works in close proximity to others, for example, psychiatrists, psychologists, and psychotherapists, if asked by a patient, how should they describe the services provided by one of the other professionals?

FURTHER READING

Responsible Advertising in Healthcare: Keeping People Safe R

Advertising compliance and enforcement strategy for the National Scheme
Australian Health Practitioner Regulation Agency (AHPRA)
December 2020
12 pages

2.5 REPUTATION MANAGEMENT

INTRODUCTION

Reputation management conflates many aspects of the principles and processes of the regulation of healthcare professionals. However, while the reputation of a regulator is all-important, it is a will-o'-the-wisp, difficult to define, complicated to manage, and presents some specific challenges.

DEFINITION

Reputation management can be defined in many different ways including:

Definition: Reputation Management
Influencing stakeholders' perception of an organisation.

ASSESSING THE REPUTATION OF YOUR ORGANISATION

As a regulator of healthcare professionals consider the following questions:

- Does the public know that your objective is public protection?
- In the eyes of your stakeholders, in terms of trust, how do they regard your organisation?
- Do your stakeholders see your process as effective and efficient?
- Do the employees value and trust the organisation?
- How does the public assess the professions you regulate as being trustworthy?

If the organisation is unable to answer these and other related questions, then market research should be undertaken to establish the state of play.

ESTABLISHING, IMPROVING, AND MAINTAINING REPUTATION

Once the current state of your organisation's reputation has been established, whether it is non-existent, good or tarnished, and in need of restoration, rather like the brand recognition of consumer goods or services, long-term investment is required as a good reputation can't be created overnight and must be built up and carefully nurtured over decades.

FACTORS INFLUENCING REPUTATION

Factors that influence the reputation of a regulator are multi-factorial and while shared with other public authorities are distinct from those of commercial businesses and other types of organisations, as illustrated in Chart 2.5 – I, below which

Chart 2.5 – I **Reputation of a regulator – Influencing factors**

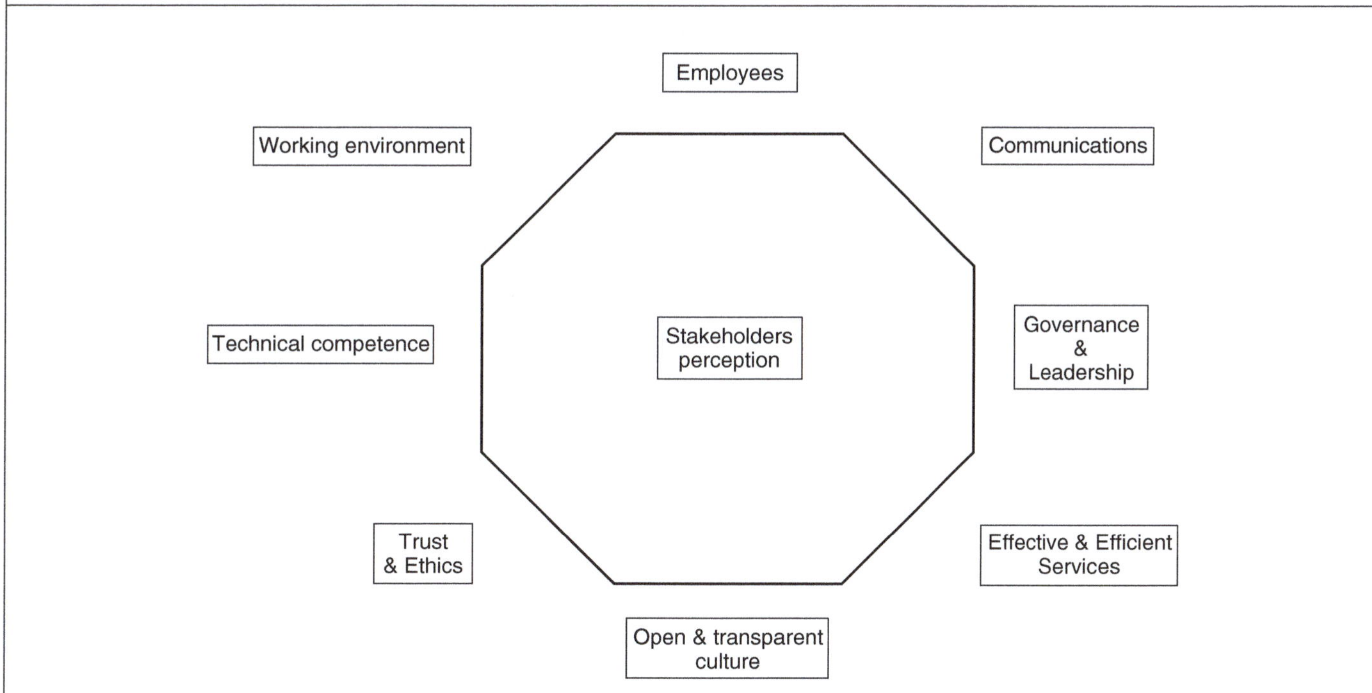

depicts the factors that influence stakeholders' perception of the reputation of a regulator.

It can be seen that stakeholders' perception is influenced by a complex confluence of factors that are drawn from every aspect of the principles and processes of regulation.

For a regulator, reputation management is made even more complex because its reputation is directly linked to the reputation of those it regulates. And while most professions are held in high esteem, history records some pertinent quotations concerning the reputation of one of our premier liberal professions, the lawyers:

1590

> *The first thing we do, let's kill all the lawyers.*
>
> Dick the Butcher

William Shakespeare, Henry IV (Part Two), Act IV, Scene II

1851

> *The one great principle of the English law is, to make business for itself. There is no other principle distinctly, certainly, and consistently maintained through all its narrow turnings. Viewed by this light it becomes a coherent scheme, and not the monstrous maze the laity are apt to think it. Let them but once clearly perceive that its grand principle is to make business for itself at their expense, and surely they will cease to grumble.*

Charles Dickens Bleak House, Chapter 39, paragraph, lines 4–6.

1906

> *all professions are conspiracies against the laity.*

George Bernard Shaw, Act 1, The Doctor's Dilemma

However, the actual management of the reputation of an organisation is, like the field of communication, one of the peripheral topics of the book. Fortuitously for inquisitive readers seeking practical guidance of what and when to manage the reputation of their regulator there is much publicly available expertise and knowledge.

CRISIS MANAGEMENT

As discussed in Section 1.2, volume 4, risk associated with crisis management or business continuity can be mitigated by preparedness by way of a business continuity action plan.

Since reputations can take decades to establish and can be lost overnight, regulators should prepare a reputation management action plan which details how they will organise, prepare, and rehearse the ways that they will manage a situation when their reputation is under threat. In particular, this should address how they will work with stakeholders such as the government and the media, remembering that if you have not already established good communications channels with the government and the media then you can't instantaneously create them.

REVIEWING REPUTATION INCIDENTS

In a similar process to enterprise complaints handling; see Section 4.4, volume 4, once the incident resulting in the use of the regulators' reputation management action plan, has been resolved the reasons for the incident should be investigated with the objective of trying to identify if a process and/or the policy of the regulator was not being correctly followed or is at fault. Where the process is not being correctly followed by employees or others such as partners, education and training should be initiated. Where it is found to be not working, then the process or policy should be changed.

A similar process should also be used where the incident was a 'close call' and the regulators' reputation management action plan was not triggered.

CONCLUSION

In the UK regulators are, and are seen to be, operating in the public sector. As a result investing resources in the management of their reputation may not necessarily be assessed as being a high priority on their agendas. However, at some time in the future if a crisis occurs and they have not invested time and effort in preparing their capabilities for such occurrences, they may inadvertently find themselves in a maelstrom of public criticism.

EXERCISES AND QUESTIONS

Exercises

- Review your crisis management plan. Is it up to date?
- Review a recent case of public criticism against a statutory regulator that resulted in the publication of a report by a third party. Where the report identifies failings or lessons to be learnt and makes recommendations for possible courses of action to improve on the failings, apply them to your organisation or one that you are familiar with. Identify any lessons to be learnt.

Questions

- How would your organisation react if it was discovered that a practising healthcare professional was not and should be on your statutory register?
- Should statutory regulators invest time and resources in reputation management and if so what percentage of their annual budget should be allocated to the task?
- Does your organisation monitor reputational near misses? If not, why not?

FURTHER READING

Doctor's Dilemma B
George Bernard Shaw
ISBN-10: 0809533995
Wildside Press (24 Nov. 2003)
First published 1911
544 pages

Organizational Reputation in the Public Sector B
Wæraas A and Maor M Editors
Rutledge
ISBN: 9781138624085
25 October 2018
264 pages

Regulation and Reputation R
National Consumers Council
Steve Brooker
Ref: PD63/06
December 2006
19 pages

Governance

CHAPTER 3

INTRODUCTION

Regulators must be well governed. Making use of the considerable amount of published research that supports best practice, the chapter explores the principles and processes of governance that are used by the board of regulators to control, direct, and manage the organisation.

The chapter has seven sections:

3.1 Governance and the role and responsibility of boards

3.2 Compositions, structure, and size of boards

3.3 Standards and competences of board members

3.4 Selecting, appointment, training, and appraisal of board members

3.5 Performance of boards, their members, and complaints

3.6 Committees and working groups

3.7 Remuneration of board members

3.1 GOVERNANCE AND THE ROLE AND RESPONSIBILITIES OF BOARDS

INTRODUCTION

Most organisations, whether they operate in the commercial, the public, or the not-for-profit sectors, are usually managed by a board comprising a group of experienced individuals. The role of the board is to control, direct, and manage the organisation, using principles and processes that are referred to as the governance of the organisation.

THE BOARD

A board can be defined as:

Definition: Board Member
Individual belonging to a board.

NOMENCLATURE

A range of terms can be used to describe a board, including:

- Board of directors
- Board of governors
- Board of trustees
- Cabinet
- Congregation
- Council
- General council
- Leadership committee

In the book, the term board will be used.

And for the sake of completeness, a board can be defined as:

Definition: Board
Group of individuals who control, direct, or manage an organisation.

To explore the subject of the governance and the role and responsibilities of boards, the following 16 topics are addressed:

1. Justification for a board
2. Governance and the role and responsibilities of the board
3. Law governing companies
4. Development of governance principles
5. Roles and responsibilities of boards
6. Oversight vs. strategic vs. operational responsibilities
7. Scheme of delegation

Operations of Regulators of Healthcare Professionals, Volume 4, First Edition. Marc Seale.

Companion website: www.wiley.com/go/seale/regulatinghealthcare

8. Vicarious liability and frolics
9. Collective responsibility of the board
10. Organisations with memories
11. Whistleblowing
12. Standing orders of boards
13. Documentation
14. Openness, transparency, and confidentiality
15. Charities and trustees
16. Governance framework
17. Operationalisation of governance arrangements

These will now be explored in further detail:

1. **Justification for a board**
All organisations have to make decisions and choices. If the organisation is comprised of just one person, then they alone must make all the decisions and choices. While consensus will sometimes be achieved, scale in terms of size and complexity will inevitably lead to differences of opinion on how to proceed. As a result someone or a group of people should have overall responsibility for making decisions about choices that others must implement even if they do not agree with it.

In some small organisations, for example, a business owned by one individual that only has a few employees, overall responsibility can be concentrated in a single individual. Others, such as religious organisations or ships, have one individual as head or captain. In other situations a single individual may be appointed by government with sole responsibility for the organisation. For example, in the UK the initial regulation of the gas supply industry following denationalisation was under the control of the head of the Office of Gas Supply (OFGAS), an arrangement that can be referred to as a corporate sole. Or, in relation to the government of a country, one individual may rest control from a democracy and install themselves as a dictator. The area is explored further in the proceeding Section 3.2, volume 4, under the topic of corporate soles.

When a single individual has overall responsibility, particularly in relation to complex or large organisations, even if they are supported by advisers, it increases the risk that they, especially if they have a dominant personality, may if unchecked make poor- or high-risk decisions, deliberate or otherwise. This will increase the possibility that the performance of the organisation, be it a business, regulator, or country, will be undermined.

As a result, most organisations appoint a board comprising of a group of experienced individuals with the collective responsibility to control, manage, and direct the running of the organisation.

2. **Governance and the role and responsibilities of the board**
The board discharges their responsibilities using principles and processes that are usually referred to as governance.

For the purposes of the book, governance is defined as:

Definition: Governance
Principles and processes used to control, manage, and direct an organisation

The term corporate governance may also be used.

3. **Law governing companies**
In most jurisdictions the principles and processes of governance are not 'just nice to have' and to be used with discretion, but are legal requirements.

In the UK, as with most other economically developed countries, the law in combination with a set of governance principles sets out best practices, particularly for commercial organisations owned by shareholders. Notwithstanding this, regulators of healthcare professionals along with other public authorities can utilise the same principles even though they were primarily devised for commercial businesses.

In the UK the Companies Act 2006 is the primary source of the law governing companies. The act codifies the principal duties of directors of boards. However, it does not purport to provide an exhaustive statement of their duties.

Most other jurisdictions embed corporate governance principles in law; a noteworthy example is in the US's Sarbanes–Oxley Act.

4. **Development of governance principles**
The UK's governance principles have historically developed in a fairly ad hoc fashion.

However, in the UK and the USA over the last 30 years governance principles and the roles and responsibilities of boards have been heavily influenced by firstly a number of high-profile commercial failures of major publicly quoted commercial companies and secondly market failures. In addition, in a strangely familiar pattern similar types of governance failures have occurred in regulators; see Chapter 5, volume 4.

As a direct result of these failures a number of public inquires have taken place. In due course the reports and recommendations of the inquireshave been a strong influence on the governance principles used by both the commercial and public sector organisations.

The three key UK reports were:

Cadbury Report
The Cadbury Report was produced by a committee chaired by Adrian Cadbury for the Department of Trade in 2019. It was published in response to the collapse of a major UK publicly listed publishing company Maxwell Communications plc.

They produced a voluntary code, the *Cadbury Code*, whose main themes are:

- The role of the chairman of the board should be separate from that of chief executive
- The majority of the board should comprise independent non-executive directors
- The majority of the membership of the remuneration committee should be non-executive directors
- The board should appoint an audit committee including at least three non-executive directors

Higgs Review
Published by the Department of Trade and Industry in the UK in 2004 the review chaired by Derick Higgs investigated the role and effectiveness of non-executive directors.

Greenbury Report
The report on director's remuneration was chaired by Richard Greenbury and was published by the Department of Trade in 1995.

Sarbanes–Oxley Act
In the USA legislation was introduced in July 2002 following the collapse of two commercial companies Enron and Worldcom and the Tyco scandal. The act, named after the two U.S. congressmen Paul Sarbanes and Michael Oxley who drafted it, aimed at improving corporate governance and accountability. The eleven titles of the legalisation focused on financial reporting and corporate governance arrangements, with the aim of increasing protection for investors in publicly traded stock companies.

In addition, other jurisdictions and organisations have undertaken reviews of governance principles. There are two notable exercises.

The Institute of Directors in Southern Africa published the Kings Report, a comprehensive review on corporate governance in 2009, since which it has been regularly updated.

The Organisation for Economic Cooperation and Development (OECD) published a report on the principles of corporate governance in 1999 and that was republished in November 2015.

5. Roles and responsibilities of boards

In commercial organisations the purpose and objective of the organisation is broadly in the gift of the board. This is because although the roles and responsibilities of the board are set down in the constitution document of the company, there is considerable greater flexibility in these areas within commercial organisations compared to public authorities.

In public authorities, the purpose and objectives of the organisation and the roles and responsibilities of the board members are more rigid and are usually set down in the legislation or rules.

This aside, both the boards of commercial and public organisations typically have the following generic roles and responsibilities:

- Devising, publishing, and communicating the organisation's strategy
- Governing the organisation by establishing broad objectives and policies
- Setting, overseeing, and monitoring operational performance of the executive against the targets of the organisation
- Undertaking adequate discussion before decisions are made
- Monitoring the effectiveness, efficiency, and ethics of the organisation
- Challenging the executive of the organisation
- Ensuring the availability of adequate financial and other resources
- Approving and monitoring the short- and medium-term financial budgets
- Requiring timely disclosure of operational and financial performance
- Delegating specific tasks to committees of the board and ensuring they are executed, for example, the risk and assurance committee
- Selecting, appointing, supporting, reappointing, and reviewing the performance of the chief executive officer (CEO)
- Recruitment of other senior employees
- Setting the remuneration package of the CEO and other senior employees
- Influencing (establishing) the culture of the organisation and monitoring the values and behaviours of the individuals of the organisation including members of the board
- Publicly communicating their support of the organisation – sometimes referred to as an 'ambassadorial role'

Boards of commercial organisations, unlike their public sector counterparts, have an additional role of:

- Accounting to shareholders for the organisation's performance

In public authorities the board and its members will often have the additional role of:

- Accounting to stakeholders for the organisation's performance

The boards of regulators in addition to their generic roles and responsibilities have sector-specific regulator responsibilities. They are:

- Setting standards
- Agreeing guidance

And for some but all boards

- Setting rules

Lastly, it should be noted that it is assumed board members are excluded from making judgment decisions; see Section 1.2, volume 4, Operating models of regulators of healthcare professionals.

6. **Oversight vs. strategic vs. operational responsibilities**
In the mantra of the governance of organisations, the responsibility of the board is described as oversight, whereas the executive under the leadership of the CEO is responsible for operations. This implies that the board should not be directly involved in the operational day-to-day management of the organisation. In turn the oversight role falls mainly on the non-executive members of the board.

The concept of oversight is complicated in boards of regulators by the ratio of executive and non-executive board membership. If the board membership is composed entirely of non-executives, how does the board deliver oversight by ensuring that the operations are functioning correctly?

That aside, this division of roles and responsibilities between the board and the executive is illustrated in Chart 3.1 – I, below. The chart depicts the division of the responsibilities of a regulator's board and the executive for oversight, strategy and policy, and day-to-day operations.In essence:

Chart 3.1 – I Division of responsibilities between board and executive

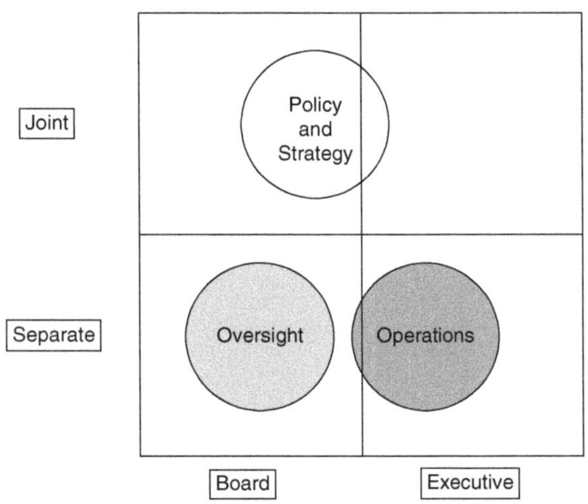

- The board is exclusively responsible for oversight of the executive
- The executive is responsible for implementing the policy and strategy and responsibility for managing the operations of the regulator
- The board is almost exclusively responsible for setting policy and strategy

However, there are two important caveats:

i. In times of crisis, the board may be tempted to stray into operational aspects of the regulator

ii. The strategy and policies of regulators are heavily constrained by their legislation

As a result a clear decision needs to be made by the regulator on the dividing line between operations, oversight, policy, and strategy. When it remains unclear or ambiguous it can be a recipe for confusion and possibly disaster.

It should also be noted that the division of responsibilities can be ambiguous. For example, responsibility for the culture of the organisation. Is it the individual responsibility of the board or the CEO or the Executive Management Team, of everyone in the organisation? Or, is it a joint responsibility?

7. **Scheme of delegation**
To help clarify and resolve the dividing line between operations, oversight, policy and strategy, boards of regulators may reserve specific takes to themselves or delegate responsibility for specific tasks to other parts of the organisation. These may be committees, the CEO, or members of the executive such as the director of fitness to practise (FTP). In terms of bureaucracy, which issues that are either reserved or delegated, should be documented in a scheme of delegation.

Definition: Scheme of Delegation
Document setting out who, in an organisation, has the authority to make a decision, or alternatively, who it is delegated to.

The scheme of delegation should be periodically reviewed, and if required, amended by the board. However, it should be noted that the question is made more complex in regulators since the legislation will often dictate what can and can't be delegated by the board.

Under normal circumstances the process of delegation works well. However, in times of crisis, for example, regulatory failure, some boards will abandon the principles of operational delegation and attempt to manage the day-to-day operations, for which they are usually not competent to do.

8. **Vicarious liability and frolics**
It is important to underline to members of the board that membership comes with important responsibilities. The consequences of not meeting them can have serious implications for the both the board as a whole and its individual members. In particular, it should be noted that board members who knowingly disregard their responsibilities and embark on a frolic can lose their vicarious liability and damage theirs and the regulators' reputation.

9. **Collective responsibility of the board**
Collective responsibility, or collective cabinet responsibility, is the principle that once a board has reached its decision then those board members who did not agree with the decision of the majority of the board should abide by the decision. This means that, for example, if a board member is questioned about the decision or position of the board, they should explain and/or support the decision even though they originally disagreed with the decision.

10. **Organisations with memories**
Board members need to understand and abide with the principle that organisations such as regulators are '*organisations with a memory*'. The practical implication of this principle is that a decision taken at a board meeting continues until it is replaced or amended by another board meeting.

11. **Whistleblowing**
The Public Interest Disclosure Act 1998 (c.23) is an act of the UK Parliament that protects whistleblowers from detrimental treatment by their employer; see Section 2.1, volume 3. The board of a regulator is therefore responsible for the principles and processes used to protect employees of the regulator who report wrongdoing or malpractice within the organisation.

12. **Standing orders of boards**
The rules and procedures for boards are set down in standing orders. In addition, the committees of the regulator should also have standing orders.

The standing orders should be regularly reviewed by the board to ensure their relevance and effectiveness.

13. **Documentation**
In terms of good governance a range of documents including standards and guidance should be maintained and made easily accessible to the public by publication. They include:

- Board papers
- Code of conduct for board members
- Conflicts of interest, deceleration, and register
- Gifts and hospitality register
- Governess framework
- Minutes of meetings
- Notice of meetings
- Register of board members interests (and senior employees)
- Rule and guidance on decision making
- Standing orders

14. **Openness, transparency, and confidentiality**
In commercial organisations, the contents of board meetings are considered to be strictly private and confidential, since the majority of issues on the agenda will be commercially sensitive or will directly affect the market valuation of publicly quoted joint stock companies.

The situation with regulators that are public authorities is entirely contradictory. Here the trust that stakeholders place in the board of a regulator is based on the principles of openness and transparency supported by the characteristics of autonomy, independence, accountability, and scrutiny, as depicted in Chart 1.4 – II, volume 1.

To maintain this trust boards of regulators must demonstrate openness and transparency, and one of the ways this is achieved is by holding board meetings in public and publishing agendas, papers, and minutes of the meetings.

However, on occasions boards will need to conduct their proceedings in private to maintain confidentiality. It is therefore imperative that clear principles and processes are adopted by the board to justify why they will on occasions conduct their meetings in private.

An example of how this can be achieved is used at the board meetings of the HCPC when a procedure is used when they discuss issues in private and a formal resolution is passed along the lines of:

RESOLUTION
The Council is invited to adopt the following: 'The Council hereby resolves that the remainder of the meeting shall be held in private, because the matters being discussed relate to the following: • Information relating to a registrant, former registrant, or application for registration • Information relating to an employee or office holder, former employee, or applicant for any post or office • The terms of, or expenditure under, a tender or contract for the purchase or supply of goods or services or the acquisition or disposal of property • Negotiations or consultation concerning labour relations between the Council and its employees • Any issue relating to legal proceedings which are being contemplated or instituted by or against the Council • Action being taken to prevent or detect crime to prosecute offenders • The source of information given to the Council in confidence • Any other matter which, in the opinion of the Chair, is confidential or the public disclosure of which would prejudice the effective discharge of the Council's functions"

Lastly, the board may establish a policy on its openness and transparency and confidentiality.

15. **Charities and trustees**
    In the UK organisations may gain the status of being a registered charity provided they meet certain criteria set by either the Charity Commission in England and Wales, the Charity Commissioner in Northern Ireland, or the Scottish Charity Regulator (OSCR) in Scotland. Once registered, the members of the board of a charity are called trustees.

    If organisations meet the criteria that charities must fulfil, they gain benefits and advantages of not paying tax on income from investments. However, there are various obligations that a charity must fulfil, including information disclosure, such as publishing a prescribed set of annual report and accounts. In addition, the trustees are usually not remunerated and are expected to provide their services for free.

    Three of the nine UK statutory regulators of healthcare professionals are registered as charities. They are the General Medical Council (GMC), Registered Charity No. 1089278, the General Optical Council (GOC) Registered Charity No. 1150137, and the Nursing and Midwifery Council (NMC) Registered Charity No. 1091434.

16. **Governance framework**
    Finally, many organisations, including regulators, draw a single reference document describing their governance structures, processes, and principles in a governance framework. This will include the working of its committees; see Section 3.6, volume 4.

17. **Operationalisation of governance arrangements**
    It should be noted that responsibility of operationalising the governance arrangements of the board rests with the secretary to the board.

CONCLUSION

The roles and responsibility of boards are complex. The principles used to govern boards are also complex and often boards are faced with conflicting challenges. The solutions to many of these challenges are partially resolved by the constitution of the board in terms of its structure and composition. These topics are discussed in the preceding sections.

EXERCISE AND QUESTIONS

Exercise

- Identify topics that boards of regulators should discuss in private

Questions

- Should UK statutory regulators of healthcare professionals be allowed to be charities?
- Who is responsible for the culture of a regulator?

LEGISLATION

Example of UK Legislation

Companies Act 2006 L
Public Interest Disclosure Act 1998 (c.23) L

Example of International Legislation

USA
Sarbanes–Oxley Act L
107th Congress
Public Law 204]
The U.S. Government Printing Office
Public Law 107-204
Public Company Accounting Reform and Investor Protection Act – Senate
Corporate and Auditing Accountability and Responsibility Act – House of Representatives

FURTHER READING

Boards That Make a Difference: A New Design for Leadership in Non-profit and Public Organizations B
John Carver
Jossey-Bass
(May 1997)
ISBN-13: 978-0787908119 ISBN-10: 0787908118
272 pages

The Cadbury Report R
Report of the Committee on Financial Aspects of Corporate Governance
Published by Gee (a division of Professional Publishing Ltd), London
ISBN: 0852589131 (Report)
ISBN: 0852589158 (Report with Code of Best Practice)
1 December 1992

Corporate Governess: Board Responsibilities R
Prudential Regulation Authority
Bank of England
Supervisory Statement SS5/16
Jull 2018
12 pages

Corporate Governance Principles and Recommendations R
ASX Corporate Governance Council
4th Edition
27 April 2019
40 pages

Director's Remuneration – Report of a Study Group R
Greenbury Report
Chaired by Sir Richard Greenbury
17 July 1995
57 pages

G20/OECD Principles of Corporate Governance R
Organisation for Economic Development and cooperation (OECD
ISBN: 978-92-64-23687-5
30 November 2015
50 pages

Governance of Regulators R
OECD Best Practice Principles for Regulatory Policy
ISBN: 9789264209008
April 2014
123 pages

Hampel Report R
Final Report – Committee on Corporate Governance
Gee Publishing Ltd, London
ISBN: 186089034
January 1998
66 pages

Integrated Governance Handbook R
A handbook for executives and non-executives in healthcare organisation
Deighan M and Bullivant J
Department of Health and NHS (UK)
Ref: Gateway Ref: 5947
16 February 2006
75 pages

King Report on Governance for South Africa, 2009 (King III) R
Chairman of Committee, Mervyn King
Institute of Directors of South Africa (IoDSA)
1 September 2009
142 pages

The New Integrated Governance Handbook 2016: R
Developing governance between organisations (GBO)
Final Report
Dr John Bullivant
Good Governance Institute
October 2016
48 pages

Ontario College of Teachers R
Governance Review Report
Governance Solutions
26 November 2018
142 pages

Regulatory Board Governance Toolkit R
International Council of Nurses, (ICN)
Jean Barry
ISBN: 978-92-95099-25-8
65 pages

Report of a Governance Review of the Law Society of British Columbia R
Cayton, H R
November 2021
39 pages

Review of the Role and Effectiveness of Non-executive Director R
Derick Higgs
Published by the Department of Trade and Industry
Printed in the United Kingdom by the Stationery Office
19585 809438 01/03
January 2003
119 pages

A Vision for the Future R
Leading in Regulatory Governance Task Force (Final Report)
College of Nurses of Ontario
December 2016
24 pages

STANDARDS, CODES, GUIDANCE, CONSULTATIONS, POLICIES, AND PRACTICE NOTES

Standards and Codes

Corporate Governance in Central Government Departments: S&C
Code of good practice
HM Treasury and cabinet Office
ISBN: 978-1-911375-85-2
21 April 2017
29 pages

Guidance

Corporate Governance in Central Government Departments: G
Code of good practice – **Guidance Note**
HM Treasury and cabinet Office
ISBN: 978-1-911375-84-5
21 April 2011
19 pages

On Board G
A guide for members of statutory boards
Scottish Government
ISBN: 978-1-78652-284-9
March 2017
73 pages

On Board A Guide for Board Members of Public Bodies in Scotland G
Scottish Executive
April 2006
118 pages

Practice Guide to Auditing Oversight G
Canadian Audit and Accountability Foundation
ISBN: 978-1-926527-03-3
91 pages
2013

New York Stock Exchange: Corporate Governance Guide G
White Page Ltd, (London)
ISBN: 978-0-9565842-6-7
First published: December 2014
358 pages

Policies

Board Declarations of Interest and Conflict Resolution Policy Pol
Social Work England
POL_BOA_004 version 1.3
March 2021

Governance Practices and Policies Pol
Law Society of Ontario
2 October 2019 (amended)
33 pages

3.2 COMPOSITION, STRUCTURES, AND SIZE OF BOARDS

INTRODUCTION

The composition, structures, and size of the boards of regulators of healthcare professional are complex. This is because certain groups of individuals can be excluded or restricted from being eligible to become members of the board due to their occupation or place of residency. Once eligibility for membership of the board has been resolved, a further decision needs to be made on whether two distinct types of board members will be used or not. Some board members, who can be engaged to work on a part-time basis, are seen as independent and are called non-executive directors. The other types of board members are called executive directors and are usually fulltime employees of the organisation. The board can then be organised using one or other of two distinct types of structures. Either a single or unitary board is used. Alternatively, two separate boards are utilised in a two-tier arrangement where one board, the executive board reports to a supervisory board.

Lastly, the overall size of the board needs to be addressed before setting the role of the chair and possibly a vice chair.

To explore the subject of the composition, structures, and the size of boards of regulators, the following 24 topics are addressed:

1. Types of board members
   - i. Non-executive
   - ii. Executive
2. Role of board members
3. Membership of boards of commercial companies
4. Evolution of membership of boards of regulators of healthcare professionals
5. Confusion between 'representation' and board responsibility
6. Geographical representation
7. Diversity of boards
8. Lay members
9. Uniformity of board members responsibilities
10. Board composition
11. Board composition of multi-professional regulators
12. Alternates
13. Concurrent membership
14. Structure of boards
    - i. Corporate sole
    - ii. Two-tier broad
    - iii. Unitary board
15. Size of boards
16. Role and responsibilities of the chair
17. Competences of chair
18. Requirement for a lay chair
19. Role of vice chair
20. Role of the chief executive officer
21. Role of the board secretary
22. Separation of the role of chair, chief executive officer, and board secretary
23. Committees of the board
24. Constitution of boards

These topics will now be explored in further detail:

1. **Types of board Members – non-executive and executive**

The governance arrangements of commercial and public organisation can make use of two fundamentally different types of board members, namely, non-executive board members and executive board members.

Non-executive board members or directors (NEDs) are distinguished from executive board members in that they are:

- Engage with the organisation on a part-time basis
- Not employees of the organisation
- Financially independent on their NED role and often have other jobs
- Paid a flat fee for their service and frequently receive no performance-related benefits
- Considered to be 'independent'

Independence of board members

For the sake of clarity, independent non-executive board members display three characteristics, namely:

- i. Have no financial and material relationship with the organisation
- ii. Not part of the organisation's executive team
- iii. Not involved with the day-to-day operations of the organisation

Executive board members in contrast are characterised by:

- i. Contracted to the organisation as full-time employees
- ii. The organisation is usually their only significant remunerated employer
- iii. Remuneration may include performance-related pay such as bonuses and share options

2. **Role of board members**
Executives and non-executive board directors have markedly different roles:

Role of non-executive board members
Characterised by:

- Strategic
- Oversight and scrutiny of the executive of the organisation
- Non-involvement in the day-to-day operations of the organisation
- Oversight of risk management

Role of executive board members
Characterised by:

- Operational
- Manage the day-to-day operations of the organisation
- Identification and mitigation of risk

3. **Membership of boards of commercial organisations**
For comparative purposes the typical board of a UK public company can be characterised by comprising two types of board members. The executive members of the board are full-time employees and typically include the CEO, chief operating officer (COO), and the chief finance officer (CFO). The majority of the board members are non-executive members. All board members are equal in stature and have full voting rights. In terms of responsibility, the executive manage the day-to-day operations of the company. The non-executive are explicitly responsible for representing and looking after the interest of the shareholders. The chair is a non-executive director and is usually engaged on a part-time basis.

Given the right competences, few constraints are placed on board membership eligibility. The exceptions are those with criminal records or have been made bankrupt.

4. **Evolution of membership of boards of regulators of healthcare professions**
The membership of boards of regulators of healthcare professionals is notably different from the boards of commercial organisations.

Historically, as professional associations were superseded by statutory regulators, board membership was exclusively drawn from members of the profession. For example, in the Apothecaries Act (1815) the warden and masters were required to be apothecaries.

In particular the membership of the board was strongly influenced by the use of principle of representation in that their role was to exclusively represent the interests of the members of the profession.

Over time the principle of a board comprising exclusively members of the profession was replaced. This was because proponents argued that a broader expertise relating to the regulators' processes, such as the employment or the education and training of professionals, should be available as it would improve the decision making of the board of the regulator.

Typically, board membership became more varied by requiring a small number of individuals to be drawn from the regulators' stakeholders including:

- Employers of healthcare professionals
- Government departments
- Higher Education Institutes (HEIs) programme providers
- Other statutorily regulated healthcare professions, typically members of the medical profession
- Professional associations

During this period, it should be noted that there was no requirement for lay membership.

5. **Confusion between 'representation' and board responsibility**
Historically in this structure of the boards of UK regulators of healthcare professionals, board members from the professions were elected. The issue of the election of board membership is explored in detail in Section 3.3, volume 4.

Challenging the use of elections reinforces the assumption that it is the role of board members to 'represent' the interest of their constituents, all of which were from their profession, and not the interests of the regulator or other stakeholders. For example, a professional member of a board of their regulator could seek to block a required fee increase on the grounds that the regulated professionals did not want to fund the regulator since they '*received no benefits from regulation*'.

To outsiders, this could be interpreted as a conflict of interest. As a board member elected from the profession it could however be seen to be looking after the interests of those they were expected to regulate, rather than the collective interests of whole of the board which is to protect the public by delivering the primary objective of the regulator.

And as a footnote the register of board members interest should help highlight and resolve any potential conflicts of interest. This is because the register should be publicly accessible and include current and historical appointments and close associations with other organisations. In some instances the register of board members interests may include the family members of the board members.

6. **Geographical representation**
Board members may be appointed or elected from specific geographic areas. For example, in candidates are required to live or work '*wholly or mainly*' in a particular geographic area. In the UK it is typically either England, Northern Ireland, Scotland, or Wales. However, this type of requirement can have the unintended consequence of reducing the number of potential candidates from the less densely populated geographical regions.

7. **Diversity of boards**
A newly emerging policy, and rightly so, is to require boards to achieve gender identity quotas. This may in due course encapsulate other areas such as age and ethnicity.

8. **Lay members**
Until the later part of the last century, the vast majority of board members of regulators were assumed to require to have the knowledge and skills of the profession. Of particular interest for today's readers, members of the public were not considered to be suitable board members. However, driven by consumerism and public concern with an imbalance of the regulatory contract, government insisted on the requirement for members of the board to include those who were not members of the healthcare profession. In essence the purpose of lay board membership is to ensure regulatory capture by the profession does not occur.

Once mandated, the new board members are referred to as lay members. The term lay emanates from the church and other ecclesiastical institutions. Those who are not clergy or ministers are referred to as the laity to distinguish them from those who are not. The term layperson, or layman or laywoman, is also used to describe a person who is not qualified in a given profession and/or does not have specific knowledge of a certain subject. Thus lay can be defined as:

Definition: Lay
Person who is not and has never been a member of a profession.

The terms community member, consumer member, and public member may also be used when the individual is a member of a board of directors or a committee.

As a result, nowadays the term 'professional board member' has been adopted, although they are sometimes referred to as '*registrant members*'. All other members of the board are lay members.

It should however be pointed out that there is a degree of ambiguity of what a lay person is. The reason for this is because of the following question:

Should an individual who is a regulated professional be eligible to be a board member of another profession as a lay member?

To expand: should a professional such as an accountant be considered to be a lay person by a nursing regulator? In contrast, should a dentist be considered a lay person by a regulator of physiotherapists? Also, should a retired and no longer registered professional be allowed to act as lay committee member when contributing to the processes of a regulator of professionals?

Another area of potential ambiguity occurs if for instance a professional has only practised their profession in a particular jurisdiction and then emigrates to a new jurisdiction but does not continue to practise their profession in their new country of residence. So, for example, should a radiographer regulated in New Zealand who migrates to the UK but does not practise there, be allowed to be a lay member of all or only some of the UK regulators of the healthcare professions?

This type of ambiguity should be avoided by clear legislation and/or rules, since, in the eyes of the public, if they were aware of these types of situation were in existence, it is reasonable to assume that they would regard it as not being in the spirit of what is meant by 'lay' participation.

9. **Uniformity of board member responsibility**
It should be noted that the legislation of regulators of healthcare professionals makes no distinction between the roles of board members who are healthcare professionals and those who are not. In essence all board members are created equal.

10. **Board composition**
Once the exclusiveness of professional board membership role is resolved, concerns then logically shift for the need to specify the requirement for the percentage of the board membership that should be lay.

There are five options relating to the ratio of professional to lay membership of boards

i. All professional
ii. Less than 50% lay
iii. 50:50:: professional : lay
iv. Less than 50% professional
v. All lay

In the UK the third option is universally adopted.

11. **Board composition of multi-professional regulators**
Should multi-professional regulators, some of who currently regulate over twenty different healthcare professions, be required to have one professional from each profession on their board? Some multi-professional regulators do and some do not. The position hinges on the argument that where profession-specific competences are required to make judgment decision, assessors can be engaged. So, for example, where a regulator does not allow board members to participate in FTP tribunal, board composition can be more flexible since

members are not required from each regulated profession. An example of this type of arrangement is the UKs' HCPC which has less professions on its board 6, compared to the number of profession it regulates, 15. It is also interesting to note that their board rarely discusses issues relating to only one profession.

12. **Alternates**

Another anomaly that arose when lay members joined the boards of some UK regulators was that some regulators introduced a somewhat unusual, or indeed perverse, process.

It was sometimes the practice that professional board members when they are unavailable to attend a board meeting would have another profession to attend in their place. These individuals were called 'alternate' board members. The justification for the arrangement was that professionals are busy people and when they can't attend board meetings an equivalent professional should attend in their place. Board members and their alternates could not both attend the same board or committee meeting but both could attend either if the other was not present.

Similar arrangements were not provided for lay members. This meant that lay board members would be unlikely to ever be in the majority as an absent professional could also be substituted by their alternates.

This meant that the regulators, by using alternatives only for professional members, were seen to be unfairly looking after the interest of their professional board members. As a result in the UK their use was discontinued by regulators such as the HPC in July 2009.

13. **Concurrent membership**

Another controversy that arose was triggered by the increase in the number of regulators of healthcare professionals. That was whether or not board members, both professional and lay, should be allowed to sit or more than one board of different regulators at the same time. Concerns focused on the issue of if one board supported a particular policy and the other board took the opposite view. If one individual was a member of both boards would they have an unsustainable conflict of interest?

In addition, it triggered the concern that if the same individual was on the boards of more than one regulator, it excluded other suitable candidates becoming board members and thus reduces participation from different members of society.

This challenge can be resolved by the drafting of the regulators' legislation to exclude concurrent membership.

14. **Structure of boards**

To quote the American architect, Louis Sullivan (1856–1924):

"Form follows function."

And when considering issues such as the structure of a board it must be remembered that one solution is not appropriate for all. The structure of a board must therefore be appropriate for a wide range of fundamentally different types of organisations, including:

- Banks and other financial institutions
- Commercial business – international and publicly owned
- Charities
- Churches
- Government Ministries
- Hospitals
- Political parties
- Research Institutes
- Start-ups – commercial
- Trade unions
- Universities

As a result boards generally adopt one of three distinct types of structures, namely:

i. Corporate sole
ii. Two-tier board
iii. Unitary board

i. **Corporate sole**

A corporate sole is a legal entity consisting of a single 'sole' incorporated office, occupied by a single 'sole' natural person. In the UK examples include the Comptroller and Auditor General and historically OFGAS. Other examples of these types of arrangements are often found in religious organisations.

ii. **Two-tier board**

In a two-tier board structure there are in effect two boards. The two boards are called the supervisory board and the management board. Alternatively they are also sometimes called the corporate board and the operating board. In the commercial sector two-tier boards are prevalent in Europe, particularly in the Netherlands and Germany where they are named the Aufsichtsrat and Vorstand boards.

There is a clear division of responsibilities between the two boards. The supervisory board is responsible for strategy and supervises or overseeing the management board. The management board manages the day-to-day operations of the organisation. The two boards meet at different times. The management board meets frequently, usually weekly, the meetings being chaired by the CEO. The supervisory board meets less frequently normally between 4 and 10 times per year.

The supervisory board is exclusively composed of non–executive directors, in that no senior, or for that matter any, employees are board members. The chair is also a non-executive director. The management board usually only comprises those who are executive directors. The Chair leads the supervisory board but does not attend the management board. The CEO and other senior employees will often attend meetings of the supervisory board but has no voting rights. The CEO reports to the chair.

This type of board structure is often used, and is seen, as a way of incorporating 'representation' of certain stakeholders into the governance arrangements of an organisation. In this context representation is seen as a desired benefit and outcome for the decision making of the board. So, for example, various stakeholder groups will sit on the board. In commercial or governmental boards, representatives may include:

- Employees
- Environmental groups
- Major shareholders
- Providers of finance
- Trade unions

A two-tier board has the advantage that it can be structured to incorporate various stakeholder groups or representatives. Its disadvantage is that it can hinder communication between the executives and non-executives and that strategic decisions that benefit all stakeholders can be blocked by one stakeholder.

In relation to regulators utilising two-tier boards, the board is responsible for making decisions and the executive has to then carry them out without formal input into the decision that they have not taken and may not have directly contributed to.

iii. Unitary board

In a unitary board there is a single board. In sharp contrast to a two-tier board, membership includes both the non-executive directors and individuals drawn from the executive. This normally includes the CEO, chief operating officer (COO), and the chief financial officer (CFO). All board members serve together as equal partners and all have the same voting rights.

The chair is a non-executive. The chair is usually excluded from being the CEO as duality is prohibited or strongly discouraged. The CEO reports to the chair. It is normal practice to have a majority of non-executives.

The advantage of this type of board structure is that it facilities communication between the executives and non-executives as all major decisions are taken in a single forum. However, it does not facilitate representation from particular groups of stakeholders. This type of board structure is more prevalent in the Australia, South Africa, USA, and UK.

A recent debate has been initiated on whether or not members of the board should be drawn from the senior executives who are employees of the regulator. The reason being that some regulators are now multimillion pound turnover organisations, and it is unusual to manage large organisations without the CEO, COO, and CFO not being members of the board.

In the UK initial proposals have assumed that the executive members would be in a minority and all other members would be non-executives. These types of arrangements would reflect in a commercial organisation and do away with the concept of a two-tiered board.

In terms of the UK regulators of healthcare professions, unitary boards were first introduced when the regulator Social Work England was established in December 2019.

15. Size of boards

What should be the size of the board in terms of the number of members? Whilst it may be conventional wisdom that two heads are better than one, anyone who has had the misfortune to participate on a committee comprising more than a dozen or so individuals will be acutely aware of the necessity of a board of the right sizes. Unfortunately there is no empirical evidence that can be used to determine the correct or optimum size of a board. However, there are identifiable challenges for boards that are either too small or too large.

Small-size challenges

Examples of the challenges of small boards include:

- There may not be enough board members to discharge all the responsibilities of the board. For example, chairing committees
- The quorate requirements for board meetings may not be met due to illness or other sudden and urgent commitments

- Unplanned board member turnover may cause problems
- A small number of members of the board members may dominate proceedings
- The totality of the competencies of the board may be insufficient
- Analysis and discussion on key issues may be poor due to lack of different perspective

Large-size challenges
Examples of the challenges of large boards include:

- The size of the board may limit participation because there is not enough time at board meetings for everyone to contribute to the discussions and debate
- Scheduling future meetings
- Board may break up into substantial factions
- Absenteeism from board meetings may increase
- Meetings have to be managed on a formal basis

Challenges to both large and small boards
Examples of the challenges for both small and large boards include:

- May dissuade applications for membership from experienced individuals
- Holding the executive to account

Correct size of boards
There is no magic formula that can be used to decide the best size of a board. However, conventional wisdom and social and psychological research currently indicates that less than 6 is too small and greater than 12 is too large. If it is assumed that the chair has the casting vote, then a board should ideally be between 7 and 11.

Despite changes that have resulted in smaller-size boards of the UK healthcare regulators, some UK examples large ones remain in other sectors. For example, the General Teaching Council for Scotland (GTCS), the independent statutory regulator of teachers in Scotland. It was established in 1965. The 27-member council comprises 19 elected teachers, 11 nominated educational stakeholder representatives, and 7 appointed lay members.

Size of the board and members' non-governance responsibilities
Some small regulators may not establish committees, and in these cases board members are often involved in making decisions that in larger regulators delegate to the executive. This may be because committees are established by small regulators and they, like their boards, are often unable, or unwilling, to delegate to their executive because of the small number of employees. For example, committee may not delegate to the executive individual decisions about admitting international applications to the register, or membership of FTP tribunals may consist exclusively of board or committee members.

In more substantive regulators, these functions will be undertaken by employees or assessors, and the board and its committees will focus on strategic issues and oversight of specific functions that are managed by the executive.

In consequence, the less that board members are involved in judgment decision, see Section 1.1, volume 4 structures and 1.2, volume 4 operating models, the less they are directly involved in the operational day-to-day management of the regulator, the smaller the size of the board can be, whilst at the same time still maintaining the boards' effectiveness and efficiency and discharging its governance responsibilities.

Board quorum
It should be noted that at the meetings of the board it must be quorate to conduct business. When the composition of the board requires different types of board members, then the rules must reflect this.

Responsibilities of specific board members
On a typical UK board of directors there are usually three specific and different roles that need to be undertaken. They are the chair, the CEO, and the secretary to the board.

16. Role and responsibilities of the chair
The chair of the board of a regulator is the leader of the board and is responsible for ensuring that it operates effectively and efficiently. The chair of regulators can be appointed by government or elected from the non-executive directors.

The role of the chair includes:

- Chairing board meetings
- Setting the draft agenda of board meetings and the allocation of the appropriate time for discussion of each item on the agenda
- Shaping the agenda of the board to ensure delivery and monitoring of the regulators' strategic intent, annual budget, and executive performance
- Setting the tone of board meetings, including the establishment of a common purpose
- Ensuring that all board members participate and contribute in board discussions and decisions and that they regularly attend the meeting of the board
- Seeking consensus when making decisions
- Obtaining appropriate information to present to the board

- Appraising the performance of the non-executive board members and where appropriate dealing with underperformance
- Motivating board members individually and collectively
- Assisting with the selection and appointing new board members
- Assisting with the selection and appointing of the chairs and members of committees
- Establishing and maintaining an effective working relationship with the CEO
- Managing the CEO and evaluating their performance against goals and objectives
- Overseeing negotiations for the CEO's terms of employment
- Drafting the CEO's job description
- Planning for CEO succession and other senior members of the executive management team
- Acting as an important link between the board and management but without necessarily preventing direct access of fellow directors

It should be noted that the role and responsibility of the chair of the board and the board itself have a high degree of overlap.

17. **Competences of chair**
The competence of the chair should be almost identical to those of board members except they must have specific competences relating to chairing.

18. **Requirement for a lay chair**
In some jurisdictions there has been consideration of the need to require that the chair of the regulator is not a healthcare professional. However, most jurisdictions assume that the role should be undertaken by the best candidate for the role.

19. **Role of vice chair**
Some boards may appoint a vice chair to act as a substitute if the chair is unavailable. Alternatively, others boards may instead appoint another board member for the duration of the meeting if the chair can't attend.

20. **Role of the chief executive officer**
The CEO is the leader of the executive management team. They are responsible for the day-to-day management of the organisation and have a strong influence on the culture of the organisation; see Section 1.2, volume 4. Unless there is a unitary board, they are expected, or are invited, to attend board meetings but have no vote.

21. **Role of the board secretary**
The secretary is to attend board meetings as the administrator of the body corporate.

22. **Segregation of the role of chair, chief executive officer, and board secretary**
It can be seen from the preceding paragraphs that the three roles of chair, CEO, and secretary require considerable time and effort and have markedly different responsibilities. Therefore, under good corporate governance arrangements one individual holding more than one of the three roles is not permitted and generally:
    - Chair should not also be the CEO
    - CEO should not also be the chair or the board secretary
    - Board secretary should not also be the chair

23. **Committees of the board**
When examining the governance arrangement and structure of a board consideration must be given to the role of its committees such as the audit or remuneration committee. The process and governance arrangements of committees is addressed in Section 3.6, volume 4.

24. **Constitution of boards**
The components of the constitution of the regulator can be embedded in the regulators' primary or secondary legislation, acts and orders, rules and standing orders. Regulators should therefore consider combining all the components into a single publicly available document.

CONCLUSION

The composition, structure, and size of the boards of regulators may be seen by an outsider as a fairly insignificant issue. However, within the world of the regulation of healthcare professionals it has been, and to some extent still is, contentious.

Over time consumerism and regulatory failure has led to political intervention to reduce the control of the regulator by the profession whose members it regulates. To achieve this the regulatory contract has been adjusted. In the UK board membership norm is a 50:50 ratio of professional to lay board members with the chairman from either. In other countries the approach can be very different, and the UK model of the composition of the board is certainly not universally accepted.

Lastly, in the UK, traditionally the board of regulators of health and care professionals have resembled a two-tier board structure. In terms of the future it is now interesting to speculate if regulators will be required to adopt a unitary board structure.

EXERCISES AND QUESTIONS

Exercises

- Historically, the councils of UK regulators of healthcare professionals consisted exclusively of members of the profession they regulated. Was it rational for the government to replace these arrangements?
- Should unitary boards be introduced by regulators of healthcare professionals?
- What are the advantages and disadvantages of a board of a regulator being chaired by an individual who is a not a healthcare professional?

Questions

- Should a member of a regulated profession be allowed to be a lay member of another healthcare regulator?
- Should a board member of regulator of healthcare professionals be allowed at the same time to be a board member of another regulator of healthcare professionals?
- If you are familiar with a regulator, in terms of the number of board members, is it the right size? Justify your view.

LEGISLATION

Example of UK Legislation

Apothecaries Act (1815) L

FURTHER READING

Board Size and Effectiveness: R
Advice to the Department of Health regarding health professional regulators
CHRE
September 2011
15 pages

OECD Corporate Governance Factbook 2019 R
OECD
2019
180 pages
Factbook about the institutional, legal, and regulatory frameworks for corporate governance across 49 jurisdictions worldwide.

A Patient Voice at the GMC; A Lay Members' View of the GMC B
Robinson, J
Health Rights, London
ISBN-13: 978-1-871715-00-2
1988
43 pages

JOURNALS AND RESEARCH PAPERS

The Impact of Board Size on Firm Performance: Evidence from the JRP
The European Journal of Finance, Volume 15, Issue 4
Paul M Guest
June 2009
Pages 385–404

3.3 STANDARDS AND COMPETENCES OF BOARD MEMBERS

INTRODUCTION

Society has high expectations of those who hold positions of public office both in terms of how they will behave and the competences that they must possess to deliver their responsibilities. The expectations of public office are laid down in the seven principles of public life and regulators have established a range of competence for their board members.

PUBLIC OFFICE

In the UK there is no precise definition of a public office but it can be defined as:

Definition: Public Office
Position or occupation created by a law or legislation to undertake a service to the public and is a position of trust.

Public office holders are individuals who are in position of authority and can be appointed or elected. They therefore include elected politicians and some individuals and occupations funded by the taxpayer. They include:

- All elected or holders of public office both locally and nationally
- Members of Parliament (national)
- Elected members of councils (local)
- Civil servants, in central and local government
- Police, courts, probation service, and NDPBs
- Administrators of government funded health, education, social, and care services
- Members of the boards of statutory regulators

Public office holders are both servants of the public and stewards of public resources. Because a degree of trust is placed in holders of public office they are expected to behave in certain ways and in particular, not abuse the trust placed in them. For example, they should not take bribes and they should treat all members of the public equally.

PRINCIPLES OF PUBLIC LIFE

To clearly codify the expectations of individuals who work as public office holders, the UK Government in 1994 established an independent advisory body, the Committee for Standards in Public Life led by Lord Michael Nolan. In due course it published a set of principles, often referred to as the Nolan principles, which laid down how individuals holding public office should behave.

The seven principles of public life, or the Nolan principles, were revised in January 2013 and are as follows:

1. **Selflessness** – Holders of public office should act solely in terms of the public interest.
2. **Integrity** – Holders of public office must avoid placing themselves under any obligation to people or organisations that might try inappropriately to influence them in their work. They should not act or take decisions in order to gain financial or other material benefits for themselves, their family, or their friends. They must declare and resolve any interests and relationships.
3. **Objectivity** – Holders of public office must act and take decisions impartially, fairly, and on merit, using the best evidence and without discrimination or bias.
4. **Accountability** – Holders of public office are accountable to the public for their decisions and actions and must submit themselves to the scrutiny necessary to ensure this.
5. **Openness** – Holders of public office should act and take decisions in an open and transparent manner. Information should not be withheld from the public unless there are clear and lawful reasons for so doing.
6. **Honesty** – Holders of public office should be truthful.
7. **Leadership** – Holders of public office should exhibit these principles in their own behaviour. They should actively promote and robustly support the principles and be willing to challenge poor behaviour wherever it occurs.

In effect these are the standards that board members of regulators must achieve. And, it should be noted that like healthcare professionals the behaviour in board members covers both their public and their private lives.

CODE OF CONDUCT FOR BOARD MEMBERS

In the UK some regulators have embedded the Nolan principles in codes of conduct for board members and employees to ensure the seven principles are consistently upheld.

COMPETENCES OF BOARD MEMBERS

Members of the board, to successfully fulfil their roles, require a range of competences.

These competences can be divided into two groups, generic competences that all board members should possess and technical competences that some but not all should have.

GENERIC COMPETENCES

The issue of which competences board members should have, has generated considerable debate and proposals from a number of organisations. An example of a competence framework for directors based on skills, knowledge and mindset from the UK's Institute of Directors (IoD) is provided in Table 3.3 – I below:

Table 3.3 – I Competences of board members

Skills
1. Strategic thinking
2. Analysis and use of information
3. Decision making
4. Communication
5. Leadership
6. Influencing
Knowledge
1. Corporate governance
2. Leadership and stakeholder relations
3. Strategy
4. Finance
Mindset
1. Ethical
2. Professional
3. Performance oriented
4. Independence
5. Aware of self and others

It should be noted that the list of generic competences is not definitive. For example, should it include collaboration and experience on knowledge of regulation?

TECHNICAL COMPETENCES

The boards of all organisations require not only generic competences but also technical competences. This can be obtained in three ways:

1. **Access to external expertise**
   From time to time a board and its committees may require access to external experts to provide specialist advice, for example, on financial or legal matters. This has the advantage that the composition of the board does not have to reflect every single eventuality. The executive should not be able to unreasonably curtail these types of requests from the board, and an annual budget should be provided for the cost of this type of expertise
2. **Technical expert board members**
   Typically at least one member of the board has financial expertise
3. **Executive board members**
   The technical expertise may reside in members of the executive, who can either be executive board members or attend the meetings as not voting members

CONCLUSION

Many organisations produce and publish standards and competences that members of boards are expected to adhere to and demonstrate. Regulators should either, adopt them wholeheartedly, or, as a group exercise review, possibly amend, and then adopt for their own specific purposes.

EXERCISES AND QUESTIONS

Exercises

- Review your organisations competences for your board members. Are they reasonable?
- Select three of the competences provided by the IoD. Without reference to external sources write a short paragraph on each. Compare with a colleague. Is there agreement or disagreement on your interpretation on what the competences mean. Why is this so?

Questions

- Should the IoD standards and competences be followed by employees and members of the executive management team of your organisation?
- Should all members of the board have to be able to demonstrate all competences? If not, what is an acceptable threshold?
- Referring to the IoD standards, select three additional competences that could be included and three that can be removed.

FURTHER READING

Competency-Based Governance: R
A Foundation for Board and Organizational Effectiveness
The American Hospital Association's, Centre for Healthcare Governance
Monograph Series
February 2009
63 pages

Competency Profile R
Instrument for the Boards of Public Bodies
Ministry of Finance and the Public Service
Jamaica
January 2017
38 pages

Ethics for Healthcare Regulators R
Enhancing compliance with the seven Principles of Public Life
Committee on Standards in Public Life
Dr Sarah Devaney
Manchester Centre for Regulation, Governance and Public Law School of Law, University of Manchester
August 2016
40 pages

Striking the Balance R
Upholding the Seven Principles of Public Life in Regulation
Sixteenth Report of the Committee on Standards in Public Life
Cm 932
ISBN: 978-1474136945
15 September 2016
92 pages

STANDARDS, CODES, GUIDANCE, CONSULTATIONS, POLICIES, AND PRACTICE NOTES

Standards and Codes

Code of Conduct for Board Members of Public Bodies S&C
Cabinet Office
June 2019
8 pages

Code of Conduct for Council Members S&C
General Dental Council
1 August 2019
19 pages

Conduct by-law S&C
Conduct of Councillors and Committee Members
College of Nurses of Ontario
20 September 2017
19 pages

Director Competency Framework S&C
Institute of Directors Academy
14 pages

Handbook and Code of Conduct for Board Members S&C
Phone-paid Services Authority
November 2019
66 pages

Principles of Public Life – Seven S&C
Lord Nolan
Committee of Standards in Public Life, UK
31 May 1995
1 page

Guidance

Board of Directors 2020 Director Profile G
Ontario College of Pharmacists
2020
17 pages

3.4 SELECTION, APPOINTMENT, TRAINING, AND APPRAISAL OF BOARD MEMBERS

INTRODUCTION

Once the eligibility of individuals to be members of a board of a regulator has been agreed, a variety of processes are used to select members to the board. Following their appointment and to ensure that the new members of the board are effective, regulators spend time and effort to train them in the principles and processes of regulating healthcare professionals. In due course, and ideally supported by periodical appraisals, board members should then have opportunities to undergo ongoing training to increase their competences.

SELECTION PROCESS

The selection of members of the board can be undertaken by three processes. They are:

1. Elections
2. Political nomination
3. Public appointment process

1. **Elections**
   Historically, elections were used to select board members, since, as discussed in the preceding sections, only healthcare professionals on the register of the regulator were eligible to become members of the board, usually with the caveat that the registrants were not subject to any ongoing FTP proceedings.

   Advantages and disadvantages of selection by election
   There are some advantages for using an election process, but these are heavily outweighed by the disadvantages.

   Advantages
   On initial perusal the use of an election process is often presented as the best method, since it clearly underlines the use of a democratic process and it also cements the relationship between the profession and the regulator. It could also be argued that the process is advantageous since professionals should also be knowledgeable about the regulation of professionals.

   Disadvantages
   However, experience has demonstrated that there are many disadvantages of using elections to select members of a board of a regulator of healthcare professionals. They are as follows:

   i. **Scarcity of candidates**
   For statutorily regulated professionals being a member of the board of a regulator is not necessary seen as 'good thing' by fellow members of the profession. This is because there are often conflicts of interests and tensions between the professional associations and the regulator. For example, in the UK and statutory regulator of the medical profession the GMC is often in direct conflict with the British Medical Association (BMA), which is both a trade union and a professional association. Professionals may therefore perceive a possible conflict of interest from being on the board of the regulator where they may be criticised as taking too harsh an attitude on FTP issues.

   ii. **Similarities of candidates**
   Candidates and therefore winning candidates are likely to be professionals with similar characteristics. For example, towards the end of their careers, economically affluent, and old.

   iii. **Lack of competences**
   Candidates for election may not be required to possess any specific competences, since all members of the profession are eligible to stand for election. Therefore the election process may result in board members who lack the required competences. In Canada, this concern has in some colleges been addressed by requiring potential candidates to be pre-screened for competences. Those who do not meet the required standards have been barred from participating in the election for the council of the professions' college.

   iv. **Low turnout**
   Frequently, the number of professionals who actually vote is very small, less than two percent of voters being quite common. For example, in June 2016 The College of Nurses of Ontario in a report on governance, reported that only 15% of the profession voted in the election to members of the college. This brings into question either, the legitimacy of board members, or, the election of candidates with controversial views or agendas, for example, the election of single issue candidates who are against statutory regulation.

   v. **Cost**
   For regulators with small registers the cost of running an election may be relatively high as a percentage of their annual income.

   vi. **Inappropriate manifestos**
   On occasions candidates have been elected who are against the principles and processes of regulating healthcare professionals, for example, the requirement to undertake continuing competence.

   vii. **Single-issue winning candidates**
   The winning candidate could on occasions only be interested in a single issue and minimise their attendance at board meetings to those where

the agenda only includes issues they were concerned with.

viii. **Influence of the professional associations**
Entirely legitimately, the professional associations were able to support candidates who would give their backing to the agenda of the association. This made it more difficult for candidates who were clearly independent of the professional association to successfully win an election.

ix. **Primacy of loyalty to electorate**
The winning candidate, not unreasonably, may feel obligated to support the views of those who elected them. However, if the regulator requires higher registration fees to deliver its objectives but the professionals do not want to pay the proposed higher fees, the elected board member may be swayed to act in the interest of the professionals rather than the interest of the regulator.

x. **Process to manage elections**
From the perspective of the regulator, the management of elections is not necessarily seen as a core regulatory process because they are held infrequently and require specialist systems and processes to organise. In the UK most regulators choose to contract out the process to a specialist supplier the Electoral Reform Society. And although an internally managed system may have the advantage of lower costs, a third party like the Electoral Reform Society also had the considerable advantage of nullifying any perception of the possibility of scurrilous practices, such as vote rigging.

Lay members

While the process to appoint members of the professions to the boards of regulators via elections was seen by the professional associations as a workable solution, although not a perfect one, the introduction of lay board membership was a catalyst for change. This was because there was no natural electorate for the role of lay members, an alternative appointment process was required to select lay board members.

Alternative process to board elections

When elections are considered not to be a suitable process to select members of the board the alternative is to use one of two different processes, either political nomination or a public appointment process.

2. **Selection by political nomination**
In this process the decision to select and appoint a board member of the regulator is in the gift of elected politicians, usually a government department or minister responsible for the regulated sector concerned.

In some jurisdictions this process of political patronage plays a significant role. For example, the process known as gubernatorial is commonly used in the states in the USA both for board members and senior executive in the regulatory agencies. This means that when a new State Governor is elected, the chair of the board and its members and the agencies senior executives may undergo wholesale change.

There is no requirement to operate a selection process from volunteering candidates because selection is effectively managed behind closed doors.

To reduce the direct influence of political patronage on appointments in some instances the legislature may request a committees of elected representatives to undertake a pre-appointment scrutiny hearing committee before their appointment is confirmed. The intention of the process is clearly more democratic and enhances transparency and will detect any conflict of interest with direct ministerial appointments. It also demonstrates that appointments are entirely based on merit of qualified candidates and that the process focuses on the needs of the regulator rather than any political agenda. However, a clear policy should be established on which appalments are subject to scrutiny by the committee and clarification on the committees' power to veto an appointment.

However, driven by the needs for checks and balances and the perception of a democratic defect, some jurisdictions have incorporated more openness and transparency of and in the process.

3. **Selection by public appointment process**
The process is predominantly used in the UK to select both professional and lay board members of regulators of healthcare professionals. The chair of the board of the regulator usually chairs the selection panel. The public appointment process, sometimes referred to as open public competition, commences by widely advertising forthcoming vacancies to the boards of the regulators on social media platforms and nowadays less so in the printed media such as national newspapers and minority media. Selection panels are organised and candidates are interviewed and selected on merit using agreed selection techniques such as competency-based interviews.

Many organisations publish standards that are guidance on the selection process, covering the minutia of the whole process from the timetable to the necessity to have non-board independent members on the interview panel.

FORMAL APPOINTMENTS BY GOVERNMENT

In the UK, Government may be involved in the final stage of the process by requiring the successfully selected candidates from open public competition to be appointed only after formal approved by a government minister. However, in some cases, this is done by the Privy Council. The process dovetails with the ability of government to intervene if a board is assessed to be not carrying out its statutory duties and regulatory failure has occurred.

OPENNESS, FAIRNESS, AND TRANSPARENCY OF PROCESS

Great emphasis is placed on the fairness of the process, and openness and transparency must be demonstrated to ensure that merit alone is used. It must ensure that the process results in diverse boards and no candidates are discriminated against.

In the UK until 2004, the Appointments Commission, a government agency, used to manage the process. The cost of the process was charged back to the regulator by the Commission. However, this was abandoned when the Appointments Commission was closed in 2012. Nowadays, the UK's PSA undertakes the role of ensuring the process is managed correctly.

TENURE OF APPOINTMENT OF BOARD MEMBERS

In the UK the tenure of non-executive board members of public authorities is term limited. In the UK the typical term of appointment is for a maximum of two terms of three or four years each, making a total of six to eight years. The policy is in place to:

1. Prevent the non-executives becoming too close to the executives and compromising the principle of independent board members. It is accepted that non-executives may take a less independent perspective over time as they develop closer working relationships with the executive. This may make it more difficult for them to challenge and supervise the work of the executive
2. Increase the number of members of the public who are able to participate in and contribute to the boards of regulators
3. Facilitate the provision of diverse and fresh talent with different perspectives to periodically join the board
4. Enable candidates to apply to become board members who may only be able to commit to a shorter period of public service

Despite this, in some instances individuals who have served maximum term of office, become re-eligible to apply after a gap of 20 years, can apply to join a board of regulators of healthcare professions.

STAGGERED APPOINTMENTS

As discussed previously, boards are considered to be '*organisations with a memory*'. This means that a decision taken at one board continues until it is replaced or amended by another board meeting.

Ensuring the principle that boards are '*organisations with a memory*' and at the same time limiting the tenure of board members by requiring them to continually leave the board at the end of their tenure and be replaced needs to be resolved. This is because if they all depart at the same time it could potentially result in the loss of the boards' corporate memory. To avoid this the legislation governing UK statutory regulators facilitates staggered appointments. The process of staggered and overlapping appointments that results in the board being gradually replaced overtime is depicted in Chart 3.4 – I, below:

Chart 3.4 – I **Board members' staggered terms of office**

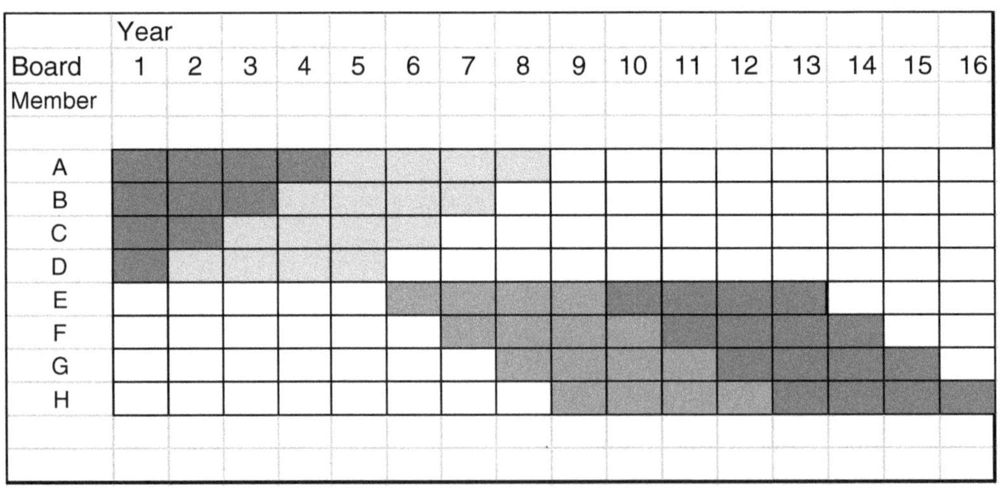

For the process to work effectively, at the point that the board is first established, the duration of the initial term of office for the majority of members must be less than the maximum term.

SELECTION OF CHAIR AND TERM OF APPOINTMENT TO THE BOARD

The legislation may constrain who is eligible to be the chair of the board of the regulator.

For example, there may be a requirement for the chair not to be a healthcare professional from the regulators' register. Alternatively, there may be no requirement in the legislation and the chair can also be a lay. Also, under specific circumstances certain types of individuals may be excluded due, for example, to the requirement on the ratio of lay to professional members. This means that consideration needs to be given to the background of any prospective chair of the board.

In terms of the selection process, a range of options are available similar to those for selecting board members. These range from selection by political nomination to a public appointment process. Another option is that the board can be responsible for electing the chair from amongst willing fellow board members.

The terms of appointment for chairs match other board members in terms of tenure. However, if the new chair has previously been a board member, the time served as a board member may directly reduce the length of tenure for the chair.

TRAINING BOARD MEMBERS

The successful onboarding of new board members and their subsequent on-going training have important ramification for the subsequent quality of the performance of board. It is therefore important for a regulator to invest appropriate resources in the process.

The training and orientation of board members can be broken down into two distinct phases. Firstly their initial one when they join the board and secondly their on-going training. The training itself can, as discussed in Section 3.3, volume 4, address two distinct types of competences, generic and technical.

INDUCTION

Like all employees joining an organisation, board members as part of the integration process should be provided with a brief period of induction. This is sometimes referred to as their 'onboarding', orientation, or training. The process usually emphasises and focuses on technical competences rather than the generic competences of a board member.

The content of their induction process can vary but may include:

- Learning about the regulation of healthcare professions
- The principles and processes of the regulator
- Meeting the executive
- Introduction of the departments of the regulator such as FTP, communications, education, and registration
- The organisation of board meetings
- Jurisprudence of regulation
- The culture of the regulator

This is often supported by an induction information pack.

Their induction process should also include meeting key stakeholders such as professional associations, practising professionals, and other regulators. In some cases a fellow board member will be appointed to be the new members' mentor.

INDUCTION OF SHADOW BOARD

Infrequently a completely new board will be required by a regulator. This occurs, for example, when a new regulator is established. On the assumption that a shadow board is appointed, all the board members can be inducted at the same time. As part of the process civil servants from the sponsoring government department or ministry may provide a valuable contribution into the process.

ONGOING TRAINING

Once a board member has been integrated into their new role they will probably be given the opportunity to be undertake ongoing training. As such, it is good practice to include a review of board members training needs as part of their annual appraisal.

BOARD APPRENTICE PROGRAMME

The board may also host an apprentice programme to help educate and train the next generation of board member for public and third sector organisations.

APPRAISAL OF BOARD MEMBERS

To achieve a high-performing organisation with high impact in terms of added value most organisations will appraise the performance of their employees on an annual basis against predetermined criteria such as goals and objectives and codes of conduct. In the UK in recent years it has become the norm that board members, including the chair, should also undergo an annual appraisal, which may include a self-evaluation, the results of which are often being reported to the sponsoring government ministry.

CONCLUSION

The days of regulators being allowed by themselves to manage the processes to appoint members of the board and the chair have been steadily eroded. Today the mutual obligations of the regulatory contract have led to the almost universal abandonment of elections, and in the UK board members are appointed by an open public competition appointment process.

EXERCISES AND QUESTIONS

Exercises

- Review the induction programme of your organisation for new board members. How can it be improved?
- Meet with one or two of your recently appointed board members. What was their view of the quality and relevance of their induction programme?

Questions

- Should members of committees have specific induction programmes?
- Should the Chair undertake a specific induction programme compared to other members of the Board?

FURTHER READING

Better Public Appointments: A Review of the Public Appointments Process R
Sir Gerry Grimstone
Cabinet Office (UK)
March 2016
41 pages

STANDARDS, CODES, GUIDANCE, CONSULTATIONS, POLICIES, AND PRACTICE NOTES

Standards and Codes

Governance Code for Public Appointments S&C
Cabinet Office
December 2016
15 pages

Guidance

Good Practice in Making Council Appointments

Principles, Guidance and the Scrutiny Process for Regulators Making Appointments which are Subject to Section 25C Scrutiny G
PSA
March 2019
51 pages

Guidance on the Appraisal of Non Departmental Public Body (NDPB) Board Members and Chair G
Scottish Government
ISBN: 978-1-78652-455-3
February 2017
9 pages

Gubernatorial Appointment Process G
Michigan Manual 2009–2010 Chapter IV – THE EXECUTIVE BRANCH • IV-6
2009–2010
2 pages

Setting Non-executive Director Terms and Conditions G
NHS Providers
25 pages

3.5 PERFORMANCE OF BOARDS, THEIR MEMBERS, AND COMPLAINTS

INTRODUCTION

Stakeholders have high expectations on how the board of regulators and their members collectively and individually discharge their duties and, in particular, what happens if they do not. This section therefore addresses the performance of boards and their members and how complaints against them are handled.

PERFORMANCE OF BOARDS

Creating and maintaining a high-performing board, or a high-impact board, is an art rather than a science. To try and satisfy the unceasing appetite for knowledge and practical skills of how to achieve this, there is an army of experts, consultants, writers, and snake oil salesmen providing the correct answer, all of which I do not intend to emulate.

On the assumption that it is unlikely, but possible, that the combined competences of the members of a board are unable to detect and rectify any challenges that exist, I would encourage all boards to periodically make use of the numerous freely available self-evaluation and assessment tools and to take prompt action once completed. For example, the board evaluation questionnaire published by the UK's National Audit Office.

RELATIONSHIP BETWEEN THE BOARD AND THE EXECUTIVE

Despite this, there is one area that should be highlighted and that is the relationship between the board and the executive. This is because the two have both different and joint responsibilities; see Chart 3.1 – I. It therefore goes without saying that the relationship between the two is mission critical for the success of the organisation.

A relationship built on a high level of trust between board and the executive is valuable where participation in board meetings is based on mutual respect and an attitude by the executive of *'Get in, get out and do not get hurt'* should be avoided at all costs.

Time and resources are required by both to establish and maintain a sound working relationship that is both efficient and effective. The working relationship should be based on the principle that the executive should be directed by the CEO and not the board. This can also be enhanced by facilitating board members to have access to employees but only under strict ground rules.

For those seeking to build sound working relationships and in particular trust, the Johari window is a technique that can be used to help individuals better understand their relationship with themselves and others. It was created by psychologists Joseph Luft (1916–2014) and Harrington Ingham (1916–1995) in 1955. Johari is derived from the combining their first names of the two psychologists, Joe and Harrington.

MANAGEMENT OF BOARD MEETINGS

It is self-evident that badly managed board meetings go hand in hand with badly performing boards. And, again whilst unpacking this topic is not a core task of the book, a range of good housekeeping issues can easily be undertaken and reported on by the secretariat.

For example:

- Frequency of board meetings lasting over four hours
- Observable commitment to openness and transparency
- Not holding committee meetings before or after board meetings
- Scheduling of morning vs. evening meetings
- Time spent on board discussion vs. executive presentations

PERFORMANCE OF INDIVIDUAL BOARD MEMBERS

The performance of a board and the performance of its members are to a greater extent overlapping and are inseparable.

These expectations of board members performance should be formally set out in standards or rules and a board code of conduct. While the vast majority of board members will match and surpass the expectations of their performance, there will unfortunately be a small minority of individuals who do not live up to the requirements for successful board participation. Typical of such concerns include:

- Communication characterised by aggression and shutting others out
- Infrequent attendance and lack of pre-notice of impending absence
- Poor or non-existent levels of contribution to board discussions

Since insight of oneself can on occasions be poor or lacking, annual appraisal of all board members can informally clear expectations on the performance of board members.

ADDRESSING POORLY PERFORMING BOARD MEMBERS

Ideally, a process to support poorly performing board members to improve their performance should be in place. In addition, before it becomes a necessity, the organisation should develop and publish a documented process to enable the removal of board members whose performance does not match expectations.

CONCERN ABOUT BOARD MEMBERS

Separate from concerns about the performance of board members during meetings of the board, concerns may be received about board members relating to their other responsibilities.

To make matters more complicated the concern may arise from events unrelated to the regulator and regulation or they may be raised by another board member. It is also not unheard of for concerns to be made to disrupt the good running of the board.

FITNESS TO PRACTISE CONCERNS ABOUT BOARD MEMBERS

From time to time concerns will be received by the FTP department about individuals who are members of the board and who are members of one of the professions that the board is responsible for regulating.

PROCESS FOR HANDLING CONCERNS ABOUT BOARD MEMBERS

However infrequently concerns may arise, it is not unreasonable for regulators to have documented processes that detail how they will be handled. Therefore, the regulator should establish policy and procedure for handling concerns and complaints about board members. It is likely that it will include the recommendation that board members should recuse themselves from all their activities relating to their membership of the board until the matters relating to the concern or complaint are resolved.

DISQUALIFICATION FROM BOARD MEMBERSHIP

Appointments and continuing membership to the boards of UK regulators can be prevented and terminated by a range of events that lead to an individual being disqualified from holding office. The events include individuals who have been:

- Convicted in the UK, and received a prison sentence or suspended sentence of three months or more in the last five years
- Dismissed, other than by reason of redundancy, from any paid employment with a public authority
- Disqualified under the Company Directors Disqualification Act 1986
- Made bankrupt or has made a composition or arrangement with their creditors
- Previously been removed from trusteeship of a charity by the courts or the Charity Commissioners
- Suspended from, or has been removed from or subject to conditions of registration of any professional association
- Terminated under certain circumstances from an earlier term of appointment as the chair or member of a public authority

REMOVAL FROM BOARD MEMBERSHIP

In the UK the Privy Council has the powers to remove a board member for a number of reasons. These include:

- Conduct or performance in board or committee meetings
- Serious and persistent insufficiency attendance
- Serious breach of the members' code of conduct

CONCLUSION

Regulators must be cognisant of the possibility that the performance of their boards and its members may not live up to expectations. They must therefore make contingencies for such occurrences including potential removal of individuals from the board.

EXERCISE AND QUESTION

Exercise

- How should the performance of the chair of the board of a regulator be appraised?

Question

- Is it reasonable that the behaviour of a board member of a regulator that is unrelated to their role of the regulator can be taken into account and may lead to their disqualification?

LEGISLATION

Example of UK Legislation

Company Directors Disqualification Act 1986 L

FURTHER READING

Fit and Proper? Governance in the Public Interest R
Professional Standards Authority
March 2013
16 pages

Simple Sabotage Field Manual B
United Sates Office of Strategic Services
ISBN-13: 9798405796871
1944, Reprinted 21 Jan 2022
51 pages

Unlocking Your Board's Full Potential R
Evaluation questionnaire
NAO
September 2009
8 pages

JOURNALS AND RESEARCH PAPERS

The Johari Window, a Graphic Model of Interpersonal Awareness JRP
Proceedings of the western training laboratory in group development (Los Angeles: UCLA)
Luft, J. and Ingham, H.
1955

STANDARDS, CODES, GUIDANCE, CONSULTATIONS, POLICIES, AND PRACTICE NOTES

Guidance

Guidance on Board Effectiveness G
Financial Reporting Council
July 2018
50 pages

3.6 COMMITTEES AND WORKING GROUPS

INTRODUCTION

The board of a regulator has a wide range of roles and responsibilities. As with many other organisations, to manage them they can be discharged by committees, panels, and in other cases, working groups.

COMMITTEES

A committee can be defined as:

Definition: Committee
Group of individuals chosen or appointed by another group and delegated to perform, investigate, consider, report, or act on a particular issue.

In the UK the regulators of healthcare professionals are prolific users of committees. The reason for this will now be explained.

LEGISLATIVE REQUIREMENT FOR COMMITTEES

Historically in the UK, the decision whether or not to have a committee was not necessarily within the gift of the board of the regulator, since the requirement for the existence of some and their particular role would be set down in their legislation. In the UK these types of committees are referred to as statutory committees.

In contrast, any committee, established by the board on their own volition, is referred to as non-statutory committees.

In addition, the responsibilities and governance arrangements of committees of regulators are complex because of the doctrine of the separation of policy or law making, from implementation; see Section 8.2, volume 1, Legal principles and process.

As a consequence, in the UK the legislation of the regulator using the principle of the separation of power may require the division of some regulatory processes into three separate components. They are:

1. The establishment of standards by the board and/or statutory committee
2. The operational implementation of the standards by the executive
3. Regulatory process that make judgments using the standards not to be made by board members or the executive

STATUTORY COMMITTEES

In the UK there was considerable variation in use, names, and responsibilities of statutory committees. Examples of statutory committees included:

- Education and training committee Section 2.1, volume 2
- Fitness to practise committee Section 3.1, volume 3
- Registration committee Section 4.1, volume 2

It should be noted that, as previously discussed in Section 2.1, volume 3, some regulators had more than one committee for the FTP process, namely:

- Interim orders committee (IoC) Section 3.2, volume 3
- Investigating committee Section 3.4, volume 3
- Health committee Section 5.1, volume 3

Another important characteristic of UK statutory committees is that they often have the power to advise the board, whether or not the board asks the committee to provide the advice in the first instance.

In addition, some multi-professional regulators may have profession specific committees, for example, in the UK historically the NMC's midwifery committee.

ETHICS COMMITTEES

In other jurisdictions, a small number of regulators may be required to form an ethics committee. For example, the Medical Council of Hong Kong has under its legislation the Medical Registration Ordinance established an ethics committee.

DEMISE OF STATUTORY COMMITTEES

Partially in response to the argument that the legislation of regulators should not be over prescriptive, in recent years the UK government considered and then decided to remove or minimise the necessity of statutory committees from the legislation of the regulators of healthcare professionals. In effect this policy transfers the responsibility for deciding what types of committees to have, from the legislature to the board of the regulator.

NON-STATUTORY COMMITTEES

Historically, non-statutory committees or committees of the board, were, unlike statutory committees, a matter of discretion for the board of the regulator. In jurisdictions where both statutory and non-statutory committees remain, the non-statutory committees tend to be more prolific and their responsibilities reflect the governance arrangements found in commercial enterprises. Non-statutory committees can be broken down into two groups, namely, non-operational and operational.

NON-OPERATIONAL NON-STATUTORY COMMITTEES

The bailiwick of these non-statutory committees reflects the governance arrangements of commercial organisation. They are established on a permanent basis and report directly to the board. Examples include:

1. Appointments or nominations
2. Audit
3. Ethics
4. Remuneration
5. Risk and assurance, or risk
6. Tribunal advisory

These will now be explored in further detail:

1. **Appointments or nominations committee**
   If established, the appointments or nominations committee oversees the appointment process for board members and sometime the CEO and senior executives.
2. **Audit committee**
   The audit committee's responsibilities include:
   - Approval of the annual report and accounts prior to approval by the board
   - Compliance
   - Liaison with the external auditors
   - Liaison with internal auditors
   - Oversight of internal controls

   Internal controls
   For accounting and auditing purposes these can be defined as:

Definition: Internal Controls
Mechanisms, rules, and procedures implemented by an organisation to ensure the integrity of financial and accounting information, promote accountability, and prevent fraud.

   For all intents and purposes the process is similar to an enterprise risk management framework. In the UK regulators are expected to publish an annual statement of internal control (SIC), which describes the effectiveness of the organisation internal controls.

   Membership of the audit committee comprises exclusively non-executive board members, plus the addition of an independent non-board member. This demonstrates their true independence from the board. It excludes the chair of the board of the regulator and should have at least one member who has expertise in financial management. It may also have a role in the regulator's whistleblowing processes.
3. **Ethics committee**
   The term has been used for committees established to oversee standards, for example, the now-replaced, UK Central Council for Nursing, Midwifery and Health Visiting operated a standards and ethics committee.
4. **Remuneration committee**
   The committee is responsible for establishing a remunerating policy for senior employees of the organisation and other groups of employees. They may also cover board and committee members' remuneration; see Section 3.7, volume 4. The chair of the board is usually not a member of the committee.

   To establish an appropriate level of wages and fees external benchmarking organisation can undertake research in the market based on a portfolio of comparative public authorities and other similar organisation. Levels of remuneration set by regulators are sensitive and controversial issues with key stakeholders and often draws comparisons between their employees and those of the professionals' they regulate. Bonuses are very rarely paid by regulators to their employees.
5. **Risk and assurance committee**
   Some boards will establish a separate risk committee although its responsibilities may be undertaken by the audit committee. It may also be called the risk and assurance committee.

   Its main responsibility will be the enterprise risk management framework, setting and monitoring the risk appetite, and the risk tolerance of the regulator.
6. **Tribunal advisory committee**
   Using the principles of the separation of powers, to ensure that there is no possibility of inappropriate interference by members of the regulators' board in the process to select and reappoint assessors, some regulators may establish a tribunal advisory committee with the specific task of recruiting, training, and appraising assessors.

CONSUMER PANEL

It should be noted that if a regulator has a consumer panel it will probably be organised along the lines of a non-operational non-statutory committee. These types of groups are explored in detail in Section 2.2, volume 4.

OPERATIONAL NON-STATUTORY COMMITTEES

The second group of non-statutory committee's responsibilities relate to the operations of the regulator. Examples include:

- Accommodation
- Communications

- Coordination
- Finance and resources
- Investments
- Legislation
- Special purposes

These types of committees may operate on a temporary basis and be disbanded once their task is completed. They may report to the board directly or to another non-statutory committee.

The propensity for a board to establish these types of operational committees can be explained by the decision of the board on where to set the division between its oversight role and stepping into the operational role of the executive. Also, in times of a crisis, boards frequently set up operational non-statutory committees.

In some instances, the executive work as an executive committee.

GOVERNANCE ARRAIGNMENTS

The governance arraignments of committees are similar to those used by boards. However, the board, having established its statutory and non-statutory committees, should specify five additional processes. They are:

1. Procedures of committees
2. Appeals process against decisions of committees
3. Chair of committees
4. Membership of committees
5. Communications

These will now be explored in further detail:

1. **Procedures of committees**
   Where statutory committees are in place the legislation is often very specific about how their process operate, leaving a low level of discretion to the committee itself. However, when not set down in legislation, the principles and processes of all the committees must be specified by the board, usually as rules or byelaws. Such arrangements usually include:
   i. Terms of reference of the committee
   The remit or purpose of the committees of regulators vary enormously from one regulator to another. It is therefore important that their purpose and of terms of reference is agreed and published by the board of the regulator
   ii. Scheme of delegation
   A scheme of delegation may also be utilised by the board to clearly establish what the committees are responsible for
   iii. Statement for the objective of the committee
   This is a brief description of the committee is required to achieve
   iv. Standing orders of committee
   The rules and procedures of committees, like those of boards, should be set out in standing orders
2. **Appeals process against decisions of committees**
   As discussed in Section 8.4, volume 1 appeals and judicial reviews, where the board of a regulator's internal appeal process is required by its legislation to delegate some of its responsibilities in a particular area to a statutory committee such as education, the board is in effect the initial 'higher authority'. An appeal can therefore be heard about a decision of the committee by the board. This has the added advantage of being fast and less costly and without the need to go directly to the courts.
3. **Chair of committees**
   The standing orders should include the process to select and appoint the chair of the committee, and also their competences and appraisal.
4. **Membership of committees**
   Members of committees can be either drawn from the board or from stakeholders such as members of the public and professionals. Again, their competences should be agreed. Their selection and appointment process, terms of office, and remuneration are generally organised on similar lines to those of board members.
5. **Communication**
   To ensure that good communications are maintained between the board and committees, the formal minutes of committees should be submitted promptly to the board after each committee meeting. The chair of the committee is then often invited by the board to answer questions relating to the work of their respective committee.

   To facilitate openness and transparency, wherever possible the meetings of the committees should be held in public. The minutes of the meetings should also be published. In addition, some committees publish thematic reviews and annual reports about the services they deliver.

   Before concluding this section, reference should be made to panels and working groups.

PANELS

When a committee has substantive responsibilities that are:

- Can be discharged by a small permutation of its members
- Frequently required

Temporary decision-making groups can be established that are often referred to as a panel. They can be defined as:

Definition: Panel
Small working group of people selected to give advice or make decisions

Panels, in a similar way to committees, can comprise solely board members or non-board members or a mixture of both.

WORKING GROUPS

On occasions the expertise of the board of the regulator will not be sufficient to address a particular issue facing the organisation. Under these circumstances a working group may be established on a temporary basis to help inform and advise the decision making of the regulator. A working group can be defined as:

Definition: Working Group
Group established by an organisation specifically to deliver a single task, that once finished, is disbanded and the work is assimilated back into the organisation.

The terms expert group or task and finish group may also be used.

TEMPORARY NATURE OF WORKING GROUPS

Working groups are usually established by a regulator to specifically deliver a single task. The group is then disbanded once its work has been completed. Any ongoing work is then assimilated back into the organisation.

THE TASKS OF WORKING GROUPS

Examples of the tasks that working groups may be established to investigate and report on include:

- Drafting and amending the standards of the regulator
- Consideration of the suitability of an aspirant group to be regulated
- Significant change to the process of the regulator

Many regulators when considering if a working group should be established set specific parameters that must be met. These may include:

- Board approval required to establish working group
- Executive responsible for drafting project brief
- Project brief approved by the board
- Chaired by board member
- Membership usually comprises board members, professionals, and non-professionals
- Recruitment to the working group is an open public appointment process against agreed competences
- Work of the group is supported by the executive
- Meetings take place in public
- Working groups are temporary arrangement and are stood down once project completed
- Members of the working group may not be remunerated, but expenses are reimbursed

The use of transient working groups has the advantage of allowing the regulator to gain considerable expertise and advice on an ad hoc basis. The working group also helps establish, build, and maintain collaborative relationships between the regulator, professional associations, members of the profession, and other key stakeholders. However, regulators need to avoid actual and the perception of undue influence by participating stakeholders which in some instances may be interpreted as regulatory capture.

POLICY

Before concluding this section consideration should be given by the board of the regulators on establishing and publishing a policy on the types of committees and working groups it will establish and related issues including their governance and organisational arrangements.

CONCLUSION

Committees have an important role in the running of regulators of healthcare professionals. To ensure that they are efficient and effective the board must ensure that the quality of their governance arrangements is on par with that of the board. They must also periodically review their necessity and arrangements to ensure that they are still appropriate.

EXERCISES AND QUESTIONS

Exercises

- For a large and small regulator in terms of number of professionals regulated, identify all their committees.
- Obtain, examine, and discuss your board's policy on reviewing the governance arrangements of its committees.

Questions

- What types of committees should a regulator have?
- Should the requirement for a regulator to have committees be set out in legislation?
- Should membership of committee include those who are not members of the board?

LEGISLATION

Example of International Legislation

Hong Kong

Medical Registration Ordinance Hong Kong L

STANDARDS, CODES, GUIDANCE, CONSULTATIONS, POLICIES, AND PRACTICE NOTES

Guidance

Guidance on Risk Management, Internal Control and Related Financial and Business Reporting G
Financial Reporting Council
Chair Nigel Turnbull
17 September 2014
30 pages

Statement on Internal Control: A Guide for Audit Committees G
National Audit Office
DP Ref: 009219-002
January 2010
16 pages

Terms of reference for the nomination committee Guidance Note G
The Institute of Chartered Secretaries and Administrators
June 2013
11 pages

3.7 REMUNERATION OF BOARD MEMBERS

INTRODUCTION

Regulators need to establish principles and processes to make arrangements for remunerating their board members.

THE REMUNERATION OF EMPLOYEES

The principles and processes used to remunerate non-executive board members are different from those used for employees.

For comparative purposes the employees of the regulator are usually engaged on full- or part-time employment contracts with a remuneration package containing a number of components. This will include a wage and usually a pension. Unlike commercial organisations, performance-related pay and long-term benefits related to the performance of the organisation are usually not provided. The employment contract may be open ended or on a one-year rolling basis.

REMUNERATION OF NON-EXECUTIVE BOARD MEMBERS

Historically, until the turn of the last century, members of the boards of regulators of healthcare professionals were rarely remunerated for their services. The strong and prevailing attitude of the day was that professionals and members of the public as board members should be considered as undertaking a public duty and that they should freely contribute their time for the benefit of society.

However, times have changed and whilst serving on a board of a regulator is still seen as prestigious and a something to aspire to, nowadays all the UK statutory regulators of healthcare professions financially compensate their board members and volunteerism has disappeared.

NOMENCLATURE

In the UK financial payments to non-executive board members for their services are described in various terms including attendance fees, compensation, fees, and remuneration.

EMPLOYMENT STATUS OF NON-EXECUTIVE BOARD MEMBERS

Non-executive board members of the UK statutory regulators of healthcare professionals are not employees of the organisations. Indeed, the legislation of UK regulators specifically excludes board members from being employed by the regulator.

As a consequence:

- They are not eligible to participate in any pension scheme that the regulator may have for their employees
- They are not covered by the UK legal framework that provides employment rights and protection to employees of employers. As a result, when they leave the board against their will they, unlike employees, are not eligible for financial compensation
- In the UK HMRC does not classify board members' fees as wages

PRINCIPLES RELATING TO LEVEL OF BOARD MEMBERS' FEES

In line with good corporate governance board members as non-executive directors should be financially independent from their earnings they receive from the organisation whose board they are members of. As peripatetic board member they must be in a position to be able to 'walk away' from a board if they are in fundamental disagreement with their colleagues and not be beholden to the income stream from their part-time position.

Regulators as public authorities can be considered as setting their fees for board members more in line with a 'gesture of good will', rather than the levels of compensation that the individuals could earn as employees of commercial organisations or in their own businesses.

TIME COMMITMENT OF BOARD MEMBERS

In the UK board members contribute to the regulator on a part-time basis. They will typically be expected to commit to being available for working for the board for between 20 and 30 days per year to attend both board and committee meetings and other ambassadorial roles.

DAILY VS. ANNUAL FEE

There are two alternative ways for paying fees to board members. They can be based either on a daily fee, or, alternatively on an annual flat fee. The advantage of a daily rate is that if a council member does not attend a meeting then no payment will be made. Daily rates also have the advantage that additional commitments by board members outside meetings of the board can be rewarded. These include the ambassadorial role of board members. However, the board member will not know at the start of a financial year what their total compensation will be. Lastly, a decision needs to be made on whether payments are made to board members for any preparation work such as reading council and committee papers before a meeting.

PROCESS TO SET THE LEVEL OF REMUNERATION

Normally the legislation of the regulator assigns the responsibility to set and change board member fees to the board. However, in some jurisdictions, remuneration policy for board members is not in the gift of the regulator but is dictated by government. As a result many regulators will assign the task of determining board members fees to their remuneration committee, see Section 3.6, volume 4, on the assumption that they have established one. The actual level of board members fees may be influenced by the wages of the professionals they regulate. However, there is little rationale to support this principle, other than to reduce the potential for criticism from some stakeholders. Once the fee levels have been set, they will need to be periodically reviewed and adjusted to reflect the prevailing rates of other and similar public authorities. Lastly, the regulator may publish their policy on remunerating board members.

REMUNERATION LEVEL FOR CHAIRS OF BOARD AND COMMITTEES

The chair of the board and the chairs of committees may receive a higher daily or annual fee compared to the rest of the council. However, such a policy of not utilising similar levels of fees may be seen by some as divisive.

FEES RELATING TO EXISTING EMPLOYMENT

In some instances the fees paid to board members can be related to their existing employer. This often applies to the chair of the board where the amount of work expected to be undertaken is significantly greater than a typical member of the board.

In these cases the fees paid are in proportion to their wages from their full-time employer. For example, if the chair is paid £100,000 per year by their employer and they are required to commit on average two days a week to the regulator. The regulator would therefore pay fees of £40,000 pa to the chair.

In some instances, the fees are paid directly to the employer. In effect this arrangement reimburses the employer for the time foregone by their employee to the regulator. This can in some case include reimbursements for pension contributions.

DECLINING FEE PAYMENTS

Some board members may waive their fees. Alternative, they may donate them to a charity. Others, for example, professionals employed by a university or hospital, will not receive the fee payment but it will be paid directly into funds used for research.

EQUALITY OF FEES

Historically, in some jurisdictions different types of members of boards were differently remunerated. For example, board members who were professionals were paid and the lay members were not paid or if paid, received a lower amount. This type of policy has now been discontinued.

EMPLOYMENT TAX

Board members, although not employees, are treated as if they were by the UK tax authority, the HMRC, who classifies the fees as earned income. This means that tax and National Insurance are dedicated by the regulator before payments are made to board members.

EXPENSES

An expenses policy will be required to cover travel, accommodation, and subsistence. Some regulators will also publish the expenses paid to board members and senior executives.

PUBLICATION OF BOARD COMPENSATION

In the UK in-line with the expectation of the transparency of regulators the actual compensation paid to all board members is normally published in the annual report and accounts of the regulators. This has an added advantage that comparative compensation paid by public authorities can relatively easily be researched and compared and contrasted.

Table 3.7 – I lists examples of fees of some UK statutory regulators in 2022/23:

Canada
Hong Kong
Republic of Ireland

Table 3.7 – I Fees of board members of regulators

Regulator	Daily fee
GMC	£300
HCPC	£200
Vets	£500
Lawyers	£200

CONCLUSION

The remuneration of members of the boards of regulators in the great scheme of things seems relatively unimportant. However, it can be seen as a contentious issue and requires time and effort to establish a defendable policy on the issue.

EXERCISES AND QUESTIONS

Exercises

- Investigate a number of regulators and ascertain if they publish the fees paid to their board members
- In your jurisdiction, do different regulators pay different or the same fees to the members of the boards and, if so, what is the justification?

Questions

- When setting the fees of board members should they be related to only other statutory regulators of healthcare professionals, charities, other public bodies or commercial organisations?
- Should members of the board be paid on a daily or annual basis?
- Should board fees be linked to the earnings of the profession they regulate?

Service Standards and Operational Performance of Regulators

CHAPTER 4

INTRODUCTION

Every one of us has numerous daily experiences of the standards of service provided by organisations and individuals. Whether it is the time waiting in a queue at the supermarket checkout, the accuracy of a utility company's bill, or the quality of a lawyer drafting a will, we all have expectations and experiences of good, bad, and indifferent services.

The regulators of healthcare professionals are service organisations and the standards of service that they provide to their users are as important as any other service provider. It is therefore entirely reasonable that standards for the services that regulators provide should be set and used to measure, evaluate, and improve their performance.

In addition to the service standards used and created by a regulator, they can also adopt standards set by other organisations such as standards organisations. Lastly, other public authorities set standards that regulators must abide by, for example, standards relating to data protection and freedom of information.

The chapter has six sections:

4.1 Service standards and operational performance of regulators

4.2 Evaluating operational performance of regulators

4.3 Standards organisations

4.4 Complaints about services of regulators

4.5 Data protection

4.6 Freedom of information

4.1 SERVICE STANDARDS AND OPERATIONAL PERFORMANCE OF REGULATORS

INTRODUCTION

The operational performance of regulators in terms of their standards of service is of great interest to their stakeholders including government, professionals, the public, and not least, their board. However, the standards of services provided by regulators are not always consistent, and can differ wildly with some performing to a high standard whilst others occasionally perform relatively less well.

If the reasons for the differing levels of service for regulators both within a sector and across sectors are better understood, then best practices for operational performance can be shared and underperforming regulators can be improved. Regulators must therefore set their service standards and evaluate their achieved operational performance against theirs and others standards. Lastly, they should take corrective action if the standards are not met.

SERVICES PROVIDED BY REGULATORS OF HEALTHCARE PROFESSIONALS

Regulators provide services that fall into two broad categories. They are as follows:

1. Services provided by the regulator to their stakeholders
2. Services provided by the regulator to internal users

SERVICES PROVIDED BY THE REGULATOR TO THEIR STAKEHOLDERS

This is the most important area of service provision, since it can be assumed that all stakeholders may at some point potentially make use of the services provided by the regulator. In addition, regulators are monopolist providers of services and their stakeholders if they are dissatisfied with the quality of service they receive, they can't use alternative providers.

SERVICES PROVIDED BY THE REGULATOR TO INTERNAL USERS

Although sometimes overlooked, services are also provided by regulators' departments or functions to its other departments or functions. For example, the finance department that will be responsible for paying employee wages both accurately and within a particular timeframe. Or the IT department will be required to ensure that new employees have access to the IT system within a short period of time after starting employment work.

Operations of Regulators of Healthcare Professionals, Volume 4, First Edition. Marc Seale.

Companion website: www.wiley.com/go/seale/regulatinghealthcare

SERVICE STANDARDS

Regulators should set and use standards for the services they provide. A service standard can be defined as:

Definition: Service Standard
Commitment by an organisation to its customers to the level of service they can expect.

The terms performance indicator and performance measure may also be used.

INTERNAL AND EXTERNAL STANDARDS

As a reminder as discussed in Section 1.2, volume 4, service standards can be set both by the regulator itself and external organisations.

USE OF SERVICE STANDARDS

The prime purpose of service standards is to enable a user of a service to know what service to expect. However, service standards are also used for other purposes, including:

- Assist the service provider to allocate resources
- Component of an organisation's management information system (MIS)
- Used by auditors and oversight organisations to measure the performance of regulators

PRINCIPLES AND PROCESSES FOR SETTING AND USING SERVICE STANDARDS

When embarking on the process to establishing service standards for their operational performance, regulators will have to take into account and decide on a range of issues. These include:

1. Identification of services provided
2. Which services to monitor
3. Tangible products vs. intangible services
4. Setting the standards for each service
5. Process – overall vs. sub-process stages
6. Generic vs. specific services
7. Clarity of measurement
8. Accuracy of measurement
9. Frequency of measurement
10. Consistency of judgment making
11. Statistical analysis of results
12. Outliers
13. Variation in demand for services
14. Irreversibly growth or decline in demand for service
15. Historical trends in performance
16. Management information system (MIS)
17. Timeliness of results
18. Publication of service standards
19. Publication of performance against standards
20. Annual review

These 20 issues will now be explored in greater detail:

1. **Identification of services provided**
The regulator should periodically conduct a review to identify all the services that it provides to both its stakeholders and internal users. It is likely that they will identify hundreds of individual services.

2. **Which services to monitor**
Some services may be considered to be relatively inconsequential, and therefore there is no requirement to set a service standard and monitor performance. However, the availability of a manned office reception may seem inconsequential until the point there is no receptionist.

3. **Tangible products vs. intangible services**
Regulators are providers of intangible services rather than tangible products.
When a tangible product is acquired by a consumer, for example, a portable radio, if it does not work it is relatively easy for a consumer to demonstrate to the supplier by returning it to the shop where it was purchased and obtaining a replacement that works. Likewise, it is relatively easy for manufacturers of products to measure the rate of their production and quality. For example, 100 widgets can be made each day that weigh 10 kg, measure 1 cm in diameter, use steel with 97.50% purity, and cost 5 Euros each to manufacture.
In comparison, when a consumer purchases an intangible service it is more challenging to demonstrate to the supplier if they are dissatisfied with the service. And in addition, measuring the rate of production and quality of intangible services is more challenging.
Despite this, the task of setting service standards for intangible services should not be set aside and should still be undertaken.

4. **Setting the standards for each service**
For each service, a decision is required to set the standard for the service both in terms of quality and quantity or

level. For example, should all or 90% of emails be answered in one, three, or seven days? Or should reliance be placed on catch-all phrases, such as 'expeditiously'?

5. **Process – overall vs. sub-process stages**
When an overall process can be subdivided into distinct individual sub-processes, should different service standards be used for each sub-process? For example, in FTP the rate of case progression.

6. **Generic vs. specific services**
Does the service standard apply to all users of the process or should there be different standards for the same process in different situations? For example, the time taken to respond to communications from the police vs. time to respond to enquiries from potential suppliers of good and services?

7. **Clarity of measurement**
Regulators must be unambiguously clear about what and how they measure their performance. For example, suppose two regulators have a service standard to answer 90% of telephone calls within 30 seconds. One regulator starts the clock running on the first ring, the other after five rings.

8. **Accuracy of measurement**
How accurate will the service be measured, for example, by hours or days?

9. **Frequency of measurement**
How frequently will the standard be measured? The frequency of evaluations can vary enormously. For example:
   - Continuous, for example, the monitoring of the time it takes to answer telephone calls
   - Periodically, for example, daily, monthly or annually?
   - Infrequently, for example, time to introduce recommendations following the publication of a government report in response to a regulatory failure

10. **Consistency of judgment making**
It is important to understand the consistent and quality of judgments made by regulators. The challenge is how can this be done?

11. **Statistical analysis of results**
Which statistical methods will be adopted to demonstrate the range and frequency of operational performance against standards? For example, the use of averages, minimum, maximums modes, and medians etc. The issue of sampling size should also be addressed.

12. **Outliers**
Will outliers be excluded or included in the data sets of results?

13. **Variation in demand for services**
When demand for a service changes significantly over a particular period of time, for example, graduating students applying to join register for the first time in early summer compared to the autumn, where should the service standards be set?

14. **Irreversible growth or decline in demand for service**
When the demand for a service is rapidly growing or declining, will the level of service be adjusted?

15. **Historical trends in performance**
What period of time will historical information be used for comparative purpose?

16. **Management Information System (MIS)**
How will the regulator's management information system (MIS), collect, monitor, record, analyse, distribute, and present actual performance against planned results? This topic is explored in the following section.

17. **Timeliness of results**
How long will it take to make service standards information available for internally use via the MIS?

18. **Publication of service standards**
Should all or only some of the regulator's service standards be made publicly available? If so, how and when will this be done?

19. **Publication of performance against standards**
Will the regulator's performance against all, some, or none of their standards be made available to the public?

20. **Annual Review**
Will an annual review of performance against service standards be published?

CONTINUOUS QUALITY IMPROVEMENT

Once the quality of a service is set, measured, and adhered to, it is tempting for any organisation to sit back on their laurels and assume that the task has been completed and they can then move onto other fields afresh. Indeed, the reputation of bureaucracies is such that one could assume that they are more likely to suffer from stasis. However, all organisation can improve the quality of their services or products by using step changes or a continuous improvement process. In Japan continuous quality improvement manifests itself in the business philosophy of Kaizen.

The benefits to regulators of healthcare professionals of continually improving their services are no different from any other organisation, and it is reasonable to expect them to do so. Regulators should therefore continually assess the effectiveness and efficiency of all their processes and their intended outcomes. Wherever possible if they are not being effective and efficient they should take corrective action to rapidly improve. As a consequence the provision of poor services and accidents and errors all provide opportunities for the regulator to better understand their processes and principles and, in turn, should facilitate quality improvement.

This is sometimes referred to as being agile or being a learning organisation. This includes retrospective evaluation.

In addition, regulators should therefore proactively encourage the entities they regulate to adopt the principle of continuous quality improvement.

RESOURCES, OPERATIONAL PERFORMANCE, AND QUALITY OF SERVICES

The operational performance and quality of a service is directly linked to the resources that are required to deliver it, both in terms of human and financial resources.

The regulators' resources includes both the knowledge and skills of the employees and the capacity of their processes. So, for example, an average FTP case costs X thousands of pounds, takes x months to complete during which a fully trained and experienced case manager is responsible for x number of cases per year.

Like nearly all organisations, regulators don't have unlimited resources and have to make decisions on where they will allocate their limited human and financial resources across competing demands. As discussed in Section 1.4, volume 4, Financial characteristics of regulators of HCPs, if the correct decisions are made regulators will deliver the required services to an acceptable quality. If the regulator makes the wrong decisions and the requirements of stakeholders, including the government and the courts, are not met and the organisation may be seen to have failed. However, as stated in the regulatory contract, regulators must have the resources to deliver their objectives and thus maintain the trust and confidence that stakeholders place in them.

Regulators must therefore measure both output in terms of the quality and quantity of services provided against standards and input measures in terms of costs. If either is below or above expectations, the government must enable the regulator to adjust its resources to ensure it remains effective, efficient, and ethical.

SERVICES PROVIDED BY EXTERNAL ORGANISATIONS TO THE REGULATOR

It should be noted that at the same time as examining regulators as providers of services, consideration should also be given to regulators as consumers of services provided by other organisations and individuals.

Examples of service providers to regulators may include companies providing IT services, law firms providing legal advice and office cleaning companies. In the UK it is common practice to set down in a legally binding contract the level of service that will be provided in a document called service level agreement (SLA). The SLAs specify service levels for both quality and quantity of services such as the seniority of the person providing the service, or the availability of services in any given 24 hour period, or the mean time to recovery of a disrupted service.

EXTERNAL STANDARDS IMPOSED ON REGULATORS

Lastly, before concluding this section, it should be remembered that regulators as public authorities may have service standards imposed on them by government or other public authorities such as the Information Commissioner's Office.

In some instances the legislation of the regulator will incorporate various service standards, for example, the time taken to complete various steps in a fitness to practise (FTP) process. However, once embedded in legislation proscriptive standards can become rapidly outdated but remain difficult to change. For example, the requirement to use letters yet remain silent on the use of electronic communication.

Government authorities, such as auditors and oversight organisations, will not only set standards but will require the regulator to either publish its performance against the standards themselves or alternatively it may collect, compare, and publish reports on the sector including individual performance against the service standards. They are addressed in Sections 6.3, volume 4.

CONCLUSION

Efficient, effective, and ethical regulators must deliver their objectives by deploying their limited resources to maximise benefits at minimal costs.

Whether it be the approval of a new education and training programme, the decision to register an international applicant or the time to conclude an investigation of a complaint about a professional, all should be completed to reasonable standards of service.

Lastly, it should be remembered that the processes of regulation are not like mass production lines for tin cans where every can is measured for conformity. However, regulators should have the ability and resources to deliver reasonable standards of services. If they fail to meet the standards and underperform, then corrective action should be taken.

EXERCISES AND QUESTIONS

Exercises

- How does your organisation measure the success of its projects?
- Investigate three regulators from different sectors. Do they use common types of service standards?

Questions

- What are the service standards for the five most important services that your organisation provides?
- Referring to your organisation, when did it last undertake a comprehensive review of its service standards? What were its findings?

FURTHER READING

OECD Guiding Principles for Regulatory Quality and Performance R
Organisation for Economic Cooperation and Development (OECD)
2005
12 pages

4.2 EVALUATING OPERATIONAL PERFORMANCE OF REGULATORS

INTRODUCTION

Regulators having established and implemented service standards for their operational processes, the results can be evaluated by either themselves or by external organisations using a variety of processes including audits, benchmarking, quality assurance, and service user feedback.

RESPONSIBILITY FOR EVALUATING PERFORMANCE OF REGULATORS

There are three contenders for who can evaluate the performance of a regulator. They are:

1. **Self-evaluation**
   The regulator can undertake their own evaluation. The work is typically undertaken by their own QA function; see Section 1.2, volume 4
2. **External evaluation commissioned by the regulator**
   The regulator can commission an evaluation using an external organisation
3. **External evaluation commissioned by government**
   Government can commission an evaluation by a named individual or a public authority such as an auditor or oversight organisation; see Section 6.4, volume 4

PROCESSES TO EVALUATE THE OPERATIONAL PERFORMANCE OF A REGULATOR

Notwithstanding who is responsible for evaluating the performance of a regulator, to state the obvious, all must select an appropriate process to undertake the evaluation. To achieve this different processes are available, including:

1. Audits
2. Benchmarking
3. Quality assurance
4. Service user feedback

1. **Audit**
   Audits can be used to examine an organisation's compliance with international standards, such as ISO or the correct use of internal standard operating procedures (SOPs).
   Financial audits are the foundation of the preparation and publication of an organisation's annual report and accounts. They are normally associated with the annual examination of the financial probity of an organisation and focus on the accuracy and record keeping of financial transactions. These financial audits are considered to be external since they are conducted by specialist auditing firms on behalf of shareholders or government.
   In contrast, internal audits, including financial audits, may also be instigated by the owners or board of an organisation.
2. **Benchmarking**
   Benchmarking is the process that compares the performance of a whole organisation or specific parts of its operations to other organisations. In regulation, an example of benchmarking would be to examine the call centre where the service standard to answers telephone calls is compared to organisations providing the same type of service. It can therefore be defined as:

Definition: Benchmarking
Evaluating the performance of one's own processes against the standards of best practice of similar organisations

   It is intuitive that customers, or the public, in a particular sector may have expectations of the quality and the level or quantity of service provided that in comparison are markedly different from other sectors. To make benchmarking results more informative, comparisons therefore tend to be made between organisations in the same sectors.
3. **Quality assurance**
   The topic of quality assurance is introduced in Section 2.3, volume 2, Quality assurance of E&T programmes. However, once a regulator has decided on the quality and quantity for all of its different services it must be able to identify if its targeted operational performance is actually being delivered and maintained.
4. **Service user feedback**
   One way to evaluate the performance of an organisation is to monitor feedback from service users in terms of enterprise complaints. The topic is explored in detail in Section 4.4, volume 4, Complaints about services of regulators.

MANAGEMENT INFORMATION SYSTEMS (MIS)

To manage an organisation operation performance information must be collected, monitored, analysed, and distributed. To achieve this organisations use MIS to measure their actual performance against planned results across two broad categories of information, namely:

OBJECTIVELY MEASURING OPERATIONAL PERFORMANCE

It is relatively straightforward for regulators of professionals to measure their processes objectively in terms of, capacity of systems, composition of components, timetable of processes, and units of service activities. For example:

- The number of units of activates performed in a given period of time
- The length of time to complete a particular process
- The number of employees working in a department
- Short-, medium-, and long-term changes over time and their causes

And provided that objective measures for operational performance have been set, then actual results compared to the desired standard can be measured.

SUBJECTIVELY MEASURING OPERATIONAL PERFORMANCE

When subjective qualities are used to measure a process, it is more complex than using objective measures. For example:

- The quality of letters to members of parliament
- The correctness of an FTP judgment
- The ethics of a regulator
- The culture of the regulator
- Preparedness for practice of newly qualified professionals
- Impact of continuing competence activities on professionals' practice

PERFORMANCE MATRIX

Therefore regulators need to include in their management information system (MIS) a combination of objective and subjective measures of their activities, abilities, and quality of performance, so that in turn they can direct resources to the most appropriate tasks.

KEY PERFORMANCE INDICATORS (KPIs)

To establish a process to measure their performance some regulators use key performance indicators (KPIs). A KPI can be defined as:

Definition: Key Performance Indicator
Quantitative measure of performance of the success of an organisation to meet its objectives.

It is relatively straightforward to select individual performance measures. However, it is more difficult to demonstrate that collectively they will enable a judgment to be made on whether or not a regulator will deliver its objectives.

BALANCED SCORECARD

To try and overcome the task of selecting KPIs some organisations use balanced scorecard. The approach seeks to select indicators of a satisfactory performance that can be objectively measured across the whole of the organisation.

CORRECTIVE ACTION

To state the obvious, evaluations of the operational performance of any organisation should result in corrective action. If this does not happen, a one-off service failure can over time lead to underperforming regulators and, in extreme cases, regulatory failure.

EVALUATING DECISIONS INVOLVING JUDGMENT

Before concluding this section, the issue of how the quality of decisions made by regulators that make use of judgments can be evaluated, requires consideration.

As described in previous sections there are six regulatory processes that involve the making of high-stake decisions based on the judgment of assessors, employees, board, and committee members. But, and this is a 'big but', how does the board and the executive evaluate if the judgments being made in the name of the regulator are good, bad, or indifferent or that they are consistent with each one another?

To some extent use can be made of:

- Feedback from legal assessors, presenting officers, legal service providers, and panel members
- Formal reviews of multiple written decisions
- Number of appeals made and the number then lost by the regulator

But since the decisions are made behind closed doors and reviews can only have access to written documentation rather than the spoken word of participants, there is a possibility that the quality assurance process will only detect major outliers; see Section 1.2, volume 4.

CONCLUSION

Within a regulator the internal evaluation of their own operational performance is often seen as a Cinderella service that is an unnecessary interruption to the more important responsibility of managing its day-to-day operations. However, this is not so. Adequate time and resources must be allocated to the important task, not least because government auditors' and oversight organisations will sooner or later address the same issues.

EXERCISES AND QUESTIONS

Exercises

- Locate a benchmarking exercise undertaken by a regulator. What lessons can you draw from it?
- Devise a balanced score card for a regulator

Questions

- How does your organisation benchmark its service standards?
- Does your organisation use KPIs; if so, do would keep them or change them and why?

FURTHER READING

Balanced Score Card in a Week B
M and P Bourne
Charted Management Institute
Hodder & Stoughton
ISBN: 0340849452
200095 pages

Developing a Methodology to Assess the Consistency of Fitness to Practise Outcomes R
PSA
Research Department of Medical Education UCL Medical School
11 June 2019
49 pages

An Inquiry into the Performance of the College of Dental Surgeons of British Columbia and the Health Professions Act R
The Professional Standards Authority
11 April 2019
107 pages

Performance Frameworks and Board Reporting II R
Review
National Audit Office
DP Ref: 009593-001
13 May 2011
32 pages

Review Conducted for the Royal College of Dental Surgeons of Ontario R
Professional Standards Authority
June 2013
50 pages

STANDARDS, CODES, GUIDANCE, CONSULTATIONS, POLICIES, AND PRACTICE NOTES

Guidance

Performance Measurement by Regulators G
Good Practice Guide
National Audit Office
DP Ref: 11264-001
November 2016
31 pages

Regulator Performance Guide G
Australian Government
Department of the Prime Minister and Cabinet
ISBN: 978-1-925364-63-7
July 2021
13 pages

4.3 STANDARDS ORGANISATIONS

INTRODUCTION

Regulators, besides setting their own standards for the service they provide, can on their own volition adopt standards devised by standards organisations.

In addition, there are a broad range of other organisations that publish recommendations that, although not necessarily specifically labelled as service standards, can be used by regulators.

STANDARDS ORGANISATIONS

A standards organisation can be defined as:

Definition: Standards Organisation
Organisations that create or enable the creation, harmonisation, and use of standards but do not themselves assess other organisations against the standards.

There are a number of international standards organisations that cooperate to establish global standards. They include:

- European Committee for Standardisation (CEN)
- International Organization for Standardization (ISO)
- International Electrotechnical Commission (IEC)

The most significant standards organisation that readers may be familiar with is the International Organization for Standardization (ISO). ISO is an international independent, non-governmental organisation (NGO) which develops standards to ensure the quality, safety, and efficiency of products, services, and systems.

In addition, in most jurisdictions there is a single standards organisation, often referred to as a national standards body. Examples of national standard bodies include:

- American Standards Institute (ASI)
- British Standards Institute (BIS)

In the UK the British Standards Institute (BSI) administers the overall process. In turn, the UK Government recognises the United Kingdom Accreditation Service (UKAS), to act as the UK's national accreditation body. UKAS operates by assessing the quality of certification organisations against internationally agreed standards such as ISO.

In turn the certification organisations assess independent service providers that certify, test, inspect, and calibrate services their own customers on a commercial basis.

This complex process is explored fully in Section 2.3, volume 2.

RANGE AND TYPES OF STANDARDS

ISO has a substantial portfolio of standards that are generally applicable to most organisations or are sector specific. They include both general standards and sector-specific standards.

GENERAL STANDARDS

These are standards that are not sector specific and can be achieved by a wide range of organisations. They include:

Business continuity	ISO 22301
Customer service complaints management	ISO 10002
Information security	ISO 27001
Quality management and continuous Improvement	ISO 9002:2016
Risk management	ISO 31000

Regulators of healthcare professionals are however not compelled by, for example, government, to achieve ISO general standards, which are in effect voluntary standards. However, encouragement for regulators to achieve them may be applied by stakeholders and if achieved them, operational and reputational benefits may flow from doing so.

SECTOR-SPECIFIC STANDARDS

ISO publishes a sector-specific standard that is of particular interest to certification organisations and regulators of professionals. This is the conformity assessment – General requirements for certification bodies operating certification of persons, ISO 17024:2012. The standard contains principles and requirements for a body certifying persons against specific requirements, and includes the development and maintenance of a certification scheme for persons.

Other examples of ISO quality sector-specific standards found in the UK healthcare delivery system include ISO/EC 15189:2012 Medical Laboratories – requirements for quality and competence. The standard is used to accredit various services including the quality and competence of medical laboratories.

OTHER EXTERNAL SOURCES OF POTENTIAL SERVICE STANDARDS

There is also a second source of material published by organisations that can influence the approach that regulators take to their service standards. This is the plethora of organisations including regulators who devise and then publish documents that include specific recommendations about service standards. Although not labelled as service standards for regulators, they can be interpreted as such. Regulators can take a pragmatic approach to these types of publications, and they should certainly proactively seek to identify them and should take them into consideration when devising and applying their own standards.

UK examples include the NHS constitution, the NHS Pledge, and the Patient's charter that set out the rights and responsibilities of patients.

IMPOSED STANDARDS

Before concluding this section, it should be noted that there are a range of other organisations like auditors and oversight organisations; see Section 6.4, volume 4, whose standards must be followed by regulators rather than having the option to adopt them.

CONCLUSION

Regulators of healthcare professionals should be cognisant of the standards published by standards organisation and also the raft of other service standards published by other stakeholders. Regulators then have the option of either measuring themselves against these standards, striving to achieve the standards or amending their own service standards.

EXERCISES AND QUESTIONS

Exercises

- Identify three UK regulators that have gained ISO standards
- Name three USA organisations that have ISO 17024:2012

Questions

- What are the benefits to a regulator of healthcare professional of meeting international quality standards such as those published by ISO?
- What action should a UK regulator take if an IGO publishes recommendation on how regulators should operate?

FURTHER READING

The Patient's Charter R
Past and future
Farrell C, Levenson R and Sharp D
King's Fund
ISBN: 1857172167
1998
135 pages

STANDARDS, CODES, GUIDANCE, CONSULTATIONS, POLICIES, AND PRACTICE NOTES

Standards and Codes

Moving Forward Together S&C
Performance scorecards
UK Regulators' Network
9 January 2020
26 pages

The Common Assessment Framework (CAF 2020) S&C
European Public Administration Network (EUPAN)
18 November 2019
95 pages

4.4 COMPLAINTS ABOUT SERVICES OF REGULATORS

INTRODUCTION

All organisations will invariably inevitably receive feedback both positive and negative from individuals and organisations who use their services. The term enterprise complaint is used in the book to describe this type of communication. Regulators of healthcare professionals are no exception to this rule. Therefore, having set their service standards they should establish a process to monitor and respond to feedback in the form of enterprise complaints from their stakeholders. Wherever possible, they should in the short term aim to rectify errors reported to them and then later investigate the causes of the complaint and take remedial action to improve their processes.

TYPES OF COMPLAINTS

It is important to differentiate between two fundamental different types of complaints that are received by regulators of healthcare professionals.

They are, firstly, complaints about the professionals that it regulators. These types of FTP complaints are examined in Chapter 2, volume 3, Concerns about professionals.

The second type of complaints that regulators receive are those about the services they provide. To avoid ambiguity, these types of complaints are referred to in the book as enterprise complaints. They will be processed by the regulators' complaints service function.

ENSURING GOOD SERVICE USER EXPERIENCE

Like all organisations, regulators should organise and manage their processes to maximise service user experience and at the same time take into account any restraints on the available resources. How to achieve good services is of great interest to commercial and public organisations alike but is beyond the scope of the book and is therefore not explored in depth. However, there are numerous publications, consultants, and organisations offering advice to those seeking assistance.

UNDERSTANDING SERVICE USER REQUIREMENTS

In parallel with organising and managing their process, regulators should proactively seek to understand the requirements of their service users with the aim of meeting their expectations. This can be achieved by investing time and resources into talking, listening, and understanding all the users of the services they provide. To do this techniques such as questioners, surveys, and mystery shoppers can be employed.

SERVICE USER SATISFACTION

Service user satisfaction can be considered to be a measurement of the degree that they are satisfied with the service they receive. To avoid dissatisfaction and enterprise complaints regulator should deliver services that satisfy or surpass service user expectations. However, it should be noted that on occasions the expectations of the users of the services provided by regulators may be set too high, and their unrealised expectations will not be satisfied. And it must be said in fairness, although far less frequently, they do receive communications from satisfied users of their services. However, despite their best endeavours regulators will inevitably receive complaints from dissatisfied users of their services.

NOMENCLATURE

It should also be noted in the context of the regulation of healthcare professionals, enterprise complaints will be received from many different stakeholders including both individuals and organisations. This generates the question of which collective term should be used to describe the source of the enterprise complaints. They include consumer, customer, patient, service user, and stakeholder. To foreshorten the debate, I have used the term service user.

However, it should be noted that the term service user can also be used to describe a patient. The difference between the two uses is that in relation to enterprise complaints it also encapsulates all stakeholders including both organisation and individuals.

HANDLING ENTERPRISE COMPLAINTS FROM SERVICE USERS

Organisations should not use a single process to manage complaints from users of their services. Rather, they should establish a series of linked processes that strive to eliminate the potential for errors and misunderstandings so that complaints are not received in the first place. Unsurprisingly, a regulator's approach to complaints from users of their services should therefore incorporate a number of processes that reflect the attributes of an effective, efficient, and ethical regulator, namely:

ACCESSIBILITY AND EASE OF USE OF PROCESS

The regulator's complaints process should be accessible and straightforward. Social media can be used to publicise the process.

APOLOGIES

At the end of the investigation if the regulator is at fault, an apology should be forthcoming.

ATTITUDE OF REGULATOR TO FEEDBACK FROM SERVICE USERS

Regulators of healthcare professionals should actively encourage and welcome service user feedback whether it is positive or negative. In terms of its reputation, regulators should be able to demonstrate their support for service user feedback, that they are committed to the process, and that they listen to complainants.

COMMUNICATION

The regulator should ensure that all complainants are kept informed and up-to-date as the complaint is investigated.

DECISION

Complainants should be informed on how the regulator will reach a decision relating to the complaint and in due course the decision and the reasoning behind it.

GUIDANCE

Clear, easy-to-use guidance on the complaints processes should be provided that is readily accessible to all users of the regulators services.

SERVICE STANDARDS FOR COMPLAINT HANDLING

Service standards for the handling of complaints should be set and publicised by the regulator.

SUPPORT

The regulator should provide personal support either using various communication tools or in person, to assist complainants to complete the process and assist with form filling and other documentation.

CORRECTIVE ACTION AND CONTINUOUS IMPROVEMENT

The ultimate goal of a regulator investigating and resolving enterprise complaints should be two fold. Firstly, in the short term taking prompt corrective action to rectify the reason for the individual complaint. Secondly, in the medium term to permanently improve the quality of the service.

The regulator should therefore use feedback from the users of its services in the form of enterprise complaints, as part of its continuous quality improvement process. To achieve this the regulator should record and classify all enterprise complaints that it receives. Wherever possible, the complaints should be analysed in terms of the quality of the service provided with the objective of trying to identify if the regulators' processes and/or its policies have or have not been correctly followed. Where the process or policy is not being correctly followed by employees or others such as partners, further education and training should be initiated. Where the process is found to be wanting, then the process or policy should be improved or replaced. And even when after investigation it is concluded that the process is not wanting, lessons can still be learnt from these 'close calls'.

All corrective actions should be assigned to a responsible named individual for timely implementation. After a reasonable period of time the required deliverables should be confirmed. In addition, analysis of all enterprise complaints received over longer periods of time, say, six months, should be reviewed to identify common themes and trends.

In a similar way that benchmarking enables evaluations of performance compared to other organisations, the number and types of complaints they receive can also be compared to other organisations.

POSITIVE FEEDBACK

While the focus of this discussion has been on negative complaints, as discussed above, some users of services will, although less frequently, also provide positive feedback. The flow of information should be treated in the same way as negative complaints.

PUBLICATION OF COMPLAINTS DATA

Regulator should collect, record, analyse, and publish enterprise complaints data internally and externally. This should include how the complaint was resolved and how long the process took.

GOVERNANCE AND COMPLAINTS

The executive management team of the regulator should receive regular reports on enterprise complaints and less frequently the board of the regulator.

INTERNATIONAL STANDARDS FOR CUSTOMER SERVICE AND COMPLAINTS MANAGEMENT

The regulator may seek and gain ISO 10002 Customer service complaints management; see Section 4.3, volume 4, standards organisations for more details.

CUSTOMER SERVICES FOR INTERNAL USERS

As previously discussed, it should be empathised that regulators provide both services to external stakeholders and internal users. For example, the services provided by the finance, HR, and IT functions to the rest of the organisation. Regulators should therefore adopt a similar approach to enterprise complaints from both groups.

PROACTIVELY SEEKING SERVICER USER FEEDBACK

From time to time regulators can proactively seek feedback from users of their services. Understanding the service experience and the degree of their satisfaction can be most informative. This can be achieved by using questionnaires, surveys, and market research organisations. The reports should be made publicly available.

However, the challenge of acquiring feedback from participants in a number of regulatory processes should be raised. For example, acquiring feedback from professionals who have been the subjects of FTP complaints or individuals whose international applications for registration was rejected may not be willing to discuss their experience. Despite this, although difficult to achieve, process should be established to seek feedback from these types of stakeholders.

BENEFIT OF INFORMING SERVICE USERS AND LEVEL OF COMPLAINTS

Before concluding this section, it is worthwhile to reflect on the benefit of informing users of services on how the service is supplied and the service standards that the service user should expect. For example, consider the electronic information that can be made available to customers by logistic organisations on the delivery of a parcel to a domestic residence, and how customer expectations can be carefully managed and dissatisfaction avoided. In a similar way it can't be overemphasised that regulators should go out of their way to inform users of their services, for example, the registration process or the handling of concerns and complaints about professionals, about how the process is progressing either by personal contact, or by the use of real-time electronic communication.

CONCLUSION

Users of the services of regulators will from time to time take the time and trouble to provide both negative and positive feedback about the service provided. Regulators like all well-managed private and public organisations should react positively to such feedback and where appropriate take swift action to correct any deficiencies.

EXERCISES AND QUESTIONS

Exercises

- What are the most frequent causes of complaints from users of the services of regulators? How do the complaints vary across different stakeholders, for example, HEIs or Members of Parliament?
- How does the executive of a regulator, that you are familiar with, report to the board about service user enterprise complaints?

Questions

- Obtain guidance provided by regulators to users of its services on how to complain if they are dissatisfied the service provided? What is your view on the quality of the guidance?
- Should regulators seek service user feedback from professionals who have been subjects of FTP complaints?

FURTHER READING

Making Complaints Count: R
Supporting complaints handling in the NHS and UK Government Departments
Parliamentary and Health Service Ombudsman
HC 390
ISBN: 978-1-5286-2066-6
15 July 220
64 pages

Principles of Good Complaint Handling R
The Parliamentary and Health Service Ombudsman
10 February 2009
7 pages

The Report of the Independent Review of Regulation, Audit, Inspection and Complaints Handling of Public Services in Scotland R
Professor Lorne D Crerar
Scottish Government
ISBN: 978075595362
25 September 2007
117 pages

4.5 DATA PROTECTION

INTRODUCTION

In the UK public authorities who handle personal data have an obligation under the Data Protection Act 2018 to protect its security. Regulators must register with the Information Commissioner's Office and can be subjected to considerable financial penalties if they lose personnel data.

PERSONAL DATA

Regulators have in their possession large quantities of personal data:

Definition: Personal Data
Information that relates to an identified or identifiable individual.

Unauthorised access to personal data, wherever by accidental loss or mischief by others, should be avoided at all costs. This is because, for example, there are dire consequences for the recipients of identity theft or cybercrime.

LEGISLATION

In the UK the Data Protection Act 1998 and 2018 (DPA) which supports the principles of the European Union's General Data Protection Regulation (EU) 2016/679, often abbreviated to GDPR, sets the legislative ground rules for the protection of personal data.

It requires that everyone who is responsible for using personal data to follow strict rules called 'data protection principles'. Those responsible must make sure the information is:

- Used fairly, lawfully, and transparently
- Used for specified, explicit purposes
- Used in a way that is adequate, relevant, and limited to only what is necessary
- Accurate and, where necessary, kept up to date
- Kept for no longer than is necessary
- Handled in a way that ensures appropriate security, including protection against unlawful or unauthorised processing, access, loss, destruction, or damage

The act also gives members of the public the right to:

- Find out what information the government and other organisations store about them
- Be informed about how their data is being used
- Access their personal data
- Have incorrect data updated
- Have data erased
- Stop or restrict the processing of their data
- Data portability (allowing citizens to obtain and reuse their data for different services)
- Object to how their data is processed in certain circumstances

ADMINISTRATION OF THE DATA PROTECTION ACT

In the UK the Data Protection Act is administered by the Information Commissioner's Office (ICO). The ICO can impose significant financial fines on organisations who lose personal data.

MANAGEMENT OF PERSONAL DATA

Within a regulator, the management of data protection is often the responsibility of the secretariat function. Their responsibility may include:

- The appointment of a data protection officer (DPO)
- Handling subject access requests

INTERNATIONAL STANDARDS FOR INFORMATION SECURITY

The International Organization for Standardization (ISO) publishes ISO 27001 Information security, a standard relating to information security and data protection; see Section 4.2, volume 4. In the UK meeting the standard has the added advantage that under certain circumstances the ICO, may be more benign on an organisation that has a data breach if they are in possession of ISO 27001.

RECORD RETENTION AND DISPOSAL POLICY

A regulator should have a clear policy on how long it should keep documents. The record retention and disposal policy should cover both physical and electronic records.

DISCLOSURE AND SHARING OF DATA

Lastly, it should be noted that data, that is protected under normal circumstances, can be legitimately disclosed or shared with other organisations provided it is specified in legislation or is supported by data sharing agreement and a data transfer agreement. From the perspective of a regulator of healthcare professionals this can be used when transferring registers. It also applies under the Common Law Police Disclosures Scheme, formerly the Notifiable Occupation Scheme; see Section 2.1, volume 3.

CONCLUSION

Although a somewhat obscure area that is on the periphery of the regulation of healthcare professions, data protection has important ramifications since losing other people's personal data is a serious matter. Regulators must establish and implement principles and processes to ensure that it does not happen and that all employees are aware of the importance of the matter, both in terms of financial fines and damage to the reputation of the organisation.

EXERCISE AND QUESTION

Exercise

- Locate your organisation's data retention and disposal policy

Question

- In your organisation how aware are you and your colleagues of the implications of losing personal data?

LEGISLATION

Example of UK Legislation

Data Protection Act 1998 and 2018 (DPA) L

Example of International Legislation

General Data Protection Regulation (EU) 2016/679 L

FURTHER READING

Report on the Review of Patient – Identifiable Information R
The Caldicott Committee
Department of Health
Ref: Caldicott 11934 CA Q 1000 1P Dec 97 (CWP)
December 1997
149 pages

STANDARDS, CODES, GUIDANCE, CONSULTATIONS, POLICIES, AND PRACTICE NOTES

Standards and Codes

Confidentiality; NHS Code of Practice S&C
Department of Health
ROCR Ref: Gateway Ref: 1656
November 2003
52 pages

Guidance

Confidentiality: NHS Code of Practice Supplementary Guidance: Public Interest Disclosures G
Department of Health
Gateway Ref: 13912
26 November 2010
15 pages

Policy

Record Retention and Disposal Policy Pol
HCPC
14 pages

4.6 FREEDOM OF INFORMATION

INTRODUCTION

Nowadays, regulators, like most public authorities, are expected to make information about themselves freely accessible to stakeholders. Regulators should establish policies and procedures to ensure that this is the case but with the caveat that where appropriate some classes of information can remain exempt from disclosure.

HISTORICAL BACKGROUND

Members of the public seeking to understand how government works have traditionally been largely thwarted by a veil of secrecy and a culture of obstruction. Even today in the western democracies, politicians while extolling the virtues of openness and transparency, government and its agencies are still reluctant to expose the machinery of their daily workings to close scrutiny by those who elect them to govern on their behalf and who are largely responsible for financing the cost of their government.

However, in recent times, in the UK and numerous other democracies, citizens have gained the right to access information about the workings of their government. That right is now enshrined in legislation. In the UK public authorities, including regulators of healthcare professionals, are required to make their information available to the public and organisations, using the so-called right to freely access information.

FREEDOM OF INFORMATION

In the UK freedom of information (FOI) can be defined as:

Definition: Freedom of Information
Legal right of the public to access certain data and information (but not personal data) held by government and its agencies, about their activities, and the requirement of government and its agencies to publish the information.

LEGISLATION

In England and Scotland there are acts of Parliament that create a general right of access, on request, to information held by public authorities

The English legislation is the Freedom of Information Act 2000 (FOIA) and establishes a public 'right of access' to information held by public authorities.

In Scotland the freedom of information law is the Freedom of Information (Scotland) Act 2002.

ADMINISTRATION OF THE FREEDOM OF INFORMATION ACT

In the UK the Freedom of Information Act is administered by the Information Commissioner's Office (ICO).

RESPONSIBILITIES OF PUBLIC AUTHORITIES

In the UK over 100,000 public authorities, including the regulators of healthcare professionals, that are required to implement the FOIA. Usually the regulators' secretariat function is responsible for the processes associated with freedom of information; see Section 1.2, volume 4.

INFORMATION AVAILABLE

The definition of information that must be made available to the public is very broad and includes all recorded information. This includes printed documents, electronic records, emails, letters, photographs, and sound recordings. If the information has been disposed of or destroyed then it cannot be provided.

PUBLICATION SCHEME

Public authorities are required to proactively publish and maintain a list of documents that are available to the public.

There are seven classes of information that public authorities should publish, namely:

1. What they are and what they do
2. What they spend and how they spend it
3. Priorities and how they are doing
4. How decisions are made
5. Policies and procedures
6. Lists and registers
7. Services provided

To support this, regulators will often draw up a publication and disclosure policy that can be used to inform employees and stakeholders on how to manage the processes and the principles used.

DOCUMENT RETENTION AND DISPOSAL POLICY

As discussed in the previous section, UK public authorities establish which information they will retain and for how long. These are normally referred to as a record retention and disposal policy.

REQUEST FOR INFORMATION

A member of the public, or data subject, who is unable to locate information can request the information from the public authority. The public authorities can request more details from the individual to enable them to locate the information if it is held. Information request must be completed with a specified timetable. Government via ministers can veto information requests.

RECERTIFICATION

When the data held about a data subject is incorrect, the data subject can insist that it is corrected.

RIGHT TO BE FORGOTTEN

Members of the public have the right to request that data held is deleted.

FREEDOM OF INFORMATION (FOI) EXEMPTIONS

The legislation exempts a range of information that does not have to be disclosed. A public interest test can be applied for qualified exceptions.

In the UK, in relation to the regulation of healthcare professionals and the FTP process in particular, a healthcare professional's observations about a complaint can be withheld by the regulator and not divulged. For example, if a member of the public raises a concern about a healthcare professional, and the professional then discloses to the regulator the mental health status of the complainant. Under these circumstances, if the information is requested by the member of the public, it may not be disclosed by the regulator. Whilst this is often an unsatisfactory state of affairs for the complainant, it does go some way to preserve procedural fairness.

In some instances rather than a case-by-case application of exemptions, automatic exemptions are applied. For example, information held by elected Members of Parliament.

VEXATIOUS AND REPEATED REQUESTS

A range of requests for information can be declined. These include requests that are abusive, frivolous, frequent, scatter-gun, and unreasonable. Because of the possibility of receiving these types of requests, a regulator should have a policy similar to their vexatious complaints policy that assists in identifying them, possibly understanding why they have been made and how to process them.

COSTS

Members of the public or organisation requesting information can be charged by the organisation providing the information. It is normally assumed that information held in an electronic format will be provided at no cost. A charge is only applicable when costs such as labour, photocopying, and postage are incurred. A maximum cost limit is set above which an FOI request can be refused. For public authorities this was £450 in 2025.

PROS AND CONS

The freedom of information legislation is not without controversy. A tussle is likely to continue between government seeking to curtain it and civil libertarians and the media seeking to extend its reach

Pros

- Enhances the scrutiny of government by the public
- Facilitates access to government information
- Right of access to information is '*good for democracy*'
- Transparency prevents unnecessary secrecy

Cons

- Inhibits policy development by government
- Encourages informal decision making, or derogatorily '*sofa government*'
- Wastes time and resources to fulfil request for information

CONCLUSION

In the UK the right of the public to access information relating to government is now enshrined in legislation, and the processes are well established. Regulators as public authorities are covered by the legislation and must be cognisant of its workings and where they must publish or have the right not to make information available to members of the public.

EXERCISE AND QUESTION

Exercise

- Review the website of a regulator and ascertain what information is provided about freedom of information.

Question

- Should some information held by public authorities, for example, the salaries of junior employees, remain confidential and not be disclosed to the public?

LEGISLATION

Example of UK Legislation

Freedom of Information Act 2000 (FOIA)	L
Freedom of Information (Scotland) Act 2002	L

STANDARDS, CODES, GUIDANCE, CONSULTATIONS, POLICIES, AND PRACTICE NOTES

Policies

GDC Disclosure and Publication Policy Version 3 General Dental Council August 2018 16 pages	Pol

Regulatory Failure

CHAPTER 5

INTRODUCTION

The chapter has one section:

5.1 REGULATORY FAILURE

INTRODUCTION

A cursory trawl of the internet will rapidly identify a litany of individual healthcare professionals, organisations operating in the healthcare delivery system, and regulators of healthcare professionals, where the expectations of stakeholders has been woefully let down by regulatory failure. These types of incidents, besides harming patients, are the primary trigger for the public and governments to lose their trust and confidence in regulators. As a result, these high-profile events often trigger government intervention and in many cases in due course have dire organisational consequences for regulators. This section examines historical examples from various jurisdictions of regulatory failures when the regulatory process has gone seriously awry. By understanding the causes of regulatory failure, counter measures can be adopted to change regulatory principles and processes that should lead to an increase to the chances of detecting and preventing similar events occurring in the future.

WHAT IS REGULATORY FAILURE?

Regulatory failure is characterised by a series of linked events that lead to a catastrophic failure of a regulator to deliver its objectives. It can be defined as:

Definition: Regulatory Failure
Process when a regulator fails to deliver its objective.

In the case of the regulators of healthcare, regulatory failure usually involves harm being caused to multiple patients because the regulator has failed to deliver their objective of public protection. Using this definition, regulatory failure rarely involves a single incident, or a single action of one individual. The process leading to the failure is often complex and often comprises many different incidents and involves, directly or indirectly, numerous individuals.

EXAMPLES OF INCIDENTS OF REGULATORY FAILURE

It should be noted that individual incidents of regulatory failure often involve a hodgepodge of events involving numerous individuals and organisations. However, to aid their examination incidents of regulatory failure can be categorised into four broad groups, namely:

1. Criminal behaviour of individual healthcare professionals who intentionally and deliberately harm their patients
2. Catastrophic failure of an individual healthcare professional who does not provide safe and effective practice and unintentionally harms their patients
3. Catastrophic failure of organisations within the healthcare delivery system often involving individual healthcare professionals
4. Poor operational performance of the regulators of healthcare professionals

For those readers seeking greater details concerning the events surrounding regulatory failures, there are numerous and often lengthy reports of the public inquiries and formal government responses to the reports. In addition, there are also books exploring the more infamous and notorious examples of regulatory failure by individual healthcare professionals and failed organisations.

Where they exist, reports and other publications relating to the regulatory failure are therefore listed at the end of the section.

When incidents of regulatory failure do occur and are detected, subsequent investigation and reports are often referred to by the name of the key individual involved, or by the name of the organisation where it occurred, or the name of the individual who chaired the committee undertaking the review. For example, Shipman or Bristol Royal Infirmary and Kennedy. In some instances more than one report is compiled,

Operations of Regulators of Healthcare Professionals, Volume 4, First Edition. Marc Seale.

Companion website: www.wiley.com/go/seale/regulatinghealthcare

not necessarily with same name, for example, Patterson and Solihull Hospital.

For the sake of clarity, and to aid their examination, examples of incidents of regulatory failure are divided into four groups referred to above. They are then listed alphabetically, firstly by country and then by either the name of a key individual, or the name of the organisation involved.

FREQUENCY OF OCCURRENCE OF REGULATORY FAILURE

From the number of public inquiries, government reports, and books that have been referenced it could appear to indicate that there are frequent significant failures of the systems to regulate healthcare professionals and organisations within the healthcare delivery system.

However, the data does not support this interpretation. In terms of the healthcare delivery system, regulatory failure is a relatively infrequent occurrence. This is because around ten percent of the population of most economically developed countries are working in the healthcare delivery system, and there are hundreds of millions of treatments occurring every year between healthcare professions and members of the public, and there are tens of thousands of organisations within the healthcare delivery system. Even if there are more than ten times the number of reported regulatory failures that are either undetected or are detected but go unreported, the numbers are still proportionally relatively small.

CHARACTERISTICS OF REGULATORY FAILURE

Is it possible to identify the characteristics of a typical regulatory failure? In general some or all the following are present:

- Standards of regulators are not adhered to
- There is actual harm or premature death to one or more patients
- Repeated similar events occur but are not initially detected
- Professional failure may go undetected and exist for sometime
- Regulatory systems and processes do not work effectively or efficiently or ethically
- Regulators are slow to react or there is an absence of reaction
- Standards of corporate governance and/or management of organisation(s) involved are below an acceptable level
- Culture or ethics of the organisation is poor and inappropriate values and behaviours are tolerated
- Raisers of concerns, complainants, consumer advocacy organisations, and whistleblowers are ignored
- Public authorities including regulators do not cooperate, share data, or communicate with one another.

However it should be noted that it can be argued that all events involving regulated healthcare professionals that result in harm occurring to patients are also failures of the regulatory process.

CAUSES OF REGULATORY FAILURE INVOLVING HEALTHCARE PROFESSIONALS

Distilling the characteristics of regulatory failure leads to the conclusion that it is caused by three types of events, namely:

1. Processes not being followed lead over time to systemic failure
2. Leadership failure
3. Professionalism failure

REACTION TO REGULATORY FAILURE

The reaction of stakeholders to a failure to regulate healthcare professionals to the required standards is to a certain extent predictable.

THE PUBLIC

- Criticise the regulator
- Lobby government to change the process and standards of the regulator
- Public may lose their trust and confidence in the healthcare profession concerned
- Seek an independent public inquiry
- Seek financial compensation

MEDIA

- Apportion blame on individuals and organisations including government
- Criticise the profession's monopoly or the perception of the profession's control of the monopoly without proper public scrutiny
- Seek to uncover similar scandals and regulator failures
- Support the position of the members of the public involved

HEALTHCARE PROFESSIONALS AND PROFESSIONAL ASSOCIATIONS

- If government in time imposes what they see to be more draconian regulation they may react with anger to the newly imposed controls

- Seek to apportion blame, particularly on the regulator, for not uncovering the failure at an earlier stage
- Support the position of members of the public involved and the media
- Trigger a decline in the moral of the profession

REGULATOR

- Criticise their legislation and by implication governed for not amending it
- Defend their reputation
- Stresses their limited resources
- Trigger their reputation management action plan

GOVERNMENT

Regulatory failure not unsurprisingly creates a maelstrom of challenges for government. The initial reaction by government to regulatory failure is often to be either highly critical of the regulator of the healthcare profession concerned, or the healthcare profession, or both.

The understandable reason for this is as follows:

1. Government sets out to resolve a specific market or social challenge by establishing autonomous statutory regulators with the intention that they will resolve the policy objective
2. The process used by government or politicians is one of delegation and the transfer of responsibility
3. The distancing of government from the day-to-day management of the regulator minimises political interference. This is good if things go according to plan. However, if regulatory failure occurs government and regulator are left in an uncomfortable position. If the regulator is seen to have failed in delivered its responsibilities, government can and will attack and prisoners will be far and few

As a result, government will often establish a public inquiry. In addition, Parliamentary Committees may undertake their own additional review.

PUBLIC INQUIRIES

A public inquiry is established by government to official review to 'establish the facts' surrounding an event or action. There are broad justifications for establishing a public inquiry that can be summarised as the existence of 'public concern' about a particular event or set of events. They can either be organised along statutory lines and follow the Inquiries Act 2005. Alternatively, a more informal and non-statutory approach can be adopted and the Inquire Act is not used. This has the advantage of allowing the inquiry to adopt a more flexible approach. Whichever one of the approaches is used, there is a degree of flexibility in how they are managed but often have common features, including a series of predictable stages. They are as follows:

ESTABLISHING THE PUBLIC INQUIRY

- Triggered by the need for a major investigation
- Convened by a government minister
- Government funds and organises the process
- Inquiry can be gifted special powers to compel testimony and the release of other forms of evidence
- The legal powers that are to be used by the inquiry are published
- Government sets and publishes the terms of reference for the inquiry
- Chair is appointed
- Members are appointed
- Provisional timetable is published
- Civil servants or others are appointed to support the inquiry

THE INQUIRY

- Evidence is obtained from organisations and individuals
- Hearings are undertaken in meetings open to the public, although they may hold private sessions
- Evidence may be given in the form of documents or by oral evidence
- The work of the inquiry may take a number of years to complete after the regulatory failure came to light and on occasion the government may have changed due to an election

REPORT STAGE

- Report of the inquiry is published
- A number of recommendations are made

RESPONSE BY GOVERNMENT TO INQUIRIES' REPORT

- After a period of reflection, government usually responds to the recommendations of a public inquiry by publishing a formal response
- Their response usually specifies which recommendations it will accept and when it plans to implement them
- Government may initiate further policy development, involving consultation and drafting changes to legislation

In turn, government may then amend legislation of the regulator or reform regulation and legislation. However, a lack of resources to amend legislation, as discussed in Section 8.4, volume 1, may mean that this occurs only after significant regulatory failures, hence the term 'tombstone legislation'.

Lastly, government may react by establishing oversight organisations, see Section 6.4.

IMPLEMENTING RECOMMENDATIONS

- Recommendations of the inquiry may be numerous ranging from a dozen to, on occasions, hundreds
- Key recommendations may be implemented forthwith, others may be delayed, or never fully implemented
- Inquiries into future regulatory failures will repeatedly refer back to similar previous inquiries highlighting the failure to implement previous recommendations

PREVENTION REGULATORY FAILURE

In his book *The Black Swan: The impact of the Highly Improbable*, Nassim Nicholas Taleb defined certain incidents as *Black Swans* because they are:

- Unpredictable events
- Low probability of occurring and extremely rare
- Beyond what is normally expected of a situation
- Has potentially severe consequences
- Widespread insistence they were obvious in hindsight

In contrast, incidents of regulatory failures are not beyond what is normally expected of a situation. They are in effect known unknowns rather than unknown unknowns. As a consequence organisations can plan to handle them and take a range of steps that can reduce the likelihood of them occurring. Nassim refers to these types of events as *Grey Swans*.

It is therefore reasonable to assume that while all incidents of regulatory failure cannot be prevented, regulators can still build robust organisations to increase the possibility of preventing some of them.

For example, regulators should proactively adopt a culture of seeking to identify areas of vulnerability. Such an area for regulators of healthcare professionals are applications from professionals who have been educated and trained in other jurisdictions.

However, preventing regulatory failure in a process comprising numerous steps will not be achieved by a single initiative or course of action by one organisation. Rather the healthcare delivery system needs to deploy its network effect using the process that collectively makes up clinical governance.

DETECTING INCIDENTS OF REGULATORY FAILURE

Regulatory failure is often a gradual but accelerating process of compounded problems. This often makes early detection difficult because the initial problem may be seen as minor and a one-off occurrence. This may result in early signals of impending disaster being overlooked or undetected by employers, services, and systems regulators, and regulators of healthcare professionals and the opportunity for timely intervention is missed.

In these situations, with the benefit of hindsight many stakeholders are unforgiving of those organisations and individuals that fail to detect the problem of regulatory failure in a timely manner.

It is therefore important that the healthcare delivery system and its regulators in particular adopt a culture of assuming that regulatory failure will occur and, as with preventing regulatory failure, will work together to detect regulatory failure.

LEARNING FROM INCIDENTS OF REGULATORY FAILURE

Regulators can learn from regulatory failure. This can be both formal, for example, the now-disbanded National Patient Safety Agency. In addition, the use of 'safe spaces' may aid the process; see Section 1.1, volume 3.

Informal methods can be used by organisation to apply the recommendation of the reports arising from regulatory failures both in their own and other jurisdictions.

REGULATORY FAILURE AND DEFAULT POWERS

Before concluding the section, as highlighted in Section 8.7, volume 1, in the UK if a regulator fails to deliver its objectives or functions, government can directly intervene, via the Privy Council, and in effect takeover the management of the regulator. This power, referred to as 'Default Powers', can exercise the powers of the regulator.

CONCLUSION

Although thankfully rare, the damage that regulatory failure inflicts on patients, the reputations of the healthcare professions, and the healthcare delivery system is usually significant and often leads to the reform of regulation.

It is therefore in the interest of all stakeholders concerned with the healthcare delivery system, to be ever vigilant and to ensure that there are systems and processes to detect them and that timely intervention is taken to shut them down.

EXERCISES AND QUESTIONS

Exercises

- Review an example of a recent regulatory failure. What role did healthcare professionals have in causing or detecting the incident?
- Is regulatory failure becoming less prevalent?
- Review publicly available information relating to Christopher Ingoldby. In your view, were reasonable decisions made by the employer and regulator?

Questions

- Should a healthcare professional who unintentionally but repeatedly causes harm to patients, be treated in a similar manner to those who intentionally cause harm?
- Some jurisdictions have no regulatory failures. Is this because their system are not detecting them?
- Was the opioid epidemic in the USA which started in the early 1990s a result of regulatory failure?

LEGISLATION

Example of UK Legislation

Inquiries Act 2005 L

EXAMPLES OF REGULATORY FAILURE

The following examples of regulatory failure are listed in four broad groups, namely:

1. Criminal behaviour of individual healthcare professionals who intentionally and deliberately harm their patients
2. Catastrophic failure of an individual healthcare professional who does not provide safe and effective practice and unintentionally harms their patients
3. Catastrophic failure of organisations within the healthcare delivery system often involving individual healthcare professionals
4. Poor operational performance of the regulators of healthcare professionals

1. Criminal behaviour of individual healthcare professionals who intentionally and deliberately harms their patients

These type of failures are characterised by a single perpetrator intentionally harming two or more victims in more than one event. The victims are often vulnerable, such as young children and the elderly, or are close to their anticipated death. Working alone often at night in a hospital setting, death is often caused by lethal injections that cause cardiac arrest. The healthcare professional is often suffering from a mental health disorder, has access to drugs, and retains them illegally. They frequently move employment and often work for charities. After their detection, co-workers will often subsequently refer to the ex-colleagues competence's making them anxious and concerned.

Australia

Reeves, Graeme Stephen

An Australian doctor specialising in obstetrics and gynaecology who practised while being disbarred. Named AKA 'the Butcher of Bega' in the press he was sent to jail in 2011. A special commission investigated the circumstances of his practice and appointment.

Special Commission of Inquiry R
Acute Care Services in New South Wales Public Hospitals
Final Report – 3 volume report and single volume overview
Peter Garling SC
ISBN 978-1-921301-81-0
27 November 2008
426 pages

Canada

Doodnaught, Dr George

An anaesthesiologist from Toronto, Canada. In February 2014, he was imprisoned for 10 years for sexually assaulting 21 of his sedated female patients

To Zero: Independent Report of the Minister's Task Force on the Prevention of Sexual Abuse of Patients and the Regulated Health Professions Act, 1991 R
Marilou McPhedran, Task Force Chair
ISBN: 978-1-4606-6543-5
15 December 2015
314 pages

Wettlaufer, Elizabeth Tracy Mae

A Canadian nurse who was convicted on eight counts of first degree murder in the province of Ontario following for a string of deaths in two nursing homes between 2007 and 2016. She injected patients with lethal doses of insulin and is one of the worst serial killers in Canadian history.

Public Inquiry into the Safety and Security of Residents in the Long-Term Care Homes System R
The Honourable Eileen E. Gillese Commissioner
ISBN 978-1-4868-3584-3
31 July 2019
Four volumes

Germany

Högel, Niels

A prolific nurse serial killer was convicted in 2015 of the murder of two patients and possibly over 100 others at clinics in the northwest German towns of Delmenhorst and nearby Oldenburg. He killed patients by unauthorised fatal doses of medications.

The Death Nurse: Why Was Niels Högel Able to Become the Greatest Serial Killer in German Post-war History? B
Karsten Krogmann
Goldman publishing
ASIN: B091L1GFCZ
20 September 2011
300 pages (German Edition)

Serial Killer Nurse – Niels Högel B
Chris Hampton
CreateSpace Independent Publishing Platform
ISBN: 1976211913
6 September 2017
36 pages

New Zealand

Green, Herbert

A scandal involving unethical research conducted by Herbert Green who intentionally undertreated women with cervical cancer and experimented on his patients without their consent or proper approval. A Commission of Inquiry from 1987 to 1988 was headed by then District Court Judge Silvia Cartwright, later High Court Justice, Dame, and Governor-General of New Zealand.

The Report of the Cervical Inquiry R
Sylvia Cartwright
ISBN 0-473-00664-2
29 July 1988
289 pages

Norway

Nesset, Arnfinn

A nurse born 25 October 1936 in Norway. Serial killer convicted in March 1983 of poisoning 22 patients with Curacit.

Republic of Ireland

Neary, Dr Michael

Dr Michael Neary, a rogue consultant surgeon, who unnecessarily removed the wombs of 129 women.

Judge Maureen Harding Clarke published a 250-page report following a two-year investigation into abnormal maternity unit practices at Our Lady of Lourdes hospital in Drogheda. The inquiry exposed a culture of obedience accorded to long-established consultants that failed to challenge the surgeon for almost a quarter of a century. Between 1974 and 1998 the high level of hysterectomies in Drogheda went almost without criticism, although one matron did raise concerns but they went unheeded.

A review by the Royal College of Obstetricians and Gynaecologists failed to detect the failings at the hospital. Dr Neary was eventually struck off Ireland's medical register after being found guilty of professional misconduct.

The Lourdes Hospital Inquiry R
An Inquiry into peripartum hysterectomy at Our Lady of Lourdes Hospital, Drogheda
Judge Maureen Hardring Clark SC
Stationery Office
Ref: Prn. A6/0246 and ISBN 0: 0755773993
January 2006
360 pages

UK

Adams, Bodkin

John Bodkin Adams was a physician who was accused and acquitted on murdering patients with overdoses of morphine in Eastbourne in the late 1950s.

Easing the Passing: The Trial of Doctor John Bodkin Adams B
Devlin, Patrick
The Bodley Head, London
Ref: ISBN 0-370-30627 9
1985
228 pages

Allitt, Beverley

In April 1991 nurse Allitt murdered and harmed a number of children at Grantham and Kesteven General Hospital in Lincolnshire. She is serving life sentence in a secure mental hospital.

Independent Inquiry Relating to Deaths and Injuries on the Children's Ward at Grantham and Kesteven General Hospital during the Period February to April 1991 R
Allitt Inquiry
Chair Sir Cecil Clother
HMSO, London
ISBN 0 11 321714 5
1 February 1994
140 pages

Angel of Death: Killer Nurse Beverly Allitt B
John Askil, Martyn Sharpe
Michael O'Mara Books
ISBN13: 9781854791825
12 February 1993
259 pages

Ayling, Clifford

GP Clifford Ayling was jailed after indecently assaulting female patients for over two decades.

Committee of Inquiry Independent Investigation Into How The NHS Handled Allegations About The Conduct of Clifford Ayling R
Department of Health

The Stationery Office
Cm 6298 and ISBN-10: 0101629826
9 September 2004
278 pages

Cream, Dr Thomas Neill

A Victorian Scottish/Canadian physician serial killer. Known as the Lambeth Poisoner, he poisoned his victims and was hanged for murder in 1892.

A Prescription for Murder: The Victorian Serial Killings of Dr Thomas Neill Cream B
Angus McLaren
University of Chicago Press
ISBN-13: 978-0226560687
1 Jun 1995
244 pages

Green, Benjamin

In May 2006 Mr Green was convicted for the murder of two patients while working as a nurse in Banbury Oxfordshire. He also harmed 15 others between 2003 and 2004 by injecting them various drugs that caused respiratory arrest.

Green, Dr Peter

On 10 July 2000 A GP Peter Green who practised in Loughborough was convicted on nine counts of indecent assault on five patients. The conviction was the culmination of concerns raised over a period of twelve years and followed three separate police investigations. Following two investigations in 1985 and 1993 the Crown Prosecution Service (CPS) took no action.

Investigation into issues arising from the case of Loughborough GP Peter Green R
Commission for Health Improvement (CHI)
ISBN 0 11 702873 8
30 August 2001
79 pages

Grigg-Booth, Anne

Nurse charged with murdering three patients in 2005 at Airedale General Hospital, near Keighley, West Yorks. Died before her trial.

The Airedale Inquiry R
Report to the Yorkshire and the Humber Strategic Health Authority
To be presented to the Strategic Health Authority Board on 8 June 2010
210 pages

Kerr/Haslam

Doctors William Kerr and Michael Haslam, who worked in the same psychiatric hospital in North Yorkshire during the 1970s and 1980s. Both were later convicted of the indecent assault of female psychiatric patients.

The Kerr/Haslam Inquiry R
HM Government
The Stationery Office
Report in two volumes
Cm 6640 and Cm 6640-I and II
ISBN 10: 0101664028 ISBN 13:9780101664028
18 July 2005
555 and 419 pages

Letby, Lucy

31-year-old neonatal nurse serial killer. Convicted in August 2023 of murdering seven babies and attempted to murder six others at the Countess of Chester hospital from June 2015 and June 2016. Independent inquiry, the Thirlwall Inquiry, was established by UK Government in August 2023.

Healthcare Serial Killer or Coincidence? R
Statistical issues in investigation of suspected medical misconduct
Royal Statistics Society
RSS Statistics and the Law Section
September 2022
61 pages

Norris, Colin

Mr Norris, a nurse who was convicted in March 2008 of murdering four elderly patients in his care in 2002.

Report of the Independent Inquiry into the Colin Norris Incidents at Leeds Teaching Hospitals NHS Trusts in 2002 R
To be presented to the Humber Strategic Health Authority
26 January 2010
76 pages

Paterson, Mr Ian

In April 2017 a UK breast surgeon Ian Paterson was convicted of carrying out over 400 unnecessary and mutilating surgical operations over a period of more than ten years; the defendant had done what no reasonable surgeon would do. He worked both in the NHS at the Solihull hospital and the Spire private hospital. He was imprisoned in 2017 for 15 years later increased to 20 years for numerous criminal offences, including wounding with intent. An independent Inquiry was established by the UK's Department of Health and Social Care in December 2017.

In spring 2023 further inquests are underway concerning some of his former patients.

Report of the Independent Inquiry into the Issues raised by Paterson R
Chairman: The Right Reverend Graham James (Lord Bishop of Norwich)
House of Commons
ISBN 978 1 5286 1728 4
4 February 2020
238 pages

At separate investigation of the main **Solihull Hospital** NHS hospital where Patterson was employed was also conducted.

Solihull Hospital Kennedy Breast Care Review R
Heart of England NHS Foundation Trust
'Kennedy Review' – Professor Sir Ian Kennedy
2013
166 pages

Shipman, Dr Harold

Dr Harold Shipman, born in January 1946, was a UK general practitioner working as a sole practitioner based in Hyde Greater Manchester. He was convicted of the murder of 230 patients of a period of 24 years. His murderous and psychopathic activities came to light via a failed attempt to forge a will of one of his patients.

Earlier at the start of his medical carer Dr Shipman stole and used a controlled drug pethidine, a morphine substitute used by drug abuses. The GMC, the UK regulator of medical practitioners, investigated but took no action, possible swayed by his assertion that he would no longer work as a general practitioner.

Later in his career he worked as a general practitioner in the North of England. He worked in a single practice. In January 2000 he was convicted of murdering 400 elderly patients by administering lethal doses of drugs. Dr Shipman committed suicide in prison in 2003.

Post Inquiry actions and impact

- Procedures for detecting and notifying unusually high number of deaths
- Stockpiling of drugs
- Issuing of death certificates

Issues of concern to regulators of healthcare professionals

- Breaking the law by healthcare professionals
- Falsifying records by healthcare professionals
- Lying to relatives of patients by healthcare professionals
- Slow and ineffectual intervention by regulator
- Regulator reviews professionals who have returned to the register following removal after a fitness to practise (FTP) case.

Harold Shipman's Clinical Practice 1974–1998 R
A clinical audit commissioned by the Chief Medical Office
The Stationery Office
2004
156 pages

Learning from Tragedy, Keeping Patients Safe R
Overview of the Government's action programme in response
to the recommendations of the Shipman Inquiry
Department of Health
London: the Stationery Office
Ref: Cm.7014
February 2007
40 pages

Safeguarding Patients R
The Government's response to the recommendations of the
Shipman Inquiry's fifth report and to the recommendations
of the Ayling, Neale and Kerr/Haslam Inquiries
The Stationery Office, London
Ref: Cm 7015 and ISBN 10: 0101701527
February 2007
143 pages

The Shipman Inquiry R
Fifth Report
Safeguarding Patients: Lessons from the Past – Proposals for the Future
Dame Janet Smith
London Stationery Office
Ref: Command Paper Cm 6394-I II III and ISBN-10: 0101639422
9 December 2004
1,178 pages

USA

Angelo, Richard

An American serial killer and former nurse at the Good Samaritan Hospital in West Islip, New York. Born in August 1962, in 1989, he was convicted of murdering several of his patients and sentenced to 50 years to life in prison.

Bradley, Dr Earl

Concerns about the paediatrician Dr Bradley's behaviour were raised at the Thomas Jefferson University Hospital in Philadelphia in 1994 and again in 1995. Investigations were conducted by the hospital but did not progress due to lack of evidence. He then relocated his medical practice to State of Delaware. In 2004 concerns were raised to the Professional Association/regulator by his office manager who was also his sister. No action was taken. In 2005 concerns were raised by a practice nurse to the Milford police in Delaware who sought a warrant for his arrest. This was rejected by the Office of the Attorney General due to an assessment that there was not enough evidence and no action was taken. In February 2010 his licence was revoked. In June 2011, following a two-year investigation, Bradley was arrested and charged with 471 offences. 2011. He was sent to prison for 14 consecutive life terms plus 165 years.

Investigations focused on service providers; in this case the hospital was unwilling to report concerns to the regulator. There was also communications failure between Government agencies, in this case the police, prosecutor's office and Professional Association/regulator. In addition, the Medical Society of Delaware was seen to be weak with an unclear remit.

Nine Bills to enhance the protection of children in Delaware were introduced on 30 June 2010. Changes included a duty to report concerns, chaperoning of children. The regulators' board membership was changed by increasing lay membership. Also, the name of the regulator was changed to better reflect its role from Medical Society to Medical Board for Licensing and Discipline.

Independent Review of the Earl Brian Bradley Case R
Final Report: Submitted to the Honorable Jack Markell,
Governor, State of Delaware:
Linda L. Ammons
10 May 2010
65 pages

The Investigation of the Failures to Report Allegations of Unprofessional conduct and Child Abuse Against Dr Earl Bradley Under Delaware Prior to 2008 R
Lawrence W. Lewis, State Solicitor
Delaware Department of Justice
Attorney General's Report)
17 May 17, 2010 page 25–26

Cullen, Charles Edmund

A nurse who during his 16-year career confessed to killing 40 patients between 1988 and 2003. However, some estimate that he could have killed several hundred patients.

Diaz, Robert

A nurse working in California who was convicted of murdering numerous elderly patients who in 1981 he poisoned using Lidocaine.

Gilbert, Kristen

A nurse from Northampton, Massachusetts, who was convicted in 2001 of murdering four patients.

Perfect Poison: A Female Serial Killer's Deadly Medicine B
Phelps M. William.
Kensington Publishing
ISBN-13: 978-0786015504
1 June 2003
480 pages

Harvey, Donald

American orderly who murdered over 50 patients in Cincinnati, Ohio, between 1970 and 1887.

Holmes, Dr. Henry Howard

Physician and serial killer. Known as the *White City Devil* he was a graduate of the University of Michigan's Department of Medicine and Surgery and operated in Chicago in the nineteenth century.

Dr H. H. Holmes: The True History of the White City Devil B
Adam Selzer
Skyhorse Publishing
ISBN-13: 978-1510713437
20 April 2017

Jackson, Viki Dawn

Nurse who killed at least 10 patients at the Nocona General Hospital in Nocona, Texas, between 2000 and 2001.

Lynn Majors, Orville

A licensed practical nurse from Linton, Indiana, convicted of murdering his patients in Clinton, Indiana. In 2017 he was only tried for six murders but is believed to have committed as many as 130 murders.

Cold Blooded Care B
The True Stories of Two Nurses (Kristen Gilbert and Orville Lynn Majors) Who Intentionally Killed Their Hospital Patients
Dan Mitrione
AuthorHouse
ISBN-13: 978-1418428273
July 29 2004
492 pages

Saldivar, Efren

The worker, Efren Saldivar, a respiratory care therapist at Glendale Adventist Medical Centre, California. He is assumed to have killed 40 to 50 unconscious patients from 1989 to 1998.

Saenz, Kimberly Clark

A nurse who was implicated in the deaths of several patients at a Texas dialysis centre.

In 2012, she was convicted of murdering five patients and injuring five others.

Swango, Dr Micheal

An American physician who poisoned over 50 patients in the 1980s and 1990s.

Blind Eye: How the Medical Establishment Let a Doctor Get Away with Murder B
Stewart, James B.
Simon and Schuster
ISBN 10: 0 684 85484 8 ISBN 13: 9780684854847
1999
335 pages

An American doctor who was a prolific serial killer; activities were allowed to continue for decades even though the healthcare system was aware of his failings.

2. Catastrophic failure of an individual healthcare professional who does not provide safe and effective practice and unintentionally harms their patients

Australia

Baily, Dr Harry

A psychiatrist who worked at Chelmsford Private Hospital in Sydney. He used '*deep sleep therapy*' that was linked to 24 deaths and 19 related suicides of patients. He committed suicide in 1985 during an investigation and before the publication of the subsequent Royal Commission.

NSW Royal Commission into Deep Sleep Therapy R
The Chelmsford Commission
Chair Hon Acting Justice John Patrick Slattery
Government Printing Services
ISBN 0724087672 (Vol 1)
1990
196 pages

Patel, Jayant Mukundray

Jayant Patel an Indian-born American surgeon who in 2010 was accused of gross negligence whilst working at Bundaberg Base Hospital in Queensland, Australia, who may have killed over 80 patients. Was convicted for manslaughter, then acquitted after a retrial.

Sick to Death B
A manipulative surgeon and a health system in crisis – a disaster waiting to happen
Hedley Thomas
Allen and Unwin
ISBN-10: 1741148812
ISBN-13: 978-1741148817
1 October 2007
448 pages

Queensland Public Hospitals Commission of Inquiry – Davies Commission R
Final Report
The Health Quality and Complaints Commission, Brisbane
Hon Geoffrey Davies AO
Dewey Number: 362.11/0994
Libraries Australia ID: 40444191
30 November 2005
558 pages

New Zealand

Bottrill, Dr Michael

The scandal occurred in 2000 relating to the under-reporting of cervical screening smear abnormalities by a laboratory that had failed to identify hundreds of abnormal smears. The Inquiry examined the practices of pathologist Dr Michael Bottrill who owned the laboratory and was responsible for reading the smears. It highlighted professional self-interest, a lack of quality assurance in the National Cervical Screening Programme.

Report of the Ministerial Inquiry into under-reporting of cervical smear abnormalities in the Gibson Region R
Duffy, A P, Barrett D K and Duggan MA
Ministry of Health New Zealand
2001
277 page

UK

Ingoldby, Christopher

A UK consultant general surgeon at Pinderfields Hospital in Wakefield, West Yorkshire, whose poor performance was first detected in 1989. This was followed by a further 84 incidents. Not until a clinical review by the NHS Executive was he dismissed by the NHS hospital in 2000. GMC investigated his performance but did not remove him from the register.

Ledward, Rodney

The regulatory failure related to 13 botched operations conducted by the surgeon at William Harvey Hospital in Ashford and the private St Saviour's Hospital in Hythe between 1989 and 1996. During the period his incompetence was known by professional colleagues and managers who failed to intervene.

The Report of the Inquiry into Quality and Practice within the National Health Service Arising from the Actions of Rodney Ledward R
Jean Richie QC
Department of Health
Stationary Office, London
ASIN: B0041CWZ8S
Ref No 54027001242518
1 June 2000
396 pages

Neale, Richard

A surgeon who was struck off the medical register in Canada in 1985 because of serious incompetence after the death of two patients. Despite warnings to this country from Canada, he practised in the Friarage hospital in Northallerton, for 10 years. After being, in effect, dismissed he continued to practice in Leicester, the Isle of Wight, and London before finally being struck off for professional misconduct in the United Kingdom in July 2000.

Committee of inquiry to investigate how the NHS handled allegations about the performance and conduct of Richard Neale R
Department of Health
The Stationery Office
Cm 6315 and ISBN-10: 0101631529
9 September 2004
372 pages

Ubani, Dr Danial

In February 2008 a German national Dr Danial Ubani was admitted to the GMC register without assessing his English language skills. Dr Ubani administered diamorphine ten times the recommended dose to a patient Mr David Grey, who subsequently died of an overdose. An independent review led by Dr David Carson of General practitioners out-of-hours services in England was then commissioned by the Department of Health.

Raising Standards for Patients New Partnerships in Out-of-Hours Care R
An Independent Review of GP Out-of-Hours Services in England
Commissioned by the
Department of Health
David Carson
22454.1P.14k.OCT 00
October 2000
88 pages

An independent review following the death of David Grey led by Dr David Carson of General practitioners out-of-hours services in England commissioned by the Department of Health.

Response to the House of Commons Health Committee Report the Use of Overseas Doctors in Providing Out-of-Hours Services: Fifth Report of Session 2009–10 R
Presented to Parliament by the Secretary of State for Health by Command of Her Majesty
CM 7904
The Stationery Office
ISBN: 9780101790420
July 2010
14 pages

The Use of Overseas Doctors in Providing Out-of-Hours Services R
Fifth Report of Session 2009–10
House of Commons, Health Committee
HC 441
75 pages
8 April 2010

USA

Duntsch, Christopher Daniel

An incompetent neurosurgeon whose licence to practise medicine was revoked due to gross malpractice that resulted in the death and maiming of several patients while working at Texas. In February 2007 he was subsequently convicted of various crimes and sentenced to life in prison.

3. Catastrophic failure of organisations within the healthcare delivery system often involving individual healthcare professionals

Alder Hay, Royal Liverpool Children's Hospital

The inquiry into the Bristol Royal Infirmary uncovered the widespread practice by members of the UK medical profession of removing and retaining organs of dead children without obtaining appropriate consent contrary to the Human Tissue Act 1961. They did not inform the parents or relatives of the deceased. The Royal Liverpool Children's Hospital, Alder Hey hospital in Liverpool was at the centre of the scandal because of its propensity to remove and store organs for 'scientific research' without consent on an industrial scale.

Royal Liverpool Children's Inquiry Report R
Michael Redfern QC
Stationery Office, London.
ISBN 9780102775013
HC 12 2000-01 PDF
30 January 2001
540 pages

Following the affair, the 1998 Human Tissues Act was replaced by the 2004 Human Tissue Act. It incorporated criminal sanctions for transgressors.

Ashworth Hospital

A high-security psychiatric hospital near Liverpool. Following the death of a patient in 1988 a report and other serious allegations, a Committee of Inquiry published a report that was highly critical of the regime, which was felt to be more custodial than therapeutic. Seven staff and two managers were relieved of their duties. A second inquiry was undertaken at the end of the 1990s following allegations by a former patient.

Report of the Committee of Inquiry into Complaints about Ashworth Hospital R
Blom-Cooper Sir L.
Cmnd 2028 – 1 and 2028 – 2
London: HMSO.
1992

Report of the Committee of Inquiry into the Personality Disorder Unit, Ashworth Special Hospital R
Fallon, Peter QC
ISBN 0101419430
Command paper 4194 – ii
London HMSO
6 January 1999
400 pages

Bristol Royal Infirmary

The events relating to the management of care of children receiving complex heart Surgery at the Bristol Royal Infirmary took place between 1991 and 1995. There was a high mortality rate of babies treated for heart conditions. 29 babies and young children died following elective surgery. Two cardiac surgeons were struck of the medical register, and one was banned from performing surgery for three years. Causes included the lack of a culture of open partnership or patient safety.

Learning from Bristol

The Report of the public inquiry into children's heart surgery at the Bristol Royal Infirmary 1984–1995 R
Professor Sir Ian Kennedy
Department of Health
Ref; CM 5207
The Stationery Office, London
18 July 2001
530 pages

Ely Hospital

Ely Hospital was a large psychiatric hospital in the Ely district of Cardiff, Wales. A 1969 inquiry into the ill-treatment of patients at the hospital led to reforms to services in the UK for people with learning disabilities.

Report of the Committee of Inquiry into Allegations of Ill – Treatment of Patients and other irregularities at the Ely Hospital, Cardiff R
Department of Health and Social Security
Cmnd 3975
Report to Parliament
HMSO
ISBN-10: 010139750X
27 March 1969
135 pages

Better Services for the Mentally Handicapped R
Department of Health and Social Security
Command paper 4683
HM Stationery Office
ISBN 13 978-0101468305
1 June 1971
67 pages

Furness General Hospital

Lessons Learned Review R
The Nursing and Midwifery Council's handling of concerns about midwives' fitness to practise at the Furness General Hospital
Professionals Standards Authority
16 May 2018
84 pages

Gosport War Memorial Hospital

450 elderly patients whose lives were shortened following the routine administration of opiates at a hospital on the South Coast of England between 1988 and 2000. A subsequent Independent Panel, Chaired by the Bishop of Liverpool James Jones, published a report on 20 June 2018. Criticism was levied against a number of public authorities including the police, the GMC, the regulator of the medical profession and the NMC, the regulator of nurses and midwives, the coroner system, and the Crown Prosecution Service. A single doctor Jane Barton was linked to the deaths, but the GMC intervened late and the doctor was not subjected to an FTP process.

Issues of Concern to Regulators of Healthcare Professionals

- Breaking the law by healthcare professionals
- Falsifying records by healthcare professionals
- Lying to relatives of patients by healthcare professionals
- Lack of insight and understanding of the ethics and belief systems of others by healthcare professionals
- Poor communication and evasiveness by healthcare professionals
- Perception of collegiate self-protectionism by the profession
- Concerns not raised by fellow professionals
- Slow and ineffectual intervention by regulator

Gosport War Memorial Hospital: R
The Report of the Gosport independent Panel
House of Commons/HMSO
Ref HC 1084
ISBN: 978 1 5286 0406 2
20 June 2018
387 pages

Infected Blood

Described as by Lord Winston '*the worst treatment disaster in the history of the NHS*' an estimated 3,000 deaths occurred attributable to infected blood, blood products, and tissues. The 2024 report's lessons to be learned and recommendations relating to healthcare professionals included candour, communication, consent, medical records, and risk.

Infected Blood Inquiry The Report R
House of Commons paper
HM Stationery Office
ISBN 978-1-5286-4685-7
HC 569 – I to VII
20 May 2024

Liverpool Community Health

In 2010 a community health service in Liverpool, implemented cost improvement programmes that put the safety of patients at risk. In addition, a culture of bullying meant that staff were scared to speak up or that incidents were ignored or not escalated. The review found that an external overview by CQC the service regulator, failed to identify problems for at least four years.

Report of the Liverpool Community Health Independent Review R
Dr Bill Kirkup
NHS Improvements
8 February 2018
78 pages

Post Inquiry Actions and Impact

In July 2018 the Department of Health established the Kark Review of the Fit and Proper persons requirements.

Mid Staffordshire NHS Foundation Trust

The serious failings at the Mid Staffordshire NHS Foundation Trust between January 2005 and March 2009 led to a public inquiry chaired by Robert Francis QC. It examined the operation of the commissioning, supervisory and regulatory organisations, and other agencies, including the culture and systems of those organisations in relation to their monitoring role of the hospitals and the professionals involved.

Central to the problem was a failure in the culture of the organisation. Other issues that the inquiry identified was that the regulatory regime allowed for overlap of functions that led to a tendency for regulators to assume that the identification and resolution of issues was the responsibility of someone else. This contributed to problems not being identified sooner and appropriate intervention taken.

Following the Francis Inquiry into the Mid Staffordshire regulatory failure the Cavendish Review recommended the introduction of Certificates of Fundamental Care.

Report of the Mid Staffordshire NHS Foundation Trust Public Inquiry R
The Mid Staffordshire NHS Foundation Trust Public Inquiry
Chair Robert Francis QC

Executive Summary	ISBN 9780 10298 1476, HC 947 2012-13	135 pages
Volumes I	ISBN 9780 10298 1469, HC 898 2012-13	692 pages
Volume II	ISBN 9780 10298 1469, HC 898 2012-13	668 pages
Volume III	ISBN 9780 10298 1469, HC 898 2012-13	434 pages

London Stationery Office
6 February 2013

Independent Inquiry into care provided by Mid Staffordshire NHS Foundation Trust January 2001 to March 2009, Vol I and II Chaired by Robert Francis QC R

Volume I	ISBN 9780 10296 4394	HC375-I	455 pages
Volume II	ISBN 9780 10296 4394	HC375-II	367 pages

London Stationery Office
24 February 2010

Patients First and Foremost

The Initial Government Response to the Report of the Mid Staffordshire NHS Foundation Trust Public Inquiry R
Department of Health
The Stationery Office
Cm 8576
March 2013
84 pages

Hard Truths: The Journey to Putting Patients First R
Government response to Mid Staffordshire NHS Foundation Trust Public Inquiry
Volume 1 and 2
Cm 8777-I and Cm 87 -II
137 and 248 pages
January 2014

Morecambe Bay

A serious failure of clinical care in the maternity unit at Morecambe Bay Hospital NHS Foundation Trust in the period 2004–2013. The result was avoidable harm and deaths to mothers and babies. The subsequent investigation by Dr Bill Kirkup, of the management, delivery, and outcomes of care provided by the maternity and neonatal services identified a pattern of failure to recognise the nature and severity of the problem, with, in some cases, denial that any problem existed, and a series of missed opportunities to intervene that involved almost every level of the NHS in England.

The Report of the Morecambe Bay Investigation R
Dr Bill Kirkup
Department of Health and Social Care
ISBN 9780108561306
London HMSO
3 March 2015
222 pages

The government response to the Freedom to Speak Up consultation, the Public Administration Select Committee report 'Investigating Clinical Incidents in the NHS', and the Morecambe Bay Investigation

Learning not blaming R
Department of Health
Cm 9113
16 July 2015
103 pages

In addition, following the completion of the inquiry, the Department of Health commissioned a report by the PSA on the NMC, the UK regulator of Nurses and Midwives. The report published in May 2018 was critical of the culture of the regulator and in particular its engagement with citizens.

Midwifery Supervision and Regulation: Recommendations for Change R
Parliamentary and Health Service Ombudsman
The Stationery Office
HC 865
ISBN 9780102987324
10 December 2013
28 pages

Midwifery Regulation in the United Kingdom R
Beccy Baird B, Murray R, Seale B, Foot C and Perry C
King's Fund
Report commissioned by the NMC
January 2015
31 pages

The Nursing and Midwifery Council – amendments to modernise midwifery regulation and improve the effectiveness and efficiency of fitness to practise processes R
Government Response
Department of Health
January 2017
34 pages

Lessons Learned Review R
The Nursing and Midwifery Council's handling of concerns about midwives' fitness to practise at the Furness General Hospital
Professionals Standards Authority
16 May 2018
84 pages

Northern Ireland

14-year inquiry into hyponatraemia-related deaths of a number of children in Royal Belfast Hospital for Sick Children (RBHSC).

Inquiry into Hyponatraemia-related Deaths R
Chaired by Mr Justice John O'Hara
Department of Health, Social Services & Public Safety
Ref: ISBN 978-1-912313-04-4
January 2018
202 pages

Shrewsbury and Telford Hospital NHS Trust Ockenden Report – Final R
Findings, Conclusions And Essential Actions
From the Independent Review of Maternity Services at The Shrewsbury and Telford Hospital NHS Trust
HC1219
ISBN 978-1-5286-3229-4
30 March 2022
250 pages

Shrewsbury and Telford hospital NHS trust, where hundreds of babies needlessly died or suffered life-changing injuries.

Vale of Levan

In 2007/8 an outbreak of bacterial infections led to the deaths of dozens of patients in a hospital in Dumbarton Scotland. The public inquiry investigated the causes, management, and clinical processes used by the hospital.

Vale of Leven Hospital Inquiry Report R
Lord MacLean
Scottish Government
Ref: SC/2014/211
ISBN 978 1 78412 843 2
November 2014
456 pages

Scottish Government's Response to the Vale of Leven Hospital Inquiry Report R
The Scottish Government
ISBN: 978 1 78544 369 5
18 June 2015
71 pages

Winterbourne View Hospital

A TV investigation uncovered abuse of adults with learning disabilities and autism at a 24-bed private hospital. In November 2014, as a result of a public inquiry the Health and Social Care Act 2008 (Regulated Activities) Regulations 2014 was introduced that updated standards relating to the duty of candour and the fit and proper persons test.

Transforming Care: A National Response to Winterbourne View Hospital R
Department of Health Review: Final Report
Gateway Reference: 18348
10 December 2012
62 pages

Winterbourne View Hospital R
A Serious Case Revie
Margaret Flynn
South Gloucestershire Safeguarding Adults Boar
4 September 2012
170 pages

4. Poor operational performance of the regulators of healthcare professionals

Canada

College of Denturists of Ontario

In May 2010, the Minister of Health and Long-Term Care of Ontario commissioned PricewaterhouseCoopers (PwC) to conduct a review of the College of Denturists of Ontario (CDO) following the receipt of numerous concerns regarding its operations. In particular, PwC investigated the adequacy of the administration and governance arrangements of the CDO, the 2010 council elections, and the finances of the regulator. The review identified a range of deficiencies in its operations. An external supervisor was subsequently appointed by the Lieutenant Governor in Council.

Operational Review and Audit of the College of Denturists of Ontario R
Ministry of Health and Long-Term Care, Ontario, Canada
PricewaterhouseCoopers (PwC)
8 March 2012
122 pages

UK – England

Care Quality Commission (CQC)

The review identified significant failings in the internal workings of CQC. Final report was published in October 2024.

Review into the Operational Effectiveness of the CQC R
Full report
Dr Penelope Dash, Independent Lead Reviewer
Department of Health & Social Care
4 October 2024

NMC
Failure of the culture of the NMC in relation to EDI, leadership, and governance. Concerns relating to nurses private lives not investigated, board unaware of problems and not detected by QA system, or the PSA the oversight organisation.

NMC Independent Culture Review R
Nazir Afzal
Rise Associates
July 2024
133 pages

FURTHER READING

Angels of Death B
Disturbing real-life cases of nurses and doctors who kill
Emily Webb
The Five Mile Press (Australia)
ISBN: 9781760063634
19 January 2015
222 pages

The Black Swan: The impact of the Highly Improbable B
Taleb, Nassim Nicholas
Random House
ISBN 13: 9781400063512
17 April 2007
400 pages

Investigating Clinical Incidents in the NHS R
House of Commons Public Administration Select Committee
HC 886
27 March 2015
75 pages

Medical Self-Regulation Crisis and Change B
Mark Davies
ISBN 13 978-1107495241
Cambridge University Press, 2nd Edition
7 April 2016
314 pages

Standards for Regulators

CHAPTER 6

INTRODUCTION

Government has a responsibility to be informed about whether or not regulatory interventions and individual regulators are delivering their objectives. To achieve this they must firstly set the standards they expect regulators to achieve. Government can then assess its regulators using qualitative and quantitative assessment tools either directly or indirectly by commissioning auditors and/or oversight organisations to ensure that regulators comply with their objectives and standards. In effect, regulators are subjected to a regulatory process. In turn, these processes have resulted in regulators evolving characteristics and attributes that enable them to meet the required standards.

The chapter has four sections:

6.1 Evaluating regulatory interventions

6.2 Standards for regulators

6.3 Characteristics and attributes of regulators

6.4 Auditing and overseeing regulators

6.1 EVALUATING REGULATORY INTERVENTIONS

INTRODUCTION

When government develops new, or modifies existing, policy, it is assumed that the investment in time, effort, and resources will result in a range of benefits. And of course with the proviso that whilst benefits are predicted to occur, negative effects can also be inadvertently triggered. Therefore, before the regulation of a sector is introduced, modified, or continued, it should be evaluated. This can be achieved using two broad approaches. Firstly, at the start of the policy development, the advantages and disadvantages of the proposed regulation can be compared. Secondly, following the introduction of regulation, the achievements of the regulatory policy objective can be retrospectively evaluated. To do this a range of evaluation methodologies can be used, including objective and compliance evaluation, cost–benefit analysis (CBA), net present value (NPV), and regulatory impact assessment (RIA), all of which are introduced in this section.

RATIONALE FOR EVALUATING REGULATORY INTERVENTION

The resources required by government are inevitably almost always scarce. Government should therefore analyse the various competing proposals for resources and invest in projects that provide the greatest good at the lowest possible cost. This means that an evaluation methodology should be used to consider the justification for investing in alternative and mutually exclusive policies or projects which are in competition for limited resources.

Regulation is normally introduced with the objective of creating and then maintaining benefits to society and the public. It is therefore important that an evaluation of regulation should be undertaken both before it has been introduced and, although frequently this not the case, retrospectively. After all, if this is not done, how would government in the first place know that its regulatory policy objectives were reasonable and that have now been successful achieved?

In relation to the regulation of professionals, examples of when these evaluations should be made include:

- Considering combing two independent regulators into one organisation
- Deciding whether or not to regulate a new profession
- Establishing a new way to educate and train healthcare professionals
- Introducing compulsory continuing competence

EVALUATING REGULATORY INTERVENTIONS

There are two broad methods that can be used to make these types of evaluations, namely, qualitative and quantitative, as detailed in Table 6.1 – I.

The different methodologies will now be expanded:

QUALITATIVE EVALUATION

Examples of qualitative evaluations include:

Operations of Regulators of Healthcare Professionals, Volume 4, First Edition. Marc Seale.

Companion website: www.wiley.com/go/seale/regulatinghealthcare

Table 6.1 – I Regulatory interventions – evaluation methodologies

Qualitative evaluation
• Net advantages vs disadvantages
• Objective and compliance
Quantitative evaluation
• Cost benefit analysis
• Net present value
• Regulatory impact assessment

Net Advantages vs Disadvantages Evaluation

The first approach is to evaluate the advantages and disadvantages of a policy using a range of categories. If the resulting advantages outweigh the disadvantages, then the policy, such as regulation, should be introduced or maintained. This process is used in Section 7.1, volume 1, Advantages and disadvantages of regulating healthcare professionals, which evaluates six broad categories, namely: communication, economic, education, social, standards, and health.

However, to state the obvious, this approach is both qualitative and subjective. To make matters more challenging, the range of categories to evaluate the advantages and disadvantages of regulation will vary across different sectors, for example, the financial services industry or the environment.

Objective and Compliance Evaluation

A second qualitative approach used in relation to regulation is to attempt to evaluate both:

1. Successful achievement of the intended policy objective of the legalisation used to establish the regulator
2. Compliance with the rules and standards of those regulated

This approach again has a number of challenges.

For example, different stakeholders may have differing subjective views on the success, or not, of the delivery of the regulators' intended policy objective. Or, in relation to the regulation of healthcare professionals members of the public and those professions regulated often have greatly differing views about the success of the regulatory regime.

In relation to evaluating compliance with rules and standards, it is challenging to link compliance to the success of regulation. For example, in relation to the regulation of healthcare professionals, there are numerous influences on how healthcare professionals behave. If their behaviour is improved, is this because of the impact of regulation or because of another influence? This issue is explored in detail in Section 1.4, volume 3, Predicting, influencing, and preventing professional failure.

In summary the challenge of seeking to evaluate the intended or actual outcome of regulation using subjective qualitative measures is that it is difficult to measure success or failure. The alternative is to use quantitative evaluation. This assumes that both regulation and regulators can be demonstrated to be unequivocally effective and efficient by the use of the processes of counting, auditing, and inspection.

QUANTITATIVE EVALUATION

When government is confronted the need to evaluate their regulatory policy, or when commercial enterprises review their strategy, both can use different types of quantitative analysis. Examples include net present value NPV, cost benefit analysis CBA, and particular in relation to regulatory evaluations, regulatory impact assessment RIA. The three calculations will now be explored:

1. **Net present value (NPV)**
   NPV calculations are predominantly used by commercial enterprises to help decide which competing projects to invest in.
   For those readers who are not familiar with the concept of NPV, it is a financial calculation that uses the principle of the *time value of money* to compare the amount invested in a project at today's prices, compared to the present value of the future cash receipts from the investment. The time value of money encapsulates the concept that individuals place a higher value on money received today compared to the option of receiving the money at some point in the future. The further away in time of the potential receipt of the money, the lower the value today.
   The calculation also encapsulates the level of risk to future cash flows by using different discount rates. The discount rate is the value that represents the risk of the project. The higher the risk, the higher the discount rate. For example, investing in UK Government securities it is reasonable to assume that it is a low-risk investment, and investors will use a low discount rate. At the other end of the investment spectrum, investing in hunting for sunken treasure in shipwrecks would be considered a very high-risk adventure requiring large amounts of capital and with a high probability of failure. Potential investors should therefore use a high discount rate to assess the likely financial returns from this type of investment project.
2. **Cost–benefit analysis**
   CBA is a process that seeks to provide the evidence that an economic, social, or environmental policy has been successful. It can be defined as:

Definition: Cost–Benefit Analysis
Systematic process for calculating and comparing costs and benefits of a decision, a policy, or a project.

Methodology

The methodology for undertaking a CBA is as follows:

i. For each project, identify options and their policy objective, including 'business as usual' (BAU) and a 'do nothing' or 'momentum' option.

ii. Assess the benefits, both monetary and non-monetary, derived from each option

iii. Assess the different types of costs for delivering each option

iv. Subtract the costs from the benefits

v. Express costs and benefits in a single currency value, i.e. £, $, or Euros

vi. Assess the risk of each option

vii. Select a discount rate to reflect the risk of the option

viii. Calculate the NPV

ix. Undertake sensitivity analysis

x. Select the option with the greatest NPV

3. **Regulatory impart assessment (RIA)**
In the world of regulation the term RIA is used to describe the CBA of a regulatory project.

An RIA is defined as:

Definition: Regulatory Impact Assessment
Explanation of the objective of the regulatory proposal, the risks being addressed, and the likely costs and benefits of options for delivering the objective.

It should be noted that an RIA and a policy impact assessment are similar. In some jurisdictions a regulatory impact statement may also be published.

Methodology

The methodology to undertake an RIA is broadly similar to that used to undertake and CBA as illustrated in Chart 6.1 – I.

LIMITATIONS OF COST BENEFIT ANALYSIS AND REGULATORY IMPACT ASSESSMENTS

CBA and RIAs require the measurement of a range of issues. This is often more easily said than done. To expand:

Measuring Costs

Government can easily edict that CBA and RIAs should be undertaken. However, it is relatively straightforward to measure direct costs but more difficult to measure indirect costs. Direct costs therefore tend to dominate regulatory arguments despite the fact that indirect costs may be more significant.

Quantifying Financial Risk

Many commercial enterprises and some governmental organisations such as regulators of utilities evaluate projects by making use of cost of capital calculations. To do this comparative risk measurements are required. While market information exists in relation to commercial joint stock companies, it is not so for public authorities. The subject is outside the scope of the book, but for those interested in the issue the UK Regulators' Network (UKRN) publishes an annual update report on the topic.

Chart 6.1 – I **Regulatory impact assessment**

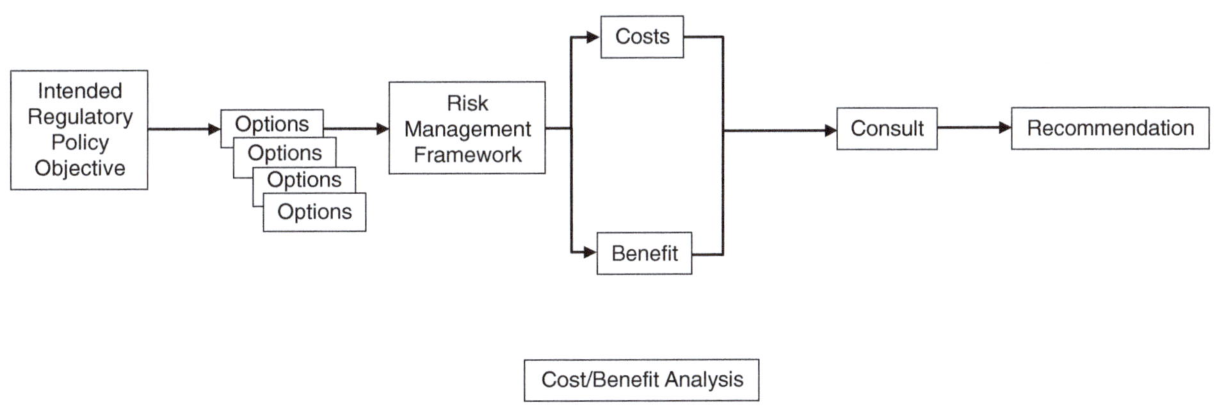

Measuring Benefits

Measuring various non-monetary benefits is considerably more difficult than measuring monetary benefits. This is because they may be more difficult to identify as they may arise in external organisations and be subjective. Challenges arise in relation to specific areas, in particular:

- Economic
- Environmental
- Social

For example, in the UK public authorities must have regard to the Equality Act 2010 and need to meet its objectives. As a consequence when evaluating regulatory interventions both regulators and government must undertake an equality impact assessment. Linking an equality impact assessment to financial projects can be challenging but remains necessary.

This leads to the oft criticism of CBA, that it is too gradgrindian.

The Cost of Regulation

Whichever method is used to evaluate regulation and regulators, it is clear that there is a cost to regulation. In essence regulation is not a 'free lunch', and there are costs associated with it. These costs are often referred to as the regulatory burden:

Definition: Regulatory Burden
Costs to an individual or organisation of complying with the requirements of a regulatory system.

It should be noted that the terms administrative burden, administrative cost, and compliance burden may also be used.

The overall cost of the regulatory burden comprised five categories of costs, namely:

1. Mitigating the regulatory activity
2. Demonstrating compliance
3. Direct costs of regulator
4. Delay costs
5. Unintended consequences

1. **Mitigating the regulated activity**
   These are the types of costs associated with meeting the regulators' rules and standards and may include, for example:
   - Additional employees to undertake mitigation
   - Educating and training employees
   - General increase in operating costs
   - Purchase of plant and equipment and its subsequent maintenance
   - Purchase of professional advice, for example, legal or accounting services
2. **Demonstrating compliance**
   This is the cost of demonstrating compliance by the use of administrative processes. For example, recording, analysing, and submitting data to the regulator or preparing for and hosting a regulator to inspect its facilities or premises.
3. **Direct costs of regulation**
   These are the costs of the regulator for items such as employee wages and its ITC systems. In turn, the regulated sector has to fund these direct costs by payment of fees or levies to the regulator.
   In the UK, for example, the financial regulator the Financial Conduct Authority charges a fee to organisations that want to provide financial services. Or, in the USA a nurse who wants to work in Virginia pays an annual fee to the state licensing board.
4. **Delay costs**
   Time lost by regulated entities or individuals to successfully complete applications and/or the regulator to make and communicate their decision. For example, a nurse may be unable to start work, or the construction and commissioning of industrial plant may be delayed.
5. **Unintended consequences**
   Regulation may have unintended consequences that drives up costs in the regulated sector or wider afield. In particular, regulation in one sector may generate unintended consequences in another sector. These can be referred to as indirect costs and can be defined as:

Definition: Indirect Cost of Regulation
Unintended costs to individuals and organisations reacting to incentives caused by regulation.

In the UK an example of this type of indirect cost effect occurred with the introduction in the early 2000s of an EU requirement to recycle domestic fridges. But because there was insufficient capacity to safely and environmentally dispose of them 'fridge mountains' of unwanted were created.

Examples of unintended consequences brought about by regulation include:

i. **Growth in the economy**
   Regulation has the potential to have significant impact on macroeconomic factors such as the rate of economic growth. This is triggered by bureaucracy

reducing the ability of commercial organisations to react quickly or diverting their limited resources away from investing in their business and thus reducing competitiveness

ii. **Labour mobility**
Regulation may reduce the mobility of workforce entering jurisdictions and therefore drive up costs

iii. **Productivity**
The productivity of employers can be reduced if they have to spend a disproportionate amount of time and effort complying with regulations

iv. **Wages and the demand and supply of labour**
The last unintended consequence cost of regulation is its impact on the supply and demand for labour. This microeconomic argument is that if the supply of labour is restricted and the demand for labour remains the same, then wages will increase; see Section 1.5, volume 4, Economics of regulating professionals

UNEVEN DISTRIBUTION AND IMPACT OF REGULATORY BURDEN

To complicate matters the burden of regulation may not have the same impact on all organisations or individuals.

For example, large organisations may be better able to manage regulatory requirements because of their large pool of resources and the sophistication of their management abilities. However, small business, charities, and voluntary organisations may suffer a greater impact compared to a larger organisation because they have fewer resources to comply with regulatory rules and standards or producing reports required by a regulator. Therefore, when undertaking an RIA the impact on various types of organisations and individuals should be assessed.

Lastly, the cost of regulation may not fall equitably across all members of society. For example, women may disproportionally have to contribute more to the cost of regulating professionals because the annual registration fee of the regulator is the same for both men and women, but women may earn less partially due to working patterns and career progression.

PROPORTIONATE REGULATION

This leads to the argument that regulation should be proportionate. The question that all regulators should ask themselves is are they using regulatory measures that are really necessary to solve the problem. If you are using a sledgehammer to crack a nut, you're probably getting it wrong.

However, there is a strong counter argument that regulators should not apply the regulatory process in a proportionate manner. For example, what is the justification for allowing a small and underfinanced water treatment plant from polluting a river because it does not have the appropriate resources?

OVERALL REGULATORY BURDEN

Clearly regulation has an economic cost. This is not to say that the regulations should not be imposed, rather that the regulatory policy objective should be achieved by the use of a minimalist interventional approach. Also, these costs can be increased if the regulator is inefficient or ineffective or the regulator imposes unnecessary requirements on the enterprise or individuals it regulates. And lastly, the regulatory burden can be contained or reduced if risk-based regulation is used by the regulator to target its limited resources into areas of high risk; see Section 2.5, volume 1.

CONCLUSIONS OF EVALUATION

When regulation and regulators are assessed as meeting their regulatory objectives, all is well and good. However, if not, the regulator is probably underperforming and its performance should be measured against specific standards for regulators, see Section 6.2. Alternatively, the cause of the underperformance may be the regulators' legislation and if further evaluation assesses it to be inadequate, it should be either revised or abolished.

Examples of these types of reviews are undertaken in the USA by the Office of Information and Regulatory Affairs (OIRA). Their reviews of newly proposed regulations include consideration of alternative options and analysis of both benefits and costs before draft regulations are adopted.

ABOLISHING OR REFORMING REGULATORS

It should be noted that whilst the preceding discussion has focused on the evaluation of the initial impact of a proposed introduction of new regulations, periodic consideration should also be given to evaluating existing regulators. This is because if the original justification for the legislation is no longer valid, it should either be revised or amended or the regulator should be done away with altogether. However, monitoring the ongoing impact of existing regulation is less frequently undertaken by government. This is for a variety of reasons including complacency and shortage of time and resources to evaluate the status quo.

In the USA, some states use such review processes called a sunset review.

Other jurisdictions try to stem the flow of new regulators by insisting that if new legalisation is required at least one other regulator is consigned to the scrap heap and eliminated. In recent times, politicians both in the UK, in 2016, and the USA, in 2017, have issued policy edicts that a '*one-in, one-out*', followed by a '*one-in, two-out*' and then a '*one-in, three-out*' policy should be followed.

These types of edicts seek to prevent government and its policymakers from creating new regulations that will increase costs to commercial and voluntary organisations and individuals. In some cases specific targets have been introduced, such that when policymakers introduced a new regulation, and where there was a cost to comply with that new regulation, that government has to remove or modify an existing regulation with double the costs to business.

In April 2011, the UK Government also introduced a '*Red tape challenge*' where it actively sought consumer input in identifying where regulations could be eliminated or reduced. This in part led to the demise in 2012 of the independent Local Better Regulation Office. It had been established under the Regulatory Enforcement and Sanctions Act 2008 to co-ordinate regulatory enforcement by local authorities; for the creation of civil sanctions in relation to regulatory offences and for the reduction and removal of regulatory burdens. Again in 2015, the UK government has sought to invigorate the process by the introduction of the Small Business Enterprise and Employment Act 2015 attempted to set targets to reduce regulation impact on small business.

These repeated efforts appear to indicate that government, whilst seeking to reduce regulation and its associated costs, often finds it difficult to achieve this end.

CONCLUSION

The public might assume that policy makers and their political masters, by necessity, make rational decision about regulation based on science, hard numbers, facts, and calculations, rather than using capricious or political judgments alone. In addition, many would assume that government has a propensity to act when they proactively detect clear signals, rather than after disasters occur.

Unfortunately, even if quantitative methods such as CBA and RIAs are available to government and its policy makers that improve decision-making related to the evaluate regulatory interventions, the reality is that subjective and qualitative judgments hold sway, rather than rationality and logic

This inextricably leads to the challenges of how to evaluate the success or benefits of regulatory interventions both before and after its introduction. And, lastly, how to eliminate unnecessary regulation altogether.

EXERCISES AND QUESTIONS

Exercises

- Identify a regulatory process that is consider disproportionate by a regulated stakeholder
- Review an RIA undertaken by government relating to the introduction of a new regulatory regime

Questions

- In the UK architects are statutorily regulated and civil engineers are not. What is the reason for this state of affairs?
- Should government include in a regulator's legislation that it must undertake and publish RIAs?

LEGISLATION

Example of UK Legislation

Equality Act 2010	L
Regulatory Enforcement and Sanctions Act 2008	L
Small Business Enterprise and Employment Act 2015	L

FURTHER READING

Assessing the Impact of Proposed New Polices R
Report by the Comptroller and auditor General
National Audit Office
The Stationery Office
ISBN 978-0-10-296531-5
28 June 2010

Better Regulation 'Toolbox' R
European Commission
November 2021
606 pages

Better Regulation: R
Making Good Use of Regulatory Impact Assessments
Report by the Controller and Auditor General
HC 329 Session 2001 – 2002: 15 November 2001
Stationery Office, London
15 November 2001
13 pages

The Business Impact Target: cutting the cost of regulation R
National Audit Office
Department for Business, Innovation & Skills and Cabinet Office
DP Ref: 11133-001
ISBN 978-1-78604-059-6
29 June 2016
48 pages

Cost–Benefit Analysis B
Economic, Philosophical, and Legal Perspectives
Edited by Matthew D. Adler and Eric A. Posner
University of Chicago Press
January 2001
ISBN: 9780226007632
345 pages

Cost of regulation rtudy R
John Tiner
Deloitte
28 June 2006
69 pages

Evaluating Costs and Benefits for Regulatory Purposes: Direct and Indirect Impacts of Regulation on Business R
A Working Paper prepared for the Regulatory Policy Committee and the Better Regulation Executive by Brian Titley Consulting Ltd
Department for Business, Energy & Industrial Strategy and the Regulatory Policy Committee
April 2015
69 pages

A framework for assessing the benefits of financial regulation R
Report prepared for financial Services Authority
Oxera, Oxford, UK
September 2006
49 pages

Framework for Regulatory Policy Evaluation R
OECD
ISBN: 13 978 9264214439
June 2014
159 pages

Making Good Use of Regulatory Impact Assessments R
Report by the Controller and Auditor General
HC 329 Session 2001 – 2002: 15 November 2001
Stationery Office, London
15 November 2001
13 pages

Measuring Regulatory Performance R
Evaluating the impact of regulation and regulatory policy
OECD
Cary Coglianese
Expert Paper No 1
August 2012
59 pages

Performance Review of the Medical Council of New Zealand R
Professional Standards Authority
June 2010
28 pages
Reducing administrative burdens: effective inspection and enforcement

Hampton Review R
Phillip Hampton
HM Treasury, UK
ISBN: I 84532 088 3
March 2005
140 pages

Regulation – Less is More Reducing Burdens, Improving Outcomes R
A BRTF report to the Prime Minister
Better Regulation Task Force
ISBN: 0 7115 0466 0
March 2005
69 pages

Regulators and the Market B
An Assessment of the Growth of Regulation in the UK
Cento Veljanovski et al.
Institute of Economic Affairs IEA,
ISBN 10 0255 36248 x
1991
243 pages

Regulatory Impact Analysis Regulatory Impact Analysis Best Practices in OECD Countries R
Edited by, Scott H. Jacobs and Rex Deighton-Smith
OECD Publications
Paris, France
ISBN 10: 9264156038 ISBN 13: 9789264156036
1997
293 pages

Rethinking Regulation: R
Report on the Taskforce on Reducing Regulatory Burdens on Business
Australian Government
ISBN 0-646-45764-0
31 January 2006
184 pages

Re-engineering Regulation R
A blueprint for reform
Stephen Booth
Policy Exchange
ISBN: 978-1-910812-XX-X
8 August 2022
73 pages

Review of the cost effectiveness and efficiency of the health professional regulators R
Professional Standards Authority
November 2012
41 pages

Smaller Government: Shrinking the Quango State R
House of Commons Public Administration Select Committee
Fifth Report of Session 2010–11
Volume I: Report, together with formal minutes, oral and written evidence
HC 537
ISBN 978 0 215 55582 3
7 January 2011
132 pages

STANDARDS, CODES, GUIDANCE, CONSULTATIONS, POLICIES, AND PRACTICE NOTES

Guidance

Australian Government G
Guide to Regulatory Impact Analysis
Second Edition
SBN 978-1-925364-31-6
20 March 2020
62 pages

Better Regulation Framework Interim Guidance G
Department of Business, Energy & Industrial Strategy
UK Government
Ref: BIS/13/1038
March 2020
44 pages

Better Regulation Framework Manual G
Practical Guidance for UK Government Official
Department of Business, Innovation and Skills
UK Government
Ref: BIS/13/1038
March 2015
90 pages

Better Regulation Guidelines G
European Commission
SWD (2021) 305 final
3 November 2021
41 pages

Equality Impact Assessment Guidance G
Equality and Human Rights Commission
ISBN 978 1 84206 2401
November 2009
52 pages

Green Book G
Central Government Guidance on Appraisal and Evaluation
HM Treasury
The Stationery Office
ISBN 978-1-5286-2229-5
2022
138 pages

Impact Assessment TOOLKIT G
A guide to undertaking an Impact Assessment and Completing the IA Template
Department for Business Innovation & Skills
Better Regulation Executive
URN: 10/901
1 April 2010
95 pages

Regulatory Compliance Cost Assessment Guidance G
OECD
ISBN 978-92-64-20964-0
April 2014
76 pages

Regulatory Burden Measurement Framework G
Guidance Note
Australia Government
Office of Best Practice Regulation
February 2016

6.2 STANDARDS FOR REGULATORS

INTRODUCTION

The purpose of standards for regulators is primarily to enable government to indicate to regulators how they will be measured to ascertain if they are achieving their objectives. To facilitate this process, many organisations in numerous jurisdictions publish standards for regulators. The section reviews these standards and identifies the specific topics that are included.

NOMENCLATURE

Somewhat unsurprisingly the world is awash with publications relating to the best practices, codes, frameworks, guidance, performance measures, principles, and standards for regulators. For the sake of brevity, I refer to this broad source of information as the standards for regulators.

SOURCES OF STANDARDS FOR REGULATORS

There are numerous stakeholders who publish standards for regulators. They include:

- Academic researchers and management consultants
- Associations of regulators, both domestic and international
- Consumer advocacy organisations
- Government
- Intergovernmental organisations (IGOs)
- Oversight organisations
- Public authorities
- Standards organisations

SECTORS COVERED BY THE STANDARDS

The range of sectors covered by the standards for regulators ranges from those that address all regulators across all sectors in many jurisdictions, to standards for regulators in only one sector or jurisdictions.

EXAMPLES OF STANDARDS FOR REGULATORS

To help identify what can be included in the standards for regulators a number of examples are now reviewed:

Assessing Organisations

Numerous academics and management consultants publish processes and standards for assessing organisation's performance, sometimes referred to as organisational health checks. An example of this is the Burke–Litwin model for organisational change.

National Consumer Council (UK)

The UK's National Consumer Council (NCC), now replaced by Citizens Advice, published a 13-point good practice guidelines for making self-regulation work for consumers and business. These included topics such as

1. Clear objectives
2. Public accountability
3. Independent board representation
4. Monitoring of compliance
5. Adequate resources

Principles of Good Regulation

UK's Better Regulation Taskforce, of the Better Regulation Commission, developed and published five principles in 1997, although it was subsequently closed in January 2008.

1. Proportionality
2. Accountability
3. Consistency
4. Transparency
5. Targeting

Regulator's Code

Published by the UK's Department for Business Innovation & Skills, now the Department of Business, Energy and Industrial Strategy, in April 2014, the code has six themes, which are as follows:

1. Regulators should carry out their activities in a way that supports those they regulate to comply and grow
2. Regulators should provide simple and straightforward ways to engage with those they regulate and hear their views
3. Regulators should base their regulatory activities on risk
4. Regulators should share information about compliance and risk
5. Regulates should ensure clear information, guidance and advice is available to help those they regulate meet their responsibilities to comply
6. Regulators should ensure that their approach to their regulatory activities is transparent

Regulator Performance Framework

Published by the Australian Government in October 2014, the framework was established with the objective of encouraging regulators to minimise their impact on those they regulate while still delivering the roles they are responsible for delivering. It consists of six outcomes-based key performance indicators (KPIs) to articulate the government's overarching expectations of regulator performance, namely, covering:

1. Regulators do not unnecessarily impede the efficient operation of regulated entities
2. Communication with regulated entities is clear, targeted, and effective
3. Actions undertaken by regulators are proportionate to the risk being managed
4. Compliance and monitoring approaches are streamlined and coordinated
5. Regulators are open and transparent in their dealings with regulated entities
6. Regulators actively contribute to the continuous improvement of regulatory frameworks

A process was then introduced whereby all Australian government regulators are expected to annually self-assess their performance against the framework. A number of regulators will be subject to an external review of their performance as part of a three-year programme, and a small number of regulators may be subject to an annual external review. External reviews are conducted by review panels comprising of government and industry representatives. This provides further accountability and transparency for key stakeholders. The framework became operational on 1 July 2015.

Regulating Better

On January 2004 the Republic of Ireland's government published a white paper setting out six principles of better regulation. They included:

1. Necessity
2. Effectiveness
3. Proportionality
4. Transparency
5. Accountability
6. Consistency

Regulators' Performance Guide

In July 2021 the Australian Federal Government published new guidance for regulators. It uses three principles, namely:

1. Continuous improvement and building trust
2. Risk based and data driven
3. Collaboration and engagement

The guidance also encourages regulators to adopt outcomes-focused (regulation) measures.

College Performance Measurement Framework (CPMF)

Published by the Ontario Ministry of Health and Long Term Care (MHLTC) in December 2020.

There are seven measurement domains:

1. Governance
2. Resources
3. System partners
4. Information management
5. Regulatory policies
6. Suitability to practice
7. Measurement, reporting, and improvement.

Each measurement domain is broken down by:

- Standards
- Measures
- Evidence
- Context measures
- Planned improvement actions

Each of the 28 colleges in Ontario is required to complete an annual report to the MHLTC. They are then reviewed by the Regulatory Oversight and Performance Unit

The Three Pillars of Profession Standards

The UK's Professional Associations Research Network (PARN) uses three standards, namely:

1. Entry standards
2. Complaints and discipline
3. CPD and positive supports (for ethical behaviour)

The Standards of Good Regulation

Originally developed and published by the Council for Healthcare Regulatory Excellence, (CHRE) in the early 2002 they have now been superseded by those published by the Processional Standards Authority (PSA). There are five standards supported by 18 topics. It should however, be pointed out that these may now have been superseded following a planned public consultation in 2024/25

General Standards

1. The regulator provides accurate, fully accessible information about its registrants, regulatory requirements, guidance, processes, and decisions
2. The regulator is clear about its purpose and ensures that its policies are applied appropriately across all its functions and that relevant learning from one area is applied to others.

3. The regulator understands the diversity of its registrants and their patients and service users and of others who interact with the regulator and ensures that its processes do not impose inappropriate barriers or otherwise disadvantage people with protected characteristics.
4. The regulator reports on its performance and addresses concerns identified about it and considers the implications for it findings of public inquiries and other relevant reports about healthcare regulatory issues.
5. The regulator consults and works with all relevant stakeholders across all its functions to identify and manage risks to the public in respect of its registrants.

Guidance and Standards

6. The regulator maintains up-to-date standards for registrants which are kept under review and prioritise patient and service user-centred care and safety.
7. The regulator provides guidance to help registrants apply the standards and ensures this guidance is up to date, addresses emerging areas of risk, and prioritises patient and service user-centred care and safety.

Education and Training

8. The regulator maintains up-to-date standards for education and training which are kept under review, and prioritise patient and service user care and safety.
9. The regulator has a proportionate and transparent mechanism for assuring itself that the educational providers and programmes it oversees are delivering students and trainees that meet the regulator's requirements for registration, and takes action where its assurance activities identify concerns either about training or wider patient safety concerns.

Registration

10. The regulator maintains and publishes an accurate register of those who meet its requirements including any restrictions on their practice.
11. The process for registration, including appeals, operates proportionately, fairly and efficiently, with decisions clearly explained.
12. Risk of harm to the public and of damage to public confidence in the profession related to non-registrants using a protected title or undertaking a protected act is managed in a proportionate and risk-based manner.
13. Regulator has proportionate requirements to satisfy itself that registrants continue to be fit to practise.

Fitness to Practise

14. The regulator enables anyone to raise a concern about a registrant.
15. The regulator's process for examining and investigating cases is fair, proportionate, deals with cases as quickly as is consistent with a fair resolution of the case, and ensures that appropriate evidence is available to support decision makers to reach a fair decision that protects the public at each stage of the process.
16. The regulator ensures that all decisions are made in accordance with its processes, are proportionate, consistent, and fair, take account of the statutory objectives, the regulator's standards, and the relevant case law, and prioritise patient and service user safety.
17. The regulator identifies and prioritises all cases which suggest a serious risk to the safety of patients or service users and seeks interim orders where appropriate
18. All parties to a complaint are supported to participate effectively in the process

Public Bodies' Review Programme

A final example of standards that can be used to measure if a regulator is meeting its objectives, is the one that can be applied to all public authorities and not just regulators. For example, the UK government has a review programme of its public bodies. The processes incorporate indicators of good practice around four sets of requirements. They are:

1. Efficacy
2. Governance
3. Accountability
4. Efficiency

Having highlighted a selection of standards published by organisations connected to the regulation of healthcare professionals various stakeholders, an important take-home message is that there is a clear distinction between the standards used in a jurisdiction that have either adopted a system of rules-based regulation or alternatively a system of outcome-based regulation.

This leads to a regulatory principle:

Principle: Standards for Outcome vs Rules-Based Regulation
The adoption of either rules-based regulation or outcome-based regulation fundamental impacts the standards applied to regulators.

USE OF STANDARDS FOR REGULATORS

It can also be seen from the above that the standards for regulators are used in different ways depending on whether or not they are voluntarily adopted by regulators or they are imposed on the regulators, and compliance is assessed by an external organisation. The options include:

1. Compliance with standards is not required or audited, but their use is encouraged
2. Compliance with standards is required, but compliance with the standards is self-assessed by the regulator itself
3. Compliance with standards is required, and audits of compliance are undertaken by independent organisations

In effect there is a spectrum of options on how to use the standards for regulators. This ranges from a laissez-faire attitude, to allowing regulators to self-assess, or to '*mark their own home work*', and lastly to the use of auditors and oversight organisations to ensure compliance; see Section 6.4, volume 4, Auditing and overseeing regulators.

CODE OF ETHICS FOR INDIVIDUALS WORKING IN REGULATION

Mention should be made of the Regulatory Affairs Professionals Society (RAPS). Founded in the USA in 1976, it publishes a voluntary code of ethics and acts as a certification organisation for individuals who are involved with the regulation of healthcare and related products, including, biologics, medical devices, nutritional products, and pharmaceuticals. The code has eight core values:

1. Regulatory compliance
2. Competency
3. Objectivity
4. Integrity
5. Honesty/credibility
6. Accountability
7. Equitability
8. Dignity and respect

Although RAPS uses a voluntary code, it is interesting to speculate whether or not similar codes should be drawn up for other sectors.

TOPICS INCLUDED IN STANDARDS FOR REGULATORS

There is no definitive list of which topics are included in the standards for regulators. Indeed, considerable variation is exhibited.

However, the standards can be divided into two groups, namely:

1. Standards containing relatively few broad statements about regulators. The topics included often reflect the characteristics of regulators
2. Standards that consist of numerous detailed requirements for regulators. The topics can be seen to reflect the desired attributes of regulators

Both will be addressed in the next section, characteristics and attributes of regulators.

LOW-, MIDDLE-, AND HIGH-INCOME COUNTRIES

Before concluding this section, attention should be drawn to low- and middle-income countries (LMIC) and the standards for their regulators impacting the healthcare delivery system. The book focuses on the principles and processes for regulating healthcare professionals that are found in high-income countries (HIC) that are predominantly economically developed and democratic.

However, numerous LMICs are confronted by corruption, lack of democratic accountability, economic deprivation, and inadequate infrastructure including communication networks, healthcare delivery, sewage, transportation, water, and school systems.

Under these circumstances should all regulators be expected to conform to the same standards that applicable to the regulators in HICs, or should they be adapted to address the actual circumstances on the ground?

CONCLUSION

Numerous organisations publish standards for regulators. Although there is a degree of variation between their standards, it is reasonable to expect that all the standards should relate to the regulators delivering their primary and secondary objectives effectively, efficiently, and ethically. And to some extent all the standards of all the various stakeholders should be of equal importance to the regulators of healthcare professionals. However, as explored in Section 4.4, volume 4, auditing and overseeing regulators, the realpolitik is that the standards of auditors and oversight organisations are of considerable greater interest to the regulators.

EXERCISES AND QUESTION

Exercises

- Referring to the KPIs, measurements, principles, standards, and topics which would you delete and for what reasons? Also, would you include others that have been missed out?
- For a low-to middle-income country (LMIC) review the state of its healthcare delivery system and its statutory regulators that impact the healthcare delivery system. What measure did you use to gauge the quality of its services?

Question

- How can an organisation that sets standards for regulators justify their approach to the process in terms of the number of separate standards they use, i.e. why do they use so many or so few?

FURTHER READING

Baring its teeth? R
An audit of the GDC's reforms
National Consumer Council
PD44/02
August 2002
26 pages

Best Practice Regulation: Principles and Assessments R
New Zealand Government Treasury
Wellington
ISBN 978-0-478-43619-8
July 2015
89 pages

Better Business Practice R
How to make self-regulation work for consumers and business
National Consumer Council
December 2000

Regulating Better R
White paper
Department of the Taoiseach, Republic of Ireland
Pin 1395
January 2004
59 pages

A Clean Bill of Health for the GMC R
An audit of the GMC's self-regulation reforms
National Consumer Council
Ref: PD85/H/01
January 2002
22 pages

Health Professions Council: An Organisational Health check R
National Audit Office
Gracie, Antonia Wijerature, Rohan
DBRef: 008807
February 2019
33 pages

Principles of Good Regulation R
Better Regulation Task Force
London, UK
ISBN: 0 7115 0438 5
December 1997, revised October 2000
11 pages

Professional Standards Bodies: Standards, Levels of Compliance and Measuring Success R
A Report for the Financial Services Authority
Professional Associations Research Network, (PARN),
25 September 2009
51 pages

Regulator Performance Framework R
Australian Government
www.cuttingredtabe.gov.au
ISBN 978-1-925237-07-8
October 2014
28 pages

STANDARDS, CODES, GUIDANCE, CONSULTATIONS, POLICIES, AND PRACTICE NOTES

Standards and Codes

Code of Ethics S&C
Regulatory Affairs Professionals Society (RAPS)
October 2003

College Performance Measurement Framework (CPMF) Reporting Tool S&C
Ministry of Health
Ontario, Canada
December 2020
64 pages

Performance Review Standards – Standards of Good regulation S&C
Professional Standards Authority
January 2016
16 pages

Regulator's Code: S&C
Department of Business Innovation & Skills
Better Regulation Delivery Office
URN: BRDO/14/705
April 2014
7 pages

Scottish Regulators' Strategic Code of Practice S&C
Scottish Government
Better Regulation Team
12 January 2015
12 pages

Standard of Good Regulation S&C
Professional Standards Authority (PSA)
January 2020
3 pages

Statutory Code of Practice for Regulators S&C
Better Regulation Executive
Department for Business, Enterprise and Regulatory Reform
ISBN: 978-0-85605-712-0
December 2007
20 pages

Guidance

Better Policy Making: G
A Guide to Regulatory Impact Assessments
Cabinet Office
Ref: 255288/0103/D24
January 2003
81 pages

Government Expectations for Good Regulatory Practice G
New Zealand Government
21 April 2017
5 pages

Regulator Performance Guide G
Australian Government
Department of the Prime Minister and Cabinet
ISBN 978-1-925364-63-7
July 2021
13 pages

Consultation

Review of the Standards of Good Regulation C
Consultation paper
PSA
June 2018
35 pages

6.3 CHARACTERISTICS AND ATTRIBUTES OF REGULATORS

INTRODUCTION

Society benefits if regulators exhibit a range of desirable characteristics and attributes. These desirable characteristics can be seen to be operating at a high level, while in turn, they are supported by more detailed attributes. Both are identified and explored in the section.

DESIRABLE CHARACTERISTICS OF REGULATORS

In the opening chapter of the book a number of topics are identified that I will now refer to as the desirable characteristics of regulators. They are listed alphabetically in Table 6.3 – I, below:

Table 6.3 – I Characteristics of regulators

1. Autonomous
2. Effective
3. Efficient
4. Ethical
5. Independent
6. Open
7. Transparent

While there is no definitive source to decide which characteristics are included in this list, it should be noted that the seven characteristics can be augmented, substituted, and replaced by others. However, within reason, it is reasonable to assume that most informed stakeholders would not raise significant objections to the list.

However, the characteristics can be seen to be at the highest level of importance and that logically there must be numerous other more specific attributes. These would include for example, an accessible web site, the timely responses to correspondence from helpful employees, and good governance arrangements.

These attributes will now be identified and examined.

ATTRIBUTES OF REGULATORS

Identifying the desirable attributes of regulators is important for three reasons, namely:

1. They help establish the service standards and the operational performance of regulators
2. It enables comparison to be made between regulators to facilitate learning and continuous improvement both within and between jurisdictions
3. It facilitates the setting of standards for regulators and the measurement of the expected deliverables of key stakeholders such as members of the public and government.

In essence the attributes are those that a perfect regulator would have. Idealistic and wishful thinking – perhaps?

ATTRIBUTES OF REGULATORS

The source for the attributes of regulators has been gleaned from the books, consultations, guidance, standards, reports and other publications referred to throughout the four volumes of the book.

ATTRIBUTES OF REGULATORS

These will now be expanded:

1. **Accountable**
   Accountable to their key stakeholders.
2. **Advisory**
   Provide advice to stakeholders about all aspects of the regulator's processes, principles, and standards.
3. **Appeals**
   Have an appeal process concerning all their important decisions.
4. **Autonomous**
   Possess the freedom to govern themselves or control their own affairs.
5. **Collaboration and cooperation**
   Collaboration and cooperation with stakeholders.
6. **Communication**
   Continually communicate in a two-way process with all their stakeholders. The communication will:
   - Accessible, clear, concise, timely, and understandable
   - Avoids jargon wherever possible
   - Encourages the public to use regulated sectors
   - Facilitate the users of their services the ability to provide feedback on their experience
   - Uses media that maximises readership
   - Uses Plain English
7. **Competition**
   Facilitate competition and reduce the impact of monopolies in the markets they regulate.
8. **Confidentiality**
   Will be open and transparent. However, from time to time there will be occasions when for perfectly legitimate reasons regulators must operate on a confidential basis. For example:
   - Making determinations that may affect the market value of commercial enterprises
   - Engaging with government on policy development and drafting of legislation

- Internal operational matters such as awarding contracts and employee HR issues
- Some tribunal process, such as addressing the health of professionals

Under these circumstances trust can be maintained with stakeholders but ensuring that clear reasons are published why the regulator is making decision in private and where appropriate publicising the decisions when they are made.

9. **Consistency**
Processes, principles, rules, and standards will be consistently applied to all organisations and individuals regulated and thus predictable.

10. **Consultation**
Consult with those they regulate, members of the public and other stakeholders when they develop their fees, guidance, operating model, policies, principles, processes, rules, and standards. They will actively encourage all their stakeholders to participate in their consultations.

11. **Contactability**
Inform their stakeholders about how and when they can be contacted.

12. **Continuous quality improvement**
Adopts the processes of continuous quality improvement

13. **Costs of regulators**
Costs of regulator will be minimised whilst at the same time they deliver their regulatory objective. In other words, regulators to minimise the regulatory burden should be both effective and efficient.

14. **Culture**
Culture of the regulator is appropriate.

15. **Data and information collection**
Seek to only collect data and information on the basis of 'collect once and use many times'. Will wherever possible utilise existing data for multiple purposes.

16. **Earned autonomy recognition scheme**
Regulators will reduce inspection and compliance monitoring to those entities and individuals that have demonstrated that they meet the regulators' standards.

17. **Education of key stakeholders**
Proactively work with key stakeholders to educate them about the regulatory process.

18. **Effective**
Be effective.

19. **Efficient**
Be efficient.

20. **Employee education and training**
Educate and train their employees in their principles and processes so they understand why and how they regulate enterprises, individuals, and sectors.

21. **Employee knowledge and skills**
Employees of regulators will have the knowledge and skills to discharge its principles and processes.

22. **Enterprise complaints**
Possess an enterprise complaints process

23. **Enterprise risk management framework**
Devise and publish an enterprise risk management framework.

24. **Ethical**
Behave ethically, in that they are, fair, honest, trustworthy, and truthful.

25. **Evidence informed regulation**
Seek to justify their own principles and processes by establishing the evidence to inform their decision making.

26. **Fees**
Level of fees will be published, supported by an explanation of how they are derived.

27. **Flexible**
    - The process of regulators will be flexible
    - They will adapt their regulatory process so that the entities they regulate are all able to achieve the standards, whatever their size, preferably using different routes rather than imposing a single solution
    - Those regulated should be able to use different approaches to achieve the regulator's objectives
    - In rapidly changing markets, regulators will not act as a constraint or impediment, rather they will swiftly adapt and will be a catalyst for change
    - Regulators will limit bureaucracy and avoid overcomplicated processes
    - Wherever possible, regulators will adopt outcome-based regulation

28. **Gaming the system**
Seek to detect and deter gaming of their processes

29. **Governance**
Governance arrangements are appropriate.

30. **Harmonisation**
Wherever possible adopt standards, rules, and processes used by other regulators

31. **Horizon scanning**
Scan the horizon of their operating environment for changes and react to those changes in a timely manner.

32. **Immediate action**
Have processes to take immediate action for serious breaches of their standards.

33. **Independent**
Independent from government, the sector they regulate, and politicians or government officials.

34. **Information sharing**
When there are no legal restrictions, will share information about those they regulate relating to compliance and risk, with the objective of facilitating others to target resources and minimise duplication of effort.

35. **Inspection of service delivery facilities**
The burden of the inspection process will be minimised.

36. **Knowledge library of regulator**
Published their knowledge library in an accessible format in a timely manner.

37. **Learning organisation**
Be a learning organisation

38. **Legislation**
    - Adhere to their legislation
    - Have a sound legal basis for all of their decisions
    - Review their legalisation on a regular basis and as appropriate seek the support of government to amend it in a timely manner

39. **Non-political**
Be non-political

40. **Objective**
Be objective and base their decisions on facts and not personal feelings and avoid the risk of arbitrary decision making.

41. **Openness**
Adopt processes that facilitate and welcome external organisations and individuals to participate and work with them.

42. **Peer review**
Wherever possible peer review will be used in the regulatory process to monitor, inspect, and assess compliance.

43. **Predictability**
Outcome of regulators' processes should be consistent and therefore predictable.

44. **Proportionality**
Apply their powers in a proportionate manner. For example, regulators may take into account the relative size or financial resources of the enterprises they regulate if they impose a fine or financial penalty.

45. **Record retention and disposal**
Retain appropriate records or dispose of appropriately.

46. **Regulatory creep**
Meet but not exceed the requirements of their legislation. Resist pressure to expand their agenda, without changes to legalisation and increases in their resources

47. **Regulatory experts**
Will be experts in their understanding and practice of regulation

48. **Regulatory process**
Publicise all aspects of the regulatory process, including: guidance, objectives, polices, processes, rules, and standards

49. **Resilient**
Are resilient in that they should be capable of adapting and evolving to enable them to operate in a changing environment.

50. **Resources**
Possess the resources to deliver their objectives to an appropriate quality and in a timely manner.

51. **Risked-based regulation**
Use a risk-based approach to target their regulatory powers and resources.

52. **Rule of law**
Operate within the rule of law.

53. **Sanctions**
Publicise why and how sanctions are imposed and the method to calculate their levels of severity.

54. **Self-assessment of operating performance**
Undertake self-assessments of their operating performance preferably on an annual basis and publish the results.

55. **Self-referral**
Encourage a culture whereby the entities or individuals regulated report concerns potential breaches of rules or standards that they themselves have identified to the regulator rather than await monitoring or audits of compliance. A 'No blame culture' should also be adopted in sharp contrast to 'Closed cultures'.

56. **Service standards**
Publish service standards and regularly report on their own performance against the standards.

57. **Service user experience**
Will be appropriate for all.

58. **Service user focus**
Provide services that service users are able to understand and use with ease.

59. **Stakeholder engagement**
Engage with all stakeholders

60. **Standards**
Their standards are:
    - Accessible
    - Clear
    - Set at a reasonable level
    - Up to date

61. **Standard operating procedures**
Develop and use standard operating procedures.

62. Supportive approach
Adopt a supportive approach to those they regulate to enable them to comply with their standards and processes.

63. Technological adopters
Wherever possible, will adopt technology to deliver effective and efficient regulation.

64. Timeliness of processes
Seek to undertake their processes in a timely manner. Regulators will publish indicative timetables relating to their processes and decision making.

65. Transparency
Facilitate the scrutiny of their processes by external organisations and individuals by removing any impediments.

66. Trusted
Are trusted.

67. Unintended consequences
Seek to avoid unintended consequences on those they regulate. The rules and processes of a regulator will not impede the efficient operations on those they regulate and at the very least aim to minimise any side-effects.

For reference, all 67 of the attributes of regualtors are listed in alphabetic order in Table 6.3 – II below:

Table 6.3 – II Attributes of regulators

Attributes
1. Accountable
2. Advisory
3. Appeals
4. Autonomous
5. Collaboration and cooperation
6. Communication
7. Competition
8. Confidentiality
9. Consistency
10. Consultation
11. Contactability
12. Continuous quality improvement
13. Costs of regulators
14. Culture
15. Data and information collection
16. Earned autonomy recognition scheme
17. Education of key stakeholders
18. Effective
19. Efficient
20. Employee education and training
21. Employee knowledge and skills
22. Enterprise complaints
23. Enterprise risk management framework
24. Ethical
25. Evidence informed regulation
26. Fees
27. Flexible
28. Gamming the system
29. Governance
30. Harmonisation
31. Horizon scanning
32. Immediate action
33. Independent
34. Information sharing
35. Inspection of service delivery facilities
36. Knowledge library of regulator
37. Learning organisation
38. Legislation
39. Non-political
40. Objective
41. Openness
42. Peer review
43. Predictability
44. Proportionality
45. Record retention and disposal
46. Regulatory creep
47. Regulatory experts
48. Regulatory process
49. Resilient
50. Resources
51. Risk-based regulation
52. Rule of law
53. Sanctions
54. Self-assessment of operating performance
55. Self-referral
56. Service standards
57. Service user experience
58. Service user focus
59. Stakeholder engagement
60. Standards
61. Standard operating procedures
62. Supportive approach
63. Technological adopters
64. Timeliness of processes
65. Transparency
66. Trusted
67. Unintended consequences

SUMMARY

To some extent the long list of 67 attributes may be considered by some to be unhelpful in that it is just one long list of factual information. To try to better understand the attributes the following two charts may be of assistance.

The first chart divides the attributes of regulators into four groups by whether the attributes can be measured qualitatively or quantitatively and whether the attribute is focused on an internal or external service see Chart 6.3 – I, opposite:

The chart is populated with four examples of attributes of regulators that are listed in Table 6.3 – II.

The second chart divides the attributes of regulators into nine groups, see Chart 6.3 – II, below:

The chart is populated with nine examples of attributes of regulators that are listed in Table 6.3 – II.

Chart 6.3 – I Attributes of regulators

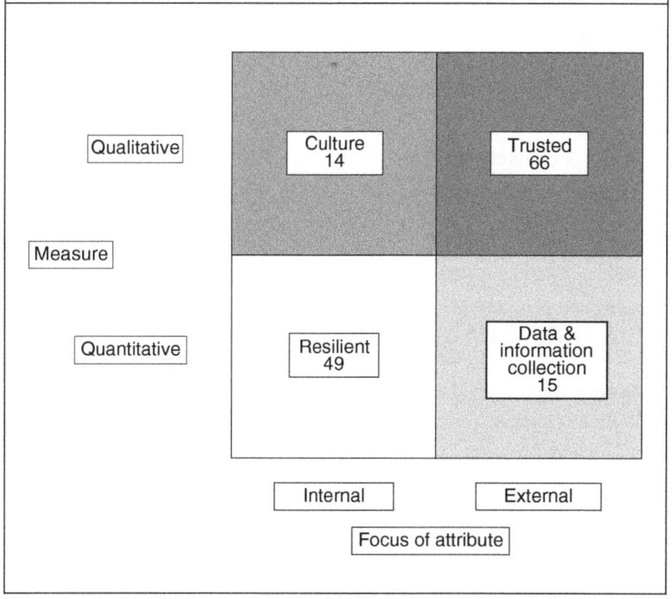

Chart 6.3 – II Attributes of regulators – populated

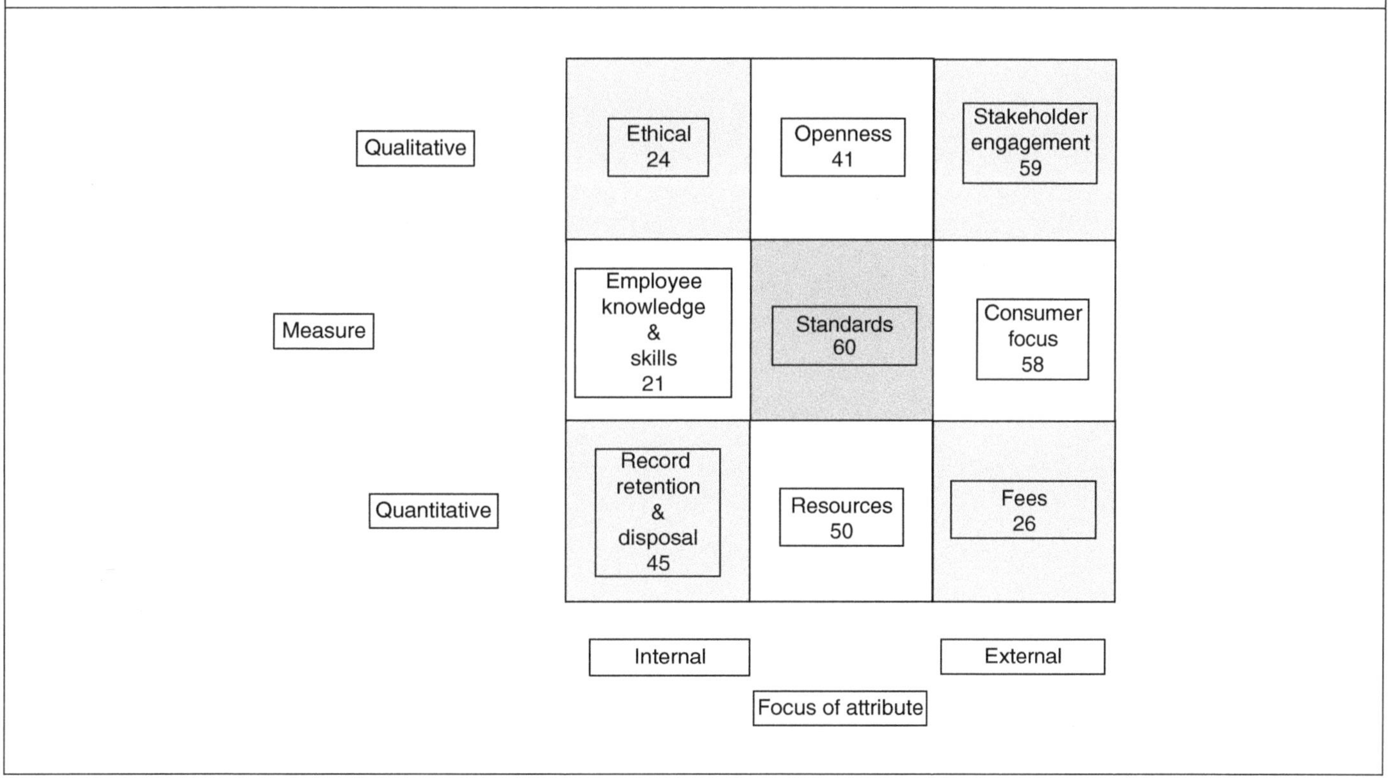

CONCLUSION

In theory there should be a positive feedback loop between the expectation of government in how its regulators will perform as set out in their standards and the characteristics and attributes that the regulators develop in order to achieve the standards. However, due mainly to regulatory failure, government does not leave the achievement of the standards to chance and has instigated audit and oversight to ensure they are indeed met. This is explored in the proceeding section.

EXERCISES AND QUESTION

Exercises

- Select five attributes at random. Does your organisation display them? If not, what is the reason for this?
- Apply a characteristic or an attribute from one of the standards for regulators to a regulator that you are familiar with. Does it meet the standard?

Question

- Of the numerous attributes identified, select the ten least important and the ten most important

FURTHER READING

Listening. Learning. Leading R
A Framework for Regulatory Excellence
Cary Coglianese
Penn Program on Regulation's Best-in-Class Regulator Initiative
University of Pennsylvania Law School
21 October 2015
122 pages

6.4 AUDITING AND OVERSEEING REGULATORS

INTRODUCTION

Governments, to reassure themselves that regulatory matters are in order, have established their own ubiquitous auditors and occasionally, in a small number of jurisdictions, oversight organisations. The remit of governments' auditors extends across the whole of the public sector. In contrast, their oversight organisations are highly specialised and operate in a single sector. Of particular interest are the oversight organisations of regulators of healthcare professionals, and they are the focus of this section.

GOVERNMENTS' RELATIONSHIP WITH REGULATORS

The relationship that regulators have with government and the legislature is explored in Section 1.4, volume 1. In particular the section addressed how regulators are accountable to government and that government can scrutinise the work of regulators by the use of government auditors and specialist oversight organisations.

GOVERNMENTS' AUDITORS

An audit is the annual process to examine the financial probity of an organisation and to check on the accuracy and record keeping of its financial transactions.

Annual audits are conducted by independent specialist auditing organisations on behalf of shareholders or government. These audits are referred to as external audits. In comparison, internal audits can also be instigated by the board of an organisation.

In the UK the audits of public authorities are undertaken by the National Audit Office (NAO). The NAO, on behalf of Parliament, is responsible for scrutinising the financial management and performance of these publicly funded organisations.

In the UK there is a statutory requirement for public authorities, including regulators, to prepare and present their audited annual reports and accounts to Parliament.

To do this the NAO audits the annual accounts of the regulators, and they are then presented to, or 'laid in', Parliament. It should be noted that the actual audit may be conducted either by the NAO or partially subcontracted to commercial auditors. And, on occasions, the NAO also conducts thematic reviews across sectors. Also in the UK, the audits can trigger further investigations and on occasions public hearings by the Parliamentary Public Accounts Committee.

VALUE-FOR-MONEY AUDITS

Government auditors may also have a responsibility to conduct 'value-for-money audits' of public authorities including regulators. Examples include the Office of the Auditor General of Ontario, Canada, and the NAO in the UK.

OVERSIGHT

Despite the formal and informal relationship between government and regulators and their scrutiny by the legislature and the work of the government auditors, a small number of governments have also established specialist public authorities to oversee and report on the performance of regulators.

In Section 3.1, volume 4, governance and the role and responsibilities of boards the term oversight is used to describe the role of a board has in overseeing the role of the executive management team (EMT). However, in the context of public authorities, the term oversight has a slightly different connotation, as illustrated in the following definition used by the Canadian Audit and Accountability Foundation:

In this context, oversight can be defined as:

Definition: Oversight
Process to review and monitor public sector organisations and their policies, plans, programs, and projects.

In particular the oversight process should ensure that the organisations:

- Achieve expected results
- Represent good value for money
- Comply with applicable policies, legislation, regulations, and ethical standards

Thus, in the context of the regulating of healthcare professionals, organisations that undertake the oversight responsibility can be defined as:

Definition: Oversight Organisation
Government organisation specific established to oversee the functions of independent regulators.

RATIONALE FOR OVERSIGHT ORGANISATIONS

Globally, there are less than half a dozen oversight organisations of regulators of healthcare professions, and the oldest, the Professional Standards Authority (PSA), was established in 2001. This raises two questions:

- What triggers their establishment?
- What is their policy objective?

TRIGGERS FOR ESTABLISHING OVERSIGHT ORGANISATIONS

The establishment of oversight organisations is usually traceable to one of three types of events, namely, operational performance, regulatory failure, or governance of regulators:

1. **Operational performance**
   These types of events relate to the regulators' operational performance and in essence they occur when regulators fail to meet their external and internal service standards. For example:
   - Delays in registration of newly qualified students
   - Slowness of the fitness to practise (FTP) process
2. **Regulatory failure**
   These often relate to poor judgment decisions by their assessors. For example:
   - Repeated application of sanctions by FTP tribunals that are considered to be unduly lenient by some stakeholders
   - The frequent rejection of candidates who are eligible to register with the regulator profession via the international application process
3. **Governance**
   This occurs when either the board of a regulator fails to discharge its responsibilities or it ventures into areas that are outside its legal responsibilities as set out in the legislation.

Reaction of government

Government is often angered, embarrassed, and frustrated by these types of events, since they have established the regulator and delegated the responsibility of ensuring that it is effective, efficient, and ethical to the board that they may have appointed. The reaction of government is influenced by the level of adverse reactions to the incidents by stakeholders, in particular: consumer advocacy organisations, the media, migrants, politicians, professional associations, the public, and the chairs of public inquiries. The reaction is often stronger when there are repeated similar incidents in a jurisdiction where there is more than one regulator.

However, the challenge for government and their civil servants with these types of events is fourfold:

1. They may not have the resources and expertise to seedily investigate the events
2. They may not want to be seen to directly interfering in the day-to-day operations of independent regulators
3. They may not want to become embroiled in potentially controversial decisions of independent regulators as they may become subjected to blame and criticism
4. If the events relates to the legislation of the regulator, it may be easier for government to commission external advocacy to address the potential for change

As a result, their solution is to establish an oversight organisation to undertake the task.

POLICY OBJECTIVE OF OVERSIGHT ORGANISATION

The purpose of oversight organisations is therefore to ensure that the regulators of healthcare professionals are indeed delivering their objectives and in particular that the regulators are effective, efficient, and ethical.

CHARACTERISTICS OF OVERSIGHT ORGANISATIONS

Although few in number, oversight organisations have a range of common characteristics that include in alphabetic order:

Accountability

They, in a similar way to the regulators they oversee, are accountable to government and the legislature.

Funding

To fund oversight organisations, there are two options. Either, their costs are paid for directly by the tax payer in the form of an annual grant. Alternatively, government gives them the powers to impose a levy on the regulator(s) they oversee. If a levy is used and there is more than one regulator, a method needs to be established to decide what percentage of the costs of the oversight organisation each regulator will be required to fund.

Governance Arrangements

Again, there are two options:

Either, a board can be appointed by either political patronage or open competition, using similar process used to appoint members of the boards of regulators.

Alternatively, the powers of the regulator are invested in a single individual and there is no board.

Powers

The powers of the oversight organisation are set out in specific legislation. This may include legal powers to intervene to require regulators to rectify their decisions which are not effective, efficient, or ethical. However, it is possible that their powers may only be to recommend and not to enforce.

Status

Oversight organisations are public authorities.

THE PROCESS OF OVERSIGHT ORGANISATIONS

Oversight organisations may have both primary and secondary processes.

Primary Process of Oversight Organisations

Although oversight organisations are not referred to as regulators, their primary process is identical to the regulatory process as depicted in Chart 1.2 – I, volume 1. This means that oversight organisations should:

- Set and publish standards for regulator
- Undertake monitoring and inspections
- Assess compliance
- Establish an appeal process
- Enforce sanctions and penalties
- Consider processes for earned autonomy

As a consequence, oversight organisations face similar challenges as the regulators of professionals including the need to resolve issues such as:

- Frequency of compliance inspections
- Use of risk-based regulation
- Setting the levels of standards
- How to select and measure the subjective attributes of regulators
- Use of self-assessment by regulators

Secondary Process of Oversight Organisations

Oversight organisations may also undertake a number of secondary processes.

- Promote good practice by publicising learning points
- Promote consistency amongst regulators
- Propose changes to legislature
- Research and publish thematic reviews of regulatory policy issues
- Review regulators' governance arrangements including their board appointment process

CONSULTANCY SERVICES AND ADVISORY ROLES

Some of the work undertaken by oversight organisations may be commissioned and paid for by government. In essence they work as the governments' advisers or consultants to undertake one-off thematic reviews or policy development. Oversight organisations may also proactively seek to undertake similar work both outside the healthcare sector and/or outside their jurisdictions. The same caveats should be considered that apply to regulators who provide, or are considering providing, these types of services; see Section 1.2, volume 4.

COMMUNICATION

Oversight organisations, again like regulators, must with limited resources communicate bi-directionally with their stakeholders. They achieve this using broadly similar communication channels and techniques used by the regulators, including:

- Publication of annual reports on the performance of individual regulators
- Publication of comparative reviews of the performance of regulators

REGULATORY CREEP

Lastly, like regulators, oversight organisations must avoid regulatory or mission creep, particularly from requests from government.

EXAMPLES OF OVERSIGHT ORGANISATIONS FROM AROUND THE WORLD

There are a small number of jurisdictions where oversight organisations have been established. They include Canada and the UK

Canada

To date, three oversight organisations have been established in Canada in British Columbia, Quebec, and Ontario.

British Columbia

Office of the Superintendent of Health Profession and Occupation Oversight.

Ontario

The Office of the Fairness Commission (OFC) was established under the Fair Access to the Professions Act 2006. It is charged with ensuring that professionals who qualified outside Ontario are not subjected to discrimination when applying to join the statutory regulated professions. To achieve this, the OFC publishes guidance and undertakes periodic audits of the regulators of professionals.

Quebec

Complaints Commissioner, Office des Professions du Québec The Office des Professions du Quebec is part of the Ministry of Justice of Quebec, Canada. Based in Montreal and established in December 2009 under chapter 26 of the Civil Code of Quebec, it is an independent oversight organisation attached to the Office des Professions du Quebec.

The main purpose of the Commissioner is to improve the process to enable professionals from outside Quebec to practise their profession in Quebec. Its responsibilities cover 45 healthcare and non-healthcare professions ranging from acupuncturists to veterinary surgeons.

The Commissioner receives and examines individual complaints from professionals about the process to grant recognition of professional qualifications obtained outside Quebec. The complaints may be from either international applications or from one of the other Canadian ten Providences or three Territories.

Following an investigation the Commissioner can impose its own decision about the granting of access to a profession. It also:

- Oversees the functioning of the overall processes for the recognition of professional qualifications
- Undertakes and publishes audits. Its recommendations on how the Orders must change and improve their processes are enforceable.
- Oversees how applicants can gain access to education and training programmes and periods of adaptation imposed on a professional.
- Promotes collaboration between the professions and HEIs.

UK

Legal Services Board

The Legal Services Board (LSB) is an independent body responsible for overseeing the regulation of lawyers in England and Wales. Established by the Legal Services Act 2007 it oversees the regulators of solicitors and barristers and six other groups such as licensed conveyors. It also oversees the Office for Legal Complaints who is responsible for administering the Legal Ombudsman. It has a broad brief including:

- Encouraging an independent, strong, diverse, and effective legal profession
- Improving access to justice
- Increasing public understanding of the citizen's legal rights and duties
- Protecting and promoting the interests of consumers of legal services
- Protecting and promoting the public interest
- Promoting and maintaining adherence to the professional principles
- Promoting competition in the provision of legal services
- Supporting the constitutional principle of the rule of law

Professional Standards Authority (PSA)

The Professional Standards Authority for Health and Social Care (PSA) is the UK oversight organisation for the nine statutory regulators of healthcare professionals and social workers in England. Established in 2001 under the NHS Reform and Health Care Professions Act 2002 as the Council for Healthcare Regulatory Excellence (CHRE) it was reorganised as the PSA in 2005. Its role is now included in the NHS Reform and Health Care Professions Act 2012.

It has five roles, namely:

1. Reports on the performance of the regulators on an annual basis using their *Standards of Good Regulation*
2. Makes referrals or appeals to the High Court against unduly lenient decisions by regulators' FTP tribunals using Section 29 of the National Health Service Reform and Health Care Professions Act 2002.
3. Undertakes research and shares best practice
4. Undertakes special investigations and provides advice to ministers to the four UK governments on regulatory issues
5. Acts as a certification organisation by setting standards for operations of voluntary registers for healthcare occupations and healthcare professions that are not statutorily regulated

Compliance with standards for regulators

Each of the UK's regulators of healthcare professions is annually assessed against the standards, and a report is then published.

Ftp process

The PSA can refer a decision of a FTP tribunal to the appeal courts when they consider the decision of the tribunal is insufficient to protect the public. The regulators have an obligation to bring to the attention to the PSA their concerns if a tribunal has been too lenient on the healthcare professional or, alternatively, that the regulator has been too tough on the professional. Confusingly the GMC can instigate an appeals to the courts if they believe the FTP tribunal has been too lenient, but currently the eight other regulators do not have this power.

Accreditation body

In the UK the PSA acts as an accrediting body. The PSA accredits voluntary membership organisations that operate certification – voluntary schemes.

Certification marks

The PSA issues certification marks for their voluntary certification schemes.

International reviews

On a number of occasions the PSA has been commissioned by organisations in other jurisdictions to assess regulators against the PSA standards.

OMBUDSMAN

In addition to oversight organisations reference should be made to ombudsmen. Ombudsman can be defined as:

Definition: Ombudsman
Individual appointed by government to represent the interest of the public.

They usually investigate complaints about public authorities and seek to resolve them often by mediation. They provide their services free of charge. Ombudsmen usually operate within the public sector and less frequently in the private sector. They intervene when members of the public and public authorities have been unable to resolve their dispute. In the UK the public sector ombudsmen include the Local Government and Social Care Ombudsman and the Parliamentary and Health Service Ombudsman, (PHSO). There are separate ombudsmen in the devolved countries of Northern Ireland, Scotland, and Wales. For example: The Northern Ireland Public Services Ombudsman (NIPSO), the Scottish Public Services Ombudsman, and the Public Services Ombudsman for Wales.

In the private sectors, examples of services provided by ombudsmen include Consumer Ombudsman, the Energy Ombudsman, and the Financial Ombudsman service.

Examples of other jurisdictions utilising the ombudsman process include Alberta in Canada. In Australia the National Health Practitioner Ombudsman has oversight of AHPRA and the national boards. It has three main roles: complaint resolution, systemic improvement, and community engagement.

However, all ombudsmen occupy an area between the internal process used by regulators to handle enterprise complaints, and governments' auditors, oversight organisations, and the courts.

NOMENCLATURE

Before concluding this section it is worth considering why the UK Government has chosen to use the term oversight to describe these public authorities, rather than regulator or inspector, since their primary processes seem very similar to those of regulators. One can speculate that the UK Governments' use of confusing nomenclature is to avoid signalling that their interests only focus on a minority of statutory regulators of professionals, whereas in theory, it could apply to all of the regulators of professionals across all sectors.

CONCLUSION

Philosophical debates can be had on the necessity for 'regulating the regulators' and like a Matryoshkas doll, they often have no firm conclusions. A similar question, of who 'regulates oversight organisations' have in consequence repeatedly occurred at the informal meetings of CEO's of regulators. Nevertheless the principle for government to establish oversight organisations of the regulators of healthcare professions has become a feature of the regulatory landscape, such that they are now becoming less rare and more prevalent. In general this policy has been supported by numerous stakeholders, ranging from consumer advocacy organisations to migrating healthcare professionals. This is counterbalanced by the perspective of some regulators, perhaps because their inception is related to significant challenges to regulators, who may see it as a contentious issue. However, looking to the future from a political perspective, once the events that trigger the establishment of an oversight organisations in the first place has been permanently resolved, should the existence of an oversight organisation continue?

EXERCISES AND QUESTION

Exercises

- Justify why an external person or organisation should be responsible for overseeing regulators and have the ability to intervene and take recourse if the regulator goes array.
- How and should oversight organisation use risk-based regulation?

Question

- Does oversight reduce the independence of regulators?

LEGISLATION

Exmple of UK Legislation

Legal Services Act 2007 L

NHS Reform and Health Care Professions Act 2002 L

NHS Reform and Health Care Professions Act 2012 L

Example of International Legislation

Canada

Ontario

Fair Access to the Regulated Professions Act 2006 L
SO 2006 c 31 – Bill 124

FURTHER READING

Entry to Practice Review R
College of Physiotherapists of Ontario
2010
61 pages

How is public confidence maintained when fitness to practise decisions are made? R
Advice to the Secretary of State
PSA
April 2019
41 pages

Inspectors and Enforcement at the Front Line of Government B
Steven Van de Walle (editor), Nadine Raaphorst (editor)
Springer Nature Switzerland AG, Switzerland
ISBN 13: 978-3-030-040574
18 January 2019
270 pages

Regulatory Enforcement and Inspections R
OECD
May 2014
ISBN 978-92-64-20810-0
70 pages

Special Report to the Minister of State for Health on the Nursing and Midwifery Council R
CHRE
11 June 2008
34 pages

State Medical Boards and Medical Discipline R
Office of the Inspector General
US Department of Health and Human Services
Ref: OEI-01-89-00560
August 1990
110 pages

Value-for-Money Audit Alcohol and Gaming Commission of Ontario R
Office of the Auditor General of Ontario
ISBN 978-1-4868-4887-4
December 2020
74 pages

Roundup

CHAPTER 7

INTRODUCTION

The chapter addresses a range of eclectic topics ranging from national emergencies, to professional indemnity insurance, to the regulation of service delivery facilities and workforce planning. However, whilst each is distinct and important in the context of the principles and processes of regulating healthcare professionals, they don't merit separate chapters of their own.

The chapter has five sections:

7.1 National emergencies, natural disasters, and epidemics

7.2 Professional indemnity insurance

7.3 Regulation of healthcare delivery facilities

7.4 Telehealth

7.5 Workforce planning

7.1 NATIONAL EMERGENCIES, NATURAL DISASTERS, AND EPIDEMICS

INTRODUCTION

Fortunately, national and international emergencies such as terrorism or natural disasters such as a tsunami or epidemics of infectious diseases like Covid-19 occur infrequently. However, these types of events can lead to unexpected surges in demand for healthcare. At the same time, there may be a significant reduction in the availability of healthcare facilities and professionals, due to loss and damage to buildings and infrastructure or the incapacitation of professionals due to ill health.

How should regulators of healthcare professionals prepare and react to these three types of, thankfully, rare occurrences?

TRIGGERS

These types of major challenges can be grouped into three categories, namely, national emergencies, natural disasters, and epidemics of an infectious disease. However, it should be noted that one category can trigger another. For example, an earthquake can lead to a famine or an epidemic.

1. **National emergencies**
   The actions of government, organisations, or individuals may cause national emergencies. These manmade events include civil unrest, political instability, terrorism, and war
2. **Natural disasters**
   The forces of nature causes natural disasters. They include earthquakes, forest fires, flooding, hurricanes, landslides, tornadoes, tsunamis, and volcanic activity
3. **Epidemics of infectious disease**
   Examples of epidemics include COVID-19, Ebola, influenza, and plague. Epidemics occurring across wide geographic areas such as the bubonic plague of the Black Death are termed pandemics

IMPACT ON SOCIETY

The impact of national emergencies, natural disasters, and epidemics of infectious diseases on society varies considerably. They include:

- Civil unrest
- Communications degradation
- Consumable resources scarcity including energy, food, healthcare services, and clean water
- Displaced healthcare personnel
- Displaced populations
- Famine
- Illness and mortality
- Infrastructure damage or destroyed including living accommodation, places of work, and transportation
- Law and order breakdown
- Secondary infectious diseases, such as cholera

IMPACT OF THE HEALTHCARE DELIVERY SYSTEM

National emergencies and natural disasters may have four types of direct impact on the healthcare delivery system.

1. **Physical damage to infrastructure**
   Facilities accommodating healthcare services may be unavailable
2. **Impact on other government agencies**
   Services provided by other government agencies may be reduced or curtailed, for example, police background checks

Operations of Regulators of Healthcare Professionals, Volume 4, First Edition. Marc Seale.

Companion website: www.wiley.com/go/seale/regulatinghealthcare

3. **Impact on regulators' operational capabilities**
Operational capabilities of the regulator may also be reduced. For example, because employees are unable to travel to work
4. **Shortage of healthcare professionals**
Large swathes of the population may be affected including both members of the public and healthcare professionals alike. At the same time the crisis may cause a sudden increase in demand for healthcare professionals, in proportion to the unexpected increase in patients. In parallel, healthcare professionals may themselves be directly affected and become incapacitated. To alleviate this eventuality, government may prioritise the provision of care to the healthcare workforce to speed up their return to work

In addition to the general impacts to the lives of the population other challenges that healthcare professionals will have to contend with if they are to continue to work may include:

- Child care required if schools are closed
- Supporting dependents

RESPONSE BY GOVERNMENT

Prudent governments should prepare contingency plans and regularly undertake preparedness simulations. Once the event has been declared to be a national emergency, natural disaster, or epidemic, governments are likely to trigger emergency executive powers. This can include overriding existing legislation by introducing emergency regulations on a temporary basis.

RESPONSE BY EMERGENCY NGOS

In response a number of NGOs are able to rapidly intervene to provide assistance with both resources and trained specialist, including healthcare professionals and members of search and rescue teams. These organisations include members of the International Federation of Red Cross and Red Crescent Societies, Médecins Sans Frontières/Doctors Without Borders, and Oxfam.

RESPONSE OF REGULATORS OF HEALTHCARE PROFESSIONALS

In the face of emergencies, disasters, and epidemics regulators of healthcare professionals may respond by changing a range of their processes. These include

- To alleviate the potential reduction in the supply of healthcare professionals, recently retired professionals may be permitted and encouraged to return expeditiously to the workforce. In the UK and other jurisdictions the legislation governing the regulation of healthcare professionals incorporates provisions to facilitate recently retired professionals to return speedily to the register under these types of emergency conditions. This may use a specific temporary emergency part of the register for the returning professionals
- If the regulator has a returner's to practise process this may be set aside or standards reduced for the duration of the crisis
- Minimise restrictions on the movement of healthcare professions attached to NGOs and International Search and Rescue Teams (ISRT) arriving from other jurisdictions
- Consider allowing more healthcare professionals to have access to prescription medicines by introducing reduced protocols and amended rules
- Waiving restrictions on the scope of practice for healthcare professionals
- Collection, analysis, and communication data relating to the event

EDUCATION AND TRAINING

Because of the possibility of physical damage to the infrastructure of education and training facilities and the availability of employees, the capacity of the education and training sector may be reduced.

In response, the government or the regulator may reduce the length of education and training required to join the profession to increase the supply of healthcare professionals. For example, in the UK during the Second World War the education and training of medical practitioners was shortened from five to four years.

Because the education and training of healthcare professionals is lengthy, these types of interventions will only occur if the impact of the crisis continues for a number or years.

Lastly, students who are close to completing their education and training may be admitted expeditiously to the profession. Students may also be encouraged to put their education and training on hold and join the workforce on a temporary basis but not as professionals but as healthcare assistants.

CONTINGENCY PLANNING AND PREPAREDNESS

In the UK, as with most other countries, government agencies have well-developed and rehearsed contingency plans on how they will deal with emergencies, disasters, and epidemics.

The UK has specific legislation for such situations, namely, the Civil Contingencies Act 2004 which provides a framework for civil protection in the UK. The act is separated into two substantive parts: part one for local arrangements for civil protection and part two for emergency powers.

However, to prevent undue concern from members of the public these types of plans may be kept under wraps and treated as highly confidential.

In response to the coronavirus, the UK Government introduced emergency legislation, the Coronavirus Act 2020. Of note, were the provisions to facilitate the practice of recently retired professionals and students who had not yet completed their education and training.

Individual regulators of healthcare professionals should also have contingency plans on how to deal with emergencies, disasters, and epidemics. These should focus on internal resources such as employees who cannot travel to work or who are incapacitated by ill health. In this type of situation a number of mitigating actions can be taken, including:

- Extend the deadlines to renew their registration
- Facilitate the provision of professional indemnity insurance
- Facilitate the return to the register of recently retired professionals
- Facilitate a rapid increase in international registrations of healthcare professionals to alleviate domestic shortages
- Fast track the registration process
- Maximise the use of ITC to replace face-to-face meetings such as board meetings or fitness to practise (FTP) panel and committee meetings
- Postpone FTP tribunals
- Postpone physical board and committee meetings
- Suspend continuing competence audits and assessments
- Suspend renewal of registration and/or fee collection

Both government and regulators should periodically test their contingency plans and their preparedness by way of simulated rehearsals. In particular, their legalisation should also be reviewed to ensure that emergency action can be taken.

GLOBAL COOPERATION

When emergencies and disasters befell other countries, it provides an opportunity for those able and willing to offer to provide assistance. In particular healthcare professionals are able to provide assistance to other jurisdictions. The onus to cooperate has been established by the WHO in the form of the International Health Regulations, an international law which has been implanted by 196 countries. Its stated purpose and scope is:

> *"to prevent, protect against, control and provide a public health response to the international spread of disease in ways that are commensurate with and restricted to public health risks, and which avoid unnecessary interference with international traffic and trade."*

Thus in response to crises caused by emergencies, disasters, and epidemics, governments are encouraged to temporarily reduce restrictions on the inward movement of healthcare professionals from other jurisdictions. For example, by facilitating the rapid movement of earthquake rescue teams through border controls.

CONCLUSION

National emergencies, natural disasters, and epidemics of infectious diseases are for most of us less than once-in-a-lifetime events. However, governments and prudent regulators should have business continuity action plans on how to deal with these types of crisis, both in terms of internal resources and capacity to deliver their regulatory functions but also to facilitate the availability of healthcare professionals.

EXERCISES AND QUESTIONS

Exercises

- What action would a regulator that you are familiar with take in the face of a national emergency, natural disaster, or an epidemic of an infectious disease?
- How does your organisation rehearse its contingency plans for a natural disaster?

Questions

- Should a regulator of healthcare professionals lower its standards of competence during a National Emergency, Natural Disaster, or an epidemic of an infectious disease?
- During the West African Ebola virus epidemic (2013–2016) what action did the UK Government take in relation to healthcare professionals?
- What measures did regulators of healthcare professionals take during the Covid-19 pandemic in 2020?

LEGISLATION

Example of UK legislation

Civil Contingencies Act 2004	L
Coronavirus Act 2020	L

FURTHER READING

International Health Regulations R
World Health Organisation (WHO)
ISBN: 9789241580410
15 June 2005, second edition 2008
74 pages

STANDARDS, CODES, GUIDANCE, CONSULTATIONS, POLICIES, AND PRACTICE NOTES

Guidance

Remote Hearing Protocol
To support the Fitness to Practice Committee Hearing during Covid-19 Emergency G
General Optical Council
9 July 2020
9 pages

Guidance for regulators on fitness to practise hearings during Covid-19 pandemic G
Professions Standards Authority
September 2020
9 pages

Guideline: Obligations in a Pandemic or Disaster, 2016 G
NZNO
ISBN: 978-1-877461-92-7
March 2020 (update)
10 pages

7.2 PROFESSIONAL INDEMNITY INSURANCE

INTRODUCTION

Infrequently, healthcare professionals cause harm or injury to their patients by their errors or mistakes. The responsibility for the financial cost of rectifying and compensating patients for these harms may become the personal responsibility of the healthcare professional. Unfortunately, due to the potential cost, it may be beyond the financial resources of the professional. To prevent this eventuality, professionals can limit their financial exposure, by purchasing an insurance contract, or, alternatively, be provided with indemnity insurance cover. Both types of insurance protection cover all or some of the costs for rectifying and compensation for the harm caused and also any associated legal costs. As an alternative, New Zealand has adopted no-fault accident compensation scheme. Notwithstanding this, regulators of healthcare professionals should consider if professional indemnity insurance should be mandated.

RISK OF HARM IN THE HEALTHCARE DELIVERY SYSTEM

Section 2.4, volume 1, identified the range of the causes of harm arising within the healthcare delivery system. It also explored the way that some of the risks of these harms can be mitigated, although, it should be noted that unfortunately, many of the risks associated with the healthcare delivery system can't be completely mitigated.

ACCIDENTS AND ERRORS

The subject of accidents and errors is explored in Section 1.2, volume 3. It concludes that under certain circumstances the healthcare delivery system tolerates their occurrence. However, from time to time, the error or mistake is so egregious that patients are able to seek compensation. To decide if financial compensation may be obtained by a patient from a healthcare professional or their employer, the clinical negligence test is used.

LAW OF TORT

A tort, in common law jurisdictions, can be defined as:

Definition: Tort
Civil wrong that unfairly causes someone else to suffer loss or harm resulting in legal liability for the person who commits the tortious act.

The victim of the harm can seek to recover their loss as damages in a lawsuit. Although a crime may be a tort, the cause of legal action is not necessarily a crime, as the harm may be due to negligence which does not amount to criminal negligence. In order to prevail, the plaintiff in the lawsuit, commonly referred to as the injured party, must show that the action, or lack of action, was the legally recognisable cause of the harm.

The equivalent of tort in civil law jurisdictions is delict.

NEGLIGENCE

Negligence is a tort which arises from the breach of the duty of care owed by one person to another from the perspective of a reasonable person.

To establish negligence the plaintiff must prove five component parts, which are:

1. The plaintiff was owed a duty of care through a special relationship (e.g. doctor–patient) or some other principle
2. There was a dereliction or breach of that duty
3. The tortfeasor directly caused the injury but for the defendant's actions, the plaintiff would not have suffered an injury
4. The plaintiff suffered damage as a result of that breach
5. The damage was not too remote; there was proximate cause to show the breach caused the damage

ESTABLISHING CLINICAL NEGLIGENCE

In the UK, to establish proof that clinical negligence has occurred, a three-part legal clinical negligence test is used, followed by the calculation of the financial worth of the damage:

1. Did the healthcare professional owe a duty of care to the patient?
2. Was the duty of care breached?
3. As a direct result of the breach, did the patient suffer harm?

Then the amount of finance that is required to compensate the patient for their pain and suffering and the financial loss they have incurred and will incur, is calculated. In many cases the amount awarded is decided by the courts.

The concept of duty of care is explored in Section 7.1, volume 1. In the UK the acceptable standard is in effect the standard of competence set by the statutory regulator of the healthcare professional.

When clinical negligence has occurred and a claim is successful, then the healthcare professional is personally liable for the financial cost of both rectifying the clinical negligence and compensating the individual concerned.

It should also be noted that an employer, such as the NHS, can be liable for the acts or omissions of its employees, provided it can be shown that they took place in the course of their employment. This is called vicarious liability and can be defined as:

Definition: Vicarious Liability
Legal responsibility of a superior for the actions or omissions of a subordinate who they have a right, ability, and duty to control.

COST OF RECTIFYING AND COMPENSATING CLINICAL NEGLIGENCE

The costs of rectifying and compensating individual patients for harms and injuries suffered may be significant and can be millions of pounds for one individual case. The cost of rectification and compensation can be in the form of a single payment or multiple smaller payments spread over many years. As a result the costs may be beyond the financial resources of the individual healthcare professional.

To gauge the scale of the costs associated with clinical negligence in the UK, in the FY 2022/23 NHS Resolution spent £2,300,000,000 settling clinical negligence claims.

PATIENT EXPECTATIONS

Because of the significant cost of rectifying mistakes and errors within the healthcare delivery system, patients expect and assume that all healthcare professionals will have appropriate insurance to cover the costs of rectification and compensation. In other words, when things do 'go wrong' patients expect their healthcare professionals to be 'insured' so that financial 'compensation' will be forthcoming.

It is noteworthy that the NHS Constitution for England incudes the statement that patients have the right to receive compensation when they have been harmed by negligent treatment.

DEFENCE PRACTICE

It should be noted that there are unintended consequences for providing insurance for clinical negligence. This is because as result of the possible risk of costly and slow court litigation, healthcare professionals may take, or avoid, action, including:

- Action
  - Undertaking unnecessary diagnostic tests and procedures
  - Prescribing unnecessary treatment
  - Unnecessarily admitting patients to hospital
- Inaction
  - Not undertaking risky procedures that if successful could result in benefits

These responses can both increase the cost of healthcare and can reduce the quality of the service provided.

This process is referred to as defensive practice, which can be defined as:

Definition: Defensive Practice
Not using standard professional practice to avoid litigation.

The term defensive medicine may also be used.

MORAL HAZARD

A counter argument to defensive practice is that by providing insurance a healthcare professional may take greater risks because someone else will bear the cost of failure. This is termed moral hazard:

Definition: Moral Hazard
Accepting greater risk because someone else bears the cost.

It should be noted that the term moral hazard has two meanings, see Section 1.5, volume 4.

INSURANCE

Insurance is a financial transaction for individuals and organisations designed to protect themselves from financial loss. The insurance is provided by an insurance company. The individual who purchases insurance is known as a policyholder. The insurance transaction involves the policyholder assuming a guaranteed and known relatively modest cost in the form of small and frequent payments to the insurance company, in exchange for their promise to compensate the policyholder in the event of a claim or loss. The loss may or may not be financial, but it must be reducible to financial terms. The policyholder receives a contract, called the insurance policy, which details the conditions and circumstances under which the insurer will compensate the policyholder. The amount of money charged by the insurance company to the policyholder for the coverage set forth in the insurance policy is called the premium.

INSURANCE FOR HEALTHCARE PROFESSIONALS

Insurance is available to try and ensure that appropriate financial compensation will be forthcoming to patients if things go wrong as a result of errors and mistakes. Insurance is of particular importance for individual healthcare professional because they may not have enough of their own financial resources available for potential claims for clinical negligence.

They can therefore protect themselves from these types of negative financial consequences.

The specific insurance available to healthcare professionals for protection against the financial consequences of a claim of clinical negligence is called professional indemnity insurance, and can be defined as:

Definition: Professional Indemnity Insurance
Protection for healthcare professionals against claims for financial compensation resulting from clinical negligence or breach of professional standards including associated legal costs.

The terms clinical negligence cover, professional liability insurance, and medical indemnity insurance may also be used. And in North America, the term used is malpractice insurance.

TYPES OF INSURANCE

Healthcare professionals are usually able to access one of two, or a combination of both types of insurance. These are:

1. Insurance contract
2. Indemnity cover
3. Combination of insurance contract and indemnity cover

INSURANCE CONTRACT

Individual healthcare professionals can purchase professional indemnity insurance for themselves from commercial insurance companies.

PROFESSIONAL INDEMNITY INSURANCE PROVIDERS

The contracts are available from commercial insurance companies who provide insurance against clinical negligence claims. It is a highly competitive well-established market. Policies are usually sold on an annual basis by insurance brokers. The sector is regulated by the Financial Conduct Authority (FCA). The insurance companies must have access to adequate financial reserves to cover their ongoing liabilities. They are also regulated by the Prudential Regulation Authority (PRA). In addition, they are also part of the Financial Services Compensation Scheme.

Individual healthcare professionals can directly purchase insurance policies. In the UK these are typically healthcare professionals who are working on a self-employed basis either on a full-time or part-time basis. In some instances an employer of a healthcare professional may reimburse the cost of the insurance to an employee or the employer may purchase on their behalf.

In addition, some professional associations may negotiate directly with insurance companies to provide professional indemnity insurance for their members. This arrangement has the advantage that the professional association will usually be able to negotiate a volume discount and any resulting financial benefits may be passed on to the individual members of the professional association. The insurance company may also benefit because the members of the professional association may be of a lower risk compared to those professionals who are not members of the association. The lower risk should result in lower premiums.

Because the provision of insurance for clinical negligence claims is a potentially important service that professional associations provide to their members, it is not an area that regulators should enter into.

INDEMNITY COVER

Indemnity cover is an alternative form of financial protection similar to insurance. It can either be provided by employers, to their employees who are healthcare professionals and in some cases healthcare occupations. They are typically employed by a state employer, for example, the NHS in the UK. Alternatively, it is available to the membership of a voluntary membership organisation established solely to provide indemnity cover.

Indemnity cover is of particular importance for healthcare professions who may not be in a position to personally fund the cost of professional indemnity insurance. For example, newly qualified nurses.

STATE-BACKED INDEMNITY COVER

In some jurisdictions such as the UK, the state as a large employer of healthcare professionals may establish indemnity schemes that directly provide clinical negligence cover for their employees or contractors. In effect, as part of their contract of employment the state finances the cost of potential compensation without recourse to insurance contracts.

In the UK, NHS bodies and organisations are responsible for any clinical negligence of their employees. There are four NHS organisations administering indemnity schemes, for those working in secondary care, namely:

England	NHS Resolution, ex-NHS Litigation Authority
Northern Ireland	HSSC Trusts and the Department of Health (Northern Ireland)
Scotland	Clinical Negligence and Other Risks Indemnity Scheme (CNORIS)
Wales	The Welsh Risk Pool.

Historically, general practitioners were excluded from such schemes, but the provision of clinical negligence cover is now being extended into primary care.

Because of its size, the NHS does not insure its risk in the market; rather the state acts as a closed system and directly funds the cost of financial compensation for harms and damages that are caused by its employees.

DISCRETIONARY INDEMNITY SCHEME

These are schemes where the provider organisation provides clinical negligence cover in the form of discretionary indemnity. It is 'discretionary' in that provision is at the discretion of the provider and may not be provided. In addition, the level of financial support is not capped. This arrangement is in stark contrast to an insurance contract.

In the UK traditional Medical Defence Organisations (MDOs) have provided clinical negligence cover for their members by way of discretionary indemnity. See Stakeholders Section 3.1, volume 1. The MDOs are a non-profit organisation (NPO), are mutual organisations owned and are managed by their members. They have no shareholders and make no dividend payments. They are specialists in the provision of services of their members compared to the general insurance market.

There are major differences between the clinical negligence cover provided by MDOs and insurance contracts and provided by commercial insurance companies. In particular discretionary indemnity schemes are:

- Not subjected to financial regulation by either the FCA or the PRA
- Not subject to the Financial Services Compensation Scheme
- Not required to disclose the adequacy of their financial reserves to meet future claims
- Do not have to disclose their financial assets and liabilities
- Higher level of risk that patients will not be compensated for the harms and damages caused by healthcare professionals

RISK AND THE PROVISION OF PROFESSIONAL INDEMNITY INSURANCE

The providers of professional indemnity insurance must also take into consideration the level of risk associated with those they are providing cover for. This is because the level of risk is not consistent across the sector and is driven by factors such as:

- Patient-specific risk
- Profession-specific risk
- Practice or context setting risk

Providers of clinical negligence cover should be able to quantify the level of risk of those they are providing services to.

If a provider incorrectly predicts the level of risk associated with those they are providing cover for they may end up providing the service at too low a price and if there are too many claims the organisation may become financially distressed. On the other hand if the risk level is predicted to be very high the provider may not be able to sell the cover as it is too expensive for healthcare professionals to purchase.As a consequence of this, a provider may decide not to participate in the market and leave provision to state-backed organisations.For the sake of completeness it should be noted that some healthcare professionals may use both an insurance contract paid for by themselves and insurance provided by an employer in the form of indemnity cover.In addition, in theory a fourth option may arise when there is no requirement for healthcare professionals to have insurance and some healthcare professional may decide not to have any. They will then be exposed to potential large financial claims where they will be solely responsible for financing. Logically, if the professional does not have enough financial resources, the harmed patient will not be paid. While historically this was more often than not the case, nowadays most jurisdictions, including the UK, do not allow this option.

COST OF PROVIDING PROFESSIONAL INDEMNITY INSURANCE

The cost of providing professional indemnity insurance is an important consideration, and the dismal signs of economics point to the logical necessity than the direct and indirect costs of its provision and the financial benefits of the clinical negligence must be equal to or lower. If not, then organisations providing the clinical negligence cover will go out of business. In other words:

Cost of providing professional indemnity insurance
≤ Cost of compensation & rectifying mistakes

In theory in a given period of time the numerous premiums are greater than the infrequent claims and a small financial return that flows to the owners of the insurance company or the MDO.

If the benefits of clinical negligence cover are too low, then harmed patients will not receive appropriate compensation.If the costs are too high, organisations will not provide the service and healthcare professionals will be unable to acquire cover. This means that they may be prevented from working and services provider to patients and/or patients will again lose out, as they may be unable gain appropriate financial compensation for their harms arising from clinical negligence.The cost of cover for some healthcare professionals will be borne by their employer, and this will not directly negatively affect their wages, in the form of indemnity cover. For example, for those working in the NHS. However, it is also important that the cost of cover does not inhibit healthcare professionals contributing to the workforce, particularly those who are self-employed, work on a part-time basis, or have low wages.

INABILITY TO OBTAIN INDEMNITY INSURANCE

It should be noted that there may be a small number of healthcare professionals who are unable to obtain insurance cover. In North America they are referred to as the '*hard-to-place*' market, in that the insurance market is unwilling to provide insurance. For example, in North America about 2–3% of the medical practitioners are unable to find providers of insurance due to their record of claims. For those who can find insurance rates can be 500% premium above the market norm. In general the consequences for a healthcare professional unable to obtain professional indemnity insurance can be catastrophic. This was exemplified in the UK in the mid-2010s when independent midwives were unable to obtain insurance.

PROFESSIONAL INDEMNITY INSURANCE FRAMEWORK

To aid you, the reader, a professional I;ndemnity insurance framework showing the relationship between the key components follows. The Chart 7.2 – I below, illustrates the relationships between risk, duty of fare, errors and mistakes, clinical negligence, claims, financial compensation, clinical negligence cover, insurance contracts, and discretionary indemnity.

TERMS AND CONDITIONS FOR THE PROVISION OF PROFESSIONAL INDEMNITY INSURANCE

The professional indemnity insurance will normally set out in detail the terms and conditions of the contract. Whilst each will have slightly different terms and conditions they will usually address the following issues:

ANY ONE CLAIM AND AGGREGATE'

There are different bases of cover. An 'any one claim' policy provides cover up to the full limit for each individual claim made in the period of insurance, whereas an 'aggregate' policy provides cover up to the full limit for all claims made in the period of the cover.

APPROPRIATENESS

The cover should ideally apply to all the activities of the particular healthcare professional. For example, an individual may work predominantly for the NHS. However, this may not be the case; see exclusions below.

CAPS TO LIMIT LIABILITY

A clause should clearly state the maximum amount of financial compensation that will be paid to each successful claimant by the provider. This amount may vary between different healthcare professions, depending on the perceived risk of the scope of practice of the profession.

CLAIMS-MADE INSURANCE

Clinical negligence claims may sometimes take years to settle. Claims made cover only protects the policy holder when they are insured and both when an incident occurs and when the claim is notified. Run-off cover is therefore required, see below.

CLAIMS-OCCURRENCE INSURANCE

Clinical negligence claims may sometimes take years to settle. Claims-occurance insurance cover claims made during the period of the policy even though the policy is no longer held by the professional. Run-off cover is therefore not required.

Chart 7.2 – I **Professional indemnity insurance framework**

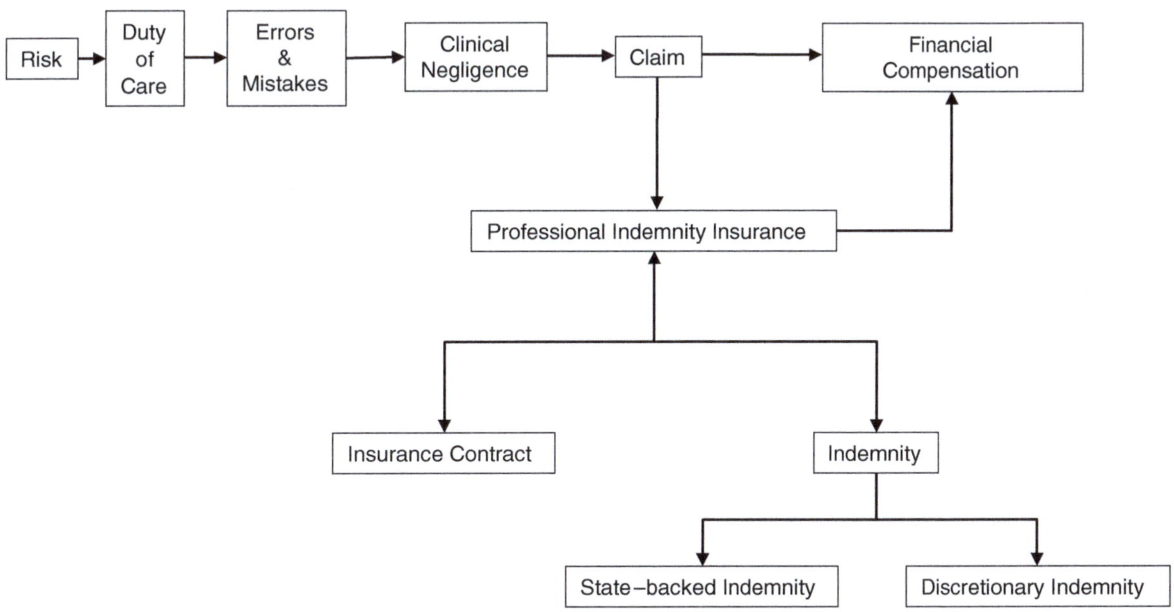

CLAIMS-PAID INSURANCE

Clinical negligence claims may sometimes take years to settle. Claims-paid cover providers cover on the same basis as claims-made cover, except that claims will only be met if they are settled (as well as accrued and reported) during the policy. Run-off cover is therefore required; see below.

EMPLOYMENT TYPE

Healthcare professionals work in a variety of different practice settings, working patterns, teams, and organisations. For example:

- Agency work
- Contractors
- Educators and trainers
- Full-time permanent
- Managers
- Medico-legal work engagements
- Overseas
- Part-time or occasional work
- Research
- Self-employed
- Students
- Voluntary work for charities and third-sector organisations

It is important that the terms of the cover provide for all these eventualities.

EXCLUSIONS – OTHER

If the harm is caused by criminal activities or deliberate malpractice, cover may also be denied.

EXCLUSIONS – SCOPE OF PRACTICE

The cover may exclude some high-risk services that can be provided by the particular healthcare professional. For example, midwifery care may not be coverable due to patient's propensity to claim. If the healthcare professional is unaware of any services that are not covered, the professional may find themselves outside the scope of cover which may have dire consequence for all parties.

LEGAL COSTS

The cover should include the legal costs of defending a claim for clinical negligence.

RUN-OFF COVER

Clinical negligence claims may sometimes take years to settle. Therefore cover should be obtained for when the event occurs, when the claim is made, and when it is settled. This is known as 'Run-off cover'. If the policy is no longer held by the professional the cover will still be provided.

SWITCHING PROVIDERS

As in any competitive markets customers for clinical negligence cover are able to switch to competing providers. However, if an individual switches to a new provider, cover should be obtained from the new provider for events arising during the term of the previous policy.

TIME LIMITS ON CLINICAL NEGLIGENCE CLAIMS

In the UK claims must be made within three years from when the incident happened or when the patient realised that they had suffered an injury. In the case of children, the three-year limit doesn't start to apply until their 18th birthday.

REGULATORS OF HEALTHCARE PROFESSIONALS AND CLINICAL NEGLIGENCE COVER

Having reviewed the options for healthcare professionals to obtain professional indemnity insurance and the details of the terms and conditions that can be included in the insurance contracts, the next issue to explore is, should regulators require healthcare professionals to possess professional indemnity insurance?

Regulators of healthcare professionals' interest in clinical negligence cover is because most members of the public expect their governments to require healthcare professionals to have clinical negligence cover. In the UK the public's expectations are met because historically European legislation and thus UK legislation required and still requires all healthcare professionals to have clinical negligence cover. However, in some other jurisdictions there is no requirement for clinical negligence cover, although some may recommend that healthcare professionals are in possession of cover.

EUROPE

EU Directive 2011/24/EU, on Application of patients' rights in cross-border healthcare, requires each member state to put in place appropriate, or a similar arrangement, for medical treatment provided on its territory. This includes a mandatory requirement for all EU healthcare professionals to have professional indemnity insurance or a similar arrangement in place.

UK IMPLEMENTATION

As a result of the 9 March 2011 the European Union Directive 2011/24/EU, the UK introduced the Health Care and Associated

Professions (Indemnity Arrangements) Order 2014 (SI 2014/1887). In Northern Ireland, the Pharmacy (1976 Order) Amendment Order (Northern Ireland) 2013 made similar changes. However, since the departure by the UK from the EU in January 2020, this is now of historical interest only.

REGULATORS' REQUIREMENTS FOR PROFESSIONAL INDEMNITY INSURANCE

Currently, in the UK the exact terms and conditions of professional indemnity insurance contracts are a matter for the regulators of each healthcare profession. However, across the nine UK regulators whilst there is consistency in the requirement to have clinical negligence cover, there is no consistency of the terms and conditions of the contracts.

STANDARD FOR PROFESSIONAL INDEMNITY INSURANCE

The Standard usually states that:

> *The professional indemnity insurance should be adequate and appropriate to the risk and scope of practice of the healthcare professional.*

The NMC tested the definition of adequacy in the High Court in a case against the Independent Midwives (IMUK/ Lucina). However, some regulators may specify specific terms such as the minimum cover.

SPECIFICATION OF TERMS AND CONDITIONS OF PROFESSIONAL INDEMNITY INSURANCE

Should a regulator of healthcare professionals that requires them to possess professional indemnity insurance specify the terms and conditions of the contract?

For example:

- Defining what is adequate and appropriate cover
- Caps to limit liability
- Run-off provision

In general, regulators are reluctant to specify terms and conditions and rely on guidance as a solution.

GUIDANCE

Many regulators solve this dilemma of what terms and conditions should be included in the insurance contacts by publishing guidance on clinical negligence cover. The guidance, it should be said, has a tendency to be vague, focusing on the need for professionals to take appropriate advice.

OPERATIONAL CONSIDERATIONS OF DEMONSTRATING TO THE REGULATOR

If the regulator of healthcare professionals requires registrants to possess professional indemnity insurance, should it proactively ensure that those professionals they regulate are indeed in possession of insurance?

There are two potential ways that this can be achieved. A system of trust can be used where at the point of joining the register, or when their registration is renewed, the professionals can be asked to confirm that they have insurance by making a professional self-declaration. This can be followed-up by random sampling to ensure that the system is working. Alternatively, all can be required to submit actual or certified documentation to confirm their cover.

SANCTIONS FOR FAILURE TO FOLLOW THE PROFESSIONAL INDEMNITY INSURANCE STANDARDS

If the possession of professional indemnity insurance is compulsory and certain terms and conditions are required, what action should a regulator take if they become aware that a professional on their register is not complying with the standards required?

What does the regulator then do if a professional makes an error but has no insurance? Should they be sent to an FTP tribunal? Given the importance of cover, lack of cover is normally deemed an FTP matter. However, deliberate non-compliance with specified terms and conditions would probably have the same remedy.

Likewise, concerns raised by a provider of clinical negligence covering from another jurisdiction may trigger an FTP investigation.

ALTERNATIVE TO PROFESSIONAL INDEMNITY INSURANCE

When clinical negligence has occurred satisfactory resolution, even when supported by professional indemnity insurance, is fraught with difficulties for all concerned. In particular, the legal costs associated with process may be astronomical. This makes alternative no-fault compensation process very attractive. Such a system has been adopted in New Zealand with their Accident Compensation Corporation system (ACC), which provides no-fault compensation for victims.

ACCIDENT COMPENSATION CORPORATION (ACC)

Since 1974 medical malpractice litigation has effectively been barred in New Zealand when the ACC was established under a radical reform of the law of tort. The ACC is a Crown Entity and is responsible to a cabinet minister via its board of directors. It is responsible for administering universal no-fault accidental injury scheme. The scheme provides financial compensation and support to citizens, residents, and temporary visitors who have suffered personal injuries.

ACC is the sole and compulsory provider of accident insurance in New Zealand for all work and non-work injuries. The corporation administers the ACC Scheme on a no-fault basis, so that anyone – regardless of the way in which they incurred an injury – has coverage under the scheme. Due to the scheme's no-fault basis, people who have suffered personal injury do not have the right to sue an at-fault party, except for exemplary damages.

ACC is primarily funded through a combination of levies and government contributions. Income is collected from four main sources, namely: employers, employees, non-earners, petrol and motor vehicles. Although the ACC is not directly concerned with regulation of healthcare professionals it is an important stakeholder since all successful claims of medical error made to the ACC are reported to the relevant registration body.

The ACC Scheme provides a range of entitlements to injured people, from contribution towards the cost of treatment, to weekly compensation for lost earnings (paid at a rate of 80% of a person's pre-injury earnings), and even home or vehicle modifications for the seriously injured. The entitlements offered by the scheme are subject to various eligibility criteria.

DISCLOSING PROFESSIONAL INDEMNITY INSURANCE CLAIMS

The issue of the disclosure of claims should be addressed since there can be causation between a claim for financial recompense and the competence of a healthcare professional. For this reason, some jurisdictions may require professions to either make public or report to their regulator all claims both successful and unsuccessful. These include both decisions of the courts, arbitration settlements, and payments by insurance companies.

PROFESSIONAL INDEMNITY INSURANCE FOR NON-PROFESSIONALS

And for the sake of completeness, for those delving into the minutiae of the subject the issue of the need to require indemnity insurance or cover for occupations and assistants may need to be resolved.

PROFESSIONAL INDEMNITY INSURANCE, COMPLAINTS, COMPETENCE, AND CONDUCT

Before concluding this section it is worth considering if there is a link between professional indemnity insurance and concerns and complaints being made against professionals.

For example, should a regulator be concerned if a professional indemnity insurance provider makes a settlement on behalf of a professional because there is a link between an insurance payment and a professional's competence or conduct? However, a payment may be related to the terms and conditions of the policy and not the validity of the claim. In addition, the claim may be settled without involvement of the professional and/or a determination of fault. However, a professional who is subject to an unusual and unexplainable number of claims should be of concern.

It is also worth considering if the provision of professional indemnity insurance inadvertently fuels the raising of FTP concerns.

The rationale for asking this question is that if a patient makes a successful complaint against a healthcare professional that is upheld by an FTP tribunal, then as a consequence are they more likely to receive financial compensation from the insurance provider? And, will the insurance provider be more likely to finance the cost of the profession defending their position in the tribunal?

CONCLUSION

Professional indemnity insurance has clear benefits for both patients and professionals. Therefore should healthcare professionals be required by regulators to have compulsory professional indemnity insurance and if so should regulators concern themselves about the terms and conditions of the insurance contracts?

EXERCISE AND QUESTIONS

Exercise

- Can you locate an example where healthcare professionals take more risky interventions because they are protected by insurance 'moral hazard'?

Questions

- Should the regulators of healthcare professionals require professionals to have indemnity insurance?
- Should regulators of healthcare professionals require all professionals to have professional indemnity insurance as a prerequisite to registration or only those who are self-employed on a full-time or part-time basis?
- What process should regulators use to ensure professionals have suitable insurance, and how frequently should this be done?
- What should the consequence be to a professional who does not have insurance? Should it be an FTP issue?
- Should the regulator specify the type of insurance required and other contractual issues such as the maximum financial compensation pay out?

LEGISLATION

Example of UK Legislation

Health Care and Associated Professions (Indemnity Arrangements) Order 2014 (SI 2014/1887) L

NHS (Clinical Negligence Scheme (Amendment SI 2014) Regulations 2014 L

Pharmacy (1976 Order) Amendment Order (Northern Ireland) 2013 L

Example of International Legislation

EU

EU Directive 2011/24/EU
Application of patients' rights in cross-border healthcare L

FURTHER READING

The Feasibility and Insurability of Independent Midwifery in England R
Flaxman Partners Ltd
Royal College of Midwives and Nursing & Midwifery Council
September 2011
69 pages

Independent Review of the Requirement to Have Insurance or Indemnity as a Condition of Registration as a Healthcare Professional R
Finley Scott – Chair of the Independent Policy Review Group
36 pages
14 July 2010
The report contained two annexes by PricewaterhouseCooper: I Policy Review Research June 2010 75 pages & II Stakeholder Engagement Exercise Key Findings May 2010 36 pages

Managing the Costs of Clinical Negligence in Trust R
Nation Audit Office
HC 305
ISBN 13: 978 1 78604 139 5
1 September 2017
60 pages

Response to the Independent Review of the Requirement to Have Insurance or Indemnity as a Condition of Registration as a Healthcare Professional R
Department of Health
14 December 2010
2 pages

STANDARDS, CODES, GUIDANCE, CONSULTATIONS, POLICIES, AND PRACTICE NOTES

Guidance

Guidance on Indemnity G
GDC
15 June 2016
3 pages

Arrangements for Clinical Negligence Claims in the NHS G
NHS Indemnity
19 pages

Professional Indemnity and Your Registration G
HCPC
Publication code 20140521POLPUB
17 July 2014
15 pages

Professional Indemnity A Requirement for Registration G
NMC
6 pages

Consultations

Appropriate Clinical Negligence Cover C
Consultation
Department of Health & Social care
6 December 2018
51 pages

7.3 REGULATION OF HEALTHCARE DELIVERY FACILITIES

INTRODUCTION

In many jurisdictions the facilities where healthcare is provided such as care homes, clinics, and hospitals are regulated. For example, in England many healthcare professions including dentists, GPs, midwives, and surgeons work in facilities regulated by the Care Quality Commission (CQC). Notwithstanding this, two of the UK's regulators of healthcare professionals, namely, the General Optical Council (GOC) and General Pharmaceutical Council (GPhC), have a dual regulatory responsibility of firstly, regulating professionals and secondly, regulating the healthcare delivery facilities or premises used by the professionals they regulate. This section explores the rationale for the anomaly.

HEALTHCARE DELIVERY FACILITIES

For the purpose of this discussion a healthcare delivery facility is defined as:

Definition: Healthcare Delivery Facility
Facility where healthcare service is provided to patients.

POWERS OF INSPECTION

Context

As discussed in Section 1.5, volume 1, the CQC regulates the quality and safely of the providers of healthcare services in England by setting standards and inspecting, rating, registering, and monitoring their facilities. The facilities include those in the NHS, commercial business, charities, and the third sector. This means that most healthcare professionals work in facilities where the service is regulated by the CQC.

EXCEPTIONS

The exception to the CQC's broad remit is the service delivery facilities of the professions that are regulated by either the GOC or the GPhC. In the case of the GOC it regulates businesses that are body corporates but has no powers to inspect their premises. On the other hand, the GPhC does have powers to inspect premises. The GPhC situation is made more complex because pharmacy services are also provided within NHS facilities, for example, large hospitals and polyclinics.

RATIONALE FOR THE ANOMALY

The rationale for why pharmacists and opticians lie outside the scope of the CQC but dentists do not, is not immediately obvious. Indeed a UK Parliamentary Committee was enquiring into the future of pharmacy in early 2025. Notwithstanding, the services do have common characteristics, namely:

1. Challenge to separate the practice of the professional from the safety and quality of the service delivery facility of the organisation
2. Specialist businesses
3. Often commercial-for-profit businesses
4. Often service provided in numerous unconnected small facilities

HISTORICAL CONTEXT

The GPhC was founded in 1852 and the GOC in 1958. In both professions there is a close relationship between the safe and effective practice of the profession and the safety of the facilities they operated from. For example, the risks posed by medicines and the need for their safe storage and dispensing.

In contrast, the regulation of the services delivering healthcare in England is a relatively new process – a process which since its introduction has been marked by the continuous metamorphosis of the organisations responsible for its delivery. From the Health Advisory Services (HAS) in 1969, to the Commission of Health Improvement (CHI), founded in 2001, to be replaced by the Healthcare Commission in 2004 and itself replaced by the CQC in 2009.

STANDARDS FOR HEALTHCARE DELIVERY FACILITIES

Whatever the organisational arrangements are to regulate service delivery facilities, the regulator should establish standards that focus on the following issues:

- Governance arrangements, which may include the necessity for healthcare professionals to be on the board of directors
- Competence and empowerment of workforce
- Environment and condition of the premises from which services are provided, including any associated premises
- Equipment and facilities used in the provision of services
- Delivery of services

INSPECTION REGIME

A regulator having establish standards for healthcare delivery facilities will then logically need to inspect the premises to ensure that the standards are being met. This is a similar process to the setting and inspection of HEI programme providers;

a range of principles and processes will need to be established. These include:

- Frequency of inspection
- Use of unannounced inspection visits
- Publication of inspections reports
- Adoption of a risk-based approach
- Types of sanctions for not meeting standards, including
- Use of financial penalties
- Use of conditions or improvement order
- Charging of inspection fees
- Use of a rating system and certification marks
- Adaptation of principles and processes to minimise impact on smaller business and start-ups to avoid disproportion burdens and costs

BUSINESSES AND PARTNERSHIPS

In some jurisdictions the businesses or partnerships that provide the services of professionals are also regulated.

By specifically referring to businesses or partnerships rather than using the term healthcare delivery facility, the regulatory framework implies a fundamental difference between the services provided by commercial organisation and those provided by publicly owned health facilities. An example of this situation is a pharmacist owned and operated within a supermarket and one operating within a public hospital providing tertiary care. The regulations may also require professionals to be on the board of directors of the business.

In some jurisdictions the regulator may issue permits to eligible business or corporations. In British Columbia these are called corporate permits.

REGISTRAR OF HEALTHCARE DELIVERY FACILITIES

The regulator may maintain a register of approved healthcare delivery facilities or businesses that meet the standards of the regulator.

COMPANY NAMES

Before concluding this section, reference needs to be made to Section 53 of the UK's Companies Act 2006, which places restrictions on the use of certain words that can be used to name companies, also referred to as businesses. These include, for example, the words dentist, nurse, physician, and physiotherapist. To use these types of names in the name of a company, authorisation is required from the relevant regulator. Companies House published guidance on the subject of naming companies.

Protected titles can also be linked to the facilities that the professional services are delivered from. For example, in the UK only retail premises registered with the General Pharmacy Council (GPhC) can use the term pharmacy.

CONCLUSION

The arrangements when multiple bodies including regulators of healthcare professionals, regulators of healthcare delivery facilities, and sometimes professional association are involved in the inspection, rating, registration, and monitoring of healthcare delivery facilities can cause confusion. Indeed, the UK Government's December 2015 report on the regulation of dental services identified a range of pertinent issues, although some can be mitigated by the use of memorandums of understanding.

All involved should therefore consider taking steps to ensure that their stakeholders are aware of their respective responsibilities and relationships and the rationale for the regulation regime.

EXERCISE AND QUESTIONS

Exercise

- Obtain an inspection report produced by a regulator on the facilities and services of a pharmacist or optician

Questions

- What is the justification for a regulator of pharmacists setting standards for the premises used by their professionals and operating an inspection regime?
- Should all regulators of healthcare professionals have powers to inspect the premises where the professionals deliver care?

LEGISLATION

Example of UK Legislation

Companies Act 2006 L

FURTHER READING

The Future of Dental Service Regulation R
Department of Health, CQC General Dental Council & others
December 2015
26 pages

The Scope of Registration R
Registration under the Health and Social Care Act 2008
Care Quality Commission
August 2013 Edition
63 pages

STANDARDS, CODES, GUIDANCE, CONSULTATIONS, POLICIES, AND PRACTICE NOTES

Standards and Codes

Standards for Optical Businesses S&C
General Optical Council
1 October 2019
35 pages

Standards for Registered Pharmacies S&C
General Pharmaceutical Council
June 2018
16 pages

Guidance

Company and Business Names G
HCPC
10 June 2019
3 pages

Guidance for Providers on Meeting the Fundamental Standards and on CQC's Enforcement Powers G
CQC
138 pages
July 2014

Use of Clinic Names G
College of Physicians and Surgeons of British Columbia (CPSBC)
July 2018
2 pages

Words and Expression Protected Under Other Legislation G
Guidance, Incorporation of Names, Annex C
Companies House
6 April 2022 (Latest update)

7.4 TELEHEALTH

INTRODUCTION

Telehealth is the use of information and communication technology to deliver healthcare and is a rapidly growing phenomenon in the healthcare delivery system. Telehealth enables healthcare professionals to provide a service from a different geographic location from that of the patient. In addition, the participants may also be in a different time zone. This separation of time and place of healthcare service providers and healthcare service has considerable benefits but raises a complex issue relating to the regulation of healthcare professionals. Namely, which regulatory regime should apply to a healthcare professional who is providing a telehealth service?

TELEHEALTH

Telehealth can be defined as:

Definition: Telehealth
Remote diagnosis and treatment of patients by the use of information and communications technology.

The terms telecare, telemedicine, and telepractice may also be used.

HISTORY OF TELEHEALTH

Until the latter part of the nineteenth century, the only way a healthcare professional could provide a service to a patient was if they were in close physical proximity to one another. For example, historically a doctor could only provide services to patients within walking distance or by using a horse. Hand-delivered letters could also be used. In due course, the introduction of steam locomotives, better roads and then the internal combustion engine allowed greater distances to be travelled between healthcare professionals and patients, but this was initially the exception rather than the rule.

However, from the early days of Morse code in the 1830s, to Alexander Graham Bell's invention of the patented telephone in 1876, telecommunications has facilitated a growing number of people to easily, cheaply, and quickly to communicate with one another across great distances without the need for close proximity.

From these humble begins, over the last 175 years telecommunications has been transformed. Nowadays, not only voice but data and moving images can, easily and at a low cost, be stored and rapidly transmitted and received almost instantaneously, anytime, anywhere on the globe.

BENEFITS OF TELEHEALTH

Assuming that the appropriate technology and energy supplies are available, the use of telehealth has resulted in the emergence of a growing range of operational benefits, including:

SEPARATION OF LOCATION OF PATIENT AND HEALTHCARE PROFESSIONAL

Telehealth can be used to enable healthcare professionals to diagnose and treat patients who are located at considerable distance from each other. A process that is sometimes referred to as the '*death of distance*'.

DISTANT MONITORING

Data can be collected from a patient and transmitted to another location where the data can be monitored and interventions triggered.

TIME SHIFTING

If a service cannot be provided on a 24-hour basis, for example, the interpretation of x-rays images at three o'clock in the morning, then the service can be provided by other healthcare professionals during their normal working day because they are located in a different time zone.

As a result there are economic benefits to be gained from telehealth service, including:

- Reduction of the need to and the cost of transporting patients to distant healthcare service facilities
- Reduction in the number of healthcare professionals required to provide a service in a particular locality

Together these benefits are resulting in the provision of improved healthcare services in terms of cost, increased capacity, and time to intervention.

PROVISION OF TELEHEALTH IN A SINGLE JURISDICTION

As the statutory regulation of healthcare professionals was established, it was assumed that healthcare professionals would practise in the same jurisdiction as the regulator, and both would be subject to the same laws and regulations.

In general the introduction and adoption of telehealth within a single jurisdiction does not within itself generate any particular novel regulatory challenges. For example, the provision of telehealth services in rural and remote areas. Whilst issues such as patient identification, confidentiality, and whether patients will actually follow the advice of healthcare professionals may be slightly more challenging than a typical patient/healthcare professional relationship, it does not require a regulator to take any special measures.

In a significantly larger jurisdiction, for example, British Columbia in Canada, the regulator of healthcare professionals and the law of the land are not compromised by size alone. This meant that before the advent of telehealth a healthcare professional based in Vancouver could only treat a patient in Fort Nelson General Hospital, located 1,009 miles to the north of Vancouver by physically travelling there. In both locations the same law prevails and the regulator, the College of Registered Nurses of British Columbia, is the same.

However, if the healthcare professional from Vancouver wanted to provide a service in Calgary, Alberta, they would have to obtain a second license. And the same constraints would apply to healthcare professionals practising in and across border areas.

PROVISION OF TELEHEALTH FROM ONE JURISDICTION INTO ANOTHER

Notwithstanding this when healthcare professional and patient are separated by distance and the service delivery is facilitated by telehealth and both reside in different jurisdictions a range of legal and regulatory challenges arise. In particular:

- The healthcare professional who is providing services via telehealth may not be subject to the standards of the regulator of the same healthcare professionals practising in the jurisdiction of the patient
- The healthcare professional who is providing services via telehealth may not possess the qualifications and/or experience that are required by the regulation in the patient's jurisdiction
- If things go awry with the provision of a service to a patient by a healthcare professional located in another jurisdiction, it may result in the inability of the law of the patient's jurisdiction to be applied to the healthcare professional
- Different legal and regulatory systems may have dichotomously opposed views on a particular issue, such that a work-related task of a healthcare professional may be legal in one jurisdiction and illegal in the other. This may result in the legal provision of a telehealth service being acceptable in one jurisdiction but illegal in a receiving jurisdiction

CHALLENGES TO REGULATORS FROM THE PROVISION OF TELEHEALTH SERVICES

The first challenge for those interested in the potential for regulating telehealth is an agreement of what constitutes telehealth. Unfortunately, there is little agreement and its definition differs across many jurisdictions.

Further challenges arise because:

- Telehealth services can be provided anonymously into the regulator's jurisdiction and a particular healthcare professional can't be linked to the service
- Telehealth services can be provided from a jurisdiction where the individuals providing the service are either not healthcare professionals or they are not regulated

For a typical member of the public if things go awry in their own jurisdiction it is challenging enough to resolve the situation by engaging with healthcare professionals, service providers and possibly regulators, and the legal profession. Unfortunately, when the delivery of telehealth is provided across the borders of a jurisdiction, if things do go awry, patients can be severely limited in their ability to seek redress.

For regulators, workable solutions are also challenging. These range from ignoring the issue, taking no overt steps to ban non in-person consultations, or seeking to ban it outright. However, no clear picture has yet emerged and, as a consequence, transgressors may go uncensored and financial compensation will remain unobtainable.

REGULATORY INTERVENTION RELATING TO THE PROVISION OF TELEHEALTH

Ideally, many regulators would like to have the ability to take action against professionals who do not meet their standards of competence and/or conduct and do not physically practise in their jurisdiction but provide telehealth services into the regulators' jurisdiction.

In this respect regulators are able to, and do, take action against a healthcare professional that they regulate who provides a service in another jurisdiction provided that the professional they regulate remains on their register. This is because, for example, a UK regulator can't take any action if the healthcare professional is no longer on the UK register.

However, for regulators to extend their reach, it seems that in the current moment in time there is only one workable solution. That is for them to seek to establish formal agreements with regulators who operate in other jurisdictions. In theory, the agreement would then stipulate that if a complaint arises against a healthcare professional who has provided a telehealth service from another jurisdiction, then the regulator of the healthcare professional will intervene and take action.

CONCLUSION

Telehealth delivers considerable benefits to many stakeholders. However, it does create unique challenges when the quality of the telehealth services delivered goes awry and the location of the healthcare professional and patient are in different jurisdictions. This has led to a small number of instances where the provision of telehealth services challenges the traditional principles and processes for regulating healthcare professionals. However, regulators can cooperate across borders if supported by formal agreements, so they can both jointly intervene if and when required.

EXERCISE AND QUESTION

Exercise

- Explain if the benefits of telehealth outweigh its disadvantages.

Question

- Explain to a politician what action a regulator can take if it can't identify a named professional who is providing telehealth services from another jurisdiction and the quality of the service is below expectable standards.

FURTHER READING

The Death of Distance 2.0: How the Communications Revolution will Change Our Lives B
Frances Cairncross
Texere Publishing; 2nd edition revised
ISBN-10: 158799089X
1 May 2001
320 pages

High Level Principles for Good Practice in Remote Consultations and Prescribing R
Co-authored by various UK regulators and others
November 2019
8 pages

On-line Consultations in General Practice: The Questions to Ask R
Royal College of General Practitioners
9 April 2018
7 pages

Regulatory Approaches to Telemedicine R
Europe Economics
17 January 2020
150 pages

STANDARDS, CODES, GUIDANCE, CONSULTATIONS, POLICIES, AND PRACTICE NOTES

Guidance

Guidance for Registered Pharmacies Providing Pharmacy Services at a Distance, Including on the Internet G
General Pharmaceutical Council
April 2019
24 pages

7.5 WORKFORCE PLANNING

INTRODUCTION

Workforce planning is undertaken by many organisations in the healthcare delivery system with the objective of forecasting the supply and demand for healthcare professionals and occupations. Other related topics for workforce planners to consider include the types of competences that practitioners should have in the future and the future capacity of educate and training programmes. The section considers how data held by regulators can be used to assist workforce planners tackle these types of issues.

WHAT IS WORKFORCE PLANNING?

Consider the following questions:

- How many nurses will be required to join the workforce in the next five years?
- How many dentists will retire over the next three years?
- What percentage of female junior physiotherapists between the age of 20 and 35 working in Hull are employed by for-profit organisations on a part-time basis?
- How many opticians should be trained in the next three years to work in Manchester compared to St Ives?
- Should society educate and train more doctors or, alternatively, physician associates?
- What competences should clinical scientists have in the future?
- Will paramedics trained outside the UK and now recruited to work on a temporary basis in the UK become permanent residents?
- What will be the net impact of emigrating and immigrating midwives over the next ten years?
- How will productivity gains in the healthcare workforce impact on service delivery?
- Will the 'trickle down' effect and roll substitution lead to productivity gains?
- Will artificial intelligence reduce the time taken by radiologists to interpret diagnostic imagery?

Workforce planning attempts to answer these types of questions so that the future supply and demand for particular categories of workers is in balance. It can be defined as:

Definition: Workforce Planning
Analysis and publication of the supply and demand for workforce competences.

It can be undertaken both by small and large organisations but also at a national and regional level by many stakeholders including employers, government, professional associations, and regulators.

REASON FOR UNDERTAKING WORKFORCE PLANNING

In economic terms, the various questions posed in the introduction to this section are all related to the issue of supply and demand for healthcare professionals. In the healthcare delivery system there are clear advantages in matching supply and demand. If it is in balance it should alleviate the pressure for wage increases where labour skills are scare and if it is not in balance, it should assist in stimulating the provision of adequate capacity for particular services.

WORKFORCE PLANNING IN A NON-COMPETITIVE MARKET

In competitive markets, government usually takes a minimal interest in undertaking workforce planning because market forces are assumed to facilitate the matching of supply and demand. For example, the UK Government does not attempt to centrally coordinate a process to match supply and demand for web site designers or piano players. Although this is the norm in the majority of economically developed countries, government does however take more interest in some more general areas, for example, the number of scientists being trained because the economic wellbeing of the nation is assumed to be linked to the availability of certain groups of workers.

WORKFORCE PLANNING IN THE HEALTHCARE DELIVERY SYSTEM

In stark contrast to competitive markets many governments frequently intervene directly in the healthcare delivery system market for both professionals and occupations. The reason for this is intervention is multifactorial and includes the following justifications:

- Importance of health to members of the public and the electorate
- Size and complexity of the healthcare delivery system
- Cost of the healthcare delivery system in relation to the GNP of a country
- Amount of resources and length of time required to educate and train healthcare professionals
- Direct funding by government of the education and training of healthcare professionals
- In the UK, the dominance of a healthcare delivery system funded at the point of use by the tax payer

- In the UK, the dominance of the NHS as an employer
- Percentage of the population employed in health
- Influence of the healthcare professions within the healthcare delivery system

Traditionally, in the UK the four NHSs attempt to match the supply and demand for healthcare professionals. This assumed that they could strongly influence the supply of professionals as it partly funded their education and training and it could control demand for healthcare professionals as it is the dominant employer. However, in recent years the UK governments have stepped back from directly funding the education and training of some healthcare professionals and instead the working of the markets is expected to balance the books. In 2025 the jury is still out on the success of this policy.

THE SUPPLY/DEMAND CHALLENGE

The central purpose of workforce planning is to match the future supply and demand for the services of healthcare professionals in a particular jurisdiction. For anyone considering undertaking this forecasting tasks, the factors that impact on both the future supply and the future demand for healthcare professionals should be understood. They include:

1. Age profile of employees
2. Continuing competence
3. Education and training capacity
4. Employers
5. Employment patterns
6. Professionals
7. Geographic distribution
8. Gender
9. Immigration and emigration
10. Internal migration
11. Job titles
12. Multi-employment
13. Part-time employment
14. Rates of pay
15. Retention rates
16. Retirement rates
17. Returners to practise
18. Sickness levels
19. Technology
20. Temporary employment
21. Unemployment rates
22. Voluntary employment

To expand:

1. **Age profile of employees**
   - By location
   - By employer

2. **Continuing competence**
   Resource allocation to continuing competence as it will impact the supply of professionals.

3. **Education and training capacity**
   This includes the number of existing and planned programmes, student attrition rates, graduate numbers, and an understanding of the destination of leavers from higher education (DLHE). The subject is explored in detail in Section 2.4, volume 2, funding and commissioning of E&T programmes.

4. **Employers**
   - Numbers, existing and planned and their location
   - Financial status
   - Employee numbers
   - Vacancy rates
   - Includes third sector and charities

5. **Employment patters**
   The historical norms of working for 40 hours per week from nine to five with four weeks paid holidays are a thing of the past. As a result the following issues now need to be taken into account:
   - Hours worked per year
   - Holding of dual roles, for example, clinical academics
   - Hours per year allocated to not treating patients. For example: management, research, education and training, and continuing competence
   - Proportion of a working life away from an occupation such as career breaks and maternity and paternity leave
   - Attrition rates for professionals leaving their profession applicable to different working patterns

6. **Professionals**
   - Number, both current and historical

7. **Geographic distribution**
   - Location of professionals by employer or residential postal address
   - Variation between urban conurbations and rural and remote locations

8. **Gender**
   - Changes in gender of the profession by age of the professionals
   - Gender geographic distribution

9. **Immigration and emigration**
   Includes both inwards and outwards movement across a jurisdiction's borders.
   - Number of healthcare professionals entering the jurisdiction
   - Permanent vs temporary emigration and immigration
   - Number of statements of professional standing issued to emigrating professionals

10. **Internal migration**
   - Impact of internal migration

11. **Job titles**
   Do job titles reflect the services delivered by practitioners?

12. **Multi-employment**
   Professionals working for more than one employer
   - Rate of changes in employer

13. **Part-time employment**

   Patterns of Part-Time Employment
   Percentages of professionals working part-time by gender and age.

14. **Rates of pay**
   Are pay demands being matched by employers?

15. **Retention rates**
   Length of time employees stay in a job or a particular employer

16. **Retirement rates**
   - Age of healthcare professionals fully retiring
   - Professional's intentions on when they may retire

17. **Returners to practise**
   Numbers, age, gender, and demographics of previously registered professionals re-joining the register. This may include those who have taken early retirement.

18. **Sickness levels**
   Period outside employment due to sickness and incapacity

19. **Technology**
   The impact on technology to either an increase in productivity leading to lower demand for labour or substitution by lower-skilled occupations compared to professionals at lower wage costs, the trickledown effect.

20. **Temporary employment**
   Many healthcare professionals are employed on a temporary basis, usually via an employment agency. This type of employment may be referred to as locums.

21. **Unemployment rates**
   Number and types of unemployed professionals who are seeking but can't obtain employment in the profession.

22. **Voluntary employment**
   Those individuals volunteering to work for no financial reward

CHALLENGES TO WORKFORCE PLANNING

There are a number of both challenging and contentious areas in workforce planning. They are as follows:

1. Sources of data
2. Access to data
3. Hard vs soft data
4. Workforce policy and workforce planning
5. International labour market
6. Internal labour market
7. Central planning
8. Skills mix
9. Redistribution of work-related tasks within the workforce
10. Productivity
11. Reallocate resources away from declining demands
12. Responsibility for workforce planning
13. Database

To expand:

1. **Sources of data**
   To undertake workforces planning analysts and researchers require access to accurate workforce data. The longer workforce data has been collected, structured, and retained, the greater its utility will be in producing

useable forecasts for workforce supply and demand. And, the data once collected can contribute to big data research; see Section 9.3, volume 4.

In relation to the healthcare delivery system there are a number of noteworthy organisations who collect and publish workforce data regularly and systematically. They include:

EU

The EU publishes data on the movement of numerous professionals in the *Regulated Professions Database*. The EU also supports the *Health workforce planning and forecast expert network*.

UK

NHS Digital publishes NHS workforce statistics for England.

In addition, it goes without saying that regulators' of healthcare professionals collect, retain, update, and manage and sometimes publish significant amounts of data workforce concerning the professionals they regulate.

In the UK data relating to the number of healthcare professionals can be obtained from five sources, namely:

- **i.** Education and training providers
- **ii.** Employers
- **iii.** Government and public authorities
- **iv.** Professional associations
- **v.** Regulators

2. **Access to data**

When considering accessing the data held by regulators that can be used in relation to workforce planning it is important to understand the relationship between the type of data collected by regulators and its accessibility.

The type of data held on a register of healthcare professionals is detailed in Section 4.1, volume 2. It falls into two broad categories. Firstly, public data that is available to all. Secondly, private data held by the regulator but not published on the register. What is critical to understand about the regulators' data is the approach they use to decide what data to collect for the register. If a 'need to know' approach is adopted the data can be relatively limited. For example, the register may contain no work address only a residential one. If on the other hand the regulator collects data, on a 'nice to know basis', the register can be significantly more useful in relation to workforce planning purposes. For example, historical employment data. It should also be noted that the accuracy of the data will be influenced by how frequently the professionals are required to update the data and to what degree they can do this on line and in real time.

When considering accessibility of data desired by organisations and individuals for workforce planning purposes, the regulator must ensure that confidential personal data is not inadvertently released. All data made publicly available must therefore be anonymised so that named individuals cannot be identified. These issues of accessibility can either be resolved within the legislation governing the regulator, or alternatively, the regulator developing and publishing a policy on access to regulators' databases; see Section 9.3, volume 4.

3. **Hard data vs soft data**

It is relatively straightforward to obtain hard workforce data such as the current number of registered healthcare professionals. However, obtaining soft data, for example, the retirement intentions of professionals, is more challenging. One solution is to use the tools of market research including focus groups, interviews, and surveys.

An example of this approach is undertaken at the Healthcare Workforce Data Centre of the Virginia Department of Professionals. Instigated by Dr Elizabeth Carter, the Data Centre collects, analyses, and publishes workforce data survey reports relating to healthcare professionals in the Commonwealth of Virginia each time a professional renews their registration. The surveys in the form of electronic questionnaires use standardised survey templates and are useful for collecting data in different jurisdictions so that results are comparable.

4. **Workforce policy and workforce planning**

Workforce planning tends to focus on 'hard' issues such as productivity, rates of pay, pensions, terms and conditions, the capacity of education and training programmes, and retirement trends.

In contrast, workforce policy focuses on issues such as:

- The culture of an organisation
- Flexibility of employees
- Flexibility of employers
- Adoption of innovation
- Quality and style of management
- Motivation of employees
- Job satisfaction

Both workforce policy and workforce planning should have a joint role to play in influencing demand and supply.

5. **International labour market**

The movement of healthcare professionals between regulatory regimes and the ethics of emigration and immigration are explored in Chapter 9, volume 3. In trying to attempt to forecast the supply and the demand for healthcare professionals the impact of emigration and immigration must be taken into account.

The reason for this is that healthcare delivery systems can't be seen in isolation to the rest of the world. In the majority of jurisdictions healthcare professionals and occupations may and do emigrate. At the same time government can encourage or discourage immigration of healthcare professionals and occupations.

6. **Internal labour market**
In a similar vein to trying to estimate the impact of emigration and immigration on the supply and demand for healthcare professionals and occupations, workforce planning should take into account any internal migration in the jurisdiction.

This may include the contrast between a metropolitan and rural and remote locations and the population's access to healthcare services and the implications for the recruitment and retention of healthcare professionals.

7. **Central planning**
Forecasting, predicting, and planning the demand for a workforce in the healthcare delivery system and how to supply it, is to say the least, not straightforward, easy or indeed possible.

For those interested in such matters there is an important lesson from history about the fable of a bureaucratic central planning regime unable to rely on market signals. In the Soviet era in Russia in the 1920s the Council of People's Commissars of Soviet Russia established a state planning function called *Gosplan*. As part of a 'planned economy' the concept and its execution had a number of inherent flaws. This included an inability to deal with productivity gains and how to reallocate resources away from areas of declining returns. One may face such a dilemma if you had to consider the impact of closing a small UK accident and emergency unit and then to relocate it into a larger hospital organisation.

Some will argue that planning for the future has to be tempered with the message that central planning does not work.

8. **Skills mix**
A particular demand for a healthcare service can be satisfied by deploying different combinations of professionals and occupations that can make use of their different portfolios of knowledge and skills. However, an increase in one, say surgeons, will not be effective, unless there is a corresponding increase in the number of operating theatre practitioners. In relation to workforce planning the challenge is identifying the most efficient combinations and ratios of available professionals and occupations.

9. **Redistribution of work-related tasks within the workforce**
This is the process of redistribution of work-related tasks among health workforce, in particular where high-cost labour supply is substituted by a low-cost providers. The issue is discussed in greater detail in Chapter 11, volume 2, Occupations and healthcare assistants. It raises two issues:

Firstly, how are decisions made to increase the supply of a particular profession when more than one profession can supply the service?

Secondly, when more than one profession can operate in the same area of the competence zone who will be allocated the task?

Practical examples of these issues are as follows:

- Should more doctors be trained to travel in emergency rescue helicopters in preference to paramedics?
- Should podiatric surgeons be employed rather than orthopaedic surgeons?
- Should the numbers of either triaging nurses or junior doctors be increased in accident and emergency departments of hospitals?
- Should radiographers be allowed to interpret images?

In theory a dispassionate analysis should be able to resolve these types of options, and civil servants or planning departments of the healthcare delivery system are well placed to furnish adequate answers. However, what about the position of professional associations? If their role is to advance the profession and in particular the position of their members, can they and will they provide dispassionate advice? This dilemma is explored in Sections 10.4 and 10.5, volume 2.

10. **Productivity**
Potential changes to workforce productivity triggered by changes in capital investment or use of technology and employment practices should all be taken into account.

11. **Reallocate resources away from declining demands**
Forecasting the decline in the provision of a service is challenging. For example, forecasting the impact on surgery by the work of Barry J Marshall and Robin Warren and on the bacteria *Helicobacter pylori* and its role in gastric and peptic ulcer disease and their rebuttal of conventional medical dogma.

12. **Responsibility for undertaking workforce planning**
Historically, in the UK many organisations undertake workforce planning often with little or no coordination or cooperation across the various stakeholders. In an attempt to address this deficit in 2008 the UK Government

established the Centre for Workforce Intelligence to facilitate workforce planning in the healthcare delivery system. Their role has now transferred to Health Education England.

Given the importance of the database by regulators, it raises the obvious question of whether or not they should have a formal requirement to undertake workforce planning in their legislation. Whilst some jurisdiction explicitly envisage a role in workforce planning for regulators, this is the exception rather than the norm.

For example, the Australian Health Professions Regulatory Agency (AHPRA) is required under Part 3 articles 18–22 of the Health Practitioner Regulation National Law Act 2009 Act, to establish a committee entitled the Australian Health Workforce (AHPRA) Advisory Council. National Boards in conjunction with the Department of Health are responsible for collecting and publishing information required for workforce planning through the registration renewal process as the National Health Workforce Dataset (NHWDS).

13. **Database**
Lastly, all organisations undertaking workforce planning need to consider the content and structure of their database and its consistency with others. This is because consistent databases facilitates comparisons with other healthcare professions databases both within the same and between different jurisdictions. They also need to decide to what extent they can use existing databases such as the registers of regulators of healthcare professionals and whether or not it will be supported by the use of voluntary or compulsory surveys on 'softer' issues such as the retirement intentions of the professionals.

CONCLUSION

The consequences for society of not being able to match the demand and supply of the workforce required by the healthcare delivery system are considerable. Failure of the process can lead to system failures as has occurred in the recent past in sub-Sahara Africa when government is unable to deliver a service. In the economically developed countries an imbalance can lead to wage inflation and shortages or reliance on agency staff, a problem that has been around for decades, a subject addressed by my late father Dr John R Seale in 1960s. The challenge for today's workforce planners is no longer a scarcity of data but how to make use of this big data.

EXERCISES AND QUESTIONS

Exercises

- In your jurisdiction, who and how is the decision made to increase the numbers of a particular profession in preference over another one?

Questions

- Should the legislation of regulators of healthcare professions require them to undertake workforce planning?
- Should regulators of healthcare professionals make anonymised data held on their registers freely available to interested parties?
- What conditions should be used by regulators make when supplying data from their register to external organisations or individuals?

LEGISLATION

Example of International Legislation

Australia

Health Practitioner Regulation National Law Act 2009 Act L

Part 3 articles 18–22

FURTHER READING

Allied Health Professions into Action R
NHS England
Chief Allied Health Professions Officer
Gateway number: 05863
January 2017
136 pages

Allied Health Services R
Avoiding Crises
National Academies of Sciences, Engineering, and Medicine
Institute of Medicine
The National Academies Press
ISBN: 978-0-309-03896-6
1989
361 pages

The Complexities of Physician Supply and Demand: Projections From 2019 to 2034 R
IHS Markit Ltd for Association of American Medical Colleges
21-023A (06/21)
June 2021
92 pages

Education, Training and Workforce Planning R
House of Commons Health Committee
First Report of Session 2012–13
HC 6-I
23 May 2012
74 pages

Equipping Health Workers with the Right Skills: Skills Anticipation in the Health Workforce R
OECD
ISSN: 25206125 (online)
15 December 2022
75 pages

EU Level Collaboration on Forecasting Health Workforce Needs, Workforce Planning and Health Workforce Trends – A Feasibility Study R
Revised Final Report
Matrix insight
29 May 2012
174 pages

Facing the Facts, Shaping the Future R
A draft health and care workforce strategy for England to 2027
Health Education England
September 2017
142 pages

Fit for Purpose – Workforce Policy in the English NHS R
The Health Foundation
ISBN: 978-1-906461
March 2016
47 pages

The Future Health Care Workforce R
David Cochrane
Project Steering Group
University of Manchester Health Services management Unit
ISBN-10: 0946250073
120 pages
May 1996

Global Shortage of Registered Nurses: R
An overview of Issues and Actions
International Council for Nurses
Buchan J Calman L
ISBN 92 950 40 120
January 2004
56 pages

Global Strategy on Human Resources for Health: Workforce 2030 R
World Health Organisation (WHO)
May 2014
43 pages

A Health Service of All the Talents: Developing the NHS Workforce Consultation Document on the Review of Workforce Planning R
Department of Health
Stationery Office, London
2000

Health Workforce Development An Overview R
Ministry of Health, New Zealand
April 2006
82 pages

High Quality Workforce R
NHS Next Stage Review
NHS (England)
Gateway Reference 10134
30 June 2008
55 pages

Horizon: 2035 – Health and Care Workforce Futures R
Centre for Workforce Intelligence
28 August 2015
15 pages

Interim NHS People Plan R
NHS
3 June 2019
76 pages

Key Changes in the Healthcare Workforce R
Rapid review of international evidence Report developed by The Evidence Centre for Skills for Health
Skills for Health
1 August 2011
124 pages

Managing the Supply of NHS Clinical Staff in England R
National Audit Office
HC 736
5 February 2016
52 pages

Medical Staffing Structures in Hospitals R
Platt Report
Ministry of Health Working Part
Chair Professor Sir Robert Platt
March 1961

NHS Long Term Workforce Plan R
NHS England
30 June 2023
153 pages

NHS Workforce: Summary of Staff in the NHS; Results from September 2014 Census R
Health and Social Care Information Centre
Kate Bedford, Bernard Horan
ISBN 978-1-78386-352-5
25 March 2015
32 pages

National Health Workforce Accounts – Handbook R
WHO
ISBN 9789241513111
12 April 2017
168 pages

Roadmap for Enhancing State Health Workforce Data: R
Implementation guide for the cross-profession minimum data set
Healthcare Regulatory Research Institute & Veritas Health Solutions
August 2023
24 pages

Supplying the Demand for Doctors R
The need to end the rationing of medical training places
Civitas: Institute for the Study of Civil Society
Edmund Stubbs
June 2016
19 pages

Supplying the Demand for Nurses R
The need to end the rationing of nurse training places
Civitas: Institute for the Study of Civil Society
Edmund Stubbs
November 2015
32 pages

Virginia's Audiologist Workforce: 2016 R
Healthcare Workforce Data Center
Virginia Department of Health Professions
January 2016
27 pages

Wakeham Review of Science, Technology, Engineering and Mathematics (STEM) Degree Provision and Graduate Employability R
Department for Business, Innovation and Skills
Sir William Wakeham
Ref: IND/16/6
16 May 2016
90 pages

Working Better with Age R
Synthesis Older Workers
Ageing and Employment Policies
OECD
ISBN: 978 92 64 40219 5
30 August 2019
80 pages

JOURNALS AND RESEARCH PAPERS

Gosplan JRP
Mark Harrison. University of Warwick. Published (in Italian) as 'Gosplan' in Dizionario del comunismo nel XX secolo. Volume primo, pp. 338–340. Edited by Silvio Pons and Robert Service. Turin: Einaudi, 2007

The Productivity of Physician Assistants and Nurse Practitioners and Health Work Force Policy in the Era of Managed Health Care JRP
Scheffler RM, Waitzman NJ, Hillman JM
Journal of Allied Health
25(3):207–217]
1 January 1996

Skill Mix in the Health Care Workforce; Reviewing the Evidence JRP
Buchan J Dal Poz Mario R
Bulletin of the WHO
2002; Vol 80–7, pages 575–580

History and Reform of Regulating Healthcare Professionals

CHAPTER 8

INTRODUCTION

The history of the development of the regulation of healthcare professionals is inextricably linked to the histories of the healthcare delivery system, the healthcare professions, and their education and training. Whilst these fields are somewhat on the periphery of the subject of the book, each has had an influence on the principles and processes of the regulation of healthcare professionals. A brief detour into each is therefore in order. The chapter then concludes by exploring what triggers governments to reform the regulation of healthcare professionals and the processes that they employ to achieve this.

The chapter has five sections:

8.1 History of the healthcare delivery system

8.2 History of the healthcare professions

8.3 History of the education and training of healthcare professionals

8.4 History of the regulation of healthcare professionals

8.5 Reforming the regulation of healthcare professionals

8.1 HISTORY OF THE HEALTHCARE DELIVERY SYSTEM

INTRODUCTION

There is a wealth of published books, reports, and research, on the history of the healthcare delivery system, in both the UK and the rest of the world. The section should therefore be seen as the briefest of introductions into what is a gigantic, fascinating, and absorbing subject.

In the UK the history of the healthcare delivery system can be undertaken by consideration of a number of its features from the 1850s to where it is at the start of the twenty-first century. At the beginning of the period the healthcare delivery system had the following features:

- The state had virtually no role in the healthcare delivery system
- Services were limited to those with the financial resources who could pay on a fee for service basis or others who could access charitable support
- Services were delivered by individual practitioners who possessed broad generalist knowledge and skills
- Individual providers predominantly worked as sole practitioners
- Hospitals and other service facilities, where they existed, were not complex organisations, often physically small and required minimal capital investment
- Practice was dependent on minimal scientific knowledge
- The understanding of how pathogens and medicines worked was minimal
- Demand for healthcare was not met due to lack of knowledge
- The system was town based
- In relation to the size of the UK's economy, the spending on the healthcare system as a share of the gross domestic product (GDP) was miniscule

175 years later at the start of the twenty-first century virtually every feature of the UK's healthcare delivery system has been radically overhauled and totally replaced.

- The state dominates the healthcare delivery system
- Services are usually available and are free at the point of use as they are universally funded by the state
- Healthcare is delivered by integrated multi-disciplinary teams of healthcare professionals
- Healthcare professionals have narrowly focused knowledge and skills
- Service facilities require large capital investment
- Scientific knowledge and discovery is at the epicentre of the system
- Some medicines are understood to the level of their relationship to the genetic makeup of individuals

Operations of Regulators of Healthcare Professionals, Volume 4, First Edition. Marc Seale.

Companion website: www.wiley.com/go/seale/regulatinghealthcare

- Demand for healthcare is not met due to lack of capacity
- The healthcare delivery system is a global enterprise
- In terms of economic size, the spending in the UK is now about 10% of GDP

IMPLICATIONS FOR THE REGULATION OF HEALTHCARE PROFESSIONALS

From the perspective of regulators of healthcare professionals every change in the healthcare delivery system has the potential to impact the professions they regulate. To identify the major trends that will impact the regulation of healthcare professionals the wheat must be separated from the chaff. This is a challenging task. For example, in a jurisdiction where the state manages the healthcare delivery system, how will the relationship between the professions and the state bureaucracy develop? Will it be one where the state and professionals are considered to be equal partners, or will the professions be seen as potential self-interested blockers of the proper management and rational allocation of funding of the system?

EXERCISES AND QUESTIONS

Exercises

- Choose one of the ten features of the healthcare delivery system that is highlighted and explore in greater detail how it changed over the last 175 years.
- Prepare scenarios, or undertake a horizon scanning exercise, for the healthcare delivery system in your jurisdiction.

Questions

- What evidence is there that the healthcare delivery system can be considered to be a global enterprise?
- How does your organisation consider and take account of potential changes in the healthcare delivery system?

FURTHER READING

Advancing our health: prevention in the 2020s R
Green paper
Department of Health and Social Care (UK)
ISBN: 978-1-5286-1545-7
22 July 2019
78 pages

Cost of Health B
Ffrangcon Roberts
Turnstile Press
1952
200 pages

Disease, medicine and society in England 1550–1860 B
Porter Roy
Cambridge University Press; 2 edition
ISBN-10: 0521552621
ISBN-13: 978-0521552622
14 September 1995
84 pages

Equity and Excellence: Liberating the NHS R
Department of Health UK Government White paper Cm 7881
ISBN: 9780101788120
July 2010
61 pages

Fit to Practice Empire, Race, Gender, and the Making of British Medicine, 1850–1980 B
Douglas A Haynes
Boydell & Brewer Ltd
ISBN 13 9781580465816
1 November 2017
256 pages

First Report of the Joint Working Party on the Organisation of Medical Work in Hospitals R
Sir George Godber Chairman
Ministry of Health
HMSO, London
August 1967

Five Year Forward Review R
NHS England
22 October 2014
41 pages

Health, Medicine and Mortality in the Sixteenth century B
Ed Webster, Charles
Cambridge University Press
ISBN 0 52122643 0
1979
393 pages

Health and Wellbeing: Delivering Together R
Ministry of Health (Northern Ireland)
16 May 2017
28 pages

A Hospital Plan for England and Wales R
HMSO
Cmnd. Paper 1604
January 1962
279 pages

Living History of Dentistry Witness Seminar 1T – The John McLean Archive B
Edited by Nairn Wilson and Stanley Gelbier
Published by the British Dental Association
ISBN978-1-291-72386-1
2014
88 pages

The making of the National Health Service B
King's Fund Historical Series
Pater, John E
Published by King Edward's Hospital Fund for London
ISBN 13: 9780900889844
1 January 1981
210 pages

Medicine and the Market in England and its Colonies c. 1830–c. 1850 B
Mark S. R. Dr Jenner (Editor), Patrick Wallis (Editor)
Palgrave MacMillan
ISBN-10: 0230506437
ISBN-13: 978-0230506435
1 October 2007
284 pages

A National Clinical Strategy for Scotland R
ISBN: 9781786520012
17 February 2016
88 pages

Next Steps on the NHS Five Year Forward Review R
NHS England
Gateway number: 06669
31 March 2017
75 pages

The NHS Long Term Plan R
National Health Service
7 January 2019
136 pages

NHS Plan R
A plan for investment, a plan for reform
Department of Health
Cm 4818-I
147 pages
1 July 2000

The new NHS modern dependable R
Department of Health
Cm 3807
ISBN 0 10 138072 0
8 December 1997
92 pages

New Politics of the NHS: B
From creation to reinvention
Klein, Rudolph
6th Edition
CRC Press
ISBN 10: 1846194091/ISBN 13: 9781846194092
2010
310 pages

Parliamentary Review of Health and Social Care in Wales R
Interim Report
July 2017
87 pages

Platt Report R
Medical Staffing Structures in Hospitals
Ministry of Health Working Party
Chair Professor Sir Robert Platt
March 1961

Revolution from Within: Transforming Health and Care in Wales R
The Parliamentary Review of Health and Social Care in Wales
January 2018
48 pages

Social Insurance and Allied Services – The Beveridge Report R
Sir William Beveridge
HMSO, London
Cmd 6404
ISBN 0108502767
20 November 1942
299 pages

Systems, Not Structures – Changing Health and Social Care R
Professor Rafael Bengoa (Chair)
Department of Health (Northern Ireland)
25 October 2016
92 pages

A Short History of Medicine B
Charles Singer and E Ashworth Underwood
Oxford University Press
Second Edition
ISBN10 0195001834
1962
854 pages

Working for Patients R
Department of Health
HMSO
Command paper 555
January 1989

8.2 HISTORY OF THE HEALTHCARE PROFESSIONS

INTRODUCTION

From pre-Christian Europe and the Indian subcontinent during the rule of Ashoka the Great, it is possible to trace the development of the healthcare professions, starting with the historical antecedents of today's doctors and nurses, through to the development of dozens of other healthcare professions. Over the millenniums the dominant changes have been the types and numbers of professionals and their social interactions and relationship with each other and the rest of society.

GROWTH

The dominant trend in the history of the healthcare professions has been the increase in both the different types of professions and the number of practitioners in each profession.

Even a cursory glance at the healthcare profession in any jurisdiction will identify that the number of different professions has increased over the last couple of centuries and that the trend in continuing and accelerating. At the same time, the total number of individual healthcare practitioners working in each profession has increased. For example, in the UK there were 18,000 general practitioners employed by the NHS in England in 1948 compared to 38,000 thousand in 2024. Compare this to the number of coal miners.

SEQUENCE OF THE EMERGENCE OF NEW HEALTHCARE PROFESSIONS

The history of the healthcare professions is dominated by the increase in both the development of novel professions and the total number of practitioners. Therefore, at the start of this section it is informative to consider the sequence of the emergence of new healthcare professions.

In ancient times there are records of bone setters, nurses, midwives, physicians, providers of medicinal substances, and surgeons. However, compared to modern times, the success of their interventions would be limited.

In the UK by the 1850s, the equivalent to today's nurses, midwives, pharmacists, physicians, and surgeons were clearly recognisable and to an extent well established in the workings of society. Although it should be noted that their titles were often somewhat different from today, for example, almoners, apothecaries, and barber surgeons. In addition, fields such as dentistry were not embedded in distinct and separate professions.

From the 1850s to the 1950s driven by developments on science and technology more professions have emerged. These include dentists and many other professions who historically were referred to as medical auxiliaries, allied healthcare professions (AHPs), professions allied to medicine, and professions supplementary to medicine. They included biomedical scientists, occupational therapists, physiotherapies, and radiographers. At the same time specialisation and sub-specialisation have continued apace across many professions, resulting, for example, in anaesthesiologists and psychiatric nurses.

Since the 1970s a third wave of professions has emerged, resulting in today's multi-professional workforce – some such as operating department practitioners who evolved from other professions, in this case the theatre nurses. Others include genetic councillors, paramedics and physician associates.

At the start of the twenty-first century, growth in the different types of healthcare professions continues apace particularly in the healthcare sciences, for example, geneticists.

DRIVERS FOR INCREASE IN NUMBERS OF HEALTHCARE PROFESSIONALS

The drivers for the increase in the number of healthcare professionals are threefold:

1. **Advancements in science and technology**
   As humankind's understanding of science increases and technology advances it has been harnessed to allow the introduction of new ways of treating disease and accidents. For example, Wilhelm Röentgen's discovery of the medical use of X-rays, the germ theory of disease, and the introduction of general anaesthetics fundamentally changed what the healthcare delivery system was able to achieve.

2. **Division of labour and specialisation**
   As discussed in Section 6.1, volume 2, Specialised practice, the limitations of an individual's knowledge and skills combined with the invisible pressures of the division of labour and the resulting in gains in productivity, led to a Balkanisation of the professions both in an increase in the number of different healthcare professionals and also specialisation and sub-specialisation of the different professions.

   At the same time specialisation has resulted in the need for the various healthcare professions to work together in multi-disciplinary teams.

3. **Societal changes to the healthcare professions**
   In parallel with the increase in the types and number of professions and professionals there have been fundamental changes to the societal aspects of the healthcare professions. This covers both the relationship between the healthcare professions and the rest of society and the relationship between the different healthcare professions. And for both, there are difference for each profession.

   So, for example, the social history of nursing in the UK is markedly different from that of the medical profession. Nursing has been strongly influenced by the dominance of the medical profession in the division of labour in the healthcare delivery system, the high percentage of women in the workforce, the subordination of women in the workplace, unequal power relationship with other healthcare professionals, and the employment relationship of nurses with the management of the NHS.

However, in recent times major changes have occurred. For example, the gender composition of the healthcare professions, which in some case was the exclusive domain of males, is no longer the case, as feminisation has occurred. As a result, where patriarchal, paternalistic, deferential, and hierarchical relationship structures were the norm and the medical profession was the dominant group, it has been gradually replaced by managerialism and multi-disciplinary teams.

CONCLUSION

The number of professions and the number of individual professionals are constantly increasing, as is the way that they socially interact with one another and society as a whole. In the same way that regulators must be cognisant of the future direction of travel of the healthcare delivery system, they should likewise consider how the professions will evolve in the future.

EXERCISE AND QUESTION

Exercise

- What difference has the feminisation of the medical profession made?

Question

- Will the number of different healthcare professions continue to grow?

FURTHER READING

50 Years of History B
Ian Moodie
The Society of Radiographers
77 pages

The Advance of the Dental Profession B
BDA
ISBN 0 902202 057
1979
289 pages

Allied Health Professions: A Sociological Perspective B
Nancarrow S and Borthwick A
Policy Press
978-1447345367
10 March 2021
252 pages

The Changing Character of the Medical Profession: An International Perspective B
Frederic W. Hafferty (Editor), John B. McKinlay (Editor)
Oxford University Press Inc, USA
ISBN-10: 0195075927
ISBN-13: 978-0195075922
30 December 1993
272 pages

Florence Nightingale B
The Women And Her Legend
Mark Bostrifge
Viking
21 October 2008
ISBN 9780670874118
647 pages

Hippocratic Oaths B
Raymond Tallis
Atlantic Books, London
ISBN 1 84354 126 2
2004
342 pages

History of the British Medical Association – 1832–1932 B
Little, Ernest Muirhead
British Media Association/Harrison and Sons Ltd
ISBN 07279 0092 7
Volume I 1932 342 pages
Volume II 1932–1981 375 pages

A History of the Nursing Profession B
Abel-Smith B
Heinemann Educational Publishers
ISBN 13 978 0435320041
7 January 1960
304 pages

In Good hands B
The History of the Charted Society of Physiotherapists 1894–1994
De Jean Barclay
Butterworth Heinemann
ISBN 0 7506 1745 4
1994
367 pages

The Making of the English Legal Profession 1800–1988 B
Richard L Abel
Beard Books Washington D.C.
ISBN 10: 1-58798-250-1
1988 – Reprinted 2005
548 pages

The Maturing Years B
A History of the Society and College of Radiographers 1970–1995
Jordan, M
ISBN 0 9503597 1 8
96 pages
1995

Medical Dominance B
Willis E
ISBN 13: 9780198257950
Allen and Unwin, Sydney
1983
256 pages

Medical Practice in Modern England: The Impact of Specialization and State Medicine B
Stevens, Rosemary
ISBN-10: 0765809567
ISBN-13: 978-0765809568
Transaction Publishers
7 Feb 2003
435 pages

The Medical Profession in Upper Canada 1783–1850: B
Canniff, William
Publisher: William Briggs
1894
688 pages

Nursing in Context: Policy, Politics, Profession B
Michael Taylor
ISBN 978-0-230-36873-6
Palgrave Macmillan
2013
174 pages

Occupational Monopoly and Modern Medicine B
Larkin G V
Tavistock
ISBN 13 978-0422783002
5 May 1983
220 pages

Open Wide B
Memoires of a Dental Dame
Dame Margaret Seward
Memoir Club publishers
2009
322 pages

The Physician Assistant: An Illustrated History B
Piemme T, Sadler A, Carter R and Ballweg R
Acacia Publishing Inc. Arizona, USA
ISBN – 978 1 935089 64 3
May 2013
113 pages

Powers of the Professions in Britain 1700–1850 B
Corfield, PJ
Routledge
ISBN 9780415222655
11 November 1999
280 pages

Professional Men – Rise of the Professional Classes in the Nineteenth-Century England B
Reader W J
Weidenfeld and Nocolson
1 January 1966
248 pages

The Professions in Early Modern England, 1450–1800 B
Servants of the Commonwealth (Themes in British Social History)
O'Day, R
Routledge
ISBN 9780582292642
21 November 2000
352 pages

Professions in Theory and History: Rethinking the Study of the professions B
Burrage M, Torstendahl
Sage, London
ISBN: 978-0803982529
21 May 2090
256 pages

The Rise of the Medical Profession: A Study of Collective Social Mobility B
Parry N Parry J
Croom Helme
ISBN-10: 085664224X
ISBN-13: 978-0856642241
April 1976
282 pages

The Rise of Professional Society, England Since 1880 B
Perkin Harold
Routledge; 2 edition
ISBN-10: 0415301785
ISBN-13: 978-0415301787
31 October 2010
632 pages

Role of Psychologists in the Health Service R
1977
HMSO, London

The System of Professions B
An Essay on the Division of Expert Labour
Abbot, Andrew
University of Chicago Press
ISBN 13 978-0226000695
15 August 1988
452 pages

8.3 HISTORY OF THE EDUCATION AND TRAINING OF HEALTHCARE PROFESSIONALS

INTRODUCTION

As education and training develops and evolves over time it has a direct influence on the healthcare professions, the healthcare delivery system, and in turn, their regulation. However, the field is beyond the scope of the book. Despite this, a brief introduction is provided on the history of the development of the education and training of healthcare professionals.

TRENDS IN THE HISTORY OF EDUCATION AND TRAINING OF HEALTHCARE PROFESSIONALS

The history of the UK's education and training of healthcare professions is explored by identifying six trends. They are:

1. Type and location of education and training
2. Level of academic attainment
3. Funding of programmes of education and training
4. Capacity of the system to education and train healthcare professionals
5. Funding of students
6. Quality assurance of education and training programmes

1. **Type and location of education and training**
   Today, the norm in the UK is that the majority of student healthcare professionals undertake their education and training at two different organisations often based at different locations, namely, university and at their future place of work.

   Historically, this was not the case and there were three different routes for those seeking to join a healthcare profession.

   The first route was used by student physicians. They were required firstly to hold a degree award by a university. However, since there were no formal academic qualifications in medicine, their education focused on the classics and ancient medical theory and practice. This was then followed by an apprenticeship with a physician. Then, in parallel with the advancement of science and technology, this evolved into the requirement to attend formal education and training initially at large hospitals. Lastly, the university campuses education component of classical education was replaced with the science of healthcare.

   The second route consisted of an initial period of education and training in the form of an apprenticeship, similar to a UK trainee solicitor undertaking articles or a pupil barrister in the 1930s. However, there was no pre-requirement to have completed a university education and to hold a degree. On completion of the apprenticeship, many, but not all, were required to join a professional association after successfully passing an examination.

   The third route, used for example, the education and training of nurses, historically assumed that it was not necessary to have completed any formal education and training and the process relied solely on learning by doing. Matters radically evolved following the successful efforts of Florence Nightingale, and over time the route into nursing shifted when students were required to attend training schools attached to hospitals. Gradually, a second major development occurred when the education and training shifted to universities.

2. **Level of academic attainment**
   The second trend has been the movement from when candidates who wanted to enter the profession were not required to hold an academic qualification to one where possession of a degree or at a minimum a diploma is now predominant.

3. **Funding of programmes of education and training**
   The length and complexity of educating and training healthcare professionals has resulted in the high cost of providing E&T programmes. As a result, the costs act as a barrier to enter the healthcare professions and can act as a deterrent to prospective students unless they can obtain financial support. As a consequence, over time government has become a contributor to the funding of many of the programmes of education and training of healthcare students.

4. **Capacity of the system to educate and train healthcare professionals**
   In the UK, until the 1950s virtually all healthcare professionals were educated and trained in the UK. However, since then the UK's capacity to educate and train healthcare professionals has been unable to match demand. This has resulted in the immigration of healthcare professionals into the UK particularly from predominantly less well economically developed countries.

5. **Funding of students**
   There has been a trend from student healthcare professionals' self-funding their education and training to them relying on financial grants provided by government.

6. **Quality assurance of education and training programmes**
   The sixth trend has been a movement from a position where there was no external quality assurance of the providers of education and training programmes, to one where multiple organisations undertake QA.

IMPLICATIONS FOR THE REGULATION OF HEALTHCARE PROFESSIONALS

The education and training of healthcare professionals has and is undergoing continual change. Whether it is the use of apprenticeships, MOOCs, or technology, regulators must keep abreast of developments to ensure that their processes and standards can accommodate future changes.

EXERCISE AND QUESTION

Exercise

- Over the next ten years, how do you envisage that the education and training of healthcare professions will evolve?

Question

- What would you change in the current process to educate and train healthcare professionals? Explain your reasoning.

FURTHER READING

Time to Heal: American Medical Education from the Turn of the Century to the Era of Managed Care B
Ludmerer, K M
Oxford University Press
ISBN-13: 9780195181364
11 November1999
544 pages

JOURNALS AND RESEARCH PAPERS

Getting a Medical Qualification in England in the Nineteenth Century JRP
Rivlin J. J.
Medical Historian, 9(1997):56–63
1997

8.4 HISTORY OF THE REGULATION OF HEALTHCARE PROFESSIONALS

INTRODUCTION

The development of the regulation of healthcare professionals has evolved over centuries. And although the pace of change varies between countries and professions, it can be seen to pass through six stages.

THE ERAS OF REGULATION

Looking back of the centuries in the UK it is possible to discern a sequence of seven eras, namely:

1. Ancient associations
2. Medieval guilds
3. Tudor state intervention
4. Voluntary membership organisations
5. Professional statutory self-regulation
6. Profession-led statutory regulation
7. Consumer-oriented regulation

The seven eras are depicted in Chart 8.4 – I, below:.

The seven eras will now be explored:

1. **Ancient associations**

For most of ancient history and before any significant scientific developments occurred, there is little evidence that health professionals formed associations for their economic and political advancement.

However, in the Greek and Roman eras, there were private associations or *collegia* that were linked to either civil or religious institutions. There is also some limited evidence that they acted to control markets to the benefit of their members. Again, during the Byzantine Empire particularly in the City of Byzantium, organisations similar to the Roman Collegia are referred to in *The Book of the Prefect*, c 900, that controlled trade and manufacturing.

However, it is difficult to gauge the economic or social influences that such organisations had, given the size of the population and volume of traded goods. Although it is contentious, there is some evidence of links between the Collegias and the emergence of the medieval guilds.

As an adjunct, the ancient Romans Cicero and Seneca developed the concept that activities that required learning such as of lawyers, physicians, and teachers should be the preserve for 'free men' or *artes liberales*. All other activities were called *operae illiberales*. Thus, there is

Chart 8.4 – I **Eras of the regulation of healthcare professionals**

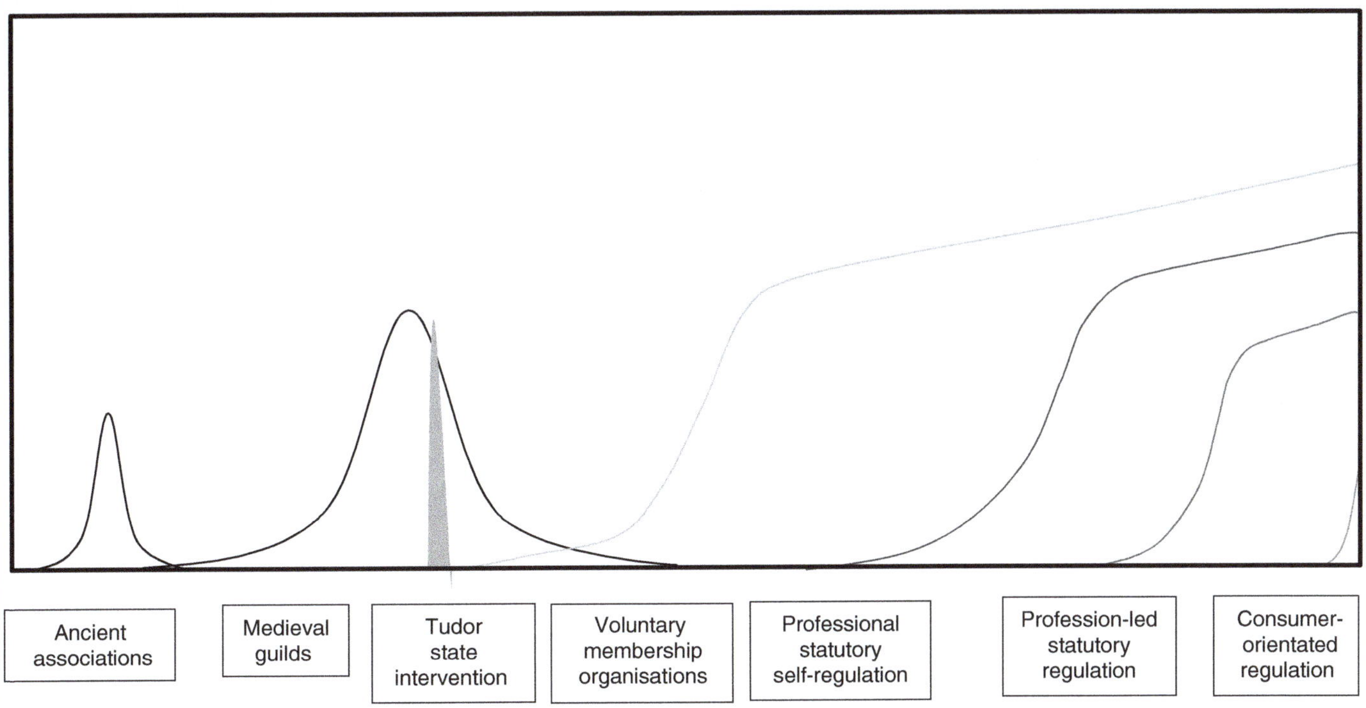

an argument that the evolution of the term liberal professions can be traced to these times. Of further interest in this area is that the Codex Theodosianus, Theodosian Code published in AD 438, makes reference to the control of the remuneration and practice of physicians.

Economic impetus to establish guilds

In parallel with the growth of the number and size of towns in the tenth century the trade in goods increased. This growth in trade offered financial incentives to those who could either create or control monopolies. Firstly, political rulers if they were able to sell markets as franchise, could extract financial rewards without the need to become directly involved in the management of the particular market. Secondly, those who were able to establish exclusive rights to operate and access monopolistic retail markets, could likewise extract excess financial rewards. This was particularly important in relation to either the import of goods into defined localities such as inside the walls of a city, or for those who manufactured goods again in a defined locality. It follows that, the more that external competition was limited, the greater the financial rewards.

Thus, there were huge economic and social incentives for associations of merchants and craftsmen operating in individual towns and cities to band together to advance their cause preferably backed-up with the power of their political patrons. The environment for the establishment of guilds was ripe for exploitation.

2. **Medieval guilds**

Under these types of market conditions, the more influential associations sought to establish themselves as guilds.

A guild can be defined as:

Definition: Guild
Association of persons of the same trade or purist, formed to protect mutual interests and maintain standards using their economic and social power.

Then, over time, if the guilds were able to negotiate successfully with either the powerful individuals or institutions of the era, such as monarchs or city corporations, they could establish in law monopolies for the provision of their services by purchasing grants of letters patents. These monopolies established by the guilds would embrace distinct geographical areas that were usually limited to a particular city or town, although the majority of towns had no guilds. Interestingly, guilds were a global phenomenon and were established in Europe, Japan, and Latin America.

Guilds were established for a broad spectrum of occupations but mainly, manufacturing, merchants who traded in commodities and retailers. Compared to the modern world guild members tended not to be providers of services but focused on manufacturing and distribution. In the UK they were an important component of civil society for seven centuries from the time of William the Conquer to the reign of George III.

In the larger cities the number of guilds increased steadily, resulting a plethora of guilds ranging from silversmiths to clockmakers and vintners. Over the centuries they often amassed considerable economic and social power. In the City of London there were over one hundred guilds or Livery companies. In some crafts fractionalisation increased the number of guilds still further.

There were also guilds for other groups, for example, religious orders and the embryonic health professions. In the UK examples of London guilds relating to the healthcare delivery system of the day are included in Table 8.4 – I, below:

Table 8.4 – I Guilds of the City of London relating to the healthcare and date of formation

Guild of City of London	Date of formation
Barbers and surgeons, City of London Livery Company	1308
Royal College of Barber Surgeons of Edinburgh	1505
Guild of surgeons	1368
The Worshipful Company of Spectacle Makers	1629
Mistery of Grossers, Pepperers and Apothecaries	1365
(Previously, the Guild of Pepperers)	1180
Society of Apothecaries	15 Dec 1673

The guilds were secretive and financially powerful. They were anti-comparative and used a welter of classic monopolistic tools including:

- Restricting the number of manufacturers and/or providers of goods or services within given locations, thus limiting supply
- Control of access to raw materials
- Price-fixing by market participants
- Limiting the number of individuals practising each occupation by requiring new entrants to undertake long periods of education and training or apprenticeships
- Restricting the introduction of new technology

Other common misdemeanours included:

- Corrupt systems of education and awards of qualifications
- Discrimination

However, membership of the guild's cartel brought not only economic advantages but also social esteem and political influence particularly in relation to local city government. Excess from profits from the economic rent seeking was then used to reinforce the powers of the guilds.

It can also be argued that the guilds did enforce quality standards that had advantages to consumers and the system of apprentices provided a highly trained and skilled workforce.

Cordwainers and city walls

So how did the medieval world dominated by guilds look like?

Let's take the manufacture, distribution of selling of shoes as an example. Before the industrial revolution a shoe maker could handcraft about one pair of shoes a day. Working from home in a classic cottage industry with little investment in any capital manufacturing equipment or stocks of goods, cobblers or cordwainers would have made shoes to order for the intended wearer rather than for stock. They would undertake all the processes required to make shoes, from cutting leather the new leather, shoetree manufacturing, and stitching.

If a number of cordwainers were able to join forces, they might pursued their city council or local Lord to grant them the right in law the exclusive right to make and sell shoes in a defined geographic area, for example, inside the walls of the said city. For the monopoly or charter, they, in return, paid an annual financial payment. The city council or Lord was able to support the monopoly by prosecuting any one breaking the terms of the charter. The guild would then restrict new entrants by not allowing the establishment of new independent shoe makers without a substantial payment to the guild.

They also required apprentices to train for many years but only with established members of the guild and provided they were men and were not immigrants from another country. They may also have required that all leather was purchased via their guild, or alternatively they may have established with another guild to be an exclusive supplier.

Competition between members of the guild was limited in that prices were in effect controlled by the guilds. There may have been some competition from cobbles established some distance away from the city, but large-scale imports would have been restricted, so potential customers looking to transact small purchases would have had to travel to distance suppliers to break the monopoly.

In return for the guilds' monopoly, consumers would receive, it was argued by the guilds, a better quality of new shoes for a given price, although lack of fast communication restricted the ability of citizens to learn about prices or quality in other markets.

Decline of guilds

In the sixteenth-century market liberalisation, the removal of monopolies, increasing international free-trade and non-guild competition, started to reduce the influence of the guilds. Scientific and technological advancements in the seventeenth century including the industrial revolution and the replacement of hand by machine manufacturing, intercity transport by canal and then the railways, acted as the final nails in the coffin for the power and influence of guilds. The world of superstition and mysticism was replaced by the rational. In the UK but less so in Europe, they became insignificant and citizens could pursue any occupation or establish business without permission from government or quasi-government authority. In the UK the guilds have metamorphosed into over 100 Livery Companies but are predominantly social and charitable organisations. Interestingly, the decline of the influence of European guilds was in some instances slow, and a few surviving well into the twentieth century.

In relation to the cordwainers, the introduction of factory mechanisation and the subdivision of unskilled labour from 1800 onwards resulted in an increase in quality of shoes, the lowering of prices, and a massive increase in the size of the market.

However, the guilds left a number of legacies. Many European cities are endowed with the history, halls, and grand buildings of the guilds. In the City of London the Worshipful Company of Cordwainers founded in 1272 still survives.

In relation to the regulation of healthcare professionals, the reasons for the general high level of disquiet by citizens in medieval times of the guilds still linger even in the modern era. In particular, some of the advantages and disadvantages of the justification for regulating healthcare professionals that are identified in Section 7.1, volume 1, hark back to the practices of the medieval European guilds.

What is of interest to those studying the history of the regulation of healthcare professionals is that it teaches us that guilds did not just neatly metamorphose into professional associations. Rather, it teaches us that the monopolistic control of markets has wide-reaching benefits to the holders of the monopoly and a level of detriment to those who have no choice other than to use services provided by monopolistic markets.

3. Tudor state intervention

In the UK during the predominance of the guilds, the first intervention by the state into the workings of the market for health occurred in 1421. A petition to Parliament during the reign of Henry V (1386–1422), from the universities of Oxford and Cambridge to restrict the practice of medicine to their graduates of physics. It also proposed excluding women from practising physic.

However, no legislation resulted.

In 1509, Henry VIII (1457–1509) came to the throne and six acts of Parliament were in due course enacted that related to the practice of medicine:

i. The first act of 1513/14 required physicians and surgeons to hold a licence. In London they were to be issued by Bishop of London and the Dean of St Pauls and outside by the Bishop of the Diocese. Applicants were to be examined by experts in physic and surgery. Graduates of the universities of Oxford and Cambridge were exempt. Unlicensed practitioners could be fined £5 per month. Interestingly, the legislation was only repealed in 1948.

ii. A second act of 1523 exempted the warden and fellows of the Company of Barber Surgeons from what was in effect military service.

iii. The third act of 1523 set parameters on the College of Physicians. In particular concerning their education and examination in physic or medical drugs.

iv. The fourth act in 1530/31 restricted competition from 'foreigner' competition.

v. The penultimate act, enacted in 1540, united the company of barbers and surgeons. The act stipulated the requirement for the members of the company to advertise their place of work.

vi. The last and sixth act of Henry VIII reign that came into force in 1542 extended the ability of non-surgeons to administer medicines relating to specific diseases.

It is possible to discern in six acts the genesis of the principals and process of today's regulation of healthcare professionals, for example, the standards to enter the profession, restriction of title and functions, advertising and unauthorised practitioners.

At the same time it should be remembered that the size of the then English healthcare delivery system was miniscule in comparison to today's monolith. For example, only 150 medical degrees were awarded by the University of Cambridge in the whole of the sixteenth century. In particular the medical colleges/guilds had limited resources and few members.

As a result the church played the major role of today's regulators of healthcare professionals, in that they examined candidates to join the professions, issued licences, and pursued and fined those practising without a licence. Their central role was supported by access to their own court system and an extensive organisation spread throughout the country of well-educated and trained personnel. These arrangements continued in the UK for the next two centuries. Meanwhile science and the professional associations grew and prospered.

4. Voluntary membership organisations

In Western Europe at the end of the eighteenth century during the age of enlightenment the philosophy of liberalism was developed by John Locke and others. This initiated a seismic shift to reduce the role of the state in the control of intellectual thinking, which in turn lead to the rise of the liberal professions.

In parallel, with the decline and influence of the guilds, the rise of the scientific societies gained momentum, followed by what we now refer to as voluntary membership organisations or the professional associations took place.

It was the age of enlightenment and scientific discovery. In this fast-changing environment society was able to organise itself as groups of individuals who got together to establish organisations whose members shared a common interest. Over time the fledgling organisations started to mature, and annual membership fees were imposed to pay for the running costs of the organisation. At first there was no way that membership could be made compulsory, but over time sets of standards were developed that prospective members were required to achieve them. As membership of the voluntary membership organisations increased the more they were able to influence the education, practice, and employment of their membership. The higher the percentage of all who were potentially members, the greater the influence the organisations were able to exert on the rest of society.

Although sometimes conveniently forgotten by vocal single-issue pressure groups (SIPGs), historically, regulation was instigated not by government or consumer organisations, but by the professions themselves. In Europe from the seventeenth century, the emerging healthcare professionals, building on the structure of the guilds whose power and influence was on the wane particular in the UK, started to delineate themselves from the uneducated rogues and charlatans, by establishing clear standards of education and training and were thus able to provide a better service to their patients in terms of probable treatment outcomes based on the emerging sciences, compared to probable outcomes from alternative treatments.

The benefit to the public of the emerging healthcare professions was increased by their ability to control entry to the profession by requiring completion of formal education and training, to exclude incompetent practitioners from their registers by reference to specific standards and the public's ability to identify those practitioners who should meet these standards by reference to a publicly available register.

As a consequence of these exacting standards, particularly the standards of education and training, the standing of the medical profession was enhanced and economic and political benefits ensured. The level of trust established between the medical profession and members of society was and remains outstanding and in many surveys of level of trust between different groups comes out on top in clear contrast to politicians, journalists, and estate agents. This had the benefit to the professions of enhanced social prestige, social standing, and social respectability. In numerous situations a process can be observed overtime of the increased upward social mobility of a profession has been achieved. In addition, the professions gained economic advantages compared to other members of society. Note the profession as a whole, not individual professionals.

However, in due course the social and economic advantages led other sectors of society to question of these unfettered benefits.

Ironically, the possibility then started to arise that due to their increasing influence the professional associations were able to gain limited statutory powers from the state, and the next stage of the regulation of healthcare professional started to emerge.

To signal their status and to gain prestige, some professional associations gained, and still continue to gain, Royal Charter Status.

These effects were then enhanced if government was persuaded by the profession to transfer powers from the state to the professional association so that it could use the law in its own right to back up its powers in relation to protecting access to the register, professional titles, and the key standards such as education and training. This legislative introduction process continued with the Apothecaries Act 1815, followed by the establishment of the GMC in 1858.

5. **Professional statutory self-regulation**
One relatively foolproof way to control access to the labour market was, like the guilds, for the voluntary membership organisations to persuade the state to enact legislation to establish laws to erect barriers to enter relevant the market. Only members of the associations could participate in the market.

Four challenges arose in this process that required cooperation between the professions and the lawmakers. They were:

   i. How to enforce the decision of the professional associations?

   ii. How to limit market access and signal membership?

   iii. How to demonstrate benefits to the state from the relationship?

   iv. How to prevent the use of the professional title by non-members?

As the strength of a voluntary membership organisation increases it is better able to extract concessions from government. This is because government is willing to proscribe powers to the organisation because society reaps clear benefits from the relationship in terms of quality. The powers usually relate to the framework for regulating healthcare professionals and focus on the standards and process of regulation and are limited in that they only apply to those individuals who are members of the voluntary organisation. In other words, there are still individuals undertaking similar functions but do not have to be members. There is therefore not a total monopoly.

To achieve these ends the need for a partnership based on a symbiotic relationship between state and the professions started to be established in the UK at the beginning of the nineteenth century, and the principles and processes used for the first time then are still maintained and in evidence today.

Apothecaries act 1815
The Apothecaries Act represents the first example in the UK of legalisation that bridges the transformation of the progenitor medieval system of guilds into primary legislation. The Act came into force on 12 July 1815. Its primary purpose is to in effect amend the Society of Apothecaries' Royal Charter into an Act of Parliament.

Apothecaries were shopkeepers who dispensed and sold medicines. They also fulfilled prescriptions from members of the Royal Colleges. Think a fifteenth century version of *Boots the Chemist*. They also visited the sick and ill at home. Many also acted as surgeons.

The apothecaries were originally a City Livery Company, incorporated by Royal Charter in 1617 when they split from the Grocers Livery Company. The Grocers, established in 1345, were responsible for spices.

The act is noteworthy in that many of its 31 clauses introduced for the first time many regulatory concepts that are at the core of statutory regulation over two hundred years later. For example, the keeping of a register and the legal requirement for prospective registrants to complete a course of education and training before entering the examinations to join the profession.

The act's main regulatory clauses are summarised in Table 8.4 – II.

Table 8.4 – II Apothecaries Act – articles
The Apothecaries Act 1815, Act of the Parliament of the United Kingdom (citation 55 Geo.III, c.194).

The table summarises the significant regulatory clauses that using the language of a modern regulator.
III
Permits entry and inspection of shops.
IV
Requires examiners and inspectors to have been members of the Society for at least ten years.
V
Requirement to provide prescriptions authorised by physicians. Failure to provide service will result in fines and potentially loss of certificate. Also mention undertakings following an offence.
VI
Permits the appointment of deputies
VII
Extends the remit of the Act from London to the whole of England and Wales
VIII
Requirement for the Society to meet or assemble to enable its powers to be legal.
IX
Appoints examiners and frequency of exams.

(*Continued*)

Table 8.4 – II (Continued)

X	Appointment of Chairman of examiners with casting vote.
	Also makes specific reference to Assistants to apothecaries.
XIV	Requirement to sit examination to become an apothecary. Those already practising when Act coming into force, 1st August 1815, do not have to sit examination. In effect a grandparenting clause.
XV	Requires five years of apprenticeship before sittings examination, be over twenty one, and have a character reference.
XVIII	Establishes a regional structure to examine assistants by holding meetings at least once a month.
XIX	Sets fees for examination and certificates for apothecaries working exclusively in London, outside London and Assistants, ten guineas, six guineas, and four and two guineas.
XX	Penalty fee of £20 for practising without a certificate. Assistants must serve apprenticeship or penalty of £5.
XXII	Establish ability to re-sit examination but within time limits.
XXIII	Register to be published each year.
XXIV	Examination fees belong to the Society.
XXV	Fines to be split 50:50 between the Society and complainants.
XXVI	Allows the charges to be placed on property to recover fines
XXVIII	Defines the scope of function of chemists and druggists and excludes them both from the Apothecaries Act
XXIX	Protects the scope of practice of graduates of the Universities of Oxford and Cambridge and members of the Royal College of Surgeons and the Royal College of Physicians.
XXX	Limits the period when action can be taken against transgressors. Fitness to practise (FTP) has to take place in the locality of the defendant and if the case is not proved the regulator has to pay them twice their costs.

The Act established a number of interesting regulatory principles. One is particularly noteworthy, in that the state granted a monopoly to a profession but then facilitated the profession to administer the monopoly on behalf of the state. At this point the principle of professional statutory self-regulating was established.

However, in 1858 the limited statutory powers assigned to a healthcare profession were considerable enhanced when the Medical Act came into force.

Medical Act 1858

The act was established on the 2nd August 1858 by the General Council of Medical Education and Registration of the United Kingdom. It enabled the setting of education standards, a register protection of title – medical practitioner and FTP/disciplinary processes that could removing individuals from the register. The Medical Act was subsequently amended in 1876 and 1886.

It should be noted that the vast majority of the board were members of the profession. However a small number of board members would be drawn from educational institutes and civil servants.

6. **Profession-led statutory regulation**

In the UK for 125 years from the 1850s to the 1980s, the model of regulation of healthcare professionals by profession statutory self-regulation was relatively stable and slowly evolved with no fundamental or radical changes.

However, in modern times a number of drivers for change started to surface and gradually came to the forefront.

It could be argued that the profession statutory self-regulation tended to have an insular relationship with their stakeholders, and contact with them was deliberately limited. As a result, there was an imbalance in the regulatory contract. In particular a perception that the professions were beset by conflicts of interest when they completely controlled the statutory regulation of their own profession and that their default position was one of '*looking after themselves*' and self-interest, rather than the public

For example, in the UK until the mid-1990s regulators focused on the conduct and behaviour of the professions with scant attention to their knowledge and skills. Only when the Medical (Professional Performance) Act 1995 was introduced, did the GMC start to take an interest in the competences of the medical profession via the publication of guidance on the duties of a doctor that in time evolved into today's *Good Medical Practice.*

As a result in a growing number of jurisdictions lay members of the board were introduced or increased but strictly remained a minority resulting in the emergence of profession-led statutory regulation.

7. **Consumer-oriented regulation**

Despite these changes, the continued trends in society such as consumerism have resulted in ever-increasing pressure for a clear separation of the regulators and the professional associations. And in particular the imposition of the inability of the professional association to control the regulator by board domination.

It is also interesting to speculate if the growth in both the number of different professions and the number of individual members of each profession brought attention to any deficiencies in the regulatory contract.

As a consequence, a gradual metamorphosis of profession-led statutory regulation has occurred in some jurisdictions, to be replaced by consumer-oriented regulation, where the ratio of professional members to lay is either 50:50 or, alternatively, in the minority.

TIMELINES

To assist the reader five timelines of various UK healthcare professions including the dentists, medical practitioners, nurses and midwives, and optomertrists and other healthcare professionals including physiotherapists and radiographers are now provided. Charts 8.4 – II to 8.4 – VI detail significant regulatory events relating to each profession listed in chronological order such as the introduction of legislation and the establishment of professional associations.

Chart 8.4 – II **Timeline dentists**

		Dentists	
Year	Month	Event	
1858		Medical Act	General Medical Council (GMC) established
1875		Dental Reform Commiittee	Sir John Tomes
1878		Dentist Act	Protects Dentis as a professional title but not the function of dentristry
1879		Dental Rergister first published	
1885		Dental Defense Union established	
1890		Representation Board	Established
1917		Dyke Committe of Enquiry	
1918		Dentis' Register	
1921		Dentist Act	Dental Board of the UK established woth overriding control of the GMC
			Protection of dentisty function introduced
1923		Dental Dressers abolished	
1932		Dental Act amended	
1947		New Dentist Bill	
1948		NHS established	
1949		Dental Professiona Bodies amalgemated	Publci Dental Setvices Assocation
			Incorpoated Denatl Soicety
			BDA
1954		New Dentil Bill published	
1956	1st July	General Dental Council (GDC) established	Dental Board of the UK abolished
			Fees £4 , 10s
		Britihs Dental Assoication (BDA) founded	
		General Dental Services Committee (GDSC)	
		Dental Auxillery Committee	
1980		Nuffield report published	
1984		New Dentists Act	
1987		Dentist allowed to advertise	Follse thretas bt MMC
2003		Counil size reducewd to 12 members	
2006	July	Dental Care professions regulated	

Chart 8.4 – III **Timeline medical practitioners**

		Medical practitioners	
Year	Month	Event	
1832	19 July	British Medical Association (BMA) founded	
1845		Medical Directory first published	
1858		Medical Act	General Medical Council (GMC) established
1859		Medical Register first published	
1878		Dentist Act	General Dental Council (GDC) established
1886		Medical Act Amendment Act	
1919		Ministry of Health and Scottish Board of Health established	
1944	July	Sir William Goodenough Interdepartmental Committee report	Review of Medical Schools
1953		Pre registration year inaugurated	
1975		Merrison Report	On regulation of the Medical Profession
1993		Calmar Report	Equalises European and UK specialist training times
1995		Good Medical Practice	First published
1998		104 council mebers of which 25 lay	
2000		Size of council rediced to 35 memebers, 40% lay	
		PMETB	Post Graduate Medical Education and Training Board

Chart 8.4 – IV **Timeline nurses and midwives**

		Nurses and midwives	
Year	Month	Event	
1887		Hospital Association establishes a non-statutory voluntary register	
	7 Dec	British Nurse's Assocation (BNA) formed	
1889		BNA voluntary register opened	
1893		BNA granted Royal Charter	Royal British Nursing Assocation
1902	31 July	Midwives Registraion Act	Central Midwives Board established
1903			Midwives Act comes into force
1904		House of Commons Select Committee	Considered the regulation of nurses
		Central Midwives Board for England and Wales	established
		Midwives Roll first published	
1916	March	College of Nurses established	
1919	23 Dec	Nurses Registration Act	Separate Acts for England and Wales, Scotland and Ireland.
		General Nursing Council (GNC) for England and Wales	
1921	30 Sept	GNC first Register published	Voluntray register
1928	28 June	College of Nurses gains Royal Charter	Royal College of Nursing
1936	1 June	Midwives Act passed	
1943		Nursing Act	Registration becomes compulsary
1945		Nursing Act	
1947		College of Midwives gains Royal Charchter	
1972	21 April	Report of Briggs Committee published	
1979	4 April	Nurses, Midwives and Health Visitors Act	
1983		UK Central Council for Nursing, Midwifery & Health Visiting	
		National Boards established	
2002	1 April	Nursing and Midwifery Council (NMC) established	

Chart 8.4 – V **Timeline optometrists**

		Optometrists	
Year	Month	Event	
1629		Worshipful Company of Spectacle Makers (WCSM)	Guild established in City of London
1895		British Optical Association (BOA)	Professional Assocation for opticians founded
1904		General Board of Opticians (GBO)	GBO Established by British Optical Association (BOA)
		Worshipful Company of Spectacle Makers (WCSM)	Responsible for examination and certification of opticians
1906		Sight-testing Options Bill	Bill that would establish the GOC fails to be approved
1923		Joint Council for Qualified Opticians (JCQO)	Formed by BOA, SMC and the Institute of Ophthalmic Opticians
1926		Dispensing Opticians	Voluntary register opened
1927		Optical Practitioners (Registration) Bill	Published by JCQO and the withdrawn
1936		Second draft bill	Withdrawn
1937 - 46		Ophthalmic Benefit Approval Committee	
1949		Interdepartmental Committee	Lord Crook
		Private members Bill	Ronald S Russell MP
1958	7 July	Opticians Act	Establishes the General Optical Council (GOC)
1960		First GOC Register published	
1979		British College of Ophthalmic Opticians (BCOO) founded	
			WCSM, BOA and the Scottish Association of Opticians merge
1986		Association of British Dispensing Opticians (ABDO)	Professional Body for Dispensing Opticians Founded
1989		Opticians Act	Amended
1995	28 June	BCOO renamed College of Optometrists	Royal Charter granted

Chart 8.4 – VI **Timeline other healthcare professions including physiotherapists and radiographers**

		Other healthcare professionals including physiotherapists and radiographers	
1920		Charted Society of Massage and Remedial Gymnasts	
1936	1932(?)	Board of Registration of Medical Auxiliaries	Rads and Physios
1939		Chiropodists join BRMA	Alos Dispensing optitions, speech therapists orthotists
1944		Charted Society of Physiotherapists	
1949/1950		Eight committeess review possibility of regulation	
1951	April	Dr V Zachary Cope Report published	
		Reports of the Committees on Medical Auxiliares	
1959		PSM Bill	
1960		PSM 1960 Act	
1961		Register opens	
1960		Speech and language therapist leave CPSM	
		Almoners leave	
		Orthoptists join register	
1966			
		Osteopathy and Chiropratic rejected	Dates????
1987		Remedial gymnasts merge with physiotherapists	
1996	April	JM Consulting report published	
2001		Shadow HPC established	

CONCLUSION

In the UK for the last 400 hundred years there has been a continuous shift in the relationship of the healthcare professions with the state, with their patients, and with each other. I argue strongly that a permanent steady state is unlikely ever to be reached. In consequence the regulation of healthcare professions needs to be periodically reformed, a topic that is explored in the proceeding section.

EXERCISE AND QUESTION

Exercise

- For the population as a whole did the disadvantages of guilds outweigh their advantages?

Question

- When professional associations started to be established, who benefited the most, the profession, members of the public, or both? Explain the rationale to your answer.

LEGISLATION

Example of UK Legislation

The Apothecaries Act 1815 L
Medical Act 2 August 1858 L
Medical Act 1876 and 1886 L
Medical (Professional Performance) Act 1995 L

Other Historical Examples of UK Legislation

An Act concerning Physicians and Surgeons L
An 3 Henry VIII c. 11 (1512/1513)

An Act that surgeons be Discharged of Constableship and other things L
An 5 Henry VIII c. 6 (1513/1514)

An Act concerning Physicians L
An 14 and 15 Henry VIII c. 5 (1523)

An Act Concerning Bakers, Brewers, Surgeons, and Scriveners L
An 22 Henry VIII c.13 (1530/1531)

Physicians Act An Act concerning the Privileges of Physicians L
An 32 Henry VIIII c. 40 (1540)

Concerning Barbers and Surgeons to be of One Company L
An 32 Henry VIII c.42 (1540)

FURTHER READING

Applications and Registration at CPSM, 1962 to 2002 R
Berrie, Tom C
HPCP Internal report
March 2010
27 pages

Departmental Committee on the Dentists Act, 1878: R
report of the Committee appointed by the Lord President of the Council to enquire into the extent and gravity of the evils of dental practice not qualified under the Dentists Act
HM Stationery Office
Cmd 33
February 1919

Dental Registration B
Being a practical Guide to the new dentist Act
Wood, Sir K
Baillière, Tindall and Cox
1921
128 pages

Doctors' Tale: Professionalism and Public Trust B
Irvine, David
Radcliffe Medical Press
ISBN-13: 978-1857759778
15 May 2003
200 pages

Educational Approval and Monitoring at the CPSM, 1962 to 2002 R
Berrie, Tom C
HPCP Internal report
March 2010
35 pages

Health for Sale: Quackery in England 1660–1850 B
Roy Porter
Manchester University Press
ISBN 13 978-0719019036
10 August 1989
240 pages

A History of the General Nursing Council for England and Wales 1919–1969 B
Bendall E, Raybould E
ISBN 0718600916 97807 18600914
HK Lewis, London
1969
312 pages

A History of the Medical Council of New Zealand 2015 B
Richard Sainsbury
Medical Council of New Zealand
2015
226 pages

Interpreting Professional Self-Regulation: A History of the United Kingdom Central council for Nursing, Midwifery and Health Visiting B
Davies C Beach A
ISBN 10: 0415230330
ISBN 13: 9780415230339
London Routledge
29 June 2000
249 pages

Licensing of Medical Practitioners in Tudor England: B
Legislation enacted by Henry VIII
Hughes, J T
Off print, Vesalius Volume XII, No 1 pages 4–11
June 2006
15 pages

Medical Discipline: Professional Conduct of the GMC 1858–1990 B
Smith, Russell
5 May 1994
Oxford University Press, Oxford
444 pages

Regulating British Medicine, The General Medical Council B
Stacey, Margaret
John Wiley and Sons, Chichester
ISBN 10 0471931896
23 June 1992
310 pages

Regulating Doctors B
David Gladstone (Editor)
Civitas: Institute for the Study of Civil Society
ISBN 1-903 386-01-2
31 May 2000
75 pages

Regulating the Health Professions B
Allsop Judith Sacks Mike, Editors
SAGE Publications, London
ISBN 0 7619 6740 0
February 2002
166 pages

Regulating Medical Work: Formal and Informal Controls B
Judith Allsop and Judith Mccarney
Health Services Management
Open University Press, Buckingham
ISBN-10:0335194044
ISBN-13:978-0335194049
1 November 1996
240 pages

Regulating the Professions B
A Public-Policy Symposium
Lexington Books
Ed Blair D B and Rubin S
ISBN 0 669 03094 5
1980
327 pages

The Regulation of the Dental Profession by the General Dental Council B
The John McLean Archive a Living History of Dentistry Witness Seminar 1
Edited by Nairn Wilson and Stanley Gelbier
Published by the British Dental Association
ISBN978-1-291-72386-1
2014
88 pages

Self-Regulation of Professionals in Health Care; Consumer Issues R
National Consumer Council
ISBN 13 978 1899581818
1 June 1999
76 pages

State, Regulation and the Medical Profession B
Moran M and Wood B
Open University Press, Buckingham
ISBN-13 978-0335157495
16 December 1992/3
150 pages

Working Party on the Statutory Registration of Medical Auxiliaries Report R
Chair Pater J E
November 1954

JOURNALS AND RESEARCH PAPERS

The Apothecaries' Act, 1815: A Reinterpretation. Part 1: The Origins Of The Act JRP
Holloway S W F
Medical History. April 1966 ; 10(2): 107–129

The Economics of Guilds JRP
Sheilagh Ogilvie
Journal of Economic Perspectives
Volume 28, Number 4—Fall 2014—Pages 169–192

English Medical Licensing in the Early Seventeenth Century JRP
Rach John N
Yale Journal of Biology and Medicine
1944 Mar 16(4):267–288

A short history of the General Medical Council JRP
Irvine, Donald
Med Educ 2006 Mar;40(3):202–11

8.5 REFORMING THE REGULATION OF HEALTHCARE PROFESSIONALS

INTRODUCTION

As the evolution of the healthcare delivery system continues apace government should periodically reform the regulation of healthcare professionals. This includes both the reform of regulators and the process that they use to regulate their sector. After reviewing the drivers that trigger regulatory reform, the section reviews the processes that are used, followed by a selection of recent examples of regulatory reforms.

REFORMING REGULATION

The reform of regulation can be defined as:

Definition: Reform of Regulation
Significant changes to the organisation of a regulator and/or the processes it uses to regulate its sector.

The implications of this definition of reforming regulation are that it:

- Involves changes to the regulators' legislation
- The process is managed by government
- Minor changes to the regulator's rules or standards are not considered to be regulatory reform

One of the implications of this definition is that because reform requires legislation to be developed, enacted, amended, or revised, it occurs infrequently and the process is slow, such that in many cases it takes decades to complete.

DRIVERS FOR REGULATORY REFORM

In essence, all matters relating to the principles and processes of the regulation of healthcare professionals, that are not working as intended, can lead to regulatory reform. Since this has the potential to embrace almost every subject addressed in the book, a number of drivers for change have been selected for examination, particularly as they have directly influenced some governments to increasingly establish consumer-orientated regulation.

The drivers for regulatory reform predominantly arise from ten areas. They are, in alphabetic order, as follows:

1. Collaboration
2. Consumerism
3. Continuing competence
4. Governance
5. Number of regulated professions
6. Oversight
7. Regulatory contract
8. Regulatory failure
9. Governments' attention
10. Legislative consolidation

The ten drivers for regulatory reform will now be explored:

1. **Collaboration**
In a particular jurisdiction the regulation of different healthcare professions is usually undertaken by more than one regulator. When government assess that there are benefits from either regulators collaborating to a greater extent, or that the number of regulators should be reduced by transferring registers, the process of reform may be instigated.

2. **Consumerism**
If members of the public as consumers of healthcare services can't act in the healthcare delivery system as informed decision makers and their interests are not being protected by regulators, reform may be initiated.

3. **Continuing competence**
In the context of the history of the regulation of healthcare professionals, the principles and processes of continuing competence are a relatively newcomer.
These days it is no longer acceptable for a professional to only demonstrate that they are competent at the time that they join the profession for the first time. As a result it has become the norm that healthcare professionals are required to maintain, revise, broaden, and raise their knowledge, skills, values, and behaviours with the objective of providing improved care for patients.
However, the principles and processes used to deliver continuing competence are not universally agreed upon and continue to evolve. This is made more complex because of the accelerating rate of change and the magnitude of change to the theory and practice of the professions in today's modern world.
When the principles and processes of continuing competence are seen by government as not working, they may introduce reform.

4. **Governance**
Historically, the guilds and voluntary membership organisations were free to decide the composition of their board. As a result, their boards consisted almost exclusively of individuals drawn or elected from the members of the profession.
However, in the modern era, as the organisations gained greater statutory powers, the argument that the professions must *'regulate themselves by themselves'*

because the knowledge and skills of the professionals are unknowable by members of the public started to be questioned.

In time the argument was lost and the concept that consumer participation needed to be implemented won the day. In essence the voice of the consumer needed to be heard and reacted to. Ensuring that the regulator's statutory powers were used in the interests of both the public and the profession, reduced the potential for conflicts of interest to arise or at the very least were reduced. Interestingly, these changes to the governance arrangements have had a secondary effect of reducing the power and influence of the professional associations.

Frustrating to many consumer advocacy organisations, these types of reform have not been achieved overnight. Initially the governance arrangements of some regulators were adjusted to include a minority of non-professionals. The reforms have continued to such an extent that in many cases the members of the professions and lay members on the boards of regulators are now equal.

However, although the changes are significant, these types of governance reforms have in numerous jurisdictions yet to be made.

5. **Number of regulated professions**
As the number of different healthcare professions has increased, government has in due course assessed their suitability for statutory regulation and then in most cases this type of regulation reform has been introduced.

6. **Oversight**
Reforming regulation by the creation of an oversight organisation has occurred in a small number of jurisdictions. As a result a similar process of reform may triggered their introduction in other jurisdictions. This is particularly likely to occur in countries with a federal systems of government that devolves regulation of profession to autonomous provinces, regions, or states.

7. **Regulatory contract**
If the obligations of professionals to society and the obligations of society to regulated professionals as described in the regulatory contract, are unbalanced, or that there is a perception that it is, the regulatory reform may be triggered.

On some instances the reform can result in the closure of the regulator and the abandonment of regulation.

8. **Regulatory failure**
The predominant trigger for regulatory reform is when a regulator, or regulators, of healthcare professions has failed to deliver its objective of public protection, and harm has been caused to patients.

And, since there are now more professions and more individual professionals, regulatory failure is occurring more frequently. As a consequence, a failure of one regulator will often result in reform to all the regulators.

At the same time the response to regulatory failure by both professional associations and regulators has sometimes been lackadaisical in both failing to constructively self-criticise, or to take appropriate action to mitigate the potential for future failure, or to recommend and implement improvements to their principles and processes.

In response to the extensive litany of regulatory failure relating to healthcare professionals over the last half century in the UK and many other jurisdictions, governments, egged on by consumerism, have reacted by reforming the legislation of regulators.

It should also be noted that regulatory failure in adjacent areas to the regulation of healthcare professionals may have an impact. For example, in the area of medicines and medical devices.

9. **Government's attention**
Government ability to reform regulation is severely limited by time and resource constraints. As a consequence, only if there is a significant imperative to do something will the attention of government be triggered and action initiated.

Reforming regulation requires government to allocate its limited resources of time and people to the process. This means that reform of regulation takes place under two different conditions. They are:

   i. There is a fundamental political shift in its attitude to regulation that is articulated in there is 'too much' or 'too little' regulation. When this is articulated in a party manifesto of a newly elected government, the possibility that reform will take place is significantly increased.

   ii. Government is confronted by serious and unpredicted crises. Under these types of conditions government's willingness to direct resources into reforming regulation is significantly increased

10. **Legislative consolidation**
In most jurisdictions as the number of regulated professions increases, the number of separate pieces of legislation has also increased. Over time, this has created the opportunity to consolidate legislation. The opportunity to consolidate legislation using omnibus models of legislation also creates an opportunity to reform regulation.

PROCESS TO REFORM REGULATION

The process to reform regulation are described in detail in the preceding sections of the book, for example, policy development and consultations.

For those seeking to study and investigate the process to reform regulation a broad range of publications is available, including:

1. Draft legislation
2. Green papers
3. Government consultations
4. Government's responses to reports of other organisations
5. Parliamentary committees
6. Parliamentary debates
7. Party manifestoes
8. Position papers of consumer advocacy organisations, oversight organisations, and professional associations regulators,
9. Publications by think tanks and research organisations
10. Regulatory reforms in other jurisdictions
11. Reports of public inquiries following their investigation into regulatory failure

EXAMPLES OF REGULATORY REFORM

There are many examples of government reforming the regulation of healthcare professionals. For those readers with a particular interest in the process, the following two examples of significant reform well illustrate the process:

Regulation of new healthcare professions in the UK in the 1960s.

In the UK from the late 1930s a number of new healthcare professions started to emerge. The cause of their emergence in the healthcare delivery system was related to:

- Expansion of science and the use of laboratories
- The use of ionising radiation for the purpose of images
- The expansion of therapies by occupational therapists and physiotherapists

Initially, some of the emerging professions were accommodated in a process of certification – voluntary. A number of these were organised by the BMA, the professional association of the medical profession in the UK.

The Government established the Cope Enquiry and its report published in 1951 recommended that almoners, chiropodists, dieticians, laboratory technicians, occupational therapists, physiotherapists, radiographers, and speech therapists should be statutorily regulated via independent boards. The proposal was resisted by the BMA whose counter proposal was that the medical profession should be in charge of their regulation.

The BMA's proposal was rejected and instead in 1960 under the Professions Supplementary to Medicine Act the Council for Professions Supplementary to Medicine (CPSM) was established, although heavily influenced and controlled by the medical profession.

There were originally seven professions, nowadays referred to in the UK as the allied health professions (AHPs):

1. Chiropodists
2. Dieticians
3. Medical laboratory technicians
4. Occupational therapists
5. Physiotherapists
6. Radiographers
7. Remedial gymnasts

AUSTRALIAN HEALTH PRACTITIONER REGULATION AGENCY (AHPRA)

Another example of the significant reform of regulation of healthcare professionals took place in Australia in 2010 when the Australian Health Practitioner Regulation Agency (AHPRA) was established; see Section 12.3, volume 3. In essence, over 90 State- and territories-based separate regulatory organisations were consolidated into a single entity.

CONCLUSION

The process to reform the regulation of healthcare professionals is never ending. From the perspective of regulators and government, it is important to be aware of regulatory reforms in other jurisdictions, since better regulatory principles and processes have few barriers for transferring from one jurisdictions to another, provided of course that there is political support.

EXERCISE AND QUESTION

Exercise

- Are there currently any indications that the UK government intends to reform the regulation of the healthcare professions?

Question

- Why does it take so long to reform regulation?

LEGISLATION

Example of UK Legislation

Professions Supplementary to Medicine Act 1960 L

FURTHER READING

Breaking the maze R
Simplifying legal services regulation
Legal Services Consumer Panel
September 2013
58 pages

Busting Bureaucracy R
Empowering frontline staff by reducing excess bureaucracy in the health and care system in England
Department of Health and Social Care
24 November 2020
32 pages

The General Medical Council: Fit to Practise? R
Hilarie Williams, Christoph Lees and Magnus Boyd
Civitas: Institute for the Study of Civil Society
Doctors' Policy Research Group
July 2014
51 pages

HM Government's Plans for Regulation R
Emily Haves
Lords Library notes LLN-2017-0090
1 December 2017
17 pages

Implementing the White Paper Trust, Assurance and Safety; Enhancing Confidence in Healthcare Professional regulators R
Final Report
Department of Health
Gateway Reference 10007
June 2008
34 pages

Integration and Innovation: working together to improve health and social care for all R
Legislative proposals for a Health and Care Bill
Department of Health and Social Care
CP381
ISBN 978 1 5286 2407 7
11 February 2021
80 pages

Legal Professions Regulatory Modernization R
Ministry of Attorney General
British Columbia
Intentions Paper September 2022
20 pages

Legislation and governance review conducted for Engineers and Geoscientists British Columbia R
Professions Standards Authority
June 2008
43 pages

The Medicines and Medical Devices Safety Review R
House of Commons
Research Briefing
Sarah Barber, Nikki Sutherland
Number CBP 9274
7 July 2021
43 pages

Meeting the Challenge: A Strategy for the Allied Health Professions R
Department of Health
Stationery Office
November 2000
43 pages

Recommendations to modernize the provincial health professions regulatory framework R
Ministry of Health British Columbia
Steering Committee on Modernization of Health Professional Regulation
27 August 2020
27 pages

Regulation of Nurses, Midwives and Health Visitors: report on a review of the Nurses, Midwives and Health Visitors Act 1997 R
J. M. Consulting Ltd, Bristol, UK
ASIN: B001AC8T50
1998
85 pages

Regulation rethought proposals for reform R
Profession Standards Authority (UK)
August or October 2016
23 pages

Regulatory Futures Review R
Cabinet Office
10 January 2017
78 pages

Report of the Committee of Inquiry into the Regulation of the Medical Profession R
Sir Alec W Merrison
Command paper 6108
ISBN 0101601808I
London, HMSO
16 April 1975
190 pages

Report on the Regulation of Nurses R
A Report on the present, a position for the future
International Council of Nurses (ICN)
Margretta M Styles
June1985
50 pages

Reports of the Committees on Medical Auxiliaries – Cope Report R
Sir Vincent Zachary Cope (1881–1974)
Ministry of Health and Department of Health for Scotland
HMSO, London, UK
Ref: Cmd. 8188
ASIN: B000X8ERC6
April 1951
227 pages

Report of the Committee on Nursing R
Chairman: Professor Asa Briggs
Command paper. 5115
SBN 10 151150 7
HMSO, London
October 1972
327 pages

Report on the Regulation of Nurses R
Report on the present, a position for the future
International Council of Nurses (ICN)
Margretta M Styles
June1985
50 pages

Review of the UKCC and the Four National Boards of Nursing, Midwifery and Health Visiting R
Department of Health, London
Peat, Marwick Mclintock
1989

Rethinking Regulation R
Professional Standards Authority (UK)
4 August 2015
27 pages

Right Touch Regulation – Revised R
Profession Standards Authority
October 2015
20 pages

Right-touch reform R
A new framework for assurance of professions
PSA
23 November 2017
219 pages

Themes and Trends in Regulatory Reform R
House of Commons Regulatory Reform Committee
Ninth Report of Session 2008–09, HC 329-I
14 July 2009
32 pages

Trust, Assurance and Safety – The Regulation of Health Professionals in the 21st Century R
Department of Health (UK)
Ref: Command paper CM 7013
ISBN 97801701227
ID 5501492 02/0721
February 2007
93 pages

STANDARDS, CODES, GUIDANCE, CONSULTATIONS, POLICIES, AND PRACTICE NOTES

Consultations

Better, safer regulation C
Our response to the DHSC consultation regulating healthcare professionals, protecting the public
NMC
June 2021
38 pages

The Future of Pharmacy Regulation in Northern Ireland C
Consultation Summary Report
Department of Health (Northern Ireland)
6 November 2017
26 pages

Modernising Regulation in the Health Professions C
Consultation Document
Department of Health
Ref: 24717 1P
August 2001
15 pages

Promoting professionalism, reforming regulation C
A paper for consultation
Department of Health
Ref: 13730
31 October 2017
51 pages

Promoting professionalism, reforming regulation C
Government response to consultation
Department of Health
Ref: 13730
9 July 2019
58 pages

Protecting Patients: A Summary Consultative Document C
General Medical Council
March 2001

Regulating Healthcare Professionals, Protecting the Public C
Consultation
Department of Health & Social Care
24 March 2021
120 pages

Regulating healthcare professionals, protecting the public C
Consultation response 9 executive summary
Department of Health & Social Care
17 February 2023
XX pages

Regulation of Nurses, Midwives and Health Visitors: Consultation of Report on a review of the Nurses, Midwives and Health Visitors Act 1997 C
J. M. Consulting Ltd, Bristol, UK
ASIN: B001AC8T50
January 1998
34 pages

Regulation of Healthcare Staff in England and Wales C
Consultation Document
Department of Health
2004

Review of Pharmacy Regulation in Northern Ireland C
Consultation Document
Department of Health, Social Services and Public Safety (Northern Ireland)
22 March 2016
35 pages

Planning and Research

CHAPTER 9

INTRODUCTION

All regulators of healthcare professionals must allocate their limited resources so that they can plan and execute their strategy to deliver their objective of protecting the public and run their day-to-day operations. This chapter looks at a range of tools and techniques that can be used to plan for the future. It also explores the role of research in this endeavour.

The chapter has four sections:

9.1 Planning processes

9.2 Scenarios

9.3 Researching the evidence base for regulating healthcare professionals

9.4 Research – ethics and integrity

9.1 PLANNING PROCESSES

INTRODUCTION

The section identifies and reviews a selection of planning tools and techniques that can be used by regulators.

WHY PLAN?

Since:

> *The future is unknowable and you can't have a memory of the future*

Could the best option be not to bother to plan?

This course of action, whilst having the advantage of simplicity and low cost, will soon result in disaster. This is because all regulators operate in conditions of financial restraint; see Section 1.3, volume 4. It logically follows that resources both financial and human must be allocated between competing and mutually exclusive projects, or the demise of the organisation will inevitably follow.

PLANNING PROCESSES

Planning processes must be implemented by regulators but which processes to use? An extensive range of options is available, as illustrated in Chart 9.1 – I. The chart depicts the range of planning processes that can be used by reference to their degree of accuracy and detail on the vertical axis and time on the horizontal axis.

Many readers will probably be familiar with various types of planning processes. From those that look far forward in time and provide the least accuracy to those that focus on the near term and are more likely to provide greater accuracy. A range of different planning processes will now be introduced:

SCENARIOS

These are descriptions of possible futures and are explored in the following section, scenarios in Section 9.2.

VISION STATEMENT

The regulator may have a vision statement.

Definition: Vision Statement
Inspirational statement of organisations desired long-term achievements.

MISSION STATEMENT

A mission statement is slightly wordier than a vision statement. They seek to encapsulate the purpose of an organisation in terms of what, why, how, and where they operate. Hence:

Definition: Mission Statement
Concise statement of the purpose of an organisation.

PURPOSE

Many public authorities including regulators will articulate and publish their purpose.

OBJECTIVES

Some organisations, particularly public authorities, also publish their primary and secondary objectives.

Operations of Regulators of Healthcare Professionals, Volume 4, First Edition. Marc Seale.

Companion website: www.wiley.com/go/seale/regulatinghealthcare

Chart 9.1 – I **Planning processes**

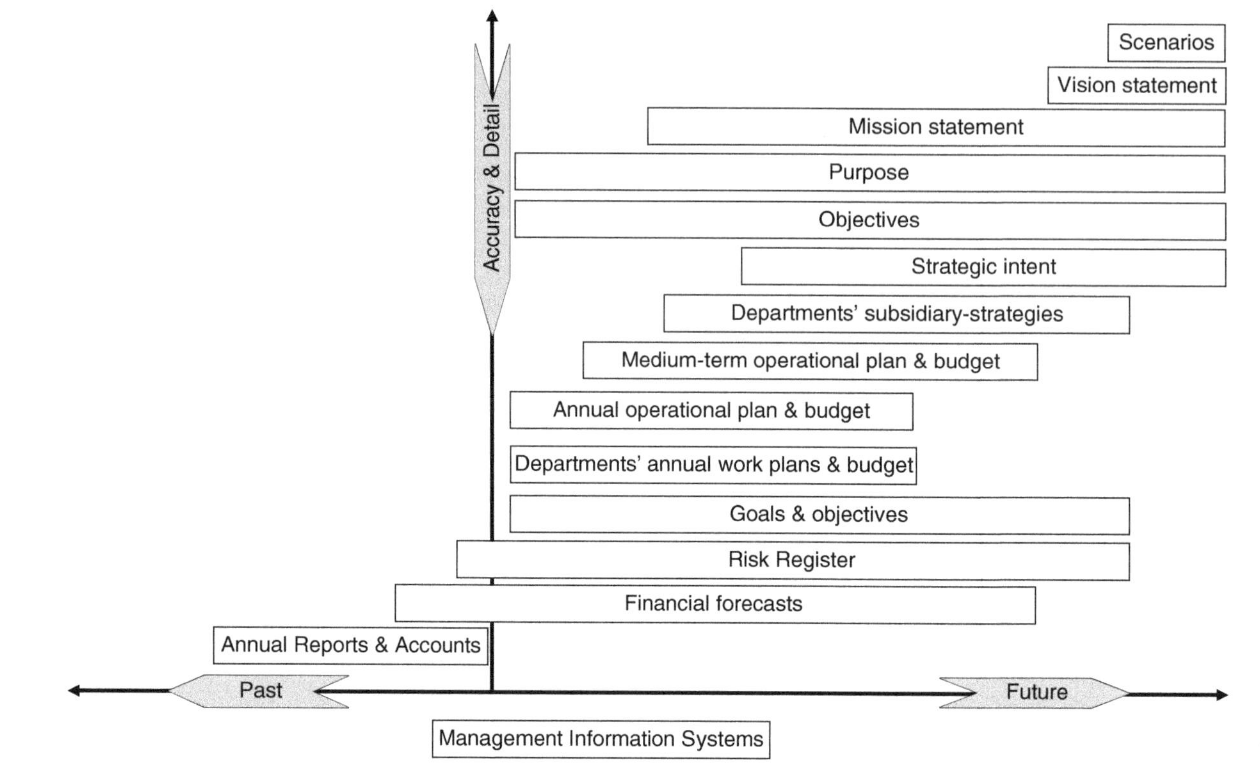

STRATEGIC INTENT

It can be assumed that most commercial organisations will have a documented strategy. However, as discussed in Section 1.3, volume 4, policy and strategy development, it may not be necessary for a regulator of healthcare professions to have a strategy. Rather, they should have a strategic intent. This sets out the organisation's ambition by combining and summarising its vision, mission, purpose and objectives within the context of its operational model.

DEPARTMENTS' SUBSIDIARY-STRATEGIES

A number of the regulators' functions or departments including communications, HR, and ICT will probably have their own strategy or subsidiary strategies.

MEDIUM-TERM OPERATIONAL PLAN AND BUDGET

Most regulators will have a medium-term operational plan. The medium-term operational plan and financial budget will be in effect a consolidation of each of the regulators' functions. The plan will probably extend out into the future for at least two years and sometimes longer for, say, three or five years. This will be heavily dependent on the forecast of the number of regulated professionals in the form of the forecast of registrant numbers and the forecast of fitness to practise (FTP) operations.

ANNUAL OPERATIONAL PLAN AND BUDGET

Although in greater detail, the regulators' annual operating plan and financial budget will be produced using a similar process used to construct the medium-term plan and budget. Each department's or function's plan and budget should articulate what they will deliver in the year ahead within the agreed financial and human resources available.

Both medium-term and annual plans will probably incorporate a sensitivity analysis to identify risks associated with the short and medium terms. The provision of all the assumptions that are used to derive the plans should form the foundation of the process and help mitigate the potential for inaccurate forecasting.

GOALS AND OBJECTIVES

A hierarchy of documented goals and objectives will probably exist flowing from the CEO to all employees.

FINANCIAL FORECAST

As the financial year progresses actual results vs budget should be reported and adjustments made as appropriate. And like the annual and medium term budget will for comparative purposes incorporate the actual results from the previous year(s).

RISK REGISTER

The risk register and mitigation should be constantly adjusted to reflect current plans.

ANNUAL REPORTS AND REVIEWS

Finally, annual reports and reviews will be published showing the results of the planning process.

MANAGEMENT INFORMATION SYSTEM (MIS)

Central to the regulators' planning process their management information system will record and disseminate planned and actual results.

CONCLUSION

The portfolio of planning processes that are available to regulators is no different from commercial organisations. Although, in the short term the risk of financial distress is low, regulators should direct adequate resources into the process to forewarn themselves of changes that must be implemented to ensure their operational performance delivers their regulatory objectives within the required financial envelope.

EXERCISE AND QUESTION

Exercise

- Compose a vision or mission statement for a regulator operating in a sector that you are not familiar with.

Question

- What planning processes does your organisation use?

FURTHER READING

Handbook of Strategic Planning B
James R. Gardner, Robert Rachlin HWA Sweenry
John Wiley and Sons Inc New Jersey
ISBN 10: 0471881279
ISBN 13: 9780471881278
1986
752 pages

Examples of regulators' plans and strategies
(Note: not included in the Appendix as reports)

General Dental Council
Corporate Strategy 2016–2019
18 pages

General Dental Council
Corporate Strategy 2020–22
Right time, Right place Right touch
27 November 2019#26 pages

GMC Business Plan 2010
Ref GMC/BP/0110
25 pages

GMC Corporate Strategy 2010–2013
Ref GMC/CS/0110
29 pages

GMC Corporate Strategy 2014–2017
Ref GMC/CS/2013-17/0114
January 2014
40 pages

National Registration and Accreditation Scheme (NRAS) Strategy
Australian Health Practitioner Regulation Agency
2020–2025
1 page

STANDARDS, CODES, GUIDANCE, CONSULTATIONS, POLICIES AND PRACTICE NOTES

Consultations

Corporate Strategy 2020–2022 C
Working with the dental team for public safety and confidence
Consultation
General Dental Council
9 May 2019
30 pages

General Dental Council C
Corporate Strategy 2020–2022
Consultation outcome report
October 2019
18 pages

9.2 SCENARIOS

INTRODUCTION

A range of planning methodologies that organisations and individuals can use to prepare for a complex and volatile future have been identified. However, they tend to be financially orientated, focus on the known knowns and the near term. One of the ways to broaden the approach to planning and to explore and prepare for a volotile,uncertain, complex and ambiguous (VUCA) future is to use scenarios.

WHAT IS A SCENARIO?

A scenario can be defined as:

Definition: Scenario
Description of a possible future.

PURPOSE OF SCENARIOS

The future is both unknown and VUCA. And change is continuous. However, by constructing scenarios, organisations can explore future environments that they may have to operate within. They can then consider how they will tackle these possible eventualities and what actions they can take today that will help in the future.

METHODOLOGY

There is no correct way to use scenarios, but there are a number of practical ways that they can be prepared.

Original developed by the military during the Second World War, the use of scenarios is often attributed to Herman Kahn (February 15, 1922–July 7, 1983), who was a founder of the Hudson Institute. Kahn was a preeminent futurist of the latter part of the twentieth century and came to prominence as a military strategist and systems theorist working at the RAND Corporation. Scenarios or scenario planning was then adopted by the international energy company, Shell. Strongly influenced by the work of Pierre Wack (1922–1997), Shell is both a renowned user and proponent of scenario planning since the 1970s. And Shell remains a veritable goldmine for information on the subject.

What exactly are scenarios?

- Scenarios are not predictions or predictions of the future. The future is unpredictable
- A scenario is usually a reactively short written story of a possible future. One to two pages of A4 paper is reasonable, although some organisations with considerable resources have been known to prepared videos of their scenarios
- Evocative titles for each scenario are recommended to aid recall and communication
- The scenario can often read more like a story rather than a series of bullet points
- They should contain limited numeric data
- Precise numerical forecast should be avoided
- Scenarios should focus on the medium-to-longer time horizon rather than the immediate future that can be left to the annual operational plan
- The time horizon of the scenario should reflect the business life of capital investments
- The scenarios need to be realistic, believable, practical, and possible. Considering the implications of 'an invasion of the earth by little green men from Mars in flying saucers' may be fun to consider but is really not a good use of one's time unless you are planning to write science fiction
- The process should use and encourage a diversity of views
- Multiple possible futures by way of more than one scenario should be prepared, preferably an even number to prevent the inevitability that too much focus will be placed on the one in the middle. Preparing four scenarios is a sound compromise
- The resources required by the organisation to prepare and develop each scenario should all be equally allocated, i.e. time and people
- Only the big-ticket issues or 'Drivers for change' that may impact directly or indirectly on the organisation should be considered
- Big-ticket issues for the future may be very small today
- Once the scenarios have been established then the way that the organisation could operate in such a scenario should be articulated

BENEFITS OF SCENARIO PLANNING

There are a number of benefits of using scenario planning. They include:

- Avoids the risk of focusing on a single view of the future
- Facilitates the organisation's thinking, understanding, and planning of how to react to the scenario if it becomes a reality
- Enables the identification of early signs that the scenario is happening
- Speeds up preparation for a reaction response

POTENTIAL PROBLEMS WITH USING SCENARIOS

Using scenarios may help an organisation to consider how the future may develop, and it should then organise its response to the possible changes if they come to fruition.

However, the process to develop scenarios is not straightforward and requires considerable effort. It should also be borne in mind that the use of scenarios and scenario planning is open to four types of criticism, namely:

1. Scenarios are an heuristic technique and lack precision
2. There is limited published scientific research assessing the practical benefits of using scenarios
3. Scenarios are subjective particularly in relation to the choice and weighting assigned to the drivers for change
4. The plans and actions arising from scenarios are difficult to incorporate into other planning methodologies such as operational plans and budget, allocating resources to capital, and other major projects

DRIVERS FOR CHANGE

If you are considering using scenario planning by creating a series of scenarios for a regulator of healthcare professionals, you may want to consider incorporating drivers for change into the process.

Definition: Driver for Change
Future events that will impact on an organisation

Drivers for change tend to be

- Significant
- Risky to the organisation
- Unpredictable

For those considering the use of scenarios in relation to the regulation of healthcare professionals, I have expedited the process by identifying 22 groups of drivers for change. However, this is entirely a subjective assessment, and generally the drivers for change are multidimensional and cannot be neatly classified as per Carl Linnaeous.

The 22 Drivers for change are as follows:

1. **Business models**
2. **Consumerism**
3. **Data**
4. **Demographics**
5. **Economic**
6. **Education**
7. **Environment**
8. **Epidemiological**
9. **Government**
10. **Healthcare delivery system**
11. **Information, knowledge, and expertise**
12. **Movement of people**
13. **Professionalism**
14. **Professionals and occupations**
15. **Profession associations**
16. **Regulation**
17. **Science**
18. **Social**
19. **Standards**
20. **Technology**
21. **Workforce**
22. **World of work**

The 22 drivers will now be expanded:

1. **Business models**

   Novel business models
   The creation of novel business models disrupts existing concepts of business and their relationship with consumers.

2. **Consumerism**

   Consumer/patient expectations
   The demand by patients for better services, choice, information, and inclusion as equal partners with professionals.

   Ethical complexity
   Ethical dilemmas change, such as the use of euthanasia.

   Genome
   Use and ownership of DNA-related technology such as stem cell research, cloning, and the ownership and exchange of DNA patient data.

   Health tourism
   Patients as informed consumers' propensity to travel to other jurisdictions to obtain healthcare.

   Inclusivity
   The demand for exacting explanations of treatment choices and outcomes and involvement in decision making by informed and knowledgeable patients.

   Markets
   Competitive markets are used to reduce the power of the monopolistic professionals, and in turn it reduces the necessity for regulation.

Patients
Impact of patients seeing themselves as active participants in their healthcare rather than receivers. The public's expectations of informed choice relates to the planning of services as well as individual engagements, see the NHS Patient's Charter.

Public assessment exchange
Routine assessment of service providers including healthcare professionals by patients and the publication of their reviews and evaluations on open access platforms on physician rating websites, for example: Dr Foster or surgeon ratings org.

Responsibility
Patient as consumers view themselves as being reasonable for their own health and wellbeing, as opposed to the state. This particularly relates to cessation of smoking, diet, and exercise.

3. **Data**

Access
Degree of unlimited access to governmental data.

Cost
The cost for accessing data.

Publication
Propensity for the availability and distribution of anonymised big data.

4. **Demographics**

Age
Average age of the global population, age distribution, and life expectancy.

Cohabitation
Children live to an older age with their parents.

Emigration and immigration and internal migration
Growth rates.

Fertility rates
Ability of the existing population to replace itself, by maintaining a birth rate of rate of 2.1.

Frail and elderly
Percentage of the population consisting of frail and elderly people.

growth
Population growth rate in countries and regions.

Size of working population
Percentage of the population in paid employment. Impact on the healthcare delivery system workforce on the unsatisfied supply for healthcare workers.

5. **Economic**

Energy prices
Price of hydrocarbon fossil fuels and alternative sources of energy.

Funding
Significant changes to percentage of GDP spent on healthcare.

Globalisation
Changes in rate of change.

Healthcare delivery costs
Percentage of countries' GDP spent on health.

Latent demand
Reducing the cost of the healthcare delivery system generates latent demand.

Manufacturing costs
Availability of and cost impact on manufacturing by new inventions such as addictive rather than subtractive manufacturing.

Productivity gains
Changes to the productivity of workers.

Rationalisation and prioritisation of intervention
Dependency on quality-of-life outcomes.

6. **Education**

Common training modules
Impact on the cost of education

Cost of education
Cost of secondary and tertiary education

Delivery of education
Rate of growth of virtual universities. The impact of badges, microcredentialing, and MOOCs on the supply and demand for traditional educational institutes

Distance learning
Prevalence of distance learning availability.

Literacy and numeracy rates
Significant changes.

Length of education programmes
Pressure from funders of education and training seeking to reduce ever-increasing costs by reducing the length of time of programmes.

Participation in education
Changes to the percentage of the population participating in secondary and higher education and the impact on an increasingly better-educated population that is knowledgeable, well-informed, articulate, and assertive. Also, see feminisation below.

Technology and education and training
Technology transforms how education and training is delivered, assessed, and credentialed.

7. **Environmental**

Climate change/the weather
Changes to the global population on communities becoming more exposed to natural disasters such as droughts and floods.

Greenhouse effect
Changes to global temperature such as food production and maritime transportation.

8. **Epidemiological**

Age-related disease
Changes brought about by the healthcare delivery system on the impact and severity of dementia and Alzheimer.

Antimicrobial resistance
Current antibiotics fail and are not replaced.

Complexity of disease
Changes to the comorbidity of diseases in populations.

End-of-life healthcare costs
Percentage of funding of end-of-life care as a percentage of the cost of an individual's whole life healthcare costs.

Inequalities
Interventions change to reduce the inequities of life span linked to affluence.

Lifestyle choices
Continued decline in tobacco usage results in decline of certain cancers in developed countries but is replaced by a corresponding increase in less well-developed countries.

Long-term survival
Enhanced healthcare results in better disease intervention services, and thus patients living longer and fuller lives, but with continuing and manageable health problems.

Neglected tropical diseases (ntds)
Potential to eliminated NTDs including malaria and river blindness.

Non-communicable chronic disease
Old diseases of 'fall ill–treated–get better' are replaced by long-lasting or chronic diseases. The propensity of the diseases of modern affluent lifestyles such as cardio vascular, diabetes, and obesity challenges continues to increase, and new ones emerge such as cancers in remission but never eradicated.

New infectious diseases
Emergence of similar diseases to Severe Acute Respiratory Syndrome (SARS) and Human Immunodeficiency Virus (HIV).

9. **Government**

Accessibility of healthcare delivery system
Government seeks to increase access to HCDS.

Funding of healthcare services
Government alters funding level of healthcare delivery system

Introduction of new and/or amended legislation
Government allocates time and resources to introduce new legislation in relation to a change in policy relating to the healthcare delivery system and/or the regulation of healthcare professionals.

Policy change
Changes to government policy impacts the regulation of healthcare professionals.

Public scandals and enquires
Public disquiet forces government to change legislation.

Rule-making powers
Pendulum swings back and forth between regulator and government

Regulated professions
Number of regulated professions.

Sin taxes
Taxes levied on socially harmful practice become the norm. The consumption of un-healthy goods, such as alcohol, fat, sugar, and tobacco, are significantly reduced; these goods lead to alcoholism, cancer, and obesity.

Universal healthcare system
Scope of coverage changed.

10. **Healthcare delivery system**

Complexity
Complexity of the Healthcare Delivery Systems changes as does the number of drugs, 6,000, and different interventions, 4,000. However, at 14,000, the number of different diseases remains similar as the 2015 WHO international classification.

Coordination
Degree of coordination between primary, second, and tertiary changes parts of the healthcare delivery system influenced by inter-professional team working and practice.

Corporatisation
Ratio of the provision of pay for service healthcare delivered by for-profit organisations vs the provision of healthcare services under a universal healthcare system changes.

Diagnosis
New technology leads to an increase in the ability to make a correct diagnose earlier in disease processes.

Fragmentation
Healthcare delivery system fragments into more and more separate pieces.

International providers
Providers of healthcare prepared to supply services into other jurisdictions from afar.

Managerialism
Reduces the independence of professionals.

Place of service delivery
Shift from tertiary hospital to home-based (domiciliary care) delivery and prevention.

Prevention schemes
In affluent countries, the increased use of routine screening results in an increase in the early detection of health problems, thereby allowing early intervention at a lower overall cost and a lower demand for healthcare.

Professional profiling
Availability of professional profiling data leads to increased patient selection of professionals.

Reconfiguration of the physical structures of the healthcare delivery system
Physical structures of the healthcare delivery system such as tertiary hospitals, polyclinics, and social services are reconfigured to provide a more efficient system.

Teams
Collaborative and integrated teams prevail, in comparison to delivery by sole practitioners.

11. **Information, knowledge, and expertise**

Capture
The knowledge of professionals becomes more and more captured by technology leading to the deskilling of existing job content, resulting in less need to use judgment.

Commoditisation
Driven by the web, information and knowledge is commoditised to become ubiquitous and distributed via the web to everyone with online data access.

Internet of everything (ioe)
Patient records available anonymised to everyone.

12. **Movement of people**

Emigration
The world's population remains in a state of hyper movement, both temporary and permanent.
Movement provides a solution to population decline in affluent countries.

Emigration of healthcare professionals and occupations
System facilitates the inward migration of the highly skilled workers to the detriment of the healthcare delivery system of the migrants' original home country.

13. **Professionalisms**

Confidence and self-esteem of professionals
Culture and organisational culture of the healthcare delivery system impacts professionals.

Professional autonomy
Continues to decline.

Provision of services
Services provided by professionals remain unable to reap economies of scale.

14. **Professions and occupations**

Costs
The wages and fees of professional's change.

Deskilling
Healthcare professionals' portfolio of work-related task radically modified as, for example, image interpretation accomplished by artificial intelligence (AI) and routine surgery undertaken by robots.

Establishment of new professions
Specialisation within professions leads to the emergence of new professions.

Feminisation of the professions
Rate of change of the number of women as a percentage of the professional workforce alters. Same impact occurs in education and training.

Geographic distribution of healthcare professionals
Decline of the willingness of healthcare professionals to work in rural and or remote areas is counteracted by increasing inducements by government funding to encourage this type of employment often as part of a migration policy.

Interprofessional practice
Continual emergence of new professions places greater emphasis on the need for professionals to cooperate, working together as teams and to understand each other's competences.

Managerialism and corporatisation
Threatens professionalism

Network of global communities
ICT costs reduces and network expands.

Specialisation
Professionals becoming more specialised.

Substitution of professionals by occupations
Work of professionals is reallocated to occupations and non-professionals to reduce costs triggered by the trickledown effect and commoditisation of services and resulting impact via the 'trickledown' effect or professional substitution by occupations.

15. **Professional associations**

Membership
Small professions struggle to maintain membership as younger generation no longer sees their relevance and the need to participate.

16. **Regulation**

Continuing competence
More compulsion for professionals to demonstrate using adaptive testing.

FTP
Pressure to reorganise the FTP and registration processes into separate organisations wanes.

Governmental intervention
Government's increasing requirement of regulators to act as an agent for their social agenda.

Harmonisation
Laws governing regulator harmonised.

Mutual recognition schemes emergence of
Accelerating trend for unilateral and mutual recognition of qualifications schemes.

Numbers of individual professionals
Changes up or down.

Quality of regulation
Regulators expected to be increasingly more effective and efficient.

Regulation
Regulation adopts standards for digital health.

Standards
The emergence of international standards for regulated professions increases.

17. **Science**

CAR T-cell therapy
Steep increases in application and cost reduction revolutionise cancer treatment.

Cell-free technology
Biological engineering enables the manufacture of proteins outside living cells.

Cost implications
Will new scientific discoveries, like the introduction of new technology, reduce costs and increase latent demand?

- In early stage of introduction may increase costs
- In later stages after the initial introduction of the new science it may lead to a reduction in costs

Human genome sequencing
Genome medicine appears and becomes aimed at the individual rather than the population as a whole. The correction of human genetic imperfections using generic engineering is mastered.

18. **Social**

Confidence in institutions of the state
Continues to decline in affluent countries

Deferential society
Trend in the public to be less respectful for authority, institutions, politicians, and professionals increases. The legitimacy of the power of the professional is questioned. Compliance with the advice of a professional may be rejected by patients who see themselves as equals with the professional. Holding professionals in esteem diminishes.

Education
Education attainment levels will either increase, stagnate, or decrease.

Feminisation
Male-to-female ratio of each healthcare profession changes from a male majority and dominance in terms of leadership, to either equality or a female-dominated profession.

The percentage of professionals taking more and longer career breaks increase as the percentage of women increase in the healthcare professions.

Health disparities and health inequities
Health disparities linked to health inequalities including culture, economic standing, ethnicity, health literacy, place of residence, race and work arrangements, change the allocation of healthcare resources to disadvantaged populations.

Individualism
Individual autonomy just keeps on growing and patients demand more input into the selection of their healthcare needs

Lifestyle trends
Demand for rational working hours means that healthcare professionals work for fewer hours during their careers.

Litigation
Society requires less confrontational and adversarial methods to resolve disputes.

Multiculturalism
Increase in diversity.

Paternalism
Evaporates.

Religious pluralism
Multifaith society.

Secularisation
Historical process in which religion loses social and cultural significance.

Self-responsibility
Individual members of the public increasingly take responsibility for their own health and wellbeing.

Social networking
Social networking becomes the norm for communicating including with professionals.

19. **Standards**

Expectations of standards
Society retains an unrealistic expectation of levels of standards both in terms of service standards and the standards of the effectiveness of healthcare intervention.

Transnational standards
Local, national, and regional standards give way to international and global transnational standards which facilitate the movement of professionals between jurisdictions.

20. **Technology**

Artificial intelligence (AI), machine learning, and deep learning
Supported by quantum computing, the knowledge and skills of professionals and the use of judgment, for work-related tasks such as the diagnosis and selection of treatment and intervention in disease processes, is commoditised.

Bonus or threat
Will revolutions in technology be drivers for beneficial or detrimental change? Consider the invention of movable type by Guttenberg in 1630, the first practical car powered by an internal combustion engine in 1886 by Karl Benz, and the World Wide Web. The three inventions impact knowledge transfer, transportations costs, and education. But are they a benefit or a detriment?

Cost implications
Will the introduction of new digital technology, likes science, reduce costs and increase latent demand?

- In early stage of introduction technology may increase costs
- In later stages after the initial introduction of the new technology it may lead to a reduction in costs

Disruptive innovation
Introduction of new technology used in specific work-related tasks is disruptive in that the requirement for knowledge, skills, and expertise is reduced and eventually disappears.

Print media
Virtually disappears, i.e. no newspapers and printed books. In addition physical delivery of post mail delivery ceases

Rate of change
What will the rate of technology change of the adoption of new technology be?

Remote diagnosis and monitoring
Technology acts as an enabler.

Robotics
Use of robotics to undertake many surgical operations rapidly increases. However, robots do not develop comprehension. Place of patient operation and location of professionals can be disaggregated.

Routine tasks
Become the domain of machines.

Superintelligence
AI far surpasses the intelligence of human beings to become super-intelligent.

Telehealth
The availability and use of telehealth increases the ability to remotely monitor, diagnose and intervene, both cross border and within the same jurisdiction

Wearable monitoring
Becomes reliable and cost effective, leading to greater self-diagnosis.

21. **Workforce**

Careers
Workers work for multiple employers during their working lives and jobs for life disappear.

Deskilling
Skills of the workforce may be eliminated or supplied by low-cost workers.

Face-to-face delivery
Declines.

Job creation
Technology creates more new jobs.

Sole professional practitioners
In affluent countries the demise of the sole family practitioner professional accelerates and are replaced by Super GP practices or GP Federations.

Workforce
The global average of the percentage of population working in the healthcare delivery system increases from 1 in 18 in 2015, to 1 in 8 by 2065.

22. **World of work**

Portfolio careers
Lifelong employment with a single employer disappears.

Productivity
Productivity of the workforce of the healthcare delivery system significantly changes.

Retirement
Change to the age of retirement.

Teleworking
Teleconferencing becomes the norm driven by low-cost solutions.

Working practices
Career breaks, part-time working, and changes in careers become the norm

Workload intensification
Increasing externally driven requirement for healthcare professionals to deliver higher-quality patient outcomes at lower cost.

CONCLUSION

The use of scenarios is a tried-and-tested methodology of exploring views about the future.

EXERCISES AND QUESTIONS

Exercises

- Create scenarios for a regulator of healthcare professionals.
- Create scenarios for the healthcare delivery system.

Questions

- Review the drivers for change. What would you exclude or include?
- Is the rate of science and technology change increasing and what if any are the implication for regulators?

FURTHER READING

The Art of the long view B
Peter Schwartz
John Wiley and Sons Ltd
1991
IBSN 0-471-97785-3
258 pages

The British Constitution B
Anthony King
Oxford University Press
ISBN 9780199232321
1 November 2007
423 pages

Global Trends 2040 R
A more contested world
National Intelligence Council
ISBN 978 1 929667 33 8
March 2021
156 pages

Insight and Industry: On the Dynamics of Technological Change in Medicine B
(Inside Technology)
Blume, Stuart S
MIT Press
ISBN 10: 0262515709
ISBN 13: 9780262515702
2003
320 pages

Life 3.0: Being Human in the Age of Artificial Intelligence B
Max Tegmark
Penguin Books
29 Aug 2017
ISBN-13 9780241237199
384 pages

Preparing the Healthcare Workforce to Deliver the Digital Future R
An independent report on behalf of the Secretary of State for Health and Social Care
Topol Review
Health Education England
February 2019
103 pages

JOURNALS AND RESEARCH PAPERS

Deep Learning for Classifying Fibrotic Lung Disease on High-Resolution Computed Tomography: A Case-Cohort Study JRP
The Lancet Respiratory Medicine
Simon L.F. Walsh
DOI: 10.1016/S2213-2600(18)30286-8
15 September 2018
http://www.shell.com/energy-and-innovation/the-energy-future/shell-scenarios.html

STANDARDS, CODES, GUIDANCE, CONSULTATIONS, POLICIES, AND PRACTICE NOTES

Standards and Codes

Guide G
A guide to good practice for digital and data-driven health technologies
Department of health & Social Care
19 January 2021

9.3 RESEARCHING THE EVIDENCE BASE FOR REGULATING HEALTHCARE PROFESSIONALS

INTRODUCTION

It is obvious that the principles and processes used to regulate healthcare professional should be constructed on a firm foundation of evidence. For example, if regulators require professionals to undertake continuing componence activities to remain competent, it should possess the evidence that the former is linked to the latter. This is because if there is no evidence, what justification have regulators to impose these types of requirements on the individuals and organisations that they regulate? To inform and improve their policy decisions and processes many regulators respond by undertaking and funding research. In addition, they can make their databases available to others undertaking research.

JUSTIFICATION FOR REGULATORS UNDERTAKING RESEARCH

Regulators should use research to seek the empirical evidence to justify their principles and processes.

This is because informed members of the public intuitively understand that, if for example, when developing a new or revised policy that is constructed on a foundations of dubious assumptions, arbitrary risk measurements, over simplifications and qualitative judgements, they will rightly regard the outputs and conclusions of such exercises to be at best highly questionable and probably indefensible.

Similarly, if regulators describe their policies and processes as being based on scientific evidence and later in due course it is exposed as being in reality non-existent, their reputation will suffer the consequences of, at the very least, being accused of being peddlers of fake news.

Regulators must avoid the accusation that their policies and processes are founded on intuition alone or are entirely arbitrary. To achieve this they must undertake or commission research and then publish the results that in turn will provide the evidence for their actions.

THE EVIDENCE BASE OF REGULATION

The purpose of the research funded or undertaken by regulators of healthcare professionals is mainly to build the evidence for the principles and processes that they use. Or, to put it another way, the research should *inform the basis for regulation*.

This is referred to as evidenced informed research, although it used to be refer to as research-based regulation, hence the definition:

Definition: Evidence Informed Research
Discovering the evidence that justifies the principals and processes used by an organisation.

This in turn leads to a regulatory principle, namely:

Principle: Evidence Informed Regulation
The principles and processes of a regulator should be informed by research.

RESEARCHERS INTO THE REGULATION OF HEALTHCARE PROFESSIONALS

In addition to regulators, a broad range of stakeholders also commission and/or undertake research into the regulation of healthcare professionals. They are predominantly individuals and organisations that have a special interest in this area and include higher education institutes, IGOs, management consultants, policy institutes, research institutes, and think tanks. The Table 9.3 – I on the next page lists named examples of these types of organisations.

CURRENT AREAS OF RESEARCH

To build evidenced informed regulation, the areas of research usually fall into five broad categories, namely:

1. Economic
2. Processes
3. Risk
4. Standards
5. Sociological

And within the five areas there are a range of issues, including:

1. **Economic**
   - Can the process to regulate healthcare professions be improved to reduce it inhibiting competition and reducing cross border mobility?
   - Is the cost of regulation justified?
   - Do different healthcare professions cost more to regulate and why?
   - Is multi-professional regulation both effective and efficient?

Table 9.3 – I Research organisations – examples

CARR: Centre for Analysis of Risk and Regulation (London School of Economics, (LSE))
Centre for Data and Analysis on Psychology Licensure
Civitas: Institute for the Study of Civil Society
Economic and Social Research Council
The European Observatory on Health Systems and Policies
The Health Foundation
Healthcare Regulatory Research Institute
House of Commons Library
Higher Education Policy Institute (HEPI)
Institute for Fiscal Studies
Institute of Economic Affairs
Institute for Public Policy Research
Institute for Government
International Centre on Nurse Migration
International Commonwealth Fund
King's Fund
National Institute of Economic and Social Research
National Institute for Health Research (NIHR)
Nuffield Foundation
Organisation for Economic Cooperation and Development (OECD)
PEW Charitable Trust
Picker Institute
Professional Associations and learned societies
Professional Associations Research Network (PARN)
Public Policy Projects (UK)
United Nations (UN)
World Health Organization (WHO)

2. **Processes**
   - What is the link between undertaken continuing competence and maintaining and improving knowledge and skills?
   - Can the FTP process be made faster whilst maintaining standards?
   - Is self-directed continuing competence effective?
3. **Risk**
   - Is the cost of regulation linked to the risk of a profession?
   - Do the different healthcare professions expose their patients to different levels of risks and if so what are they?
4. **Sociological**
   - What is professionalism?
   - How do student professionals become professionals?
   - What are the best governance arrangements for a regulator of healthcare professionals?
5. **Standards**
   - Will transnational standards emerge?
   - Can AI be used to predict and identify professionals who in the future are more likely to transgress standards?
   - Should standards for advanced practitioners be established by regulators?

RESEARCH INTO THE CARE PROVIDED BY HEALTHCARE PROFESSIONALS

Mention should also be made of the strong and important link between evidenced informed practice and research. Clearly, considerable resources are directed into research that in due course results in the evolution of the body of knowledge of the profession. Since, in the UK regulators of healthcare professionals are not the keepers of the body of knowledge of the profession, they are an interested observer of its evolution, rather than an active participant in the research process. However, this assumes that the programmes of education and training and the professional associations do indeed embrace new science, technology, and the delivery of improved healthcare.

TYPES OF RESEARCH TECHNIQUES USED BY REGULATORS

The Holy Grail of research is to use the scientific method to find empirical evidence that is indisputable 'hard evidence'. For some subjects of interest to regulators that can be relatively easily quantified, for example, financial and economic, a range of research techniques are frequently used, including experimental quantitative studies where all variables are controlled and errors are removed or limited and randomised controlled trials.

Unfortunately, many of the areas of interest to regulators of healthcare professionals relate to the behavioural sciences. Since regulation can't be treated as a petri dish, research in this area relies on quantitative studies which are often criticised for being unable to defend their conclusions by statistical analysis, even if supported by systematic reviews and meta-analysis of numerous data sources.

DISSEMINATION OF RESEARCH FINDINGS

Once regulators have completed their research they should aim to contribute to the not inconsiderable library of published research by publication. This can be achieved in a number of different approaches including:

PUBLICATIONS

In terms of publications, there are a number of dedicated journals, including:

- CLEAR Exam Review
- Journal of Economic Perspectives
- Journal of Governance and Regulation
- Journal of Medical Regulation (JMR)
- Journal of Nursing Regulation
- Journal of Patent Safety and Risk Management
- Journal of Regulatory Economics
- *Professional Licensing Report*, published by CLEAR
- Professions and Professionalism
- *Registrar Magazine*, Toronto, Canada
- *Regulation* magazine Cato Institute
- *The Regulatory Review*Penn Program on Regulation
- Research in Accounting Regulation
- *Risk and Regulation* magazine – Centre for Analysis of Risk and Regulation – LSE
- Yale Journal on Regulation

CONFERENCES

There are also a number of annual and biennial conferences organised by national and international regulatory organisations. These include CLEAR and IAMRA. They provide a venue for sharing research findings into the principles and processes of regulation, as well as a venue for exchanging best practice and meeting regulatory practitioners from around the world.

SPENDING ON RESEARCH

How much money should regulators spend on funding or commissioning research? Regulators with small registers and/or budgets are probably not going to be in a position to invest their limited financial resources in the funding of research although they may be able to analyse and publish using their own data source. They may also have the option of jointly working as a member of a research consortium. That aside, it would not be unreasonable for a regulator to allocate 1–2% of its annual budget to research.

DATA POLICY AND RESEARCH

Regulators generate, collect, structure, retain, and consume considerable quantities of data. Their databases also have the potential to be of assistance to third parties undertaking research. Regulators should therefore have a policy on making their databases accessible, which it goes without saying that the policy must abide by all data protection and freedom of information legislation.

In relation to the regulation of healthcare professionals, of particular interest to researchers is data relating to:

1. Alternative processes for acquiring competences	Section 1.7, volume 2
2. Approval and monitoring of E&T programmes	Section 2.2, volume 2
3. Concerns	Chapter 2, volume 3
4. Continuing competence	Chapter 7, volume 2
5. Emergence of new healthcare professions	Chapter 11, volume 3
6. Fitness to practice	Chapter 3, volume 3
7. Initial registration	Section 4.4, volume 2
8. International application processes	Section 9.3, volume 3
9. Renewal of registration	Section 4.8, volume 2
10. Return to practise	Chapter 8, volume 2
11. Specialised practice	Chapter 6, volume 2

The EU's 2024 establish regulations for the European Health Data Space (EHDS) to support this type of data sharing.

COMMON DATA SETS

By publishing anonymised data online at no cost researchers can now sort, analyse, and match data held by regulators from their registries, records of the FTP process, and continuing competence. However, for researches the degree of the inconsistency of data capture by regulators is a challenge. This is because even in the same jurisdiction different definitions and terms are used to describe the same or slightly different processes.

USE OF OPEN DATA

Much data held by government and its agencies is of great value to many stakeholders, and the regulators of healthcare professionals are no exception to this rule. In recent years particularly the western democracies, government egged on by organisations such as the Open Knowledge Foundation and the Open Data Institute, have imposed a requirement to make data available to interested parties, preferably at no or at minimal cost.

An example of how data can be provided to third parties is the UK's NHS Digital Health and Social Care Information

Centre (HSCIC), which is a UK-Government-funded agency which holds much interesting data.

BIG DATA

In recent years the subject of so-called big data has become an area of growing interest and controversy. What exactly is big data and what interest is it to regulators of healthcare professionals? Big data can be defined as:

Definition: Big Data
Extremely large and complex data sets that may be analysed computationally to reveal patterns, trends, and associations.

The interest has arisen because of the combination a range of developments including:

- Storage of structured and unstructured data sets
- Increased availability of unrestricted access to data sets
- Lower-cost computing and telecommunications
- The development of the web
- The development of social media
- Recording of human behaviour
- The development of the Internet of Everything (IoE)

The value of the big data is enhanced by the provision of meta data, or a description of how the data is structured and concerns about the privacy of data and its disclose by matching data from multiple sources requires carefully consideration.

Big date, by linking data sets, provides the opportunity to increasing our understanding of how and why things happen the way they do and in particular, how humans may behave given a particular situation. This includes:

- Patterns
- Trends
- Associations

In relation to the regulators of healthcare professionals the potential use of their databases which contain information relating to demographic, education and training, employment, and location, if joined to other databases, could provide a powerful tool for the use of workforce planners.

CHALLENGES OF USING BIG DATA

The major challenges of big data is how to extract information in a timely and cost-efficient way. It must also address a number of intractable questions, which, although not the subject of this book, include:

- Data discrimination
- Data ownership
- Data privacy
- Data security

BIG DATA AND THE HEALTHCARE DELIVERY SYSTEM

Big data facilitates the linking of a number of large and complex databases. These can include:

- Diagnostic data: biometrics, electronic patient records (EPR), and hard copy records
- Education and training demand and supply
- Financial records such as insurance claims, government payments to citizens and healthcare workforce, and payments to healthcare providers
- Health outcomes
- Monitoring of equipment-to-equipment and human-to-equipment data
- Patient outcomes
- Pharmaceutical prescribing
- Population demographics
- Procedure provision and utilisation
- Processes of the regulators of the healthcare delivery system
- Service provision including capacity, location, and use
- Service user demographics
- Service provision and utilisation
- Treatment outcomes
- Research and development findings
- Web and social media usage
- Workforce data

One can envisage that in the not too distant future it will be possible to link the provision of a healthcare service to patient outcomes.

CHALLENGE OF THE DOMINANCE OF WESTERN CENTRISM

Those using outputs derived from researching the evidence base for regulating HCPs should be cognisant of the dominance of the source and application of funding for research being focused on the western model of regulation and in particular the USA. As a result most research and grey literature is published in the English language and focuses on the regulation of healthcare professionals using protection of function. Even when the publishers are IGOs, the descriptions focus on the baseline of the western model and the differences of alterative models, rather than the other way around. Challenges are highlighted in non-western models, and resolution is assessed as how to move to the western model.

THE REGULATION OF THE NON-HEALTHCARE PROFESSIONS

Before concluding the section, it should be emphasised that there is a rich vein of research that takes place of the regulation of other non-healthcare professions and occupations, both of which should not be overlooked.

CONCLUSION

Although researching the evidence base for regulating healthcare professionals is an important and significant area, the book takes only a relatively cursory glance at it. Those readers interested in delving more deeply into the subject will easily be able to uncover much published research.

EXERCISES AND QUESTIONS

Exercises

- Devise a research project that would evidence how long it takes for the standards of a professional to fall below required standards if they either stop working or alternatively undertake no continuing competence activities.
- Select a topic that a regulator should research. Locate three doctoral theses relating to the topic.

Questions

- To what extent does published research influence the development of regulation?
- In your view what percentage of their annual budgets should regulators of healthcare professionals spend on research?
- Should regulators be required to collect data using the same terminology?

FURTHER READING

Ambitious for change: R
Research into NMC processes and people's protected characteristics
NMC
20 October 2020
127 pages

British Government Publications: An Index to Chairmen and Authors R
4 volumes 1800–1982
Richard, Stephen
London: Library Association
ISBN 10: 0853657432
1 September 1981–1984
186 pages

Directory of British Official Publications: Guide to Sources B
Richard, Stephen
Mansell - 2nd Edition
ISBN-13: 978-0720117066
1 December 1984
431 pages

The Health & Care Professions Council equality, diversity and inclusion data 2020 report R
Dr Izzy Moore, Ms Leah Bitchell and Dr Rachel Lord
Cardiff Metropolitan University
29 October 2020
28 pages

Health-Related Reports: A key to full titles R
Rob Caley
Avril Roberts Learning Resource Centre
Liverpool John Moores University
20 December 2011
29 pages

Researching Health: Qualitative, Quantitative and Mixed Methods B
Saks, Mike and Allsop, Judith (Editors)
SAGE Publications Ltd; Third edition
ISBN-13: 978-15264 2428 07
11 May 2019
590 pages

A Review of Research into Health and Care Professional Regulation R
Cardiff Unit for Research and Evaluation in Medical and Dental Education
Bullock A, Browne J, Poletti C, Cserző D and Russ E
29 March and 4 June 2020
110 pages

STANDARDS, CODES, GUIDANCE, CONSULTATIONS, POLICIES, AND PRACTICE NOTES

Policy

UK Policy Framework for Health and Social Care Research Pol
NHS Health Research Authority and others
4 November 2022 (Updated)
40 pages

9.4 RESEARCH – ETHICS AND INTEGRITY

INTRODUCTION

Research must be undertaken with integrity and, when it involves human beings, those involved must abide by specific ethical standards. As a consequence, healthcare professionals who are researchers must follow and meet the standards of conduct of their profession and standards of integrity and ethical research set by regulators and other organisations.

THE HISTORICAL CONTEXT OF ETHICS OF RESEARCH

There are a number of infamous cases where healthcare professionals have participated in research where ethical standards were totally lacking or inappropriate.

SECOND WORLD WAR

During the Second World War criminal human experimentation was conducted by the Nazis. Following the war and the conclusion of the Nuremberg trials, a global code for ethical guidance on research was adopted. The ten points of the code were given in the section of the verdicts of the trial entitled 'Permissible Medical Experiments'. They are:

1. The voluntary consent of the human subject is absolutely essential.
2. The experiment should be such as to yield fruitful results for the good of society, unprocurable by other methods or means of study, and not random and unnecessary in nature.
3. The experiment should be so designed and based on the results of animal experimentation and a knowledge of the natural history of the disease or other problem under study that the anticipated results will justify the performance of the experiment.
4. The experiment should be so conducted as to avoid all unnecessary physical and mental suffering and injury.
5. No experiment should be conducted where there is an a priori reason to believe that death or disabling injury will occur; except, perhaps, in those experiments where the experimental physicians also serve as subjects.
6. The degree of risk to be taken should never exceed that determined by the humanitarian importance of the problem to be solved by the experiment.
7. Proper preparations should be made and adequate facilities provided to protect the experimental subject against even remote possibilities of injury, disability, or death.
8. The experiment should be conducted only by scientifically qualified persons. The highest degree of skill and care should be required through all stages of the experiment of those who conduct or engage in the experiment.
9. During the course of the experiment the human subject should be at liberty to bring the experiment to an end if he has reached the physical or mental state where continuation of the experiment seems to him to be impossible.
10. During the course of the experiment the scientist in charge must be prepared to terminate the experiment at any stage, if he has probable cause to believe, in the exercise of the good faith, superior skill, and careful judgment required of him that a continuation of the experiment is likely to result in injury, disability, or death to the experimental subject.

In due course the World Medical Association (WMA) developed the Declaration of Helsinki that incorporates and expands on the Nuremberg Code.

TUSKEGEE SYPHILIS STUDY

From 1932 to 1972 United States Public Health Service conducted an infamous unethical research on African-Americans who had syphilis. The participants were promised free medical care which was not provided. Over 125 died although they could have been successfully treated with penicillin which was available from 1947.

THE REGULATION OF RESEARCH

In response to the scandal the Belmont Report, published in September 1978, establishes three principles. They are as follows:

1. **Respect for persons**: Protecting the autonomy of all people and treating them with courtesy and respect and allowing for informed consent. Researchers must be truthful and conduct no deception
2. **Beneficence**: The philosophy of 'Do no harm' while maximising benefits for the research project and minimising risks to the research subjects
3. **Justice**: Ensuring reasonable, non-exploitative, and well-considered procedures are administered fairly – the fair distribution of costs and benefits to potential research participants – and equally

RESEARCH STANDARDS

Standards relating to research can be located in two distinct publications. Firstly, there may be national laws such as the USA's National Research Service Award Act of 1974. Secondly, those issued by regulators of healthcare professions and those of other organisations. For example, the European Code of

Conduct for Research Integrity published by All European Academies (ALLEA).

In the UK three organisations influence, provide financial support, and coordinate research. They are the Health Research Authority, Medical Research Council, and NICE.

STANDARDS OF REGULATORS

Topics relating to the ethics of research are usually, embedded in their Standards of Conduct. They include:

- Avoid harm to patients
- Confidentiality of patients
- Conflicts of interest
- Informed consent
- Right of withdrawal

GUIDANCE ON RESEARCH

A number of regulators publish guidance on research.

INTEGRITY OF RESEARCH

Research must be carried out with integrity. For example, if the results of research are falsified or plagiarised.

FAILED RESEARCH

There is growing acceptance that research that failed research or negative results should also be published.

PUBLICATION OF BIAS

Publication bias is a type of bias occurring in the world of published academic research. While the elimination of flawed studies is entirely reasonable there appears to be a tendency for researchers and publications to select certain outcomes such as an important finding, as opposed to research with no particular results, called a null result. Many factors contribute to this type of publication bias. For example, once a result is well established in the sector, it may become non-newsworthy to publish papers with null results, however strong the research.

There are also incentives for researchers not to submit their papers with null results since they may have made a mistake, or, that no one will be interested

Identifying unpublished studies is obviously difficult. However, some publications now require that research submitted for publication must be pre-registered prior to the collection of data and analysis. Other options include the detection and control for publication bias by placing less credit on small and non-randomised studies as they have a high probability for error and bias. The issue is also important in relation to literature reviews since they will themselves be biased if the original literature is influenced by publication bias.

CONCLUSION

Healthcare professionals who are involved in undertaking research must not only abide by the standards of their regulator but also in some instances those of other organisations.

EXERCISES AND QUESTIONS

Exercises

- Obtain the standards of conduct for a healthcare professional. Is it clear what standards the professionals should use when undertaking research?
- Does the Declaration of Helsinki and the Nuremberg Code still apply, or should they be replaced?
- Investigate the research undertaken by the German anaesthesiologist Joachim Boldt.

Questions

- Should regulators of healthcare professions publish their own standards on the ethics of research or should they rely on the standards of other organisations?
- If you are a healthcare professional, or studying to become one, when did you learn about the ethics of research? Was it adequate?

LEGISLATION

Example of International Legislation

USA L

National Research Service Award Act 1974

Public Law 93-348, 88 Stat. 342 July 12.1974

FURTHER READING

Belmont Report: Ethical Principles and Guidelines for the Protection of Human Subjects of Research R
National Commission for the Protection of Human Subjects of Biomedical and Behavioural Research
Federal Register (USA)
Ref: DHEW Publication No. (OS) 78-0012
30 September 1978
40 pages

Human Experimentation and the Law B
Nathan Hershey and Robert D. Miller
Lippincott Williams and Wilkins
ISBN 13 978-0912862194
1 April 1976
173 pages

Research: The role and responsibilities of doctors R
GMC
ASIN B001OZ32U
2002, withdrawn April 2010

STANDARDS, CODES, GUIDANCE, CONSULTATIONS, POLICIES, AND PRACTICE NOTES

Standards and Codes

Declaration of Helsinki S&C
Ethical Principles for Medical Research Involving Human Subjects
World Medial Association
June 1964 and versions October 2013

Ethical standards for research during public health emergencies:
Distilling existing guidance to support COVID-19 R&D S&C
WHO
2020
4 pages

The European Code of Conduct for Research Integrity S&C
ALLEA – All European Academies
ISBN 978-3-00-055767-5
2017 (Revised edition)
11 pages

Nuremberg Code S&C
Trials of war criminals before the Nuremberg military tribunals no control council law No. 10
Volume Two the Medical Case
Pages 181–183
OCTOBER 1946-APRIL 1947
U. S. Government Printing Office
896 pages
20 August 1947

University of Cambridge Policy on the Ethics of Research Involving Human Participants and Personal Data S&C
University Research Ethics Committee
July 2020
6 pages

Guidance

Ethical Guidelines for Nursing Research G
William L. Holzemer
International Council of Nurses, ICN
ISBN 9295005767
2003
40 pages

Good practice in research and Consent to research G
GMC
4 May 2010
14 pages

Research ethics: RCN guidance for nurses G
RCN
Publication code 002 013
March 2004
19 pages

Future of the Regulation of Healthcare Professionals

CHAPTER 10

INTRODUCTION

The chapter has one section:

10.1 FUTURE OF THE REGULATION OF HEALTHCARE PROFESSIONALS

INTRODUCTION

I have consciously attempted not to bowdlerize the book by suggesting that all issues relating to the statutory regulation of professionals are agreed and uncontroversial.

However, before concluding, I would like to briefly explore my predictions for what I believe will be the 'Big issues' relating to the regulation of healthcare professionals that in the future will be controversial and will need to be resolved.

WHAT ARE THE 'BIG ISSUES' IN THE REGULATION OF PROFESSIONALS TODAY?

The future is unknown and to quote Niels Bohr, the Danish physicist and Nobel Laureate:

> *"Prediction is very difficult, especially if it's about the future"*

And, to quote John Kenneth Galbraith:

> *"The only function of economic forecasting is to make astrology look respectable"*

Matters are also made more complex as the world at the start of the twenty-first century is, to quote the acronym, definitely VUCA.

- **V**olatile
- **U**ncertain
- **C**omplex
- **A**mbiguous

This aside, gazing into the distance, is it possible to make any sense of what might be coming down the road in the world of regulating healthcare professionals?

There are 18 'Big issues'. Here they are:

1. **Emergence of transnational standards**
   Will the emergence of transnational standards relating to the regulation of healthcare professionals across the globe continue apace? If this is probable, how will regulators ensure that they influence their development?
2. **Revising, broadening, and raising standards**
   Is enough emphasis placed on revising, broadening, and raising the standards of healthcare professionals, as opposed to establishing the standards? If this is the case, how exactly can regulators change the standards of those they currently regulate?
3. **Compliance with continuing competence standards**
   What percentage of a profession actually maintain, revise, broaden, and raise their competences and values and behaviour throughout their professional careers?
4. **Methods to maintain continuing competence**
   There is no doubt that competences are perishable and the argument for and against regulators setting standards for continuing competence has been resolved. However, the issue of what activities should ccontinuing competence actually consist of, has still not been resolved.
5. **Link between continuing competence and fitness to practise tribunals**
   Is there a demonstrable link between continuing competence and the safe and effective practice of professionals, i.e. does investment in continuing competence maintain, revise, broaden, and raise standards and thus reduce the likelihood of a professional becoming subject to a complaint and thus trigger a fitness to practise tribunal?
6. **Proactive seeking underperforming and failing professionals**
   Should regulators invest more resources in proactively seeking out underperforming and failing professionals?
7. **Prevention agenda**
   How should regulators of healthcare professionals divide their limited resources between inspection, improvement, and enforcement of standards? And in particular, should

Operations of Regulators of Healthcare Professionals, Volume 4, First Edition. Marc Seale.

Companion website: www.wiley.com/go/seale/regulatinghealthcare

they increase resources to try and reduce the percentage of professionals falling below the required standards?

8. **Government intervention and oversight**
Government has for a number of years expected regulators to take on a wider agenda, one that has tended to reflect government's social policies and at the same time it has been dissatisfied with the performance of regulators. To this end, oversight organisations have been established in a minority of jurisdictions.
The question for the future is, will the level of government intervention continue to be required and will oversight be extended?

9. **Ensuring legislation is effective, efficient, and ethical**
Will government have the time, resources, and inclination to ensure that the legislation governing regulators is amended and reformed so that they remain effective, efficient, and ethical?

10. **Structure of regulators**
Is the structure used by regulatorsoptimal? For example:
    - Should the organisation and management of FTP tribunals be integrated with, or independent from, the organisation that sets the standards of regulated professionals?
    - Should more multi-professional regulators be established?

11. **Extending statutory regulation of healthcare occupations and assistants**
To what extent should or will more healthcare occupations and/or healthcare assistants be brought into some form of statutory regulation?

12. **Costs of regulation**
Will there be more pressure to ensure that the regulators are both effective and efficient and that their direct costs are reasonable and that indirect costs are minimised?

13. **Governance arrangements**
Will the traditional board be superseded by unitary boards where the executive participates as equal with the non-executive board members?

14. **Structures and the cost of education**
How will education and training programmes for healthcare professionals evolve over the next quarter of a century?

15. **The future of the nature of professionals and the professions**
    - Will the role of professional associations and the services they provide, stand the test of time?
    - Will the advancements in science and technology negate the necessity for some or all of the healthcare professions?
    - Will the regulatory contract with its resulting economic advantages bestowed on professionals but funded by the rest of society, survive?
    - Should, and can, the professions evolve, rather than suffer extinction as was the fate of the dinosaurs and the dodos?

16. **Focus on regulatory burden**
Can an increased use of risk-based regulation reduce intervention by regulators?

17. **Asymmetrical knowledge base**
Will technology, the internet of everything, robotics and instant free communication, eliminate the asymmetrical knowledge base between members of the public and healthcare professions, leading to a decline in the number and influence of healthcare professionals and reduced regulation?

18. **Rule-making powers of regulators**
Will greater rule-making powers be delegated by government to regulators or will its desire be to remain in control persist?

CONCLUSION

In conclusion, to quote William Ford Gibson the American—Canadian writer of science fiction:

> *"The future is here – it's just not evenly distributed"*

EXERCISES AND QUESTIONS

Exercises

- Review the list of 'Big Issues'. Which would you remove and what others would you include?
- Identify your top five issues. Explain why have you selected them.

Questions

- Select one of the issues and explore in detail your views on how it may evolve.
- Do all the issues apply in your jurisdiction? What should be included that is specific to your jurisdiction?

Epilogue

For those readers who have read the four books from cover to cover, well done and many congratulations. I hope that you have now become more familiar with the principles and processes of the regulation of healthcare professionals and also that you have gained a better understanding of how they relate to one another. For those of you who have made use of the books by way of a reference guide and have dipped in and out of its various sections, as opposed to ploughing the whole way through, I also hope that it has helped provide an answer to your specific questions, or if it has not, that it has triggered a desire for you to develop your own views and ideas.

To quote Pliny the Elder (AD 23–AD 79) in his dedication to his encyclopaedia *The Natural History*:

> *"And because the public good requires that you should be spared as much as possible from all trouble, I have subjoined to this epistle the contents of each of the following books, and have used my best endeavours to prevent your being obliged to read them all through. And this, which was done for your benefit, will also serve the same purpose for others, so that any one may search for what he wishes, and may know where to find it."*

I worked in the world of the regulation of healthcare professionals on a full time for twenty years. Throughout the time I repeatedly encountered the same questions being asked about the principles and processes for regulating healthcare professionals, or, it was evident that those concerned should have known what the answers were in the first place. For example:

- Board meetings of regulators received papers without any contextualising of how and why they related to the broader regulatory arena or the 'bigger picture'
- Conferences on regulation repeatedly debating the same issues year after year, often ignoring the principles and processes of regulation
- Governments in different jurisdictions investing their time and tax payers resources in addressing the same regulatory problem without apparently understanding the principles or processes of regulation
- Self-declared 'management consultants' or 'experts' partially reinterpreted the principles and processes and repeatedly repackaged their interpretations and then selling them for a king's ransom to ill-informed purchasers

Therefore, a number of years ago, when I embarked on the task of writing this book, I set myself two challenges. They were:

Firstly, to craft an easily accessible reference guide to enable individuals to understand the principles and processes that are used in the regulation of healthcare professionals without the need to search many different and sometimes contradictory sources.

Secondly, to write a single source reference guide that could provide the foundations for a number of reparative tasks including:

- Assisting government establish and refine its regulatory policy
- Briefing and commissioning management consultants, experts, and gurus
- Designing learning and developing programmes for new employees or board members of regulators
- Identifying and selecting areas for research including doctoral thesis
- Planning the contents and agendas for regulatory conferences
- Setting the agendas for the board meetings of regulators of professionals

I certainly do not claim to be a panjandrum and I do not think that I have discovered anything particularly original or profound, rather the books have placed in logical order some obvious facts. On reflection, and if I am not suffering from pollyannaism, I hope that I have partially achieved these two challenges.

COMPLEXITY OF THE REGULATION OF HEALTHCARE PROFESSIONS

Before concluding this book, I have one final point to make concerning the complexity of the regulation of healthcare professions.

Operations of Regulators of Healthcare Professionals, Volume 4, First Edition. Marc Seale.

Companion website: www.wiley.com/go/seale/regulatinghealthcare

Many industries and organisations are complex. For example, the satellite industry, the pharmaceutical industry, or the management of hospitals. However, in my view the regulation of healthcare professionals is not overtly complex, but at the same time it is not axiomatic. Indeed, I have been known to say in an unguarded moment:

> *Regulation of healthcare professionals is at the end of the day just a process for writing names of individuals in a book and crossing them out when they do not meet standards*
>
> **Marc Seale**

This may seem heterodox, but there are however three areas of complexity.

Firstly, as I state in Section 3.1, volume 1, it is my long-held view that the regulation of healthcare professionals is

> *"An uncomplicated operating model, operating in a complex stakeholder environment"*

Secondly, regulation is a 'team sport' and as such requires the complex cooperation and coordination of:

1. Consumer advocacy organisations
2. Educators and trainers of professionals
3. Employers of professionals
4. Healthcare professionals
5. Professional associations
6. The public
7. Regulators
8. The State comprising the legislature, executive/ government, and the judiciary

Thirdly, when assessors must make complex judgments at the interface of the eight process used by a regulator to statutory regulate professionals.

— 0O0 —

FINAL WORD

You should now be in a better position to explain what is happened, why it is happening, and to select a solution to solve the problem that you are facing.

And that, dear reader, is the end of the four books.

Lastly, if you have any comments, criticisms, or suggestions on the contents of the book, please feel free to contact me via LinkedIn.

Legislation Index

Operations of Regulators of Healthcare Professionals, Volume 4, First Edition. Marc Seale.

Companion website: www.wiley.com/go/seale/regulatinghealthcare

Organisation Index

Operations of Regulators of Healthcare Professionals, Volume 4, First Edition. Marc Seale.

Companion website: www.wiley.com/go/seale/regulatinghealthcare

People Index

Operations of Regulators of Healthcare Professionals, Volume 4, First Edition. Marc Seale.

Companion website: www.wiley.com/go/seale/regulatinghealthcare

Subject Index

Operations of Regulators of Healthcare Professionals, Volume 4, First Edition. Marc Seale.

Companion website: www.wiley.com/go/seale/regulatinghealthcare

Q

R